The Sunrise Serenade
A World War II Bomber Crew Story

Jerry Penry

The Sunrise Serenade

Dedicated to the memory of
Vince & Marie

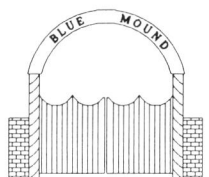

Published by
Blue Mound Press
P.O. Box 150
Milford, Nebraska 68405

© Jerry Penry, 2000
All rights reserved. No part of this book may be reproduced or transmitted
in any form or by any means electronic or mechanical including photocopying,
recording, scanning, or by any information storage and retrieval system
without permission in writing from the Publisher.

First Printing - August 2000.

371/1000

ISBN: 0-9679041-0-2

Printed by
Service Press
P.O. Box 606
Henderson, Nebraska 68371

Cover Photo: Official U.S. Air Force photo of Crew #61 from the 452nd Bombardment Group (H) of the U.S. 8th Air Force, standing in front of their plane, the *Sunrise Serenade*, B-17G, Serial No. 42-37949. Photo taken at Revetment No. 29, U.S. Air Force Station 142, Deopham Green, England. Photo date: ca. March 20, 1944.
Standing left to right: 2nd Lt. John J. McGrath, navigator; 1st Lt. Francis C. Smedley, pilot; 2nd Lt. William J. Hewett, copilot; 2nd Lt. George D. Griffin, bombardier. Kneeling left to right: S/Sgt. John G. Brown, right waist gunner; T/Sgt. Norbert E. Rhodes, engineer; S/Sgt Raymond E. Dean, tail gunner; S/Sgt. Harry C. Shoffner, left waist gunner; T/Sgt. Andrew Senetsky, Jr., radioman; S/Sgt. Robert A. Lalumiere, ball turret gunner.

We did not win it because destiny created us better than all other peoples. I hope that in victory we are more grateful than we are proud. I hope we can rejoice in victory – but humbly. The dead men would not want us to gloat.

- Ernie Pyle, 1900-1945.
World War II journalist.

Contents

1. A Call For Your Country..1
2. The Crew Comes Together..7
3. Specifications of the Plane...15
4. Before the Arrival of the Sunrise Serenade....................................21
5. The Bombing Missions...27
6. The Final Mission...51
7. A Mother's Worry...57
8. The Ultimate Sacrifice..63
9. An Eagle in a Sparrow's Nest...67
10. In The Belgian Underground..73
11. Two Officers Stay Together...79
12. Away From the Battle Fronts...91
13. The Tiger's Tale..103
14. The War Comes to an End..113
15. After The War...121
16. Fighters, Flak and Fear...127
17. A Tale of Two Smedleys...135
18. Behind the Plane's Name..137

Official Documents..139
Planes of the 452nd Bomb Group..150
Acknowledgements..159
Bibliography...161

Drawing credits - The various drawings and maps shown in this book, unless otherwise noted, are the work of the author.

Introduction

Many books have already been written about various aspects of World War II. It has been the war that has gained the most attention and notoriety from authors worldwide, and its topics remain endless. The logistics, tactical information, battle plans, statistics and other war-related data will always be available through archives for authors to compile in the years to come. However, the individual stories of bravery, courage, desperation, and sadness that affected millions of people worldwide, which truly portrayed the War for what it really was, are quickly disappearing with time. For the most part, the majority of these stories have gone untold, and many are now gone forever with the passing of those men who were fortunate enough to have survived the War.

The crew of the *Sunrise Serenade* does not stand out as having experienced the War any differently than any other bomber crew. Each man first left his home and family to train and then commit his knowledge and experience to help win the War. The expectations of all bomber crews were enormous, but through their willingness to die for their country, if need be, and the determination to win at all costs, they were victorious. Sadly, most bomber crews that were shot down during the War have only become statistics as time passes. The tragic circumstances surrounding many bomber crews exceed those pertaining to the crew of the *Sunrise Serenade*; however, the story of the *Sunrise Serenade* represents what it was like to be part of a typical bomber crew.

My involvement in writing this book is a result of having known the brother of the pilot from the *Sunrise Serenade*. A veteran of the 2nd Armored Division, Vincent A. Smedley always wondered what had happened to his younger brother and only sibling, Francis C. Smedley. I met Vince and his wife, Marie, in the 1980's near Atkinson, Nebraska. Our ages differed by over 50 years, but we shared a common interest in many things, and our relationship soon developed into a close friendship. Vince felt a need to talk about his experiences of the War to anyone who would listen. It was not because he suffered from the effects of the War, but rather it centered around a deep love for his country and a desire to preserve the stories and memories of those who had participated in the War. The information that Vince would reveal to me about the War was often only in bits and pieces. Being a young man in my early twenties, I had no real prior knowledge of what the War had entailed. During high school I had learned about the War in a history class, but it was never brought to life in a personal way. The War seemed so distant and irrelevant to me, so I just politely listened to Vince's stories while we enjoyed each other's company.

As the years progressed and our friendship grew, I offered to compile his story if he would write down everything he could remember. The result was an unpublished manuscript titled "*My Life in the 2nd Armored Division*", which Vince proudly shared with friends and family. When I presented the finished copy to him during Memorial Day weekend of 1993, he openly wept while holding it in his hands. He was not weeping because the story had brought back painful memories, but rather he was showing his relief of having his story finally preserved for future generations.

During our many conversations, his focus would almost always turn to a framed 18" x 24" picture which hung on his dining room wall. In this picture was a large plane with 10 young men posing in front. The nose of the plane revealed its name, the *"Sunrise Serenade"*. Although Vince knew the names of all of the crew, he personally knew only one, its pilot, Francis C. Smedley. His younger brother was only 20 years old when he became the pilot of the *Sunrise Serenade*. Vince would talk about his brother's plane and crew, but the many details pertaining to his brother's last flight as well as those pertaining to the other missions flown were mostly unknown.

In March of 1997, Vince died due to the effects of cancer. After his death, Vince's wife, Marie, gave me the picture of the *Sunrise Serenade* and its crew. I knew there was much more to be told about the plane and its crew, but I had no idea how I would proceed to obtain this information. Over the course of the next year, I desperately searched and finally located six living crew members and also the wives of those crew members who had already died.

Sadly, Marie Smedley died in September of 1999, as I was well into writing this book. She was intently involved with the progress of the story and often remarked "*What would Vince have said?*" at every new piece of information that was uncovered. Once when I let her hold actual pieces of the plane, which were acquired from the crash site in Belgium, it was her turn to weep. She realized what that moment would have meant to Vince.

This book is the result of having personally interviewed well over one hundred combat veterans of the United States Eighth Air Force who proudly served during World War II. Their stories helped to form the framework of the 452nd Bombardment Group as I tell their story while focusing on one crew, the *Sunrise Serenade*, who lived and flew alongside them. Later many of these same men struggled to survive together in the prisoner of war camps. There will never be another generation in American history like these men.

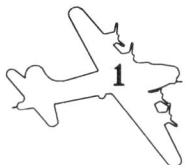

A Call For Your Country

The events leading to World War II were escalating many years before the United States became involved. In fact, most of those events took place while the majority of U.S. servicemen who would eventually serve in this War were still finishing their public school education. That was the case for most of the young men who would later form the crew of the *Sunrise Serenade*. Their willingness to serve their country at such a young age was a tribute to the sense of patriotism instilled during the previous war. Yet immediately after the first World War, the stage became set for another one of greater proportions; although no one believed another world war could actually happen.

Germany, the principal defeated nation of World War I, bitterly resented the territorial losses and reparations payments imposed upon it by the victorious nations as a result of the Treaty of Versailles. Some of the restrictions imposed upon Germany called for a cease in its compulsory military service for its people, a reduction of its military to just 100,000 people, and a stop to the production of all war-related material. In addition, Germany was required to make extensive financial reparations to its victims, not only through monetary measures, but also by giving its victims access to Germany's valuable natural resources. Italy, although one of the victors during World War I, found its territorial gains far from enough either to offset its involvement in the War or to satisfy its future ambitions as a world power. Japan, also a victor, was unhappy about its failure to gain control of China, since they perceived their participation in the War should have resulted in their own territorial gains. Japan needed territorial gains to supply it with the natural resources that they did not possess to become a world power. Three other major participants, the United States, France, and Great Britain, attained their wartime objectives by mainly reorganizing Europe and the rest of the world powers, and also reducing Germany to a non-military nation.

It did not take long for Germany to overcome that objective. Several factors led to the rebuilding of Germany into another military power as the rest of the world stood silently by and watched. First, the French and the British frequently disagreed on policy during the postwar period, and were unsure of their ability to defend the peace settlement negotiated after the War had ended. Although the Treaty of Versailles seemed good on paper, it lacked the necessary direction for enforcement. The United States was present at the signing of the Treaty of Versailles, but never ratified the agreement. It instead chose to sign another treaty with Germany in June of 1921 known as the Treaty of Berlin. This left enforcement of the Treaty of Versailles entirely up to the European countries. Secondly, the United States became disillusioned by the Europeans' failure to repay their massive War debts owed them, and retreated into isolationism. This isolationism continued through the depression of the 1930's, when the United States was no longer interested in dealing with foreign affairs to a large extent. Lastly, almost no one believed that another world war would ever be fought again, or at least during his or her lifetime. World War I, with its 30 million casualties, was hoped to have been enough reason to prevent another one from happening again. It was hoped to have been the War to end all wars, so no one believed that any country would dare do anything to spark another one.

In the early 1930s, the government in Germany laid the kindling for that spark to ignite. A severe depression, like the one known to the United States, greatly affected Germany. The moderate parties of a struggling Germany could not agree on what to do about it, so large numbers of voters turned to the German National Socialist (Nazi) Party. This new party's leader, Adolf Hitler, preached a racist brand of fascism. He promised to overturn the Treaty of Versailles and secure additional land that was taken from the German people immediately after World War I in an attempt to boost the depressed economy and people. In 1933 Hitler became the German chancellor, and in a series of subsequent moves he established himself as dictator.

Germany immediately began to rebuild itself into a nation of military strength under Hitler's leadership. He eagerly tried out his new weapons on the side of right-wing military rebels in the Spanish Civil War (1936-39). This venture brought him into collaboration with Italy's Benito Mussolini, who was also supporting the Spanish revolt. Treaties between Italy, Germany, and Japan in 1936-37 brought into being the Rome-Berlin-Tokyo Axis. Japan had realized the opportunity to expand its territory in the Pacific while Germany and Italy would be doing the same in Europe. Only twenty years earlier, the Italians and Japanese were fighting against the Germans.

Germany launched its expansionist drive with the annexation of Austria in March of 1938. The British and French were overawed by Germany's rearmament, and accepted Hitler's explanation that the status of Austria was an internal German affair. The United States had severely impaired its ability to act against aggression by passing a neutrality law that prohibited material assistance to all parties in foreign conflicts.

Germany soon annexed Czechoslovakia, and then threatened Poland. Only after this latest threat of aggression did the British government pledge to aid any country whose independence was threatened by Germany. France already had a mutual defense treaty with Poland, so it, too, became directly involved with the conflict with Germany. Meanwhile distrust between Germany and Russia was growing, because neither Hitler nor Joseph Stalin trusted each other. Yet, on August 23, 1939, the Nazi-Soviet Pact was signed, with both nations agreeing not to go to war against each other. By September 1, 1939, the German armies marched into Poland, which was also something the Russians had secretly been considering. Two days later the British and French surprised Hitler by declaring war on Germany, but they had no firm plans to deal with the situation militarily. Although Poland had one of the world's largest armies, it had inherent weaknesses in organization and outdated equipment resulting in the Germans overrunning it in just 18 days.

In an unrelated act of aggression to that of the Germans, the Soviet Union showed their military strength by declaring war on neighboring Finland on November 30, 1939. This act of aggression by the Russians brought to an end the uneasy and rapacious peace between Germany and Russia. Hitler then approved the German invasion into Norway and Denmark on April 2, 1940, fearing that Russia might also try to take these countries first. Denmark surrendered at once; the Norwegians, however, were now aided by 12,000 British and French, and held out until May 3rd, although a German victory was never in doubt. Sweden quickly declared itself to remain a neutral country throughout the War since they were now within reach of both the Russians and the Germans. On May 10th, German airborne troops landed inside Belgium and Holland to seize airfields and bridges. By May 26, 1940, the British and French trying to stop the Germans were pushed into a narrow beachhead around Dunkerque, France, and the following day the Belgian king surrendered. Destroyers and smaller craft of all types rescued over 338,000 French and British soldiers from Dunkerque in a heroic sea lift that brought them safely to England. France was soon overrun by the Germans, and signed an armistice with Germany on June 25, 1940, that gave Germany control of northern France and the Atlantic coast.

England was one of the only remaining obstacles left for Germany to conquer, but the British fighting spirit resolved to defend their country to the end, if necessary. The United States was shocked by the fall of France, and began the first peacetime compulsory enlistment for military service in its history and greatly increased its military budget. Public opinion, although sympathetic to helping Great Britain, was overwhelmingly against getting into another world war.

German invasions became more persuasive as 1940 wore on. In August of 1940, Germany launched daylight air raids against Britain, but they failed to reckon with a new device known as radar, which greatly increased the British fighters' effectiveness by alerting the arrival of the German planes. Due to heavy losses, the Germans had to switch to night bombing at the end of September. The German high command made a critical mistake when it decided to stop targeting British air fields and other military installations and switched to bombing civilian targets, which they had hoped would break the morale of the British people. By May of 1941, over 70 major raids had been made on Britain's major cities, but the damage inflicted was too indiscriminate to be militarily decisive and it only served to strengthen the morale of the British civilians. Also, the heavy losses inflicted upon the German bombers during the Battle of Britain was a terrible defeat for the German high command, so Germany directed its attention toward northern Africa. Also, a massive attack to the East on the morning of June 22, 1941, directed more than 3 million German troops to invade Russia. The German front line stretched more than 1,500 miles as it pursued Russia as its next victim. For the time being, the German high command was hoping that its Italian ally could provide most of the men and equipment for the African campaign.

While Germany and Italy were involved with the War on European and African soil, Japan was showing signs that they, too, were anxious to annex new territory by military might. Japan was a small, aggressive nation, fiercely proud, and with few natural resources. The presence of the American naval fleet in the Pacific would hinder any plan of annexing new territory by Japanese military might unless the American presence was greatly reduced.

The unprovoked attack by the Japanese on December 7, 1941, at Pearl Harbor, Hawaii, immediately brought the United States into the world conflict. – *Collection of the author.*

An unprovoked attack by the Japanese against the United States at Pearl Harbor, Hawaii, on December 7, 1941, finally brought America into the War. Germany subsequently declared war on the United States on December 11, 1941, since the United States had declared war upon Japan, Germany's ally.

Prior to the bombing of Pearl Harbor, all men between the ages of 18 and 35 were required to register with their local draft board. At this time only one year of service was required if a person chose to volunteer for service. After the bombing of Pearl Harbor and the declaration of War on Japan and Germany, the situation greatly changed; men were now being called for active service by the draft. There was no shortage of volunteers immediately after the Japanese attack, although some chose to wait until they were actually called for active duty. Very few men refused the call to serve their country when their draft number came up. Everyone knew that total victory in the War had to be achieved to preserve their own freedom and way of life, as well as that for others fighting to save their own countries.

One of the major commitments made by the United States to the War effort was that of heavy bomber aircraft. The bombers could penetrate the Germans behind their established lines of defense while the upcoming ground assaults were still in the planning stages. This is where the famed Boeing B-17 Flying Fortress first came into use. Initially being provided for the Royal Air Force of England, they were soon almost entirely used by the United States Air Force after England had built up its own type of heavy bombers.

A B-17 Flying Fortress bomber required a crew of ten well-trained airmen. Each position required individual advanced training before the men could come together as one effective crew. Each man who eventually became part of the crew of the B-17 known as the *Sunrise Serenade* began his training separately. This separate training lasted between one and two years before they all could come together as a crew. As each airman's individual training was completed, they parted company with the fellow airman they had grown to know during this training, and reported for duty at an assigned airfield to become part of a new bomber crew.

The men making up the crew of the *Sunrise Serenade* came from different places amid different circumstances. The pilot of the plane, Francis C. Smedley, came from the small town of Oconto Falls, located in northeastern Wisconsin. Flying had been a dream of his from early childhood as he and his brother, Vincent, would spend hours crafting wooden airplanes or drawing sketches of them on paper. The War gave Francis an opportunity to become a pilot as well as providing an income to help for his mother, whose husband had left the family while the boys were very young. His training to become a pilot took him to various places including the cities of Santa Ana, Merced and Visalia, California. At Sequoia Field in Visalia, California, he soloed for the first time on November 20, 1942. Advanced training took him to La Junta, Colorado, where he learned to fly his first bomber, the B-25 Mitchell. A final phase of training took him to Roswell, New Mexico, where he learned to fly the B-17 bomber for the first time in July of 1943. The much larger B-17 had four engines compared to the B-25's two engines, but Smedley soon adjusted and fell in love with the famed B-17. Smedley was seemingly born to fly and absolutely nothing would keep him from his childhood dream.

For many young men the call for their country came in the form of a Western Union telegram. Francis Smedley received his call on April 1, 1942. – *Collection of the author.*

For the copilot, William J. Hewett, the military had already been familiar to him. A Clevelander, Hewett graduated from Shaker Heights High School in 1935 and went directly into what was then called the Case School of Applied Science (now Western Reserve), graduating in 1939. While at Case he applied to the Army Air Corps for their pilot training program in June of 1939. Hewett would have gone immediately had he been accepted; however, his height of 6'6" put him over the height restrictions of that time. Hewett instead joined the E Troop of the 107th Cavalry (Horse Mechanized) of the Ohio National Guard, which had recently been mobilized. Horse Cavalry units were mechanized by supplying them with vans so that horses could be strategically positioned. The unit was taken into federal service in March of 1941 at Camp Forest, Tennessee, which was located near Nashville. After the attack on Pearl Harbor, Hewett was immediately sent to Fort Ord, located near Santa Monica, California, to join the unit. While at Fort Ord, Hewett won a Citation for Heroism for saving the lives of two people whose boat had capsized in the Pacific surf. After a change in height regulations for flyers, as well as the intervention of a priest who sought a waiver for Hewett, he was allowed to enter Air Force Cadet training in 1942. Bill Hewett was commissioned a second lieutenant in the Army Air Corps in August of 1943 just before helping to form the crew of the *Sunrise Serenade*.

Many future B-17 pilots, including Francis Smedley, first learned to fly in these Trainers at the Merced Army Flying School at Merced, California. - *Collection of the author.*

John J. McGrath, the navigator aboard the plane, came from the small town of Langhorne, Pennsylvania, which is located just outside of Philadelphia. After high school, McGrath received a business degree at Banks Business College in Philadelphia and also worked for both the Sears & Roebuck and the Fuller Brush companies. In 1940 he obtained a job at the Rohm & Haas company which made a variety of items, including the plexiglas noses for the B-17 bombers with which McGrath would soon become familiar. At the start of the War, he enlisted in the Army Air Corps at New Cumberland Base near Harrisburg, Pennsylvania. Basic training for John McGrath was at Jefferson Barracks near St. Louis, Missouri; aviation mechanics school was at Biloxi, Mississippi; and then pre-flight school was at Santa Ana, California. Training to become a pilot at Visalia, California, was hampered due to continuous fog, and only those few in his class who had prior experience passed the class; therefore McGrath was not among them. He then decided to attend navigation school, so he returned back to Santa Ana. Unbeknownst to McGrath his future pilot, Francis Smedley, had also been at Santa Ana and Visalia during some of the same time periods. John McGrath finished his training in navigation at Houston and also at San Marcos, Texas, before he would join a bomber crew. McGrath joined the crew of the *Sunrise Serenade* a short time after the initial crew had gotten together and replaced a man named Chester Story.

The bombardier, George D. Griffin, grew up on a dairy farm near Roxbury, New York. At a very young age he developed a love for baseball and continued to play during his years in high school and college up to the time he enlisted in the Army Air Corps. Bombardier pre-flight training for Griffin was at Arlington Field near Houston, Texas, and the majority of his bombardier schooling was conducted at Big Spring, Texas. Upon arrival at Big Spring, all cadets were entrusted with one of our nation's most closely guarded secret at the time, the Norden bombsight. Griffin was required to take a special oath promising to protect the secret of the sight with his life if necessary. Bombardier school lasted from 12 to 18 weeks during which a student dropped approximately 160 bombs, both in daytime and at night. Precise records were maintained of Griffin's hits and misses on the targets. Upon graduation from bombardier school, Griffin trained with another crew from the 452nd Bomb Group in the United States whose pilot was Jake S. Colvin. After arriving in England, George Griffin transferred to the crew of the *Sunrise Serenade* and became this plane's bombardier while flying combat missions.

The enlisted men aboard the plane also attended various schools for specialized training. Norbert E. "Dusty" Rhodes, the engineer (also known as the upper turret gunner), came from the small town of Williamsburg, Pennsylvania, which is located east of the city of Altoona. Prior to the War, Rhodes worked for Piper Aircraft at the nearby Peterson Airport where he helped build airplanes; it was here that he first developed a love for airplanes. Because of his admiration for planes and flying, as soon as he was able, Rhodes immediately enlisted into the Army Air Corps at New Cumberland, Pennsylvania, and then headed to Fresno, California, for basic training. The main part of his training to become an engineer and gunner for a heavy bomber was at the air base near Lincoln, Nebraska. Also, some of his training was done at Fort Myers, Florida. Engineer training required Dusty Rhodes to know every detail about the operation of his plane in the event that the crew experienced trouble during flight.

The radioman on the *Sunrise Serenade*, Andrew Senetsky, Jr., came from a small town known as Dickson City, Pennsylvania. This town is located just north of the much larger city of Scranton in the northeastern part of the state. Senetsky knew that his draft number would soon be called, so he enlisted at Fort George Mead, Maryland, with the hope of getting into the Army Air Corps, instead of being placed in another branch of service if he waited for his draft number to come up. He then went to Miami, Florida, for aptitude testing and then on to Jefferson Barracks near St. Louis, Missouri, for basic training. After basic training he traveled to an airfield near Great Falls, Montana, for more training and then to Sioux Falls, South Dakota, for radio school. After radio school was completed, Senetsky finished his training at a gunnery school in Wendover, Utah. This school enabled him to become proficient in shooting the .50 caliber machine guns aboard the plane that he would soon be aboard. Wendover would also be the site where Colonel Paul W. Tibbets and the rest of his B-29 crew trained to drop the first atomic bomb on Hiroshima, Japan, a few years later to help end the War with that country.

Andrew Senetsky mastered the Browning M2 machine gun at Wendover, Utah, during training. His position aboard the plane was a dual role as a gunner and radioman.
- *Collection of Andrew Senetsky.*

Harry C. Shoffner, the left waist gunner, grew up in Coffeyville, Kansas, and had been in the Kansas National Guard for a few years preceding the War. Early in 1940 he attended an aircraft school in Kansas City, Missouri. While attending this school, Harry Shoffner was introduced to a girl named Mary Lou from Lawrence, Kansas, through a friend of hers who was also attending the same school. Harry and Mary Lou were married on December 20, 1941, just two weeks after the attack on Pearl Harbor. Shoffner soon went to work for Consolidated Vultee Aircraft Company, (later named Convair) in San Diego, California. Their son, Larry, was born in October of 1942 during the same time that Harry Shoffner was drafted into the Army Air Corps. Shoffner left for active service when his son was only three weeks old. A couple of the specialized courses that Shoffner participated in before becoming part of a bomber crew was the Airplane Mechanic Course at Amarillo, Texas, and the Aerial Gunnery Course at Las Vegas, Nevada. Shoffner's training was much quicker than the rest of the crew since he had already taken basic training and other courses while being part of the Kansas National Guard. Because of his absence, Mary Lou and Larry moved back to Lawrence, Kansas, to be closer to her family to wait for her husband's return. Harry Shoffner would be the only crew member of the *Sunrise Serenade* with a child.

John G. Brown, the right waist gunner, left his home in Abingdon, Virginia, for a job as a ship fitter's helper on the docks in the ship yard in Portsmouth, Virginia. Brown took the job immediately after graduating from high school since it was a job with the National Defense, and he could support his country. One day his entire team at work was transferred to the midnight shift in an area where most of the welding was taking place. This position could have secured Brown a job away from the battle fields for possibly the duration of the War, but the work was not to his liking. He was constantly blinded by the intense and harmful flashes of the welders, so the next morning he told his boss he was quitting to join the Marines. The Marine quota was full that month, so Brown decided to enlist in the Army Air Corps instead. It turned out to be a decision that he never regretted, since no one could have ever predicted the terrible fighting inflicted upon the Marines by the Japanese during the War. John Brown attended basic training at Miami, Florida, and then traveled to Aircraft Mechanics school at Gulfport, Mississippi. His final training was at the gunnery school in Laredo, Texas, before joining the crew of the *Sunrise Serenade*.

The tail gunner, Raymond E. Dean, also had dreams of becoming a pilot, but during his cadet physical he failed to pass the eye exam. During his childhood on a farm near Valier, Montana, Dean built many models of airplanes in the hopes of someday flying. Dean enlisted in the Army Air Corps and attended basic training at St.

Petersburg, Florida, where he obtained a chance to take a test for Aerial Gunnery school. This time he passed the physical with 20-20 vision and later traveled to Harlingen, Texas, for aerial gunner training. The next phase of his training took him to Myrtle Beach, and also to Greenville, South Carolina, where he learned to use gun turrets on B-25 and B-26 bombers. Ray Dean's final training before joining the crew of the *Sunrise Serenade* took him to Salt Lake City, Utah, where he trained on turrets for B-17 and B-24 bombers.

The tail gunner, Raymond E. Dean, received part of his aerial gunner training at Harlingen, Texas, before being transferred to other sites for additional specialized training.
- *Collection of Gwendolyn Dean.*

Robert A. Lalumiere, the ball turret gunner, was a Haverhill, Massachusetts, native and attended Haverhill High School before being drafted. He worked after school making juke boxes. Realizing his draft number would soon be called, he tried to join the Air Corps and attend pilot's school, but was told that his "overbite" would prevent him from flying, so he waited for the draft. He entered the military on December 31, 1942, at Ft. Devens, Massachusetts. Coincidentally, they assigned him to basic training with the Air Corps in Miami, Florida. After basic training, he went to Aircraft Armorer's school in Denver, Colorado. He then attended an advanced armorer's school in Kingman, Arizona, where he received his instructions to be assigned to the crew of the *Sunrise Serenade*. Bob Lalumiere soon was on his way to the state of Washington to meet with the other men coming together under a pilot named Smedley.

James E. Gallagher was the "11th man" with the crew of the *Sunrise Serenade* who substituted in the ball turret location for Robert A. Lalumiere in April of 1944. Gallagher entered the Armed Forces at age 17 immediately after finishing high school in Pittsburgh, Pennsylvania, making him the fourth crew member from that state. Training to become a ball turret gunner took Gallagher to many of the same places that Lalumiere had trained, but neither were at the same base at the same time since Gallagher's training was about a month later. Jim Gallagher's training with a B-17 bomber crew while still in the United States took place with another crew, and he did not come to meet the full crew of the *Sunrise Serenade* until after they had already flown many combat missions.

The background of these eleven men, who at one time or another comprised the crew of the *Sunrise Serenade*, was typical of crew members from all of the B-17s. Through the events surrounding the *Sunrise Serenade* and other B-17 bombers of the 452nd Bomb Group, one sees that these crews were, however, far from typical. Their bravery and courage helped the United States defeat Germany in one of this country's most devastating wars.

The insignias of the 8th Air Force (center), 452nd Bombardment Group (left), and the 730th Squadron. This order represents the chain of command the crew of the *Sunrise Serenade* served under in combat.

The Crew Comes Together

The United States Army Air Force activated the 452nd Bombardment Group (H) on June 1, 1943, at Geiger Field, Washington, with plans to have the Group be at full strength by August 25, 1943. Immediately the Group was divided into four squadrons: the 728th, the 729th, the 730th, and the 731st. On June 13, 1943, the Group began to grow when 192 enlisted men reported for duty at Camp Rapid, located near Rapid City, South Dakota. A new Commanding Officer, Lt. Colonel Herbert O. Wangeman, with eight months of distinguished service overseas in the United Kingdom was introduced to the Group on June 18, 1943. On October 8, 1943, the 452nd Bomb Group began to move from Camp Rapid to Pendleton Field, Oregon. The four squadrons each left Camp Rapid by rail in Pullman cars made into troop trains.

The 452nd Bomb Group was just one of the twenty four B-17 Heavy Bomber Groups that would eventually become stationed in England as part of the United States Army's Eighth Air Force. In addition to the B-17 Groups, four Medium Bomber Groups, nearly twenty Fighter Groups, and nineteen Heavy B-24 Bomber Groups would also make up parts of the mighty Eighth Air Force in England. The 452nd Bomb Group would be among the last of the B-17 Heavy Bomber Groups to arrive in England, but the timing of its arrival would later prove to be at a critical time in the War's history.

While the 452nd Bomb Group was forming at Camp Rapid in the summer of 1943, most of the airmen who would eventually comprise the crew of the *Sunrise Serenade* were receiving their own training as part of the 396th Bomb Group. The pilot, Francis Smedley, was at the United States Army Air Base in Moses Lake, Washington, in August still finishing his pilot training. At this time he was assigned to the 594th Squadron of the 396th Bomb Group. Smedley seemed to adjust fairly well to the new camp as indicated in a letter he wrote home dated August 20, 1943, just after he had returned from a trip back to Wisconsin to visit his family.

> *"...Now at Moses Lake. The country is flat, barren, and not a tree for miles. The post is five miles out of town and quite a fair-sized city in itself. It's a new camp, and the barracks are little tar-paper jobs. We are about a mile from the flight line and everything is spread around. Our mess cost $1.60 per day (what a gyp joint). If you fail to salute an officer they fine you $10.00. All in all it's pretty rough, but I'll make it all right. I'm to meet the crew tomorrow or the next day. As yet I haven't got a co-pilot or navigator..."*

By August 25, 1943, the crew began to come together and included several men who would later transfer to other crews. The first four men to greet each other as fellow crew members were Francis C. Smedley - pilot; Leon R. Kleopfer - bombardier; John Collier - radioman; and Norbert E. Rhodes - engineer. A few days later Raymond E. Dean came aboard as tail gunner. On September 6, 1943, William J. Hewett joined the crew as their co-pilot, and by September 17th the rest of the crew comprised of Harry C. Shoffner, John G. Brown, Robert A. Lalumiere and an unknown navigator had joined the crew, bringing it to their total of ten men. In an effort to bring some immediate unity to the crew, Smedley bought the crew all different-colored baseball caps, which gave the crew something to laugh about as they jokingly called themselves the "Rainbow Crew".

A few of the newest Air Force bombers, the B-29's Super Fortresses, arrived at Moses Lake for the Rainbow Crew to inspect. For a brief moment Smedley was hoping that he might be able to fly one of the massive planes, which at that time were just coming off production lines and not being flown in active service. A minimum requirement of 400 hours flying a four-engine plane was necessary for a pilot to be considered a candidate for the new B-29's. The crew would instead be assigned to one of the newest models of the Flying Fortress, which was the B-17G, also just coming from the production plants.

On September 18, 1943, the crew joined in a formation comprised of eighteen B-17's on a practice mission over the Pacific coast. The crew learned what it was like to fly in a tight formation while Lockheed P-38 Lighting and Bell P-39 Airacobra fighter planes simulated the German *Luftwaffe* as they dived upon the planes. Formation flying took great skill, since all the planes were staggered both vertically and horizontally. Usually a minimum side distance of 50 feet from wing tip to wing tip was required in a tight formation. Minimum distances also had to be held in the front and back of the planes as well as above and below. These close flying formations left no room for error; so the pilots rarely had any time to relax.

The crew really began to come together with the assignment of Chester L. Story as the replacement for the original navigator. Story had already been in the Army for eight years and held the rank of 1st Lieutenant since 1941, making him the highest ranking officer in the crew. He had also been an instructor in navigation, so the crew was thankful that they were assigned such a knowledgeable airman. As the airmen continued to fly with each other on a daily basis, they became more unified as a bomber crew. The crew made a trip to Seattle after receiving a pass to leave the base. While in Seattle the men began to learn more about each other, now being away from the confines of the formal military bases. They bought themselves a 2-month-old puppy, part Collie and part German Shepherd, which became their unofficial and temporary mascot.

The four original officers of the *Sunrise Serenade* posed for a picture while in training at Pendleton, Oregon, on October 25, 1943. Left to right - Chester L. Story (navigator), William J. Hewett (co-pilot), Story's wife, Francis C. Smedley (pilot), and Leon R. Kleopfer (bombardier). - *Collection of the author.*

On October 15, 1943, forty-six crews from the 396th Bomb Group were officially transferred to the 452nd Bomb Group. Among those crews making this transfer would be the crew of the *Sunrise Serenade* who were designated as Crew #61. The 452nd Bomb Group would become the Group with which the crew would continue their training and eventually who they would serve with in combat. The 46 crews of the 396th Bomb Group joined the 24 crews of the 452nd Bomb Group who were just completing their own Third Phase ground school training at Pendleton Field, Oregon.

On October 21st the crew of the *Sunrise Serenade* finally left Moses Lake, Washington, and flew to Pendleton Field at Pendleton, Oregon. During the night of October 30th, the crew obtained more night flying time. During this flight a dangerous situation occurred which could have ended in disaster. A letter written home by Francis Smedley recalls the events of that flight:

"...Lt. Vallee our Flight Commander had scheduled Lt. Hess and myself for night transition. We both were to make two landings and then we would be checked out at night. Hess and I decided he would take the first shift, so he climbed into the pilot's seat with Vallee in the co-pilot's. Everything went swell, we took off and circled the field for the first landing. In the meantime I had gone up to the nose and seated myself as far up in it as I could. We came around the approach and I noticed we were a little low and with not too much air speed. I didn't think anything of it until I saw a fence directly in front of us (the landing lights were on). The next thing I knew, we hit with a helluva bang that shook the airplane like it would fall apart. The Flight Commander gave it full power and we pulled up to go around. About this time we were all hoping the engines wouldn't quit on us, and they didn't. I don't know what made me do it, but I went back to look at the tail (which hit the ground first) and found that the tail wheel mounting was broken all to hell. I went back to tell the Flight Commander not to land as the tail wheel wouldn't hold, and asked him to look at it, which he did. After informing the control tower of our situation, we were told to buzz the tower so they could see our main landing gear and see if it was all right. By this time the big wigs on the field were down at operations wanting to know what was wrong. The colonel called us on the radio and instructed us to fly around to burn up most of the gas we had in the tanks, and also to get our bombs off. In our terms to salvo them, which we did. It was about this time that I got the idea of putting a splint on the tail gear to brace it so we wouldn't tear out the bottom of the ship. Well we took the barrels out of the .50 caliber waist guns and had some one inch rope. So we made a swell splint on the strut. To make a long story short we came in and landed and the strut held. All the crew were in crash stations and as soon as the ship stopped we all piled out as fast as possible in case of fire. My gosh they had all the meat wagons out, and fire trucks that were on the field. The runway was lined with jeeps and plenty of "brass" in them. Boy what a show! Vallee was congratulated for making such a good landing with a wrecked ship, and I was congratulated for using my head and saving the tail end of the ship by using the .50 caliber barrels for splints. They said it was the first time anyone ever thought of doing that. We had a split crew comprised of half of mine and half of Hess's. Well I can say my crew put on a great show. My engineer and gunner helped me fix the tail strut, and my tail gunner had to show them how to salvo the bombs, and my radioman stuck at his post at the radio. All I can say is my crew gave a grand show and I'm proud to be one of them. They now say they won't fly with anyone but me. I don't know of any greater compliment..."

The Group continued their training which was now increasing, since only two months were left before they would fly to England and join the other many groups who were doing their part to fight the War. On November 4, 1943, the Group transferred to the airfield at Walla Walla, Washington. The airmen were so busy rising before sunrise and retiring late in the evening that they had very little time to write letters home. The once daily letters written by Francis Smedley to his mother were now becoming weekly instead. On November 10, 1943, Smedley wrote home and described the crew of their plane.

> "Starting with the bombardier who operates the bomb sight and is our gunnery control officer. This chap's name is Leon Kleopfer. He is a California boy about 24 years old and a good singer. Next we have Story, "Chet" for short, and he's our navigator. Besides his job of navigating, he also fires one of the forward guns. Chet is about 31 years old and a 1st Lt., and always ready for lots of fun. When it's time to work he really works hard. Now we come to the pilot and co-pilot. Well you know about the pilot, so I'll go to the co-pilot. As the word implies he's the pilot's assistant and must be able to take over any time. He is also in direct charge of the crew with the pilot's supervision. Well, that takes care of the four officers and now for the six enlisted men. First is Sgt. Rhodes, whom we call "Dusty". He's our engineer and a darn good one. He is also a gunner. Next is the assistant engineer who is Sgt. Brown and again the word explains itself. The lad is from Virginia and he's a good joker. Now we come to the radio operator who is a fellow by the name of Collier. John for short or "Sparky". He's a corporal like Vince. His assistant is Harry Shoffner who is a Kansas boy and has a child and never goes up without his pair of baby shoes pinned on his flying suit. Next is the armorer and his assistant. The armorer is Bob Lalumiere from Boston, Massachusetts. His main duty is a gunner and his assistant is Ray Dean who is a boy my age from Montana."

The positions on the plane by the gunners were as follows: John Brown - right waist gunner; Harry Shoffner - left waist gunner; Bob Lalumiere - ball turret gunner; and Ray Dean - tail gunner. As implied by Smedley's letter, it didn't take long for the crew to begin calling each other by nicknames. Smedley was often referred to as "Smed", "Pappy" or "Skipper". Other associated names for crew members were "Sparky" for John Collier; "Tiger Bob" for Robert Lalumiere; "Brownie" for John Brown; and "Deanie" for Ray Dean.

In mid-November the crew of the *Sunrise Serenade* moved to Redmond, Oregon, to conduct more maneuvers. The move to Redmond, located in the heart of the lumber industry, was a welcome change from the barren land at Pendleton. The crews were now responsible for the care and maintenance of their own plane, which included refueling, ammo loading, cleaning the guns, and other general maintenance that did not require a mechanic. Flying at high altitudes was done on a daily basis for 6 hours straight. Since the base was located in the Pacific Northwest, the weather was generally overcast or rainy. This simulated the typical weather that would be normal once the crews reached England. This weather did, however, often restrict the much-needed flying time that the crews had to have for training. On one particular day in November the crews could not fly, so part of the crew of the *Sunrise Serenade* decided to go rabbit hunting with their .30 caliber carbine rifles and their .45 caliber automatic pistols. The hunt was somewhat successful with the boys getting one rabbit, which they chose not to eat because of a sore on its leg. Ray Dean also demonstrated his markmanship by shooting from at least 50 feet away the individual wires on the fences the crew had been forced to crawl under earlier during the hunt. Other hunts also took place during that dismal November weather. Leon Kleopfer and another airmen went up into the mountains and spent the afternoon hunting for deer. The two men spotted a large buck which they estimated to have weighed 225 lbs., but it was too far out of range to fire a shot. They did, however, succeed in bringing back a smaller buck to the base.

The left waist gunner, Harry C. Shoffner, poses near the tail of a B-17 used in training while in the States. - *Collection of Mary Lou Shoffner.*

As the rain, fog, and snow continued to hamper the training progress at Redmond, Oregon, the crews became impatient and began to wish that they were back at the other less scenic bases in eastern Washington. On November 20, 1943, Francis Smedley took time to reflect that it had been a year ago on that date that he had taken his first solo flight in a Ryan Trainer at Sequoia Field, California.

One day the commanding officer of the Group reportedly called the officers together to put an end to the fraternization between the officers and the enlisted men who ranked below them. Many of the officers allowed the enlisted men of their crew to address them by their first names which was looked poorly upon by the commanding officers. The hot-tempered navigator from the *Sunrise Serenade*, Chester Story, stood up and said that he wanted out of the Group because of the no fraternization rule. Shortly after the incident he transferred to another Group, and John J. "Mac" McGrath became the permanent navigator with the crew. It was not unusual for individual crew members to switch crews due to personality conflicts with their own crew, or because they were closer friends with another crew. The various individual airmen were routinely around each other in living quarters and other activities while not flying with their assigned crews. Friendships developed quickly while playing cards, baseball, or sharing other similar interests. While switching crews was not encouraged by the commanding officers, they none-the-less did want each crew to perform as one unit without having personal arguments getting in the way of their duties.

In early December the commanders of the Group decided that the air crews would be much better off leaving the Walla Walla, Washington, and Redmond, Oregon, areas and head for better flying conditions at Rattlesnake Air Base near Pyote, Texas. The trip to Texas included having to fly over the Las Vegas, Nevada, area. As the crew of the *Sunrise Serenade* was flying near Las Vegas the plane unexpectantly developed "engine trouble", so the crew landed at an airfield near the city. The decision to fake engine trouble was unanimous since it might be the last time the crew would ever have fun together in the States. The consequences of such a move were great, but one engine did show slight signs of a small oil leak to hopefully help justify their unscheduled stop. The crew immediately headed for the sights of the big city where they would eventually spend three nights. At the El Rancho hotel and casino the crew personally met actress Dorothy Lamour who was performing, and who actually gave some of the men money for gambling. Most of the crew wasted no time in trying their odds at the casino games where Bill Hewett won $75, and another member of the crew won $100 at the craps tables. Francis Smedley did not fair so well at his try at gambling, but did manage to save his final $11 from being lost. Meanwhile some of the crew who were not interested in gambling, quickly became friends with the young girls who were walking around making change in the casino. Soon, almost the entire crew with their neatly pressed uniforms were trying their best to catch the attention of some of the pretty girls in the casinos. Each evening the crew enjoyed themselves at several shows taking in as much entertainment as possible before resuming their journey to Texas.

One of the highlights of the crew's unscheduled stop in Las Vegas was meeting the 29-year-old actress Dorothy Lamour. - *Collection of the author.*

While at the Las Vegas airfield checking on the plane, Francis Smedley was approached by a staff car with an Army Air Corps major in it. Smedley feared being reprimanded by the major for not being at Pyote, Texas, with the rest of his Bomb Group. To Smedley's surprise the major didn't even bring up the situation regarding his crew and plane being there, but instead started to talk about planes and flying. Smedley asked him whether he had ever been to La Junta, Colorado, where he had received part of his training, and the major replied that he had indeed been the director of flying there. This then gave the two men something in common to talk about, which brought much relief to Smedley, who had been fearing the worst. As the two men continued to talk, Smedley suddenly realized that this was the man who had reprimanded him for flying at 14,000 feet instead of the prescribed 3,500 at La Junta during his training. Both men laughed since this situation was well in the past. Seeing that Smedley was wearing his .45 caliber pistol, the major ended up inviting him to join him for target practice at the firing range.

During the entire time at Las Vegas, Smedley worried about what his punishment would be upon their arrival at Pyote, Texas. After arriving three days late, a captain approached the crew upon their landing and asked them where they had been. Smedley quickly stepped forward and replied that they had stopped in Las Vegas. The captain lightly laughed and while grinning and shaking his head he asked "There are lots of nice women there, aren't there?". Smedley meekly replied "Yes Sir", and then the captain asked if the stop had been caused by engine trouble. Smedley again slowly replied "Yes Sir", and the captain just smiled and said "That's all", and turned around and left the crew. The men stood looking at each other in a state of bewilderment and shock as they each breathed a sigh of relief that they had not been severely punished.

On December 14, 1943, the crews were greeted with a frost covering the ground at Pyote. As they assembled into formation for more training, the crews knew that their days of training in the States were coming to an end. The formation flying that morning took them over northern Texas which was surprisingly covered with snow that day. The previous few days had been ones of intense training where the crews had been airborne for an average of 8½ hours per day. They repeatedly flew both at high and low altitudes and dropped practice bombs on selected targets. On a good day the number of bombs a crew should drop on a target would be about ten. During these last few days of training the crew of the *Sunrise Serenade* had succeeded in dropping a total of 34 bombs on one single day. That intense day of training started at 10:00 a.m. and continued until almost 8:00 p.m. The plane had to land and reload four times for more bombs, then fly off to release over another target. After landing for the final time, the crew then had to refuel their plane and do other necessary duties before sitting down for dinner at 10:30 p.m. that evening. Francis Smedley had written home that his body, which was in prime physical condition, had now become greatly fatigued due to the constant flying.

During a break from flying, John Brown and Bill Hewett went to the firing range at the Pyote airfield to qualify to use a Colt .45 pistol that most of the airmen were issued. Every time the crew changed bases the Air Force had taken their side arms and given them new ones for no particular reason. The weather was cold and not cooperating so the two men were hurrying. One of the many safety procedures being strictly enforced at the firing ranges was the Raised Pistol rule, which meant that the person shooting had to have the muzzle pointing up at all times until instructed to commence firing. Hewett and the range officer did not quite see eye to eye on this rule, which created some tension as the men were shooting. Brown didn't even think either of them came close to qualifying that day, but the range officer passed them in order to keep from having them come back. By the time the men would enter combat, all of the bomber crews were ordered not to take their pistols with them on missions. Several reasons were given which mainly had to do with being taken prisoner. It was thought that by not carrying a gun any airman having to parachute from a plane would be met with less hostility on the ground, and also their guns would have been confiscated by the Germans and possibly used against other Allied troops. The chances of a downed American airman making it out of occupied German territory, even with a gun, were very remote anyway.

The air crews received their final inspection on December 16th and 17th by flying two last missions at Pyote. The crews of the 452nd Bomb Group left Pyote and flew to the air base located at Grand Island, Nebraska, for additional training. At Grand Island the crew picked up their overseas flying equipment and then boarded a train for Camp Shanks at Nyack, New York. Smedley, however, stayed with the *Sunrise Serenade* at Grand Island since he would be flying it to England. At Camp Shanks the men boarded the luxurious ocean ship known as the *Queen Elizabeth* on the last day of 1943 and also the first day of 1944. John McGrath volunteered to help supervise with the passenger loading since he was promised a pass if he would help, but he never got it. Some of the men had milled around on the dock, which proved to be to their advantage since those who had already boarded the ship were not allowed to leave once aboard. Much to the displeasure of those already aboard, many men were celebrating the coming of the new year outside the confines of the ship. The next day the ship pulled away from the dock and began its long voyage across the Atlantic Ocean toward England.

Most of the pilots had remained with their planes and left the airfield at Grand Island, Nebraska, on December 26th. The route to England would take them along the eastern coast of North America and then across the Atlantic Ocean and into England from the north. This northern route required much less travel over the Atlantic Ocean. After leaving Grand Island, the pilots then flew to Presque Isle, Maine, where they were then passed by the Air Transportation Command. Part of the Air Echelon flew to New Foundland, while others flew to a base located at Goose Bay, Labrador. From those locations they flew to Nutts Corner, Ireland, which was located near Belfast. After refueling at Nutts Corner, the planes then flew to their new base at Deopham (pronounced *Dee-Fum*) Green, England. Francis Smedley was not alone in the *Sunrise Serenade* as he flew it across the United States, the Atlantic Ocean, and finally to England. For an unknown reason the ten men aboard the plane with Smedley were from many different crews and also at least one member of the ground crew. Accompanying Smedley was Jake S. Colvin, Donald B. Bird, Ray W. Rottler, Robert F. Hausman, Thomas E. Murray, Zenas R. Cole, James J. Doherty, Ralph S. Hayes, and Charles Moravec. Colvin was a fellow pilot and friend of Smedley and Hayes was the Squadron Commander as well as a pilot.

The men traveling aboard the *Queen Elizabeth* soon realized that the stately appearance of the ship did not necessarily mean that they were going to travel in complete luxury. Half of the estimated 18,000 men aboard were quartered on the Promenade deck, while the other half were placed in staterooms. At the end of each 24-hour period the situation was reversed, so everyone was treated equally. Two meals were provided each day, which generally did not meet the young men's large appetites. To supplement their less-than-adequate meals, many men formed long lines at the ship's store in order to purchase more food. Most of the time the food was greasy and those who had never traveled by ship soon became seasick, which sometimes made the entire ship a mess. Conditions were generally clean though, and other than those getting sick, most men eventually settled in for the journey. Many men passed the time just enjoying a time of needed rest, or just walking along the deck. For many men the trip was either one of great riches or poverty as they exchanged money while playing blackjack and other card games. The *Queen Elizabeth* traveled unescorted during the six days at sea while it zig-zagged to thwart any German submarine attacks. Reportedly two days of travel were lost due to this evasive action taken a couple of times. A common rumor circulated among the airmen that Hitler had offered a quarter million dollar reward for any submarine U-boat crew that could sink either the *Queen Elizabeth* or the *Queen Mary* on its way to England loaded with American troops.

The entire crew of the *Sunrise Serenade*, except the pilot who flew the plane, traveled across the Atlantic Ocean aboard the *Queen Elizabeth*. - *Collection of the author.*

On the evening of Sunday, January 8, 1944, the ship dropped anchor at a harbor located in northern Scotland. To everyone's relief the ship had not come in contact with any German U-boat submarines. For the next two days the airmen debarked the ship to board waiting trains to take them to their new air base. The Deopham Green airfield was located near the small village of Attleborough, which is southwest of Norwich. With everyone now settling in at their new base, the crews immediately began extensive training to familiarize themselves with flying in group and squadron formations. Every crew member attended his respective ground schooling every day to further develop his specialized tasks. The month of January was long and hard for the air crews since every day was more practice flying and then more schooling. Most were eager to start flying actual combat missions, but their commanders knew that those extra days spent in additional training would eventually prove to save more lives.

Although the *Queen Elizabeth* was luxurious, the estimated 18,000 men aboard had to take turns sleeping in the State rooms while the other half slept on the Promenade deck every other night during the six day voyage. - *Collection of the author.*

During the month of January, Leon Kleopfer left the crew of the *Sunrise Serenade* to join the crew of a plane named *Invictus*. His replacement at the bombardier position was George D. Griffin, who had transferred from Jake Colvin's crew who were flying aboard *Cock O' the Walk*. Griffin was an excellent bombardier and made a fine addition to the crew. He generally went by the name of "Don" and soon held the nickname of "Grif" by his fellow crew members. A final change in the crew positions also came in January when the radio operator, John Collier, left to join the crew aboard the Flying Fortress known as *Inside Curve*. His replacement was Andrew Senetsky, Jr., who had earlier been flying as the radio operator on a plane piloted by William Hess. Because Senetsky was only a staff sergeant in rank on Hess's crew, his position was then given to an airman named Ken Raske, who had already achieved the technical sergeant rank needed to become a full-time radio operator. When this position came up on Smedley's crew, Senetsky was able to be promoted to a technical sergeant and thus became the permanent radio operator aboard the *Sunrise Serenade*. During this pre-combat time the crews began another specialized training of their own in the art of obtaining passes to cities like London and Cambridge. It was not long before those who were returning from passes to London informed those waiting to take their turn where the best places to visit were to have a good time.

Finally, after a month of anticipation, the crews were told of their first combat mission. Most were ready to get the mission under way even though approximately 200 heavy bombers of the 8th Air Force had been lost since their arrival in early January. The reports of other bombers being shot down by the Germans did bring some anxiety to airmen, but most were not even close to being prepared for what they would soon experience. For many airmen it was a sense of self-denial; they repeatedly told themselves that being shot down or even being killed would never happen to them.

That was understandable since the average age of the crew at the beginning of their combat missions was 22 years of age. Bill Hewett was the oldest member of the crew at 26, followed by Harry Shoffner 25, John McGrath 25, Andrew Senetsky 22, George Griffin 22, Norbert Rhodes 22, Bob Lalumiere 21, John Brown 21, Francis Smedley 21, and Raymond Dean 20. Jim Gallagher would later join the crew at age 19. This group of very young men were soon to take the controls of a 22 ton airplane loaded with over 4,000 pounds of explosives.

CREW POSITIONS

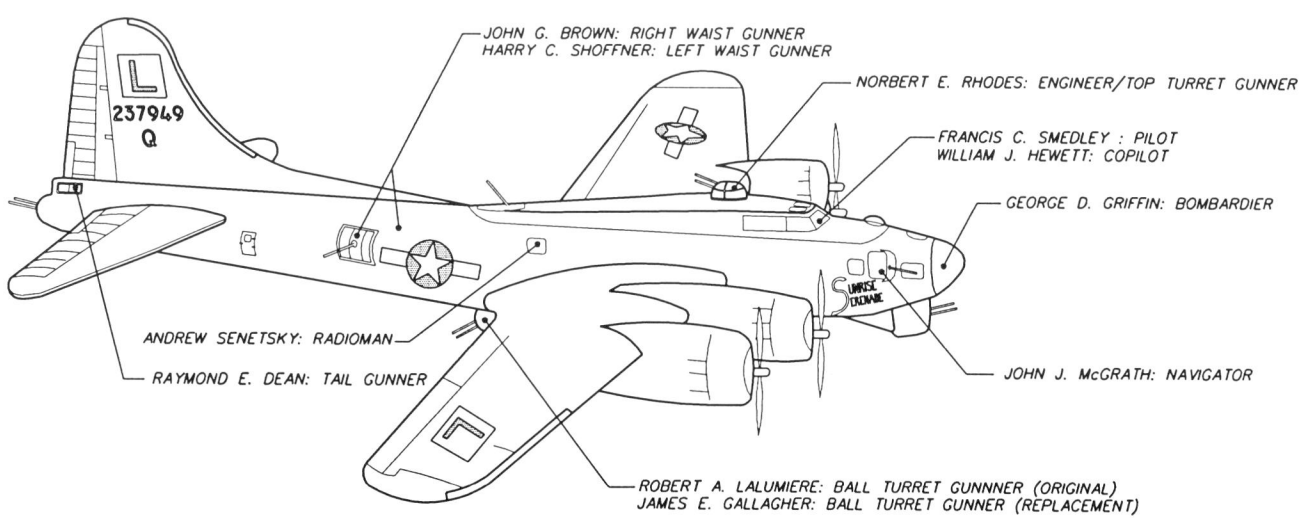

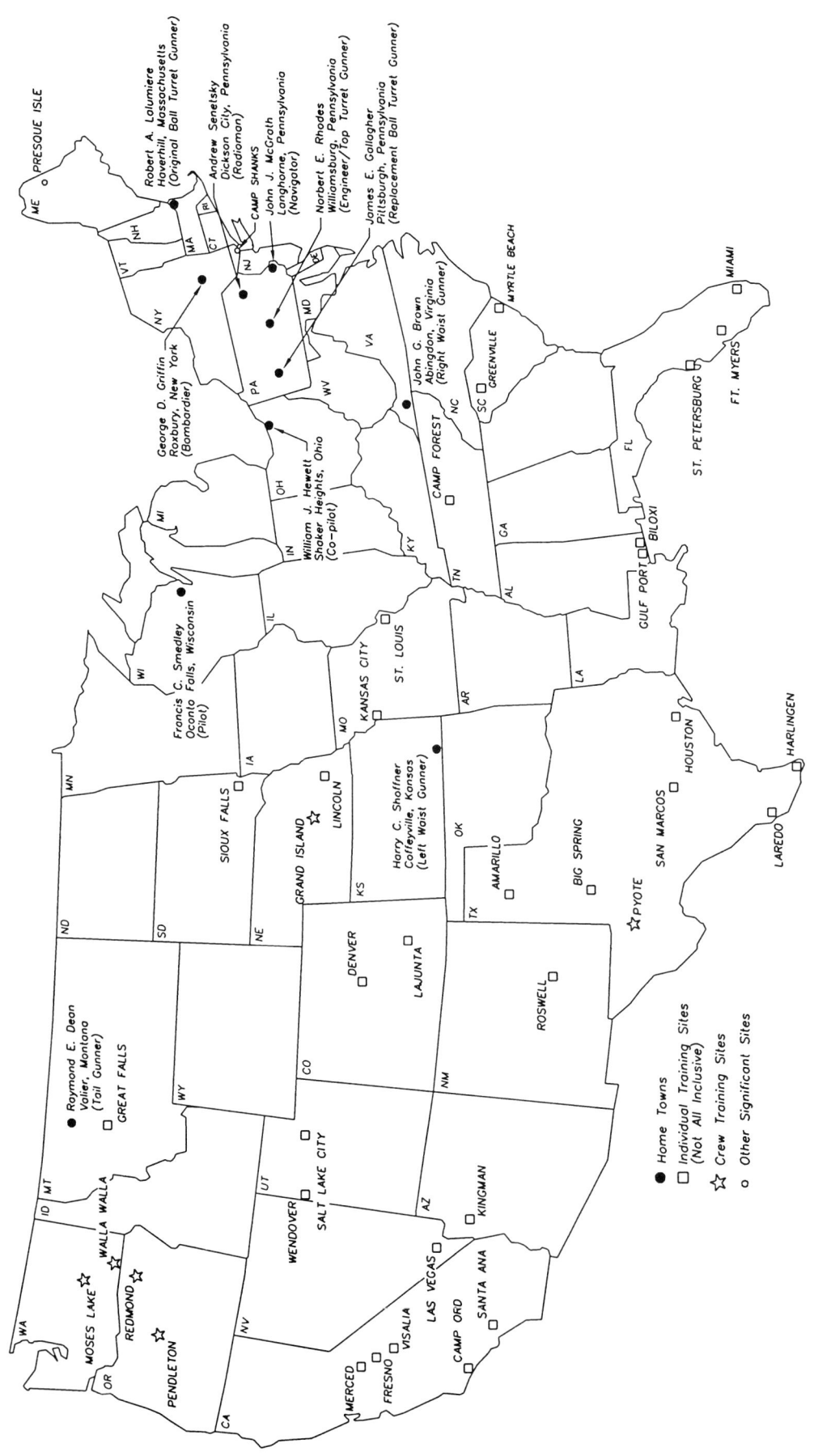

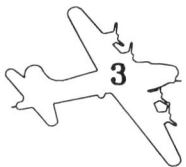

Specifications of the Plane

Production

The *Sunrise Serenade* was designated as a B-17G Flying Fortress. The "G" model was the newest and most prevalent design of the B-17 that flew in combat during World War II. Of the 12,731 B-17's that were produced, 8,680 of them were the B-17G model built from September 1943 to July 1945. The most noticeable difference between the B-17G and its predecessor the B-17F was the addition of the chin turret which carried two additional .50 caliber machine guns. The correct name given by its manufacturer for this type of bomber was the Model 299, but the Armed Forces designated it the B-17. The "B" designated it as being a bomber, and the "17" fitted an unused number for a new type of bomber. During the first showing of an early model of the B-17 in July 1935, a *Seattle Times* newspaperman named Richard L. Williams was reported to exclaim "Why it's a flying fortress!" and the name was soon forever associated with the plane. A few B-17G's were redesigned in 1945 and became known as B-17H's. These planes were specially equipped to carry a lifeboat under the fuselage to aid in search-and-rescue operations at sea.

The B-17 Flying Fortress was originally built only by the Boeing Aircraft Company, but since production during the War needed to be increased, both the Vega Aircraft Company (a subsidiary of Lockheed), and the Douglas Aircraft Company joined in the production known as the BVD pool. Of the total number of all models of B-17's produced, Boeing built 6,981; Vega had 2,750; and Douglas ended with a total of 3,000. Boeing built the most B-17G's, having constructed 4,035; while Vega produced 2,250; and Douglas 2,395. The *Sunrise Serenade* was built in the B-17G-20-DL 42-37894 to 42-37988 production block of planes by the Douglas Aircraft Company at Long Beach, California. Of the 94 planes in this block, nine were sent to serve with the 452nd Bomb Group. In order of lowest serial number, these nine planes eventually became known by their crews as *Lucky Lady, The Worry Bird, Princess Pat, Sunrise Serenade, Dinah Might, Mavoureen, Paper Doll, The Hard Way,* and *Delta Girl*. All nine of these planes would be shot down within the first three months of combat against the Germans. Only the plane known as *Princess Pat* stayed in the air longer than the *Sunrise Serenade*, but only by 11 days. With every new block of planes being built by the three companies, new changes were continually being developed to improve the design. During the block of planes with the *Sunrise Serenade*, the improvements made to the B-17's included adding a removable cockpit windshield panel, and also incorporating a change in the National insignia on the plane. The estimated cost for every new B-17G model of the Flying Fortress coming off the mass production lines was just over $238,000, although some early figures were as high as $259,000. Improved manufacturing equipment cut the cost to just $188,000 by the end of the War. At peak production approximately 45,000 workers were assembling the B-17's at a rate of just over 16 completed aircraft per day. These assembly plants operated 24 hours a day throughout the War.

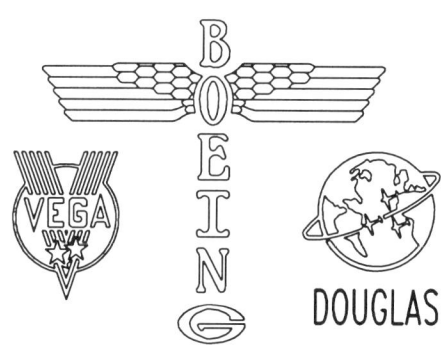

Two other major aircraft manufacturers, Vega Aircraft Company (a subsidiary of Lockheed) and Douglas Aircraft Company, joined the Boeing Aircraft Company to meet the wartime demands for B-17's. The trio became known as the BVD Pool.

Configurations

The wing span of a B-17G was 103 feet 9.38 inches from wing tip to wing tip. The length was 74 feet 8.9 inches if the plane was equipped with an earlier version of the tail turret like the *Sunrise Serenade*, or 5 inches shorter if it had the newest Cheyenne tail turret. The height of the plane was 19 feet 2.44 inches, which had remained a constant for all models used during the War. The weight while the plane was empty was approximately 44,000 lbs. Top speed was 302 mph, and normal cruising speed was at 160 mph. To lift these massive planes off the ground, the plane utilized four 1200 hp Wright R-1820-97 "Cyclone" nine-cylinder radial engines which operated at 2300 rpm at 25,000 feet. These engines were equipped with exhaust driven turbo-superchargers, which were installed under engine nacelles. Each individual engine held 37 gallons of oil. The maximum altitude was 35,600 feet, which often made for a very cold trip since the planes were not pressurized. The total range that a B-17G could travel with fully loaded fuel tanks was 3,750 miles. The fuel tanks, which were located in the wings, carried 2,780 gallons, and fuel was consumed at a rate of 200 gallons per every hour of travel. Extra tanks (called "Tokyo tanks"), sometimes mounted under the wings, extended the total to 3,630 gallons. These main fuel tanks were specially made to withstand penetration from enemy bullets with a double membrane of self-sealing rubber lining inside the tanks. After a bullet passed through the membrane, the hole was immediately sealed preventing any loss of fuel. The fuel itself was a special high octane, which was rated on a performance number scale as 100/300.

The bomb load varied with each particular mission depending on the planned target, but a normal bomb load was approximately 5,000 lbs. Several different types of bombs were used throughout the bombing campaign. General purpose bombs and demolition bombs were simply high explosive bombs, which created a massive explosion. The bombs available during the time the *Sunrise Serenade* flew in combat came in the following sizes: 100 lb., 250 lb., 500 lb., 1000 lb., and 2000 lb. The 100 and 250 lb. bombs were used against airfields, while the 500, 1000, and 2000 lb. bombs were used against targets such as aircraft factories and other industrial targets. An experimental 4000 lb. bomb was designed to be carried under the wing of a B-17. Most general purpose bombs had a .01 second delay, which brought detonation immediately after the bomb had penetrated the building roofs, but before actually striking the ground. This was hoped to bring maximum damage from the force of the explosion instead of just leaving a large crater. Fragmentation bombs were designed as anti-personnel bombs and were frequently used against targets that supported the German ground forces. These bombs came in the 20, 120, and 500 lb. sizes. The outside of the fragmentation bombs were scored with rings which, upon detonation fragmented into many pieces, which covered a large area. Another type of bomb that was used was called the incendiary bomb. These bombs were designed to start massive fires in industrial areas. The chemical mixture inside the incendiary bombs had good adhering qualities and the resulting fire could not be easily extinguished.

The armament inside the B-17G's which were used to protect them against the German fighters consisted of thirteen .50 caliber M2 Browning machine guns. Two of these guns were located in the chin turret, two in the ball turret, two in the tail turret, two in the upper turret, one in each side of the nose, one in each side of the waist area, and one through the top of the radio compartment. The Browning .50 caliber machine gun could fire 750 rounds per minute with an effective penetration range of 3,500 feet.

Crew Positions

The normal crew size of a B-17G was 10 men, but was later reduced to 9 several months after the crew of the *Sunrise Serenade* was no longer flying. This reduction in the size of a B-17 crew occurred later in the War when the Air Force decided that one waist gunner could handle the guns on both sides of the plane at this position. The shortage of qualified airmen and also the reduction in the number of German fighters attacking the Flying Fortresses helped to decide the change in the crew size. The pilot, Francis C. Smedley, was the aircraft commander and his job was to physically fly the plane. His copilot, William J. Hewett, was also expected to know all of the operational characteristics of the plane and assist Smedley in flying the plane. In the event that Smedley was killed or injured to the extent that he could not fly the plane, the entire duties would be taken over by Hewett. Before each mission the pilot and copilot would sit in their seats and go through a complete list of checks before the plane could take off. This system of checks took nearly an hour to complete and was very repetitious, but it often alerted the pilots to a problem which could have put the entire crew in jeopardy. The presence of two pilots in one plane seemed wasteful to other air forces, but the physical demands placed upon a pilot while flying a Flying Fortress were enormous. The plane could be flown from either seat, so Hewett often took over for Smedley, especially during long bombing missions.

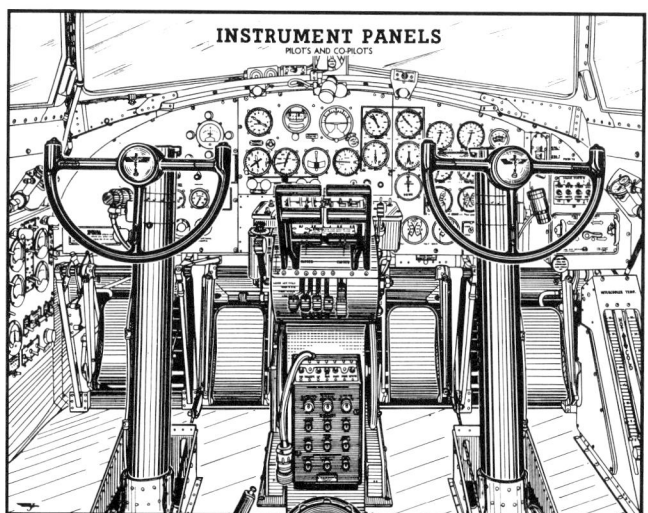

The B-17 could be flown from either seat although the pilot normally sat on the left side with the copilot on the right side. Before each mission the pilot and copilot went through a long series of instrument checks before take-off.
- *From the B-17 pilot training manual.*

Smedley also developed his own system of training the rest of the crew to fly the plane, which was not authorized by the Air Force. While flying in safe conditions, each member of the crew was often given a chance to fly the plane. Smedley wanted the rest of the crew to have at least some knowledge of flying the plane in case both he and Hewett were unable. The pilot and co-pilot of any B-17 had to have good leadership skills to help the entire crew develop as one good team. During the War the average age of bomber pilots was 21 years old. Smedley turned 21 just before beginning the combat missions. At that young age, the crew of the *Sunrise Serenade* were not without occasional disagreements, but they respected each other and performed their duties exceptionally well during flight.

The navigator's assignment was to get the plane over the intended target. Merely getting to the right city was not good enough since the Air Force was wanting to bomb specific targets such as aircraft factories, industrial plants, or bridges that would hopefully expedite the end of the War. Every mission had its flight plan laid out in advance for the navigators. The routes often consisted of a series of check-points where the planes should change course. Routes to and from the targets were hopefully planned to avoid known concentrations of anti-aircraft batteries. John J. McGrath had a table in the rear of the nose compartment where he calculated the course that the plane should be taking. He radioed the information to Smedley who then changed the course if necessary based upon these instructions. Navigators often utilized visual reference to the ground that matched their maps. However, the weather often made visual observations of the ground impossible, so the navigator relied upon dead reckoning which included using true airspeed, winds aloft, heading and time to calculate a new position from the last known position. McGrath also had to navigate by use of radio signals and celestial observations from the night sky. Sometimes his navigation depended upon using a combination of all of these methods. A gyro-magnetic compass and a radio compass were two vital instruments used by the navigator. Throughout each mission, McGrath would inform Smedley of their position and the time estimates to various check points. His main goal was to reach the IP (Initial Point) which was the start of the bomb run. It was also McGrath's duty to operate the two cheek guns when he could leave his table.

The bombardier controlled the bombing of enemy targets. It was George D. Griffin's job to accurately place the bombs on the intended target if the entire mission was to be deemed a success. His main tool was the Norden bombsight, which was a top-secret device and heavily guarded throughout the entire War. The Norden bombsight compensated for a variety of factors including altitude, airspeed, ground speed and drift of the plane. Once the IP was reached, the bombardier would fly the plane through the bombsight linked to the autopilot of the plane. It was then that Griffin had to fly the plane straight and level to the MPI (Main Point of Impact) amidst a barrage of flak. His view was the best in the entire aircraft since he was sitting behind the bombsight in the plexiglas nose.

Once the target was reached, he would attempt to line it up in the telescope of the bombsight. Two sets of crosshairs showed drift left or right of the target and the other showed the rate of closure. When the two indicators came together, the bombs would automatically release and head for the target.

George Griffin also operated the Bendix chin turret guns by remote control when he was not operating the bombsight. The chin turret guns were needed to help defend the plane during head-on attacks. During most of 1943, the German fighters found that the head-on attack against the B-17's was the most successful tactic in which to fire upon the huge planes without receiving much return fire. The fighters would come toward the B-17's at a slightly lower altitude than what the bombers were flying. This low position could not be fired upon by the upper turret gunner or the two cheek guns located on both sides of the nose. The addition of the chin turret solved many of the problems that had aggravated the bomber crews when under a frontal attack by the German fighters.

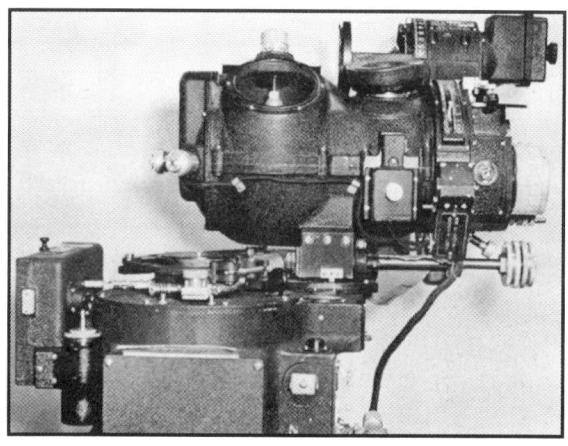

The most valuable instrument aboard a B-17 was the highly secret Norden bombsight, which enabled the planes to accurately hit their intended targets. - *Air Force photo.*

Norbert E. "Dusty" Rhodes, as the plane's engineer and upper turret gunner, was specially trained to have a wide knowledge of how the *Sunrise Serenade* operated and also how the equipment operated that was aboard the plane. His training enabled him to service the plane in the event that the crew had to make an emergency landing away from their base and normal ground crew. Rhodes was also very knowledgeable regarding every detail associated with the guns aboard the plane and also the bomb racks. Every mission could encounter unforeseen problems due to mechanical failures or problems caused by the plane being hit by the German fighters or flak. The B-17's were a mass of electrical systems, hydraulics, oxygen lines, and a variety of other systems that required someone with detailed knowledge of the plane to be able to improvise in the event of a problem. It was also the duty of the engineer to operate the upper turret during combat situations. The upper turret was located just behind the pilot and copilot above the flight deck, making the cockpit very noisy, especially when Rhodes fired the guns in the forward position. The guns on the upper turret had an automatic shut-off mechanism if the gunner was firing over the propellers or toward the tail of the plane. The turret guns could only be elevated to 45 degrees, which left a blind spot directly overhead. The engineer's seat was just behind those of the pilot's so the engineer often became a third man in the cockpit as he stood between the pilots. As the plane was started, the engineer stood in this position to check the fuel and engine gauges. He then maintained watch over them periodically during the flight to determine if all the engines were working properly.

The radio operator's position was one of three positions which were isolated from the rest of the crew. Andrew Senetsky's seat was located behind a wall at the rear of the bomb bay area. The radio room was considered to be the safest place in the plane in the event of a crash landing or ditching at sea. Upon orders from the pilot, the rest of the crew would all meet in the radio room in the event of an eminent crash. This room contained emergency equipment and other tools. One of his first duties before take-off was to make sure that the radio was properly tuned to the right frequencies. All radio transmissions made by Senetsky were secretly entered in Morse code to hopefully confuse the Germans. His position became the lifeline for the entire crew in the event that they developed trouble, such as going down at sea, and had to relay their position. After bombing the target, Senetsky would relay the information back to the base so that the leaders would have first-hand knowledge of the mission before the planes returned. It was crucial to have the information back as quickly as possible so the planning for the next day's mission could begin. Senetsky also listened for messages coming from headquarters, such as a decision to abandon the mission or turn to a different target. An antenna called the "fish bowl" was a lead ball attached to a long wire that could be lowered at different levels out of the plane for better reception. During formation flying this antenna would not be extended very far from the plane, but in other areas it could extend at least 25 feet. Andy Senetsky remembered an incident during training at Walla Walla, Washington, when a radioman from another plane forgot to retract this antenna before landing. The fully extended wire and lead ball struck a parked car which caused much excitement from its owner. Another function of the radio operator was to activate the cameras located beneath his floor. These cameras took pictures of the bombing while in progress, which gave headquarters an idea of the extent of damage to the target. While not at his radio, Senetsky operated a .50 caliber machine gun that was hung from a swivel and pointed out of the roof of his compartment. The field of fire from his gun was somewhat limited, but it did give the crew one more weapon against the German fighters.

Another isolated position on the plane was the tail gunner's location. Raymond E. Dean was located at the very rear of the plane where he protected against enemy aircraft coming from the rear. After the *Sunrise Serenade* became airborne, Dean would leave the radio room and crawl around the rear wheel to his guns. His legs were doubled back with his knees resting on padded supports while in a kneeling position. The tail gunner often saw a lot of action while firing his guns at German fighters coming in from the rear. Early models of the B-17 had just a ring with a bead for the gun sight, but later models were improved to have a compensating sight. The compensating sight required the gunner to recognize the type of enemy aircraft and feed this information into the gun as he fired. The rear attack was successful for the German fighters since they could often hide in the contrails left by the many bombers in formation. Dean had his own escape hatch near the tail of the plane in the event that the plane needed to be evacuated.

The final isolated position was the ball turret which was considered to be about the worst position on a Flying Fortress since it hung exposed below the center of the plane. The specifications for being a ball turret gunner usually required the smallest man on the crew to fill this position. For Robert A. Lalumiere, and later James E. Gallagher, this position aboard the *Sunrise Serenade* had them completely away from the rest of the crew. The ball turret position required a great amount of bravery since the occupant had to deal with being in a very tight place, and also did not have the luxury of having his parachute attached to him. His field of fire was a complete 360 degrees on the horizontal plane and 90 degrees on the vertical plane. An exception to this field of fire were those locations when an automatic shut-off mechanism prevented the gunner from shooting at his own plane, such as at the propellers. Once inside the ball turret, the gunner's body was in a fetal position with his back against an armor plated door. Only when his guns were pointed straight down could he exit through his door and into the floor of the plane. On several occasions the ball turret became jammed on other B-17's and the gunner could not escape until the plane landed. A hand crank could raise the ball turret in an emergency, but sometimes the tongue and groove metal section was also damaged. If the ball turret became stuck and the landing gear could not be lowered upon landing, the gunner was crushed upon impact. Another serious problem was the location of the ball turret, which presented a weakened spot in the underside structure of the plane. Many Flying Fortresses were known to have broken apart at the ball turret location upon impact with another plane sending the gunner to his death while still inside the ball. The ball turret was operated by a system of pedals and grips, which controlled the movement and firing of the guns.

For John G. Brown and Harry C. Shoffner much of the trip over enemy territory was done while standing behind their waist guns. Their bodies filled a larger target area, so the waist gunners incurred the largest number of casualties during the War. As Brown manned the right side of the plane, Shoffner stood slightly staggered on the left side behind him. The right waist gunner's position was closer to the front of the plane. Earlier models of the B-17 had the waist gunners directly behind each other, which often caused them to bump into each other during intense moments of combat. A large plexiglas window was an improvement over earlier models of the B-17 which afforded a large view of the area outside their plane and helped to keep cold air from swirling in. As their guns blazed away at German fighters, the empty shell casings from the two guns piled up on the floor, and at times they completely covered it. Later in the War canvass bags were used in an attempt to catch the falling casings. The guns were hand-held, but were also supported by bracing on the plane. Unlike other guns on the plane, the waist guns did not have an automatic shut-off mechanism, so the waist gunner could conceivably shoot his own plane if he wasn't careful. In August of 1944, the two waist gunner positions was reduced to just one man who operated both sides.

Plane Markings
Each individual plane had certain markings to distinguish it from another plane. Usually the pilot had the honor of naming the plane, but often, to be fair, the crew would all put names into a hat and draw out the winning name. Francis Smedley chose the name for his crew's plane, and the rest of the crew felt that it sounded good as well. Dusty Rhodes, with the assistance of John Brown, painted the name "*Sunrise Serenade*" on the nose so that everyone would recognize their beloved plane. Two members of the 452nd Bomb Group's ground crew, Dan and Tom Birkbeck, were very talented artists and did most of the more elaborate art work on many of the other planes. The original crews were afforded the opportunity of naming a plane since they were the first ones to fly the new planes. Replacement crews coming into their Group later, often had to fly whatever plane was available to them. Sometimes replacement crews flew many different planes, most of which were already well used and beat up by the time they were assigned to them. Most of the planes had names to them, but sometimes the crew never got around to painting them on, or their plane was shot down early. Popular nose art designs included beautiful or even risqué portraits of women, cartoon characters, the name of the pilot's wife or girlfriend, popular songs of that era, or references to the War itself.

The Army Air Corps leadership did not officially use the names given to the bombers as a way to recognize them, although the crews preferred to use the names. Each bomber had its own serial number, which properly identified it, and distinguished it from all the others. The serial number assigned to the *Sunrise Serenade* was 42-37949, although the tail number was just 237949. The "42" at the beginning of the serial number indicated that construction for the plane had been budgeted in the year 1942. The actual construction of the *Sunrise Serenade* occurred during the late summer of 1943. By dropping the "4" and the dash, the remaining six digits represented the tail number. During the flight formation before a mission, the *Sunrise Serenade* would have been referred to as plane "949" on the flight schedule, which was the last three digits of the tail number. Most veteran airmen do not recall the entire tail number on their plane, but many can still remember the last three digits.

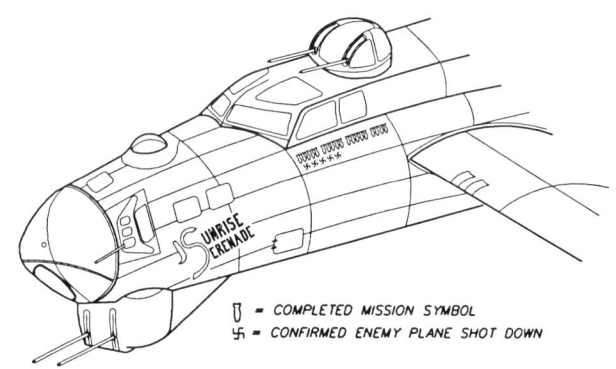

FRONT MARKINGS

Bomber crews often painted the name they gave their plane on the nose. Individual bomb symbols and swastikas below the cockpit window represented the number of missions flown and the number of enemy aircraft they had shot down.

Above the number on the tail was the insignia representing each individual Bomb Group. The 452nd Bomb Group was assigned a square with the letter "L" inside the square. This square was white with a black letter on olive drab colored planes like the *Sunrise Serenade*, but these two colors were reversed on later natural metal colored planes for better visibility. This same marking was also affixed to the top surface of the right wing, so it could be seen by planes flying from above. The Square indicated that the plane belonged to the 3rd Air Division of the 8th Air Force. Under the 3rd Air Division were fourteen Bomb Groups each displaying the square insignia with a different letter inside. On D-Day only, black and white stripes were added around the wings and fuselage on 452nd Bomb Group planes. In January 1945 two parallel yellow horizontal bands were added on the vertical tail and on the wings for the rest of the War. The 3rd Air Division was further broken down into Combat Wings (also referred to as Bomb Wings). The 96th, 388th and 452nd Bomb Groups all made up the 45th Combat Wing since their bases were all in close proximity to each other. The 1st Air Division was the other 8th Air Force unit utilizing the B-17's from bases in England. The planes from this division were identified by a letter inside a triangle for the Bomb Group insignia.

Below the tail number on a B-17 was the "Call" letter for each plane. This individual letter identified it during radio transmissions from other planes. This letter varied on each plane, and on the *Sunrise Serenade* it was "Q". The letter "Q" was derived from a system of lettering planes from each squadron in sequence and had no special meaning. When either Francis Smedley or Bill Hewett contacted the control tower, they would identify themselves as "Q for Queenie". Each squadron also had a letter/number code assigned to it, which was intended to be displayed in large figures on the fuselage, but those planes from the 452nd Bomb Group did not display theirs. This was due to certain Combat Wing commanders either deeming them unnecessary or not issuing the details to their particular Groups. Had the 730th Squadron displayed this letter/number combination it would have been shown as "6K".

Certain bomb groups also had nicknames for their entire group such as "The Sky Scorpions" for the 389th, or "The Bloody Hundredth" for the 100th, but the 452nd, like most of the other groups, did not have a nickname. Other markings on the planes were symbols for completing missions and also for downing enemy aircraft. The symbol for a completed mission was represented as one vertical bomb. These were usually placed in groups of five below the pilot and co-pilot's windows. A swastika symbol painted below the bomb symbols represented one confirmed enemy aircraft shot down for each swastika. Variations to these symbols included a horizontal bomb which was placed on those B-24 bombers who participated in the low-level Ploesti, Romania, oilfield bombing, or a large bomb symbol for bombers participating in the D-Day invasion. A box with a parachute symbol would indicate a supply mission. Certain crews went a step further to paint a star above the bomb symbol to represent that they had flown as group or squadron leader during that mission. A Purple Heart symbol indicated that their plane had sustained heavy damage during that mission. Most of these additional markings that accompanied the bomb symbol were rarely used by the crews. Occasionally the swastika symbols were also painted below the particular gunner's location who had been credited with downing the plane. Most crews preferred to have them displayed in just one location to show crew unity.

Individual crew names were also sometimes painted below each airman's window giving a personal feel to his position.

During the early part of the War, all B-17's were painted in camouflaged colors. The upper surface of the plane was dark Olive Drab and the underside was Neutral Gray. It was intended for these two colors to either blend in with the ground when looking down upon the planes from above, or match the color of the sky when observing the plane from below. The *Sunrise Serenade* was painted in these two basic colors, with the other markings such as tail number, call letter, bomb symbols, or other small markings painted either yellow or white. By January 1944 the camouflage paint scheme was discontinued since its original purpose was no longer of great importance. The Germans generally knew that the heavy bombers were coming due to their advanced radar detection, and the camouflaged paint often faded and did not match the surroundings anyway. The newer Flying Fortresses arrived in England in their natural metal finish, which gave them a bright silver look. The top of the nose and inside edges of the engines on these unpainted aircraft were painted a matte finish in green to reduce glare for the pilots. Most of the identifying symbols on the natural metal finish planes were painted black. The decision to leave the B-17's unpainted proved to make the planes a little lighter, which slightly improved performance. The most important factor arising from this decision to leave the planes unpainted was the extra time being saved at the production plants by not having to paint the planes. That added time produced more B-17's to help fight the War that was heating up in Europe.

TAIL MARKINGS

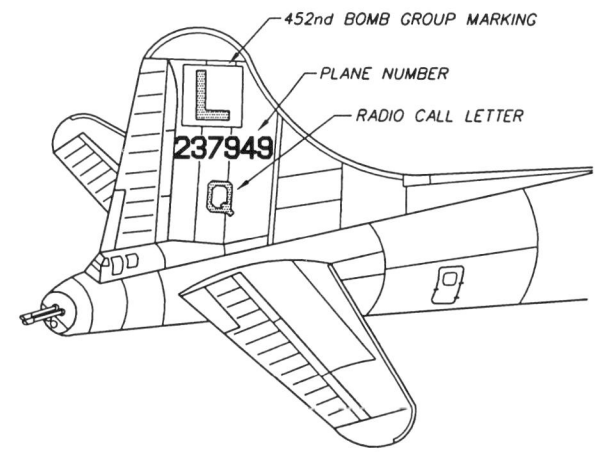

The markings on the tail identified the Bomb Group to which the plane was assigned, its tail number, and the Call letter used during radio transmissions.

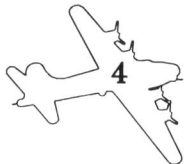

Before the Arrival of the *Sunrise Serenade*

Much had already taken place on the continent of Europe before the crew of the *Sunrise Serenade* arrived. By 1944, World War II was in its fifth year, with the United States having been involved just the previous two years. One of the first major bombing missions conducted by the United States Air Force in WWII had actually occurred against the Japanese on April 18, 1942. Lt. Col. James H. Doolittle trained 16 volunteer aircrews in B-25 Mitchell bombers and launched his attack from the aircraft carrier *Hornet*. The successful attack upon the Japanese mainland was seen as retribution for the attack upon Pearl Harbor four months earlier.

The American Air Force bombing campaign against Germany, however, did not fully materialize until late in the summer of 1942. While the air war over occupied German territory was becoming a full-scale battleground, the crew members of the *Sunrise Serenade* had not even met each other. Many events occurred in the War before the arrival of the *Sunrise Serenade* and before the 452nd Bombardment Group became part of the mighty 8th Air Force.

On August 17, 1942, the United States 8th Air Force flew its first bombing mission utilizing the B-17's from a base at Polebrook, England. Eighteen B-17's left the base; six flying along the French coast as a diversionary tactic to draw the German fighters away from the main force. The remaining 12 planes flew to bomb the Sotteville railroad marshalling yards at Rouen, France, which was located just across the English Channel. Four squadrons of Royal Air Force Spitfires joined the group to provide fighter support against the German *Luftwaffe*. The bombing was considered a success; at least 50 percent of the bombs hit their intended target, and only two planes received damage.

The first three missions by the 8th Air Force gave the impression that the B-17 could not be touched by the German fighters or flak coming from the ground guns. However, on their 4th mission to bomb the docks at Rotterdam, The Netherlands, on August 21, 1942, the 8th Air Force had finally met reality. Twelve planes were dispatched, with three having to turn back due to mechanical trouble, leaving the other nine to continue without them. The remaining B-17's were running 16 minutes late for their rendezvous with another Spitfire fighter escort, and their present escort had to turn back due to shortage of fuel. Given the impending circumstances, a recall was issued to bring the bombers back home. As they were just starting to turn around, they were attacked by a group of over twenty Focke-Wulf 190 (FW-190) and Messerschmitt 109 (Me-109) German fighters. A 20-minute battle ensued, resulting in the B-17 crews knocking down two enemy planes with the probability of five more, and damaging six additional planes. One Fortress named *Johnny Reb* lagged behind from the protection of the main group formation. Five German fighters seized the opportunity and attacked the lone B-17. A 20mm shell went into the cockpit, wounding both the pilot, 2nd Lt. Richard F. Starks, and the co-pilot, 2nd Lt. Donald A. Walter. Despite the attack, the crippled B-17 was still able to make it back to England. Walter later died from his wounds, and became the first combat casualty of the 8th Air Force bomber crews during World War II. Although loss of life was encountered on this mission, it did prove that the B-17 crews could stand on their own against the German fighters without having their own fighter escorts.

The Lockheed P-38 Lighting fighter became the first American escort plane for the B-17 bomber crews. Later they were joined by Republic P-47 Thunderbolts and the famed North American P-51 Mustangs. The fighter support was crucial for the bombers so they could focus on their mission without having to deviate from their precise bombing runs. Anti-aircraft fire producing flak was something that neither the bombers nor their escorts could prevent. Normally both the German and American fighter planes would stay clear of the flak as the bombers flew through it alone. This gave the fighter planes on both sides a brief opportunity to regroup themselves. As tempting as it was to break formation away from the flak, the bomber pilots continued their steady and level course right into the heavy black puffs of smoke from the exploding shells. Once the bombers had dropped their bombs on the intended target and began to fly out of the range of the flak guns, the German fighters would then reappear as would the American escort fighters to resume their respective roles as pursuer and escort.

The first loss of B-17 planes by the 8th Air Force occurred on September 6, 1942, on a mission to Meaulte, France, when two planes went down. The first of these planes was named *Southern Belle* and would be the first of thousands of B-17's to follow a similar fate during the course of the War in Europe. The first B-17's lost in combat during the War, however, were at Pearl Harbor, Hawaii, when the Japanese attacked. Coincidentally, a group of B-17's were arriving in Hawaii from California at the same time the battle was taking place. Small bombing missions against the Germans continued throughout the remainder of 1942, occasionally losing a few planes, with a daily high loss of six planes on December 20, 1942, at Romilly-sur-Seine, France. Altogether, the 8th Air Force had listed approximately thirty bombers as MIA (Missing In Action) from September 6 to December 30, 1942. Of these losses, twenty-eight were B-17's. The success of the bomber crews upon their German targets was usually very accurate, however the vast territory controlled by the Germans, and also their ability to quickly rebuild damaged areas seemed to many that no amount of Allied bombing could ever make a decisive difference in the War.

The first B-17 casualties of World War II were at Pearl Harbor, Hawaii, during the attack by the Japanese on December 7, 1941. - *Collection of the author.*

The new year of 1943 started out with a mission to St. Nazaire, France, on January 3rd, which resulted in a new daily high loss of seven planes. This port city was located in western France in the Bay of Biscay and was one of five German submarine sites in the bay. This city had been named "Flak City" by earlier bomber crews after their initial raid to the city on November 9, 1942, had made them aware of the many anti-aircraft guns defending the city. One of the bombers to go down on the January 3, 1943, raid was relentlessly attacked by fighters as it limped alone across the Bay. With several of the crew already dead, and others parachuting into and drowning in the icy-cold water, the pilot was able to set the plane down onto the water's surface. Meanwhile the top-turret gunner put on a show of stubborn valor, refusing to leave his gun position while continuing to fire at the German fighters overhead. Other B-17 crews witnessed his guns still blazing away as the plane sank below the surface, taking him with it.

The January 3, 1943, mission to St. Nazaire introduced a new bombing technique for the B-17 crews. Prior to this date, the bombardiers would release their bombs individually, but on this date all bombardiers released simultaneously when they saw the bombs leave the lead plane. This resulted in greater accuracy and a more concentrated strike on the target. The most skilled bombardier and pilot flew in the lead aircraft, which set precedence for the remainder of the War.

A couple of weeks later from January 14-24, 1943, the Allied commanders Franklin Roosevelt and Winston Churchill and their strategists held a meeting known as the Casablanca Conference. Much-needed coordination between the Allies was achieved; however, the meeting did not go without some blaming and insinuations about how each country was fulfilling their part in the War. Britain's Churchill sent a memo to his Secretary of State for War noting that "*the Americans have not yet succeeded in dropping a single bomb on Germany.*" Churchill was referring to the actual country of Germany and not the various other countries the Germans had taken over. Although the English had previously bombed Berlin on August 24-25, 1940, in retaliation of the Germans' bombing London, the strength of the German defenses was much more fortified now 2½ years later. The British were also critical of the daylight bombing campaign, saying that it should be ended in favor of night bombing due to the heavy losses being inflicted. The Americans, however, knew that the Norden bombsight would not be effective at night, so they continued to bomb during the day, while the British bombed at night. Three days after the Casablanca Conference, on January 27, 1943, the American forces sent their first bombers consisting of fifty-five B-17's, to German soil toward the port city of Wilhelmshaven. This city was located on the North Sea in northwest Germany, and was the site of the U-boat submarine construction yards. The bombing mission was aimed at one of Germany's greatest weapons, submarines, since they were sinking hundreds of Allied shipping vessels. Three planes were lost that historic day; one B-17 was shot down by fighters and two B-24's collided with a German FW-190. A return mission to "Flak City" on February 16, 1943, resulted in a new daily high loss of eight planes. This mission was also the *Luftwaffe's* first experimentation with dropping clusters of small, time-fused, fragmentation bombs into the 8th Air Force bomber formations. Although the incident quickly secured the attention of the nearby bomber crews, the German fighter carrying the bombs miscalculated his release and the bombs missed their mark.

Prior to take-off for a return mission to Wilhelmshaven ten days later on February 26, 1943, the American press was given approval to be involved in the trip. Six war correspondents from "The Writing 69th" flew with the 8th Air Force that day. All of the correspondents were eager to fly in the Flying Fortresses; however, some of the planes also flying that day were the B-24

Liberators. A public relations officer succeeded in persuading only one reporter to fly on one of the B-24 planes coming from a different base. Among those flying on the famed B-17's was Walter Cronkite, who later went on to be a distinguished news reporter. The B-17's would make better headlines, in the eyes of the reporters, than the B-24's which were seemingly not as glamorous. Even though the B-24's proved to be every bit as successful as their counterpart, the size of the B-17, combined with all of their armament, was very impressive. A total of seven planes were lost that day, including the B-24 which carried the lone war correspondent, Robert B. Post, from the *New York Times*.

Nearly two months later on April 17, 1943, the largest attacking force of B-17's up to this date was sent to bomb the Focke-Wulf plant at Bremen, Germany. This force, which was comprised of 115 planes, lost sixteen that day, which doubled the previous daily high loss and was 14 percent of the total group. Another 39 planes were damaged. The assault by the *Luftwaffe* fighters was relentless all the way to and back from Bremen, especially on the lead planes that were trying to focus on the bomb runs. Many B-17 crewmen were already calculating their own odds against returning to base safely. Counted a success, the attack upon Bremen seriously disrupted the production of aircraft and the plant was later moved deeper into Germany.

Bombing operations continued against the German-held cities throughout the spring and summer of 1943, with the American forces continuing to lose planes and men. One 35-day period between May 21 and June 25, 1943, was especially bad for the 8th Air Force. Missions to Wilhelmshaven on May 21st lost thirteen planes; to St. Nazaire on May 29th lost fourteen planes; to Wilhelmshaven on June 11th lost eight planes; to Bremen on June 13th lost twenty-seven planes; to Huls and Antwerp on June 22nd lost twenty planes; and to targets of opportunity over Germany on June 25th eighteen planes were lost. These six missions resulted in the loss of 100 planes. The damage, however, being inflicted upon the German industrial targets was increasing, though still not enough to subdue the German army. Around this same time the 452nd Bomb Group, of which the *Sunrise Serenade* would become associated with, was being activated on June 1, 1943, at Geiger Field, Washington.

Between July 25 and August 12, 1943, another six days of intense battle against the Flying Fortresses took place over the cities of Hamburg, Kiel, Kassel, and other German targets. This resulted in a six-day loss of 114 aircraft and 1,140 crew members. The Germans were also taking massive losses, but neither side showed any sign of giving in to the other. The round-the-clock bombing by the American and British forces gave the Germans no rest, and strikes could be expected at any time of the day. One particular night raid by the British on Hamburg in July of 1943 resulted in at least 50,000 German civilians being killed due to firebombing. Unfortunately, civilians become casualties of war; though, the majority of adults were fueling the German army by working in factories to make the weapons of destruction that prolonged the War.

By August of 1943, the Americans were ready to inflict large-scale assaults upon the Germans, even at the expense of losing many planes and men. More planes and crews were arriving to build up the fighting forces stationed in England. The ten young men of the *Sunrise Serenade* were just now coming together as a full crew in the States, and were intently reading the news reports coming from Europe.

The Lockheed P-38 Lightning twin-engine fighter became the first American fighter to escort the B-17 bomber formations.
- *Collection of the author.*

On August 17, 1943, a force of 376 B-17's was dispatched from various bases to bomb the German cities of Regensburg and Schweinfurt. Regensburg was the site of a major factory which built the Messerschmitt fighters, and Schweinfurt held the plants which produced ball-bearings that were needed in many German military vehicles. The Regensburg-Schweinfurt mission took a terrible toll on the B-17 fighting forces, having a total of 60 planes go down -- 24 at Regensburg and 36 at Schweinfurt. The loss was staggering; 16 percent of the entire force was lost. Of those planes that did return, 17 had to be scrapped, and 121 needed major repairs before they could fly again. Crews watched everywhere as their fellow friends and crew members plummeted to the earth, many of them dying in the process. The German fighters had found that the most successful attack on the B-17's was from a head-on position. At this time most of the B-17's that were flying did not yet have the frontal chin-turret guns that were just arriving on the new B-17G models in August and September. While the German fighter pilots were devising new techniques against the Flying Fortresses, the strategy being used against the Germans by the gunners aboard the American bombers remained virtually the same.

A few weeks later on September 6, 1943, the Air Force sent 338 B-17 bombers to attack various targets, especially the ball-bearing works at Stuttgart, Germany. Another group of 69 B-24 bombers was dispatched as a diversion to hopefully draw the fighters away from the main force. The weather over the bombing sites was terrible, and none of the planes could see the target. The Flying Fortresses were severely attacked by more than a hundred German fighters, which separated the formations. Through a break in the cloud cover, forty-six B-17's dropped down to release their bombs into the center of the city. The rest of the planes looked for targets of opportunity to bomb. Because of the cloud cover, the formations had attempted no less than three bomb runs, which consumed so much gas that many were unable to make it all the way back to their respective bases. The Air-Sea Rescue pulled 118 crew members out of the English Channel that day from the planes that never made it across. The loss for the raid on Stuttgart was 45 planes, which accounted for 13 percent of the total force. The loss of planes was staggering since the intended target had not been directly hit.

One month later on October 8, 1943, a force of 399 bombers were dispatched to the target destinations of Bremen and Vegesack, Germany, which resulted in losing 30 planes, or nearly 12 percent of the planes. Clearly any crew that was lucky enough to make it past ten missions was on borrowed time. The next day, October 9, 1943, saw 28 more planes go down at targets over Anklam, Marienburg, Danzig, and Gydnia. The following day resulted in 31 more planes going down on a mission to Munster, Germany. A return mission to bomb Schweinfurt for the 8th Air Force four days later on October 14, 1943, resulted in losing 60 planes and 600 experienced crew members. The German *Luftwaffe* seemed to be getting stronger despite the continuous raids on aircraft factories by the Allies.

The months of October and November in 1943 began to see a shortage of qualified crew members, due to the heavy losses being inflicted by the Germans. The crew of the *Sunrise Serenade* was still training at bases in Washington and Oregon during this time. If being in the Air Force had once seemed glamorous to any crew member still training in the States, the news reports describing the reality of War were continuously being spread in the newspapers. These losses were just too great to assume that those airmen being shot down in Europe were merely the result of inexperience. If nothing else, the continual loss of planes and crews told those still preparing in the States to take their training seriously. Even with these high losses of planes, a few veteran aircraft did continue to escape the German fighters and anti-aircraft guns. A plane known as *Hells Angels* had become the first Flying Fortress of the 8th Air Force to complete 25 missions on May 14, 1943, and on May 17, 1943, the crew of *Memphis Belle* became the first crew to complete their required 25 missions and be sent home with their airplane. The plane known as *Knockout Dropper,* became the first 8th Air Force Flying Fortress to complete 50 combat missions on November 16, 1943, and later also became the first B-17 to complete 75 missions. Both *Hells Angels* and *Knockout Dropper* were from the 303rd Bomb Group and the M*emphis Belle* was from the 91st Bomb Group. All three of these planes began flying combat missions in November of 1942.

The pilot of the *Memphis Belle*, Capt. Robert K. Morgan, bids farewell to Generals Devers and Eaker as he and the rest of his crew depart England for a public relations tour in America. Morgan and his crew were the first to complete their required 25 bombing missions and be sent home with their plane.
- Collection of Robert K. Morgan.

After the demoralizing loss during the second Schweinfurt mission, the B-17's stayed closer to home and did not attempt to penetrate deep into Germany for the remainder of 1943. The long range of the fighter escorts was not yet available, and without them, the bombers would continue to sustain heavy losses. High losses did continue to occur, however, over closer cities like Bremen, Munster, Paris, and Solingen. By the end of 1943, the 8th Air Force had lost at least 979 bombers during that year, putting the 1942-43 total loss of planes over 1000. This meant that over 10,000 crew members had either been killed, taken prisoner, or been reported missing. Very few airmen were able to evade capture and make their way back to England after getting shot down. This total loss of airmen did not reflect the many planes with crews that crashed on take-off or crashed on English soil. Also, a large number of bombers that made it back to base had to be scrapped due to excessive damage.

Besides the thousands of bombs being dropped, the planes also dropped millions of leaflets over the cities in an attempt to persuade the German soldiers to surrender. The leaflets described what kind of treatment the Germans would receive from the British and Americans at the prison camps. Many Germans saw the promise of full meals and relaxation as a far better alternative than continuing to fight while being dirty, tired, and hungry, and surrendered to the Allied ground forces. Some of these German prisoners felt they were so well taken care of in the United States that they returned to live there after the War ended.

The beginning of 1944 immediately saw terrible losses for the American 8th Air Force, with nineteen planes lost on January 4th; twenty-five on January 5th; and twelve on January 7th. By January 10, 1944, the majority of the 452nd Bomb Group, including the crew of the *Sunrise Serenade*, had arrived at their base at Deopham Green, England. The next day, 663 planes from other bases were sent to bomb various German targets at Oschersleben, Halberstadt, Brunswick, and Magdeburg. To support the bombers, the Air Force also sent 592 fighters as escorts on the bombing missions. Due to bad weather, over half of the force had to be recalled, although many had actually succeeded in dropping their bombs. The mission that day lost 60 planes, which was again over the 10 percent loss mark. This mission was important in two different ways -- the bombers had reached within 90 miles of Berlin, and also the P-51 Mustangs had escorted the B-17's the entire mission.

Reaching the capital city of Berlin had long been a goal of the 8th Air Force and would represent both a strategic and psychological victory. The ability of the P-51 fighters to escort the bombers during the entire mission meant that the B-17 crews would always have assistance in fighting off the German fighters. Prior to this date the *Luftwaffe* would wait until the American escorts had to turn back due to a shortage of fuel and then attack the bombers without an escort.

Bad weather during January of 1944 continued to lighten the attack against the Germans, but raids were still made whenever possible to continue the bombing campaign. The crew of the *Sunrise Serenade* and the rest of their Group were now training on English soil to do their part, as so many other crews had done before them. The 452nd Bomb Group had been training in England for just less than one month before being assigned to their first mission on February 5, 1944. During their short period of training in England, approximately 150 bombers from various other Bomb Groups had been shot down by the Germans during nine combat missions. This included twenty-two bombers going down the day before the 452nd was ready to fly their first mission. Up to this point in time, over 1,200 bombers had already failed to return to their bases since the beginning of the American bombing campaign in 1942. The damage inflicted by the American and British bombers upon the German occupied territory was extensive, but the worst was yet to come for the 8th Air Force in terms of high aircraft losses.

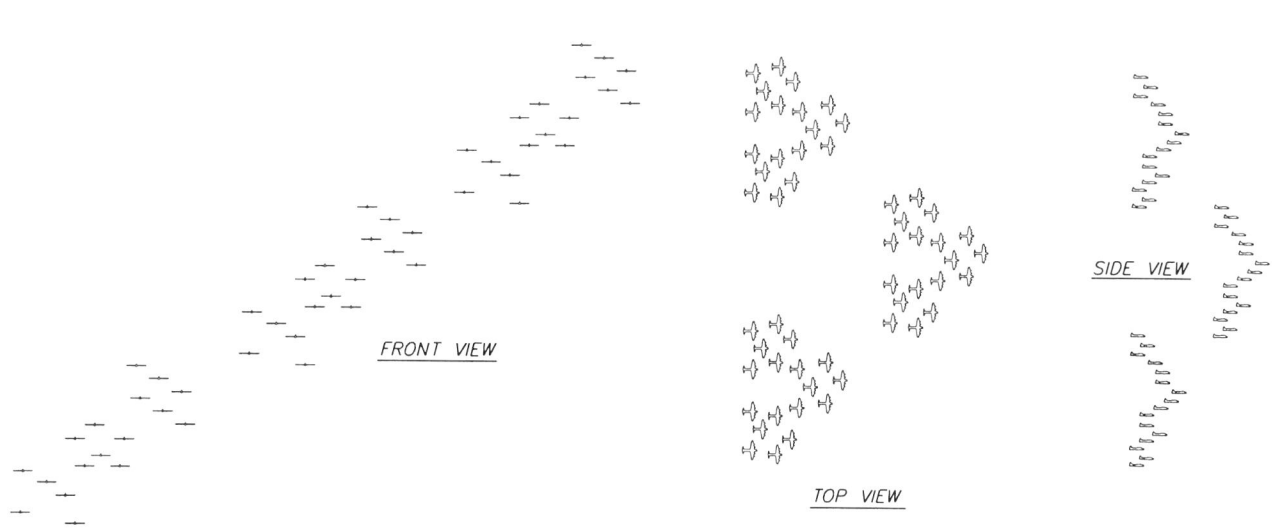

A bomber pilot was required to fly his plane in perfect formation that often left only 50 feet between his plane and others, whether to the side, above, or below. This tight formation was essential to repel enemy fighter attacks, and to provide a higher concentration of hits on the intended target. Flying in overcast weather that obscured visibility created some very tense flights. This diagram represents a large formation of 54 bombers from three squadrons (High, Lead and Low).

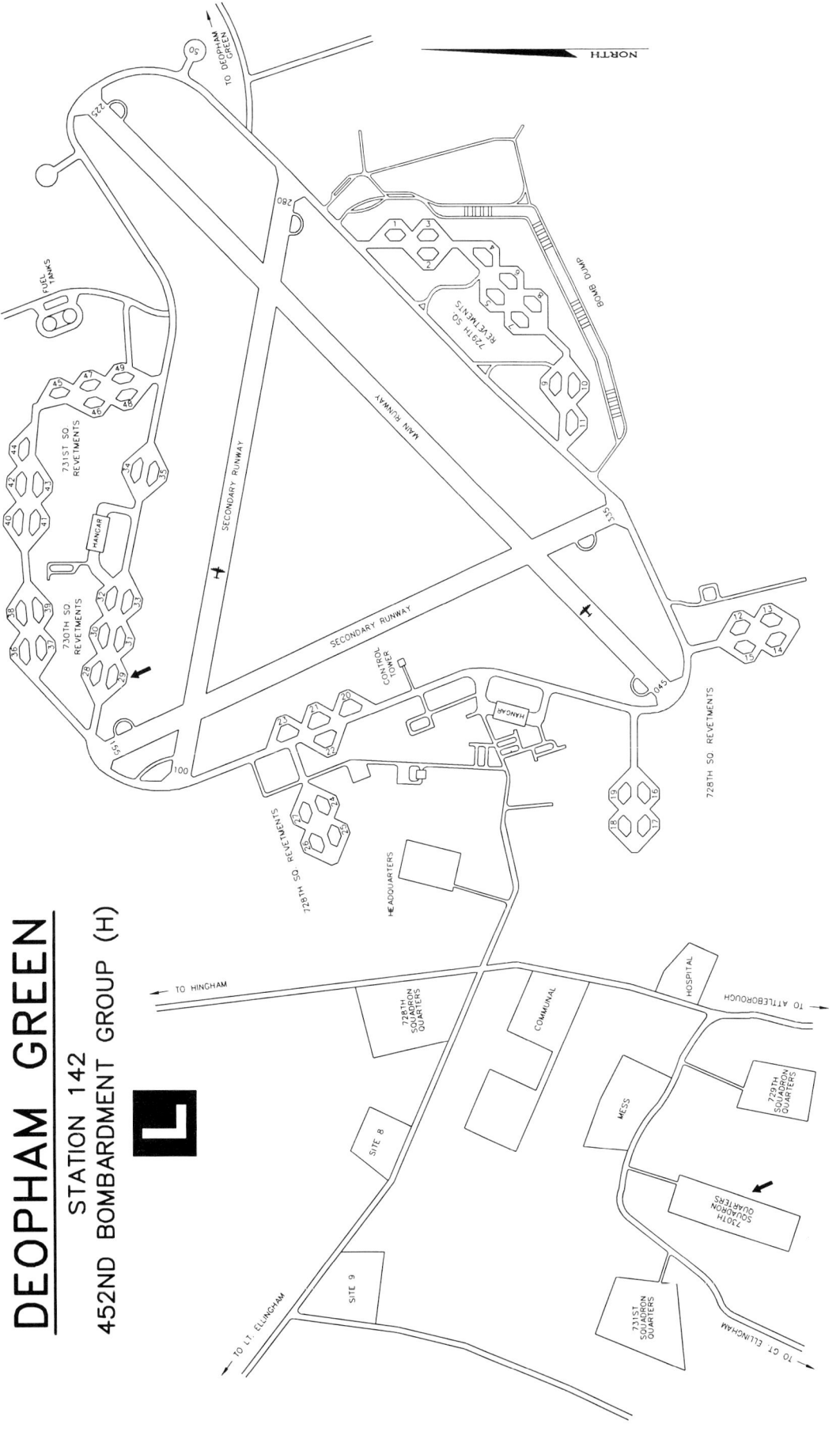

DEOPHAM GREEN
STATION 142
452ND BOMBARDMENT GROUP (H)

The Deopham Green airfield was located approximately 12 miles southwest of Norwich, England. The main runway was 6,000 feet long with two additional secondary runways which were 4,200 feet long. The living quarters were located west of the runways to provide better protection in the event the Germans tried to bomb the runways and planes. The entire base was abandoned after the War and most of it has returned to farm ground. Arrows on the map point to the area where the crew of the *Sunrise Serenade* lived with other members of the 730th Squadron and also to the location of Revetment No. 29 where the *Sunrise Serenade* was parked when not flying. The above map was drawn by the author through the assistance of a detailed map of the former airbase provided by Martin J. Jeffery who currently lives at the site.

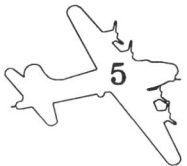

The Bombing Missions

Even though the *Sunrise Serenade* was part of the 452nd Bomb Group, the plane and its crew did not participate on every bombing mission flown by that Group. This was also true for the rest of the planes and crews comprising the 452nd Bomb Group. Many of the crews wanted to fly on every mission to quickly bring an end to their required quota of missions, but their Commanding Officers had utilized a system of rotation to keep the crews alert and well-rested before every mission in which they would actually participate. The crews soon realized that even though they may have been scheduled to be part of a particular mission, many factors often resulted in the mission not counting toward their quota. Among these factors were having to be called back because of unsuitable flying weather, mechanical problems with the plane, or sometimes being an extra plane in formation. Extra planes flew with the formation from their Group until just before crossing over the English Channel. If no planes had to drop out of formation due to unforeseen problems, the extra planes would return to base, usually at the disappointment of the extra crews, since such a mission did not count toward their quota.

Many other crews were shot down from the 452nd Bomb Group as they participated in the bombing missions along with the crew of the *Sunrise Serenade*. The crews often socialized together, and even may have shared the same living quarters. Because of the bonds developed between crews, the events pertaining to the missions flown by other planes of the 452nd Bomb Group, even when the *Sunrise Serenade* was not flying, are also detailed in the following account of the bombing missions. The crew of the *Sunrise Serenade* attempted to participate in a mission nearly thirty different times, but many of these attempts would not materialize due to unforeseen circumstances. Only nineteen combat missions were successful enough to be credited toward their quota of thirty missions before they were shot down. Each of these successful nineteen missions is indicated by the mission number, which is common only to the crew of the *Sunrise Serenade*. The 452nd Bomb Group would eventually participate in 250 different missions as a Group before the end of the War. These mission numbers for the Group as a whole run consecutively. The first mission of the *Sunrise Serenade* did not occur until the third mission flown by the Group.

The first combat mission flown by planes of the 452nd Bomb Group occurred on February 5, 1944. As the bomber crews assembled in their respective briefing rooms to go over the details of the morning mission, the transition from training to combat had now arrived, and the airmen were ready to get the mission underway. The crew of the *Sunrise Serenade* was not selected to fly on either of the first two missions, but were eagerly awaiting their turn.

After take-off at 8:00 a.m., the Group began to assemble into formation. At 11:43 a.m. the Flying Fortresses passed over the selected target at Romilly, France, but due to solid cloud cover, no bombs were dropped. As the planes passed over the secondary target with their bomb doors open, another squadron of B-17's was spotted below the 452nd's lead squadron, so the bombs were again held. The Group then decided to plot a course back toward England and return to base without dropping any bombs. The mission was not a complete failure since the participating crews did have their first real experience with anti-aircraft flak, which luckily did not hit any planes. The following day the Group again flew toward Romilly, France, for their second mission. The 452nd flew as the high group with the 388th Bomb Group leading, and the 96th Bomb Group flying in the low position. These three groups made up the 45th Combat Wing of the 3rd Air Division. The target at Romilly was again completely clouded over. The secondary target at Soissions, France, was also obscured, so the planes again returned to base without dropping any bombs on the enemy. No planes or crew members were lost on either of these missions; however, one plane did crash on take-off on the second mission.

Sunrise Serenade Mission #1

The first mission flown by the crew of the *Sunrise Serenade* occurred on February 8, 1944. The men were awakened in the early morning hours and informed that Smedley's crew would be flying. The first stop was the mess hall for breakfast. The crew then either loaded into a truck or rode bicycles to the briefing room where they learned the necessary details for that day's mission. A large curtain covered the map of the intended target until everyone was seated in the open room and the leader had everyone's full attention. Once the curtain was pulled back to reveal the target, the necessary details pertaining to that mission were then thoroughly explained. A separate room known as the "POW Room" was where each man received an Escape & Evasion kit, which contained European currency, maps, and high-energy candy. Also included in the kit was a picture of themselves wearing civilian

TARGET LOCATIONS OF THE SUNRISE SERENADE

1. Frankfurt, Germany. February 7, 1944
2. Posen, Poland. February 20, 1944
3. Posen, Poland. February 24, 1944
4. Berlin, Germany. March 3, 1944
5. Berlin, Germany. March 6, 1944
6. Augsburg, Germany. March 18, 1944
7. Brunswick, Germany. March 23, 1944
8. Cherbourg, France. March 26, 1944
9. Bordeaux, France. March 27, 1944
10. Chateaudun, France. March 28, 1944
11. Achmer, Germany. April 8, 1944
12. Courcelles, Belgium. April 10, 1944
13. Augsburg, Germany. April 13, 1944
14. Luneberg, Germany. April 18, 1944
15. Lippstadt, Germany. April 19, 1944
16. Coastal France. April 20, 1944
17. Dijon, France. April 25, 1944
18. Northern France. April 27, 1944
19. Clermont-Ferrand, France. Apr. 30, 1944
20. Brussels, Belgium. May 1, 1944

clothing. This picture could later be used by members of the Belgian or French Underground to make false identification papers for the airman. These items were stored in the pockets of their flying suits while flying combat missions. The POW Room was also where each man put all of his personal items into a large envelope identified with his name. In the event that he was taken prisoner or killed, these personal items would be shipped to a holding place in the States. After the War was over, the men or their families contacted the holding place to retrieve their items. After the briefing, the men obtained their parachutes and guns and went to their airplane where each man performed the necessary checks on instruments and equipment before take-off. The machine guns were normally removed from the planes until the crew was actually ready to fly a combat mission. This same procedure was repeated before every mission.

A formation of approximately twenty-one B-17's leave long trails of condensed water vapor "contrails" while flying at a high altitude. One plane decides to pull out of formation, probably due to mechanical problems. - *Collection of Sylvester Petri.*

On the crew's first mission they experienced their initial barrage of flak coming toward them. The experience of war became a reality when it became apparent that someone was trying to kill them. Deep inside, everyone was terrified, but no one wanted to let the other members of the crew down by openly displaying his fear. The primary target for this mission was Frankfurt, Germany, and would prove to be the first time the 452nd Bomb Group would lose planes and crew members. The mission had trouble from the beginning when the lead plane, *The Worry Bird,* developed engine trouble approximately ten minutes before the Initial Point, causing them to abort. The pilot of this plane was 1st Lt. Earl W. Truex, and his co-pilot that day was the 452nd Bomb Group's Commanding Officer, Lt. Col. Herbert O. Wangeman. *The Worry Bird's* No. 3 engine went out and could not be properly feathered. Feathering an engine was a procedure used to shut down an engine that was causing trouble. A propeller on a properly feathered engine had to be completely stopped, otherwise they would start what was known as a "windmilling" effect and slow the plane down. The drag produced by the movement of the propeller slowed down *The Worry Bird* so much that the crew decided to return to base alone. German fighter planes seized the opportunity to attack the lone plane near Caen, France, which caused the crew to make a crash landing. The top turret gunner managed to bail out and escape, while the rest of the crew was immediately taken prisoner by the Germans.

Since the 452nd Bomb Group was still relatively inexperienced in actual combat missions, the lead plane's departure from the rest of the Group caused confusion regarding how to continue to execute procedure in the event the lead plane aborted. The high and low squadrons overran the lead squadron and no bombs-away signal was seen. Since the primary target was missed, the planes then flew to Kaiserlautern, Germany, where the Group released their bombs on an enemy target for the first time.

Three other planes from the 452nd Bomb Group also failed to return that day from the 8 hour and 40 minute mission. A plane piloted by 2nd Lt. Eno Compton, Jr. dove into the ground shortly after takeoff about two miles east of the airfield. Since the plane was only about 500 feet above the ground, there was no time for the crew to bail out. Upon impact, two 500 lb. bombs and eleven 100 lb. bombs exploded, killing the entire crew. A nearby pilot of another plane reported seeing Lt. Compton's cockpit on fire just before they crashed. The crew aboard *Dixie Jane*, piloted by 2nd Lt. Lake H. Jameson, was forced to bail out when their plane ran out of fuel and subsequently crashed near St. Pierremont, France. Two crew members escaped, seven were taken prisoner, and the right waist gunner, Sgt. Harold C. Golub, was killed when his parachute failed to open. Another plane, flown by 2nd Lt. Robert O. Lorenzi, was attacked and shot down by enemy fighters near Le Cardonnois, France, during their return to England. Four crew members managed to escape, six were taken prisoner, and the bombardier, 2nd Lt. Abe W. Rosenthal, was killed. At the completion of the mission, twelve men from the 452nd Bomb Group had given their lives for their country.

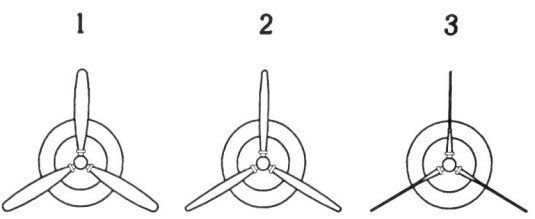

Feathering the propeller on a disabled engine was often necessary to prevent excessive vibration from a windmilling propeller and also to lessen the amount of drag on the plane. The pilot could rotate the individual propeller blades 90° relative to the wing of the plane, which prevented them from turning in the wind.

After returning from each mission, the men headed to the "Hot News" room where the crew was interrogated about what they had seen during the mission. Details about the planes that were lost, locations of flak guns, and the number of enemy aircraft seen were all very important details for their leaders to know. Red Cross women provided sandwiches and doughnuts to the hungry men who had eaten very little since their early morning breakfast. Often a bottle of cognac or a cup of coffee helped to calm the nerves of those who were still shaken by what they had seen.

On February 10, 1944, the 452nd Bomb Group flew to Brunswick, Germany, after having to cancel an attempt on this city the previous day. This was the fourth mission for the Group, with the Sunrise Serenade not participating. A total of five planes failed to return that day from the target.

The B-17, The Belle of Broadway flown by 2nd Lt. Milton Turner, was leading the Group when the plane named Bad Check, piloted by 2nd Lt. Walter S. Tiska, apparently overran the formation and pulled up into the bottom of Turner's plane. The impact of the two planes caused Tiska's plane to break in two. All crew members of Tiska's plane were killed except the tail gunner, Sgt. Louis T. Haas, who managed to survive and was then taken prisoner. Turner's plane suffered damage, which resulted in the ball turret being knocked off the plane, taking the ball turret gunner, S/Sgt. Adam G. Bomba, to his death. The tail gunner from Turner's plane, S/Sgt. Claude Westerfield, suffered wounds and subsequently died when the armor plating of the plane crushed his stomach during the impact.

Planes from the 452nd Bomb Group bank to the right as they fly toward another German target - Collection of the 452nd Bomb Group Association.

The third plane lost was known as Hard to Get, flown by 2nd Lt. Kenneth D. Smith. It was shot down by German fighters near Hildesheim, Germany. The fighters were successful in knocking out three of the plane's engines, which caused it to become engulfed in flames. Seven crew members were taken prisoner and the navigator, bombardier, and radioman were killed.

Another plane referred to as Dinah Mite was the fourth plane lost that mission. It was being flown by 2nd Lt. Thomas F. Sharpless. It had been borrowed from a pilot named 1st Lt. Clyde T. Boy, Jr. whose crew was on a three-day pass. The plane was attacked by German fighter planes and made a crash landing after the rest of the crew had bailed out. The plane landed in a marsh area off Holland known as the Zuider Zee. Less than a year earlier this plane had been on the production line in the United States as the next plane being built behind the Sunrise Serenade. All crew members of Dinah Might were taken prisoner except the navigator, 2nd Lt. John J. Lyons, who was able to escape and return to duty. The Dinah Might was found nearly intact when the marsh was drained many years later.

The final plane to go down that day was Delta Girl, which was being flown by 2nd Lt. Hugh E. Noell, Jr. This plane was the highest in the formation and was also attacked by German fighters. Twenty-millimeter cannon fire coming from an Me-109 knocked out the top turret and three of the engines. The two waist gunners and the tail gunner were killed from enemy fire while still aboard the plane. The rest of the crew, with some wounded, managed to bail out and were taken prisoner. The highly damaged plane crashed near Dankern, Germany.

By the end of the day the Group was again mourning the loss of their fellow airmen and friends; seventeen were killed during the mission. The number of airmen who lost their lives during the last two missions was now at 29. The presence of the empty bunks in the huts served as a constant reminder of those gone until replacement crews could arrive to fill the spaces. The men that were killed during the first missions were well known among the entire Group since they had all trained together before coming to England.

On February 12, 1944, the Group flew a practice mission over England. The next day, February 13th, the fifth mission flown by the 452nd Bomb Group was to a primary target in Northern France near Calais. Very heavy flak damaged several of the planes, but all returned safely to base.

The crew of the Sunrise Serenade was on a three-day pass to Cambridge and also London, England, at this time. While in Cambridge, the crew learned first-hand what it was like to participate in an air raid, as the city was on high alert due to nearby London being under the threat of a bombing attack. After arriving in London, John Brown, the right waist gunner, recalled a memorable event:

> "We were finally given a 72-hour pass and every one made a bee-line for London in general, and Piccadilly Circus in particular. Dusty Rhodes and I arranged to overnight at the NCO Club, but Bill Hewett, for whatever reason, wound up with no place to stay. So Dusty and I tried sneaking Bill up to our room. It would have worked too except for one disgruntled G. I. who ratted on us. So Bill was politely but firmly asked to leave, as were Dusty and I. We did not let it spoil our fun for that was what it was all about, and believe me we did have fun. That was our one and only trip to London."

Bad weather caused a planned mission to be cancelled on February 17th. During the night of February 18th, the nearby city of Norwich, England, was bombed by the German *Luftwaffe*, which reminded the crews that even though they were not flying missions over German-occupied territory, the danger was still present.

Harry Shoffner took this photo while flying aboard the *Sunrise Serenade*. The plane is #239814 from the 96th Bomb Group that was one of the three groups in the 45th Combat Wing. The plane was shot down on February 21, 1944, with five of the crew killed and the other five taken prisoner. Note the barrage of flak above the plane - *Collection of Mary Lou Shoffner.*

Sunrise Serenade Mission #2

The next mission for the Group was to Posen, Poland, and also a target of opportunity at Rostock, Germany, on February 20th. Off the west coast of Denmark, approximately 25 enemy aircraft attacked the Group, with at least four of these being Ju-88's, each firing a rocket into the formation. This was a tactic often used by the German fighters to try to break up the Group's tight formation. After firing the rockets, the fighters fired upon the Fortresses with their 20mm guns. A plane piloted by 2nd Lt. Billy L. Huffman, named *Mavoureen*, took major damage which resulted in a bailout for the crew. Witnesses from other planes observed nine parachutes open, but most were over open water. Huffman was killed when he decided to stay with the plane, which subsequently crashed near Haldagerlille, Denmark. Most of the other crew members drowned, but the waist gunners, Sgt. Thomas E. McDannold, and Sgt. George T. Smith, survived and were taken prisoner. McDannold could only surmise that he and Smith were probably better swimmers than the rest, which saved their lives.

Harry Shoffner, the left waist gunner of the *Sunrise Serenade*, noted in his diary that their crew witnessed two planes from another bomb group collide in mid-air with at least one of them blowing up. Their own plane had many holes in it from the German fighters and a large piece of one wing tip was missing after this mission. The *Sunrise Serenade* crew also claimed to have unofficially brought down two enemy aircraft during this mission.

Prior to this mission the pilot's brother, Cpl. Vincent A. Smedley from the 2nd Armored Division, had obtained a 3-day pass and visited his brother and crew at the base. The night before, Vincent was given a 2nd Lieutenant's uniform so that he could slip his way into the officer's club with the other officers. The next morning Vincent boarded the *Sunrise Serenade* with the rest of the crew as they prepared for the mission. Just as the plane was taking off, Vincent jumped out of the plane and laid low on the tarmac as the plane's tail went over him. During the interrogation after the mission, Francis Smedley was reprimanded by a superior officer for allowing a member of his crew to abandon the plane. Vincent quickly spoke up saying that it was he who had left the plane. The officer then directed his attention toward Vincent and wanted to know just who he was wearing a 2nd Armored Division patch on his uniform at an Air Force base. The incident was thoroughly explained and no disciplinary action was taken.

———

The next mission for the Group was to Brunswick, Germany, on February 21, 1944, with the crew of the *Sunrise Serenade* not participating. No planes were lost on this mission; however, a few enemy fighters attacked the formations, which resulted in Sgt. Abel Tamez being wounded when a cannon shell hit his ball turret.

The next mission that the crew of the *Sunrise Serenade* attempted to fly in was to Schweinfurt, Germany, on February 22nd. This mission was recalled due to bad weather just as the Group approached the coast of France, so the planes loaded with 1,000 lb. bombs turned around and headed back to their airfield. Francis Smedley, the pilot of the *Sunrise Serenade*, decided to write a letter home that day to his mother, since he had not had been able to find the time to write for a few weeks.

> "Mother Dearest, Hello mom, this is your younger son again and this time making a good report. I saw none other than that big brother of mine. After some time of trying to get in touch with each other we finally made it. I need not say we both were very happy. I wrote Vince and said I would meet him at the Bell Hotel at 5:00 p.m. I arrived in Norwich around 2:00 and for the life of me I didn't know what to do until 5:00. I've never had the time drag so. About 4:30 I dropped over to the Hotel, as I walked through the doors I saw a fellow standing sort of in the corner, the light wasn't too good, and I wasn't sure of myself. But as I walked up to him, I was sure it was good old Vince. I can say this, he hasn't changed a bit. It sure did my eyes good to see the old boy again. My co-pilot, Bill Hewett, navigator "Mac" McGrath, and the bombardier Don Griffin also came into town and the five of us went out to see the town. After paying our respects to a few "Pubs" we went to the dance. Again I'll say it did me good to see him dancing and having a swell time. Vince came back to the field with me that evening and spent the next day and a half with me. Sunday I had to fly so it rather cut our visit short. Vince started talking shop with my armorer "Dean" and he seemed to get a big kick out of everything. I showed him through my ship and he met all the crew. Bill Hewett and I took Vince down to the train at 3:00 Monday. I have a pass coming up and plan to spend it with him. Well mom here it is February and your birthday is rolling around and this time I won't be able to help you celebrate it like we used to when Vince and I were in high school, and down in Winnetka in Apt. 204. Well mom say hello to everyone for me and give Duff my love, or something. Tell him he's lucky he's not drinking this English beer. May you always be happy and well. Your younger son, Francis."

The two brothers did get together once more a short time later. Francis visited his brother's base and was afforded the opportunity to operate a tank, which he found quite different than being the pilot of a B-17. This meeting was the last time that the two brothers would ever see each other again.

Another attempt at Schweinfurt was scheduled for the next day, February 23rd, but was again recalled due to weather. The actual air temperature at 26,300 feet was 42° below zero, making it very difficult for the airmen to function inside the unheated planes. The airmen wore heated flying suits, but they were not able to keep every part of their body covered to avoid getting frostbite. One area that was susceptible to frostbite was the face, particularly the cheeks. A bare hand touched against the side of any metal surface would adhere itself to the metal at these extreme temperatures. The instinctive reflexes needed by the gunners to shoot at enemy fighters was considerably slowed due to the often bulky clothing. Under the large gloves worn by the gunners was a nylon glove that closely fit the contour on the hand. These gloves allowed the gunners to work on their equipment without getting their hands stuck to the bare metal. Often the guns turned white due to the extreme cold temperature. Many airmen realized that it was indeed possible to both freeze and sweat at the same time during a tense mission.

The cold weather also affected the ground crews. They worked on the planes at the airfields during the nights and had no choice but to endure the cold to prepare the planes for the next mission. The ground crew members also had an affection for the plane, just like the men who flew aboard her. They were the unsung heroes of the 8th Air Force who diligently worked on the planes to get them ready for each flight. Everything from fueling the plane, washing the windshield, to loading the bombs and gun boxes were just a few of the many duties they performed. For every one combat airmen it was estimated that there were about twenty ground support personnel. Rest for the ground support crews was usually obtained while the air crews were flying.

The unsung heroes of the Air Force were the ground crews who diligently worked to prepare every plane before each new mission. - *Collection of the 452nd Bomb Group Association.*

Sunrise Serenade Mission #3
On February 24, 1944, the crew of the *Sunrise Serenade* participated on the eighth overall mission for the 452nd Bomb Group with the target again at Posen, Poland. The weather was good that day, and approximately 1,000 Air Force bombers escorted by American fighters took to the skies to bomb targets at

Brunswick, Oschersleben, Bernberg, and Leipzig, in addition to the 452nd's target at Posen. Approximately 25 enemy aircraft attacked the Group near the Danish coast, which resulted in several planes taking direct hits. The battle lasted nearly four hours as the German fighter pilots matched their guns against the .50 caliber machine guns on the Fortresses. One plane known as *Lady Satan*, being piloted by 2nd Lt. Harold G. Holland, was damaged by flak and then attacked by rockets from German fighters. After the entire crew bailed out, the plane crashed near Jornsdorf, Germany. One waist gunner, Sgt. Thomas G. Raines, had been shot and later died. The other crew members were all taken prisoner after safely landing on the ground. The mission to Posen had required the crews to be in the air for nearly 12 hours, so everyone was relieved to be finally back on the ground. The Group claimed to have shot down 10 enemy aircraft, damaged 5, and had probable hits on at least 6 others that day. This particular day was the heaviest assault taken by the 8th Air Force up until that time. It was also the start of what would historically become known as "The Big Week" for the mighty 8th Air Force. Massive bomber raids were conducted on February 24th, 25th, 26th, 28th and 29th. Extremely bad weather was the only reason for not flying on the 27th.

Loading the bombs into the Flying Fortresses was not an easy task and required several men working together on each plane. - *Collection of the 452nd Bomb Group Association.*

The ninth mission flown by the Group was to Regensburg, Germany, on February 25, 1944. Most of the crews that had participated in the previous day's mission to Posen, including the *Sunrise Serenade*, remained at the base to obtain rest. The 452nd flew in the high squadron in the 45th Combat Wing and was attacked by approximately 30 enemy aircraft from the French coast all the way to Augsburg, Germany. The target at Regensburg took a direct hit, and aerial photos indicated that there would be no need to return to this target in the near future. The 452nd Bomb Group claimed to have shot down three enemy aircraft and two others were damaged. The Group lost no planes, but one crew member, F/O Pete A. Rosko, died from wounds received while aboard a plane. His funeral was held in Cambridge four days later. The 8th Air Force lost a total of 31 heavy bombers from various other Groups on the February 25th missions.

The German ground crews had to work in the same weather conditions as the Allies. The plane being loaded is a Heinkel He-111 medium bomber. - *Collection of the author.*

The next mission was to Brunswick, Germany, on February 29, 1944, and lasted 7 hours and 30 minutes. The plane named *Cock O' the Walk*, flown by 2nd Lt. Jake S. Colvin, received several hits from flak over the target before it dove down into the clouds. The plane crashed near Bienrode, Germany, with four crew members killed, including the pilot and co-pilot, and the other six taken prisoner. Jake Colvin had flown over to England with fellow pilot and friend Francis Smedley while their respective crews arrived by ship. The bombardier of the *Sunrise Serenade*, George Griffin, had once been part of Colvin's crew during training. Another plane named *Invictus* flown by 2nd Lt. Frank S. Stephens, crashed on the runway after returning from the mission. All crew members of this plane were safe after the incident.

The conclusion of that week on February 29, 1944, saw over 2,000 planes bomb Regensburg, Augsburg, Furth, and Stuttgart. The large-scale attacks destroyed or damaged at least one half of the German aircraft factories which had been mostly untouched during the previous months. Those five days in February changed the direction of the War for the Allied fighting forces, but it came with a high cost. Approximately 244 bombers and 33 fighters were lost, which meant nearly 2,500 experienced crewmen were either killed or taken prisoner.

Sunrise Serenade Mission #4

After a two-day pass to Norwich, the fourth flight flown by the crew of the *Sunrise Serenade* was one to remember. The target on March 3, 1944, was the German capital of Berlin, which either excited most airmen of the Group, or frightened them. The German *Luftwaffe* and ground anti-aircraft crews would be out in their strongest opposition to defend their most-favored city. This historic 7-hour mission was recalled due to bad weather, but it did count as a mission for the participating crews. Since they had come within 45 minutes of reaching the prized city of Berlin. Harry Shoffner recorded the events of that day in his diary:

> *"Up at 2:00 a.m. The 'Sunrise Serenade' on the logs again - Mission Berlin. We turned back on account of weather - mission counted. It was the coldest I have ever been, being 50° to 59° below zero. Brother that was cold. The heated suit didn't do its job. The mask froze up, the mike froze up, frost in the oxygen tube, and my gun froze up. God did I have trouble."*

———

On March 4, 1944, the 452nd Group attempted another mission to Berlin, Germany. The crews awoke at 2:30 a.m. and began the same ritual that they had performed the previous morning. The morning briefings before each mission were held in rooms separating the officers from the enlisted men. The smell inside the room was a mixture of hair oil, shaving lotion, sweat, and cigarettes as the men listened intently to the details of the mission. The second attempt to bomb Berlin was called back just 15 minutes from reaching the Initial Point of the bomb run. Thirteen planes from the 95th and 100th Bomb Groups, however, did not receive the message to turn back apparently due to communication problems and continued toward Berlin. These planes were the first American bombers to succeed in bombing Berlin. During the attack the 95th Bomb Group lost four planes, while the 100th Bomb Group lost one plane.

The *Sunrise Serenade* had pulled into formation as their Group was assembling over England for the second mission to Berlin. Just as the planes headed out across the English Channel, the oxygen system dropped dangerously low in the *Sunrise Serenade*, so the crew had no choice but to drop out of formation and turn back. Without the oxygen system properly working at high altitudes, the crew would have become unconscious and died. It was the first time that the crew had to abort a mission, and this one would not count for them.

A Flying Fortress from the 452nd Bomb Group named *Breaks of the Game*, piloted by 2nd Lt. Arthur Mittman, was shot by an Me-109 fighter, which caused it to explode in the air and break apart. The main part of the plane then crashed northwest of Berlin. The entire crew was able to bail out, but the engineer died when he hurriedly left without a parachute, and the radioman died from wounds while descending. The remaining eight crew members were taken prisoner.

The most beautiful sight for a bomber crew was having an escort of American fighter planes. The crews referred to them as "Little Friends". A formation of eighteen P-47 Thunderbolts are in this photo. - *Collection of the author.*

On the way back to Deopham Green, Francis Smedley decided to buzz a B-24 bomber base with the *Sunrise Serenade*. Harry Shoffner, flying at the left waist gunners position, described the incident as flying so low that they took paint off the belly of their ship. Unauthorized 'buzzing', which was a display of the pilot's flying talent to fly low to the ground, was done as a thrill to excite or frighten those on the ground as the low flying aircraft roared by. Buzzing was also done over fighter bases by bomber pilots to show their appreciation for the fighter support given during a previous mission. Often those in charge turned a blind eye toward such incidents. However, on July 19, 1944, a B-17 from the 95th Bomb Group buzzed the 78th Fighter Group's base. The pilot of the B-17 flew in low and then pulled up over the control tower, but failed to see a warning light mast above the tower. The impact sheared off part of the wing and tail. Four men were killed in the incident, including an airman in the barracks. General James H. Doolittle issued an order stating that unauthorized low flying was strictly forbidden, and the strongest action would be brought against any further perpetrators.

Young men acting as boys, nevertheless, continued to buzz airfields or do "hedge hopping" whenever they thought they could get away with it. Hedge hopping was the act of flying low to the ground until a hedge line was met, then the pilot would swoop over the top of the trees and then fly back low to the ground again. The crew of the *Sunrise Serenade* always knew when they were about to fly low because Smedley would start singing the popular song "Shoo Shoo Baby" over the intercom. This practice started while they were still training in the States and continued during combat. Smedley generally chose the prime time to display his flying talents just after the planes had returned from a mission and had crossed the English Channel. On one particular mission when the *Sunrise Serenade* was flying as the lead ship in formation, their roommates flying *The Big Noise* decided to radio Smedley that they needed to drop out of formation. Their pilot, Bill Denham, secretly wanted to do some hedge hopping of his own without letting the other crews know about it. As the crew of *The Big Noise* were enjoying their low flight along the ground, they were shocked to see Smedley and the *Sunrise Serenade* flying off their right wing and even lower! Smedley's skill while flying a B-17 in the air was often compared to that of a race car driver handling a fast car on the ground. He could do almost anything with the plane as though it were a part of him. His dream upon finishing their required missions was to fly low along the Thames River in London and under the London Bridge as a final display of his talent. This act, if it had been carried out, would have resulted in Smedley being court-marshaled since this area was strictly a no-fly zone and heavily guarded.

By early 1944, the silver colored B-17's were increasingly outnumbering the older and original olive drab colored planes, which had mostly been shot down. The plane in the center, #2102650, was later destroyed on the ground at Poltava, Russia, on June 21, 1944. - *Collection of Sylvester Petri.*

Sunrise Serenade Mission #5

After a day of rest, the target on March 6, 1944, was once again the capital city of Berlin. The Air Force commanders were not going to give the Germans any time to rebuild their most prized city. At the morning briefing many bomber crew members were stunned at having to return to Berlin for the third time in four days. Having survived the trip the two previous times was luck, but many knew their luck could surely not continue. By this time many airmen had developed a certain ritual that they followed before every mission. Any deviation from this ritual that had brought them safely back from the previous mission was seen as a sign of bad luck. The fear and reality of dying caused many men to resort to these rituals and also to possess items carried on every mission as a lucky charm.

Lucky charms were needed as Focke-Wulf and Messerschmitt fighter planes attacked with brutal force in order to save their city of Berlin. Pressure had been applied to the *Luftwaffe* from Hitler himself to do a better job of protecting the German homeland. The *Luftwaffe* pilots were being called cowards for not being more aggressive in stopping the B-17's from destroying German strongholds. The German fighter planes pressed their attack all along the trip to the target and on the way back to England. German pilots displayed many skilled maneuvers not yet witnessed by bomber crews. Flak over the target ripped holes in countless B-17's as they opened their bomb bay doors to release their bombs. The plane named *Hell's Cargo*, piloted by 2nd Lt. Howard Sweeny, received excessive flak damage and subsequently was shot down by fighters. All crew members were able to bail out of the plane, which crashed near Fassberg, Germany. The copilot, 2nd Lt. John J. Buel, reportedly hit his head on a rock while landing in his chute. This story was furnished by the Germans; however, this so-called rock could have very well been the butt end of a rifle wielded by a German soldier or angry area resident. He later died of this wound at a German hospital. The rest of the crew were taken as prisoners. On the return trip, a plane named *Flakstop*, piloted by 2nd Lt. Charles F. Wagner, was shot down by German fighters near the Dutch-German border. The pilot and four other crew members were killed, one crew member was taken prisoner, and four managed to escape and return to England.

Yet another plane, piloted by 2nd Lt. Robert C. Schimmel, was damaged by flak and subsequently attacked by German fighters on the March 6th mission to Berlin. With the No. 4 engine on fire and danger from explosion eminent, Schimmel ordered the entire crew to bail out while he continued with the plane. Soon after the crew left the plane, the fire went out and Schimmel no longer saw the danger. He flew the plane, known as *Evanton Babe*, back to England alone where he safely landed. One of his crew died when his chute failed to open, seven were taken prisoner and one escaped. While in the prison camp, his copilot heard from newly arriving prisoners that Schimmel had safely returned to England. This greatly angered the copilot, thinking that his pilot had needlessly ordered the rest of the crew to bail out too early. It was not uncommon for the pilot and copilot of the same plane to be in total disagreement over various issues even without having an incident such as this. Harry Shoffner of the *Sunrise Serenade* recorded the events of that day in his diary:

> *"Mission to Berlin. We made it this time - saw lots of Germany. The flak barrage over Berlin was something to talk about. Looks like hundreds of guns. Missed the target however - our Group did. It wasn't so cold today. We had a clear target and should have blasted the hell out of it, but I don't*

know what is wrong with our Group's bombardier. We had a wonderful escort today – P-47's, and P-38's. Those P-47's sure run the Jerries ragged. Buzzed the country after we got back. Maybe we will fly again tomorrow."

The term "Jerries" was often used to describe the German fighter pilots or Germans in general, which was a carry-over from World War I. The successful mission to Berlin was extra special to the crew of the *Sunrise Serenade* since they were all awarded with the Air Medal for completing their fifth bombing mission. Many of the airmen that participated on this monumental mission were interviewed by reporters from many different newspapers and magazines. John G. Brown was quoted as saying, "*We really set Berlin on fire and it will take the entire Atlantic Ocean to put it out.*" At least two members of the crew, Francis Smedley and Norbert Rhodes, both wrote lengthy stories about the mission for their hometown newspapers.

The Air Medal was awarded to the crew of the *Sunrise Serenade* after their 5th mission on March 6, 1944. An oak leaf cluster (2 shown on the blue & gold ribbon) was awarded for each additional 5 missions. - *Collection of the author.*

On March 8, 1944, the 452nd Bomb Group continued its quest for Berlin; business as usual for the crews. By this time the city appeared to be in a state of total ruin with fires raging out of control and buildings reduced to rubble. The intended target was Erkner, located in the southeastern part of Berlin. The Germans had anticipated that this target would be bombed, so they created their own ground smoke screen to obscure the target. With this target hidden, the Group flew a little farther south and bombed a factory at Werndorf. The *Sunrise Serenade* had flown with the formation as far as the enemy coast as an extra plane in case someone had to drop out. No planes dropped out, so the crew flew back to England to await another chance to complete a mission of their own. The crew had pulled the arming pins on the bombs and threw them out. They had prematurely thought that they would be participating on the mission so arming the bombs was a common practice while flying toward the target. Luckily they landed back at the base with the bombs on board without incident. From that point on the pins on the bombs were usually kept available just in case a similar situation would occur. The pilot of the *Sunrise Serenade*, Francis Smedley, and some of his crew spent the remainder of the day flying the engineering officer over to a base near Liverpool.

As the rest of the Group continued to Berlin, once again enemy fighters were out in high numbers to do whatever they could to lessen the attack. The plane piloted by 2nd Lt. Glenn T. "Tay" Butterworth known as *Mon Tete Rouge* (French for *My Redhead*), was attacked by four German fighters firing their 20mm shells into the plane. The cockpit, as well as the navigator and bombardier's area, were hit, killing the bombardier, 2nd Lt. Orville E. Robertson. The pilot made a crash landing along the Weser River. The surviving nine crew members were taken prisoner. Butterworth was flying Lt. Hal Fulmer's plane that day instead of his usual plane named *Tangerine*.

A plane being flown by 2nd Lt. Durwald L. Sorenson, named *Dixie Jane,* was also attacked by fighters. This plane was also not Sorenson's regular plane either, but was borrowed from another pilot since his was being repaired. Sorenson made a crash landing near Zerbst, Germany, with the crew aboard. The radioman was thrown from the plane upon impact and died of a broken neck; the ball turret gunner and tail gunner died from wounds received from the 20mm shells. The remaining seven crew members were taken as prisoners. Sorenson had trained and graduated with Francis Smedley at the Army Flying School in Merced, California, the previous year.

Another plane to go down that day was *Sleepy Time Gal* being flown by 2nd Lt. Theodore J. MacDonald. This plane suffered hits to the engines, knocking out two of them. A fire ensued in the nose and bomb bay areas of the plane, and MacDonald ordered the crew to bail out. Since the navigator's chute was riddled by 20mm shells, MacDonald gave him his parachute and rode the plane down for a crash landing in a swamp near Nienburg, Germany, with the bombs still aboard. MacDonald survived the crash only by quickly exiting the plane minutes before it blew up, and he was then taken prisoner. The rest of the crew safely landed on the ground in their parachutes, but German rifle fire killed the co-pilot and bombardier. The remaining seven crew members were also taken prisoner.

A plane known as *Invictus,* being flown by 2nd Lt. Frank S. Stephens, also fell victim to the Germans on March 8, 1944. This plane broke up in mid-air while on fire with the bombs still aboard. The crew managed to bail out, but the copilot, 2nd Lt. William H. Mary, was killed.

The rest of the crew were taken prisoners. Among the crew of *Invictus* who were taken as prisoner was the bombardier, 2nd Lt. Leon R. Kloepfer. Kloepfer was the original bombardier aboard the *Sunrise Serenade* while still in training before being replaced by George Griffin.

The plane known as *Hank from Dixie,* being flown by 2nd Lt. Henry L. Wilson, also was shot down by enemy fighters on the Berlin mission. The plane exploded in the air and crashed near Toeppel, Germany, just after the crew bailed out. The navigator and bombardier were reportedly lynched by the Germans upon landing, since their bombs had been released upon civilian houses. The remaining eight crew members were taken as prisoners.

One other plane flown that day by Lt. J. R. Miller experienced mechanical problems in the engines, and the plane started descending due to loss of power. Miller gave the order to possibly prepare to bail out as the bombs were being released. Some of the bombs became wedged in the open bomb bay and a few incendiary bombs were rolling around. Upon seeing this, the navigator, bombardier, engineer, and radioman all decided to bail out. The bombardier, 2nd Lt. Roger A. McGuire, was killed and the other three were taken prisoner. The remaining bombs were eventually freed and dropped, and the remaining six airmen returned to England with their plane. The 8th Air Force lost 37 bombers and 18 fighters during the March 8th bombing missions.

On March 9, 1944, the 452nd Bomb Group continued their march to Berlin, having completed their fifth consecutive mission to Berlin. Very few, if any, enemy fighters appeared, but flak was heavy. No planes were lost on this date from their Group; however, a total of eight bombers were lost from other Groups.

During the month of March 1944, the number of missions required to be flown by each individual airman was raised from 25 to 30. Certain commanding officers of the 8th Air Force stated that the missions being flown over enemy territory were getting easier, therefore the B-17 crews had less chance of getting shot down. One of the real reasons for the change was the fact that the replacement crews arriving in England in 1944 still did not cover the heavy losses inflicted upon the bomber crews during the latter part of 1943. With the planned D-Day invasion just a few months away, the leaders wanted to keep the experienced crews around as long as possible. This change did little to boost the morale of the already stressed airmen, especially those who had already seen the worst of the German *Luftwaffe* and ground artillery. Certain provisions were made for those airmen who had already completed over half of their missions, and they could still finish on their 25th mission. None of the air crews from the 452nd Bomb Group had completed over half yet, so everyone was required to complete 30 missions. Later in the War this quota was again raised, requiring the completion of 35 missions. This quota was shortened by a few missions for certain crews who were at greater risk by routinely flying as lead plane in formation.

After the March 9th mission the next five days were days of rest for the crews. On March 10th Francis Smedley again found time to write a letter home to his mother.

> *"Dearest Mom, Hello everybody, this is your son Francis again and still in jolly old England. Since my last report from the E.T.O. quite a bit has happened. First off, I'm now the proud owner of the Air Medal, which was awarded for completing five missions over enemy territory. I believe you read about the Eighth Air Force making a call on Berlin, well your son has now seen the German capital. It was quite a show, but that's past now so don't worry or fret now. Remember I'm still going to school and it was just another lesson. My gunners are really on the ball! My tail gunner 'Ray' Dean, shot down a Ju-88 (a twin engine fighter). His name, along with the ball turret "Bob" Lalumiere who shot down a Ju-88 and a Me-109 (a single engine job) and the top turret "Dusty" Rhodes who got a FW-190 (a single engine job) appeared in all the big time papers back in the States. By the way the ship's name is the 'Sunrise Serenade' your favorite number, remember. Anyway watch for her name I'm sure she'll make more news in the near future. My waist gunner John Brown also made the papers and this time the front page of Stars and Stripes, a paper for all GI's in the E.T.O. But it too went to the States for publication. He made a statement about the raid on the Nazi capital. The fighters were not claimed on that raid. All those notes made us plenty happy, enough said. A few days ago we (my crew and I) took a trip over to the other side of the Island and due to weather and a misunderstanding we stayed a few days. We landed at an RAF field and they treated us swell or I should say like kings. A squadron leader took me all over the field, (he's the same rank as our majors), bought me drinks and I couldn't pay for a thing. My opinion of RAF boys has gone up 1000% since I've had the chance to get to know them. When we finally took off I gave them a buzz job that I believe they won't forget. Well mother dearest I must close and hit my old sack (bed) as it is now 10:00 p.m. May God look after you all and keep you well. Say hello to everybody will you please. Your loving son, Francis."*

On March 11th, a small ceremony was held at the airfield where five airmen received the Purple Heart and also the Air Medal. Harry Shoffner wrote in his diary that his crew found five bottles of wine that day, and apparently none of it was wasted.

The Junkers Ju-88 was a four-seat German fighter/bomber. Both Ray Dean and Bob Lalumiere had each shot one down while flying aboard the *Sunrise Serenade* during their first 5 missions. This captured plane bears American markings.
- Collection of the author.

On Sunday, March 12th, the weather was too bad to fly, so most airmen attended church services. The services were very important to the airmen since their lives were held in the balance on every mission. Before every mission many men took communion to help ease their mind about what lay ahead for them.

The next day the *Sunrise Serenade* was scheduled to fly a mission to the coast city of Calais, France, possibly to bomb some German V-1 or V-2 Rocket sites under construction. The mission would probably see very few fighters, but flak would be protecting the site. At the last moment the mission was cancelled, so any chance at another close and easy target would have to wait. The crew flew a practice mission over England on March 14th to keep them alert.

On March 15, 1944, the bombers of the 452nd Bomb Group struck Brunswick, Germany, for their sixteenth mission, with the their Group leading the entire 8th Air Force. Again, the crew of the *Sunrise Serenade* would have to wait while some of their friends were adding another mission to their own quota. No planes were lost on this date during the entire 8-hour mission. Harry Shoffner of the *Sunrise Serenade* wrote in his diary that the entire mission was a "Milk Run" after talking to returning airmen who had participated in the bombing mission. The crews did not engage contact with a single enemy fighter plane or even see one the entire trip. The German fighters were, however, in the area as the American fighter escorts bagged 35 German aircraft that day and had kept the German pilots well away from the bomber formations. The entire fighter escort was one of the largest deployed and airmen said that it was a beautiful sight that day. It was not uncommon to see bunches of 40 to 60 American fighter planes flying together. With the American fighters only losing five of their own planes, the loss ratio was seven German fighters downed to every one American fighter.

The next day the 452nd Bomb Group flew as the low group in the 45th Combat Wing to a target at Augsburg, Germany. The crews awoke at 2:30 a.m. and took off shortly after daybreak. The crew of the *Sunrise Serenade* was eager to add another mission to their total since it had been ten days since their last one. It was difficult for crews to see other crews adding to their own quota while they had to stay grounded. As the *Sunrise Serenade* became airborne, a gasoline leak was discovered. Soon after they assembled into formation the leaking gasoline continued and an estimated 270 gallons of fuel had already been lost. Smedley decided to reluctantly drop out of formation at the request of his engineer, Dusty Rhodes, and at about 2,000 feet above the water George Griffin jettisoned the bombs. As the bombs exploded, the concussion from the explosions rocked the plane. For a brief moment during this flight, the crew realized that their opportunity to attempt to land their disabled plane in Switzerland was indeed an option. This could have meant that they would then be spending the rest of their time sitting out the War in a neutral country. Realizing that the War couldn't be won with that kind of attitude, the crew voted to return to England. The *Sunrise Serenade* returned to Deopham Green, and the crew disappointedly did not get to count the mission toward their quota.

As the rest of the formation continued, an estimated 25 twin-engine and 5 single-engine enemy fighter planes attacked the formation for approximately 30 minutes near Strasburg. The fighters came in from all directions using a large variety of tactics as they fired upon all of the planes. Rocket attacks were common and also at least one unsuccessful aerial bombing attempt by a fighter was made. 2nd Lt. George B. Callow was borrowing Lt. John Pesch's plane, *Eastward Hup,* that day. German fighters knocked out three engines, causing it to crash near Le Titre, France. The crews' regular plane, *Miss Anonymous,* had to remain at the base due to needed repairs. The left waist gunner, S/Sgt. Bailey Pullen, took a bullet in his head during the battle and was killed. Eight members of the crew, including Callow, became POW's, while the bombardier was able to escape into the French Underground. Had the crew of the *Sunrise Serenade* decided to continue in the formation and then fly their damaged plane to Switzerland, they would have undoubtedly been easy targets for the German fighters and probably would have been shot down. The decision by the crew to return to base had been wise since they would have probably been shot down as a straggler away from the protection of the main formation of planes and escort fighters. That night while the crews were enjoying themselves in their respective clubs, the red ball went up signaling a mission for tomorrow. After finishing their drinks the men made their way back to their huts to get some much-needed rest for the next mission.

When March 17th arrived, the planned mission was cancelled, evidently due to inclement weather. The crew spent time checking over their beloved plane during the day. The navigational instruments inside the plane were calibrated and other mechanical areas such as the guns were inspected. The only planes from the 8th Air Force flying that day were 135 P-47 fighters who attacked enemy airfields in nearby France.

Sunrise Serenade Mission #6

The following day, March 18th, the 452nd Bomb Group made a return trip to Augsburg, Germany. This was the 18th mission overall for the Group. Harry Shoffner summed up the events of that day in his diary:

> "Mission to Augsburg. Took off at approximately 9:30 a.m. and it was a long trip there and back. The bombing was done visually, and we did some very good bombing. We hit the target for an assembly plant for Me-410's. We saw huge fires from 24,000 feet, so it must have been a hell of a fire. Flak wasn't very bad, although it was accurate. Enemy fighters were very few, for we had a wonderful fighter escort of P-47's, P-38's, and those P-51's. They probably took care of all enemy fighters. However, one fighter did come in at our formation and let loose a barrage of cannon shells, but they missed the ship. We saw one ship 'ditch' in the Channel. I guess he ran out of gas. The mission was pretty much a 'milk run', but very tiresome".

The plane that they saw ditch in the Channel was from another Group. The 8th Air Force effectively had 678 bombers release their bombs over their targets with 43 planes lost that day.

The next day, March 19th, the Group did not fly, so the Air Force took the official photos of the crews standing next to their planes. The photo of the *Sunrise Serenade* revealed two swastikas painted below the cockpit window that credited them with downing only two enemy aircraft. The crew had actually shot down as many as four at this time, but receiving credit was often difficult when many other planes fired at the same enemy planes. This day had special meaning to the pilot, Francis C. Smedley, who became a First Lieutenant, making him the highest-ranking officer on the *Sunrise Serenade*. During an official ceremony at the airbase, the engineer of the *Sunrise Serenade*, Dusty Rhodes, was given the honor of pinning Smedley's silver 1st Lieutenant bars to his uniform.

On March 20, 1944, the 452nd Bomb Group flew as lead group in the 45th Combat Wing formation that was leading all 8th Air Force formations that day. Most of the crew of the *Sunrise Serenade* was taking the day off for needed rest, except for George Griffin who flew as the bombardier on 1st Lt. William D. Hess's crew. Near the target area, the formations had become spread apart due to poor weather. Most of the planes from the 452nd Bomb Group dropped their bombs in the Frankfurt area, with two planes having been able to attack targets of opportunity through the cloud breaks. Around 1:30 p.m., the plane known as *Passionate Witch,* flown by 1st Lt. Robert Cook, was attacked by three Me-109's, and five FW-190's about fifteen miles northeast of Paris, France. During the attack, Cook kept turning his B-17 into the attacking planes. His crew was able to shoot down two of the FW-190's, and possibly severely damaged at least one other. The attack upon *Passionate Witch* was relentless nearly all the way back to England. Many of the crew inside the plane had been wounded as the plane limped along toward the English Coast with over two thousand bullet holes in it. Cook directed his plane toward the first available airbase at Dunsfold, in southern England, and made an emergency crash landing. His plane, now a total wreck from the enemy attacks, sat empty and alone on the grass field at Dunsfold. On the evening of March 25, 1944, a British Lancaster bomber (BIII ND572 PM-M), piloted by Fred Browning, made an emergency landing at the same airfield and crashed into the parked plane doing further damage.

The B-17 (far right) known as "Passionate Witch" and piloted by Robert Cook, was parked at an airfield near Dunsfold, England, when it was struck by a crippled British Lancaster on March 25, 1944. - *Collection of Robert Cook.*

The March 20th mission also claimed the life of an experienced bombardier on a plane known as the *Shed House Mouse,* flown by 1st Lt. James C. "Big Jim" Reynolds. After the bombs had been dropped on the target, one B-17 with presumably a new crew aboard had one of their 300 lb. bombs hung up in the bomb bay. At the moment that the bomb was finally freed, this plane had become directly over the *Shed House Mouse* and the bomb struck its nose. The impact tore most of the nose away, and also struck 2nd Lt. Lawrence H. "Andy" Anderson in the head, killing him instantly. His navigator, 2nd Lt. Frank Kottlowski, could only watch in horror as the plane then became lost in bad weather and ran out of gas, but was able to crash-land in a plowed field near Dulverton, England.

Anderson was very well liked among the other airmen and was a very positive thinking person. He routinely carried his Bible on combat missions and was devoutly religious. His crew members found his Bible next to his body and placed it on him after covering him with a parachute.

Lawrence H. "Andy" Anderson was killed when a bomb from another B-17 was mistakenly released over his bombardier's position aboard the *Shed House Mouse* on March 20, 1944. The plane was later rebuilt and became known as *The Reincarnation*. - Collection of the 452nd Bomb Group Association.

The mission that day to Frankfurt also resulted in five airmen being wounded and eight planes receiving battle damage. Initially only five planes came back, which sent anxiety into those awaiting their return, but the report finally came in that all crews had safely returned.

Since the crew of the *Sunrise Serenade* was not scheduled to fly, Francis Smedley flew to another base to pick up Lt. Elliot Eakin's crew who had previously crash-landed there. The crew of this plane, *Inside Curve*, were no strangers to the crew of the *Sunrise Serenade*, especially the radioman T/Sgt. John "Sparky" Collier who had once been part of their crew during training. The only planes flying missions that day from the 8th Air Force were fifty-six B-24's from the 2nd Air Division. The next day the crew also did not fly, so Francis Smedley took time to write home.

> "Mother Dearest, Hello Mom, I received your package, you know the 5 lb. one. Enclosed are some pictures of my crew and one of your son, yep, that's me, believe it or not. Yesterday we took a trip down to southern England and dropped in at an RAF base. They sure treated us swell. You can bet anytime any of our aircraft land at their bases they take dam good care of us. Between drinking and shooting the bull we looked over their ships and equipment and I can say that it is dam good. Boy the food was tops and even fresh milk, something darn hard to get in the E.T.O. Well mom, there's not much to say. You know how it is. Hush, hush, and all that stuff. I'm still waiting for my pass so I can drop down and see that big brother of mine. I hope he doesn't get too impatient with his kid brother. Well mom in order to send the photos I can't write too much. Say hello to all the folks back there. May the good Lord always look after you and keep you well. Your younger son, Francis."

The next mission for the Group was on March 22, 1944, to once again attack the city of Berlin. The Group was led by their new Commanding Officer Lt. Col. Marvin F. Stalder. The formations encountered heavy flak over the target and also a lot of flak on the return trip back to England. To everyone's relief they were not attacked by any German fighters on this mission. A total of 657 heavy bombers made the trip to Berlin that day from 28 different bomb groups. Twelve bombers failed to return, but none were from the 452nd Bomb Group. The *Sunrise Serenade* again stayed on the ground; however, Bob Lalumiere and Raymond Dean substituted on other crews. This was Lalumiere's eighth mission, Dean's seventh, and the 20th overall mission for the 452nd Bomb Group. After arriving back at the base, Bob Lalumiere made the following assessment during the interrogation of the mission:

> "I think we did a pretty good job. There were breaks in the clouds, and I could see the city through it. I don't think there was a hellava lot left of the target. Hitler must have moved a long time ago to new quarters."

Another airmen commented that the American fighter support was so good that they resembled flocks of blackbirds all flying together.

Sunrise Serenade Mission #7

The seventh mission credited to the crew of the *Sunrise Serenade* occurred on March 23, 1944. This mission proved to be rough for the 452nd Bomb Group, having five of their planes lost to enemy fighters and flak. The target was at Brunswick, Germany, and was best summed up in Harry Shoffner's diary that day as he observed from his left waist gunner's position:

> "Mission to Brunswick, my 7th. Flak was not bad going in, but terrible over and all the way back. Damned lead navigator must have led us over the Happy Valley. We had quite a violent attack by enemy FW-190's and Me-109's. There must have been 30 or more of them. They flew right through our formation taking two or three 'Forts' with them. One crashed into a 'Fort' and cut it right in two. However, all of the enemy didn't get through our formation. Those that saw them said it was quite a bit of battered junk that fell out of the sky. I didn't get a shot at those planes the first time, but I did later. I'll admit when I saw those 190's and 109's come through our formation I was really scared. Our fighter escort had just left us and they sneaked through out of the haze. Later our fighters showed up in scores and we had no more enemy fighter attacks, only flak. I've gotten over my fear of flak after the second mission. Occasionally I duck when those big ones go off and splatter the ships. There is no telling how many missions we will have to make. I just hope I have a chance to bail out when the time comes."

Of the five planes that went down that day, three planes had crew members killed. 1st Lt. Robert J. Brennan was flying *Duchess of Fubar* when the German fighters swept through the formation. His plane took many direct hits, including one that hit the ball turret gunner, S/Sgt. Euel T. Drake in the chest, killing him while at his guns. The rest of the crew bailed out, but the parachute of the radioman, T/Sgt. Walter R. Purcell, failed to open, and he was killed upon impact with the ground. The engineer and the tail gunner were wounded by enemy fire as they floated to the ground, while the plane crashed near Rengershausen, Germany.

The plane being flown by 2nd Lt. Charles C. Young Jr. known as *Star Eyes* was attacked by German fighters. After a brief period of being on fire, the plane exploded into a huge fireball before any of the crew could bail out. The explosion from the incendiary and fragmentation bombs threw the men and pieces of the plane in all directions near Rodenbeck, Germany. Miraculously the engineer, navigator, and a waist gunner all had their parachutes attached to their harnesses at the time of the explosion and were blown clear of the wreckage and were able to open their chutes. The engineer later died due to a broken back and other injuries from the explosion. The navigator, 2nd Lt. Edward S. Wodicka, suffered many injuries from pieces of the plane hitting him, including having a leg nearly severed off. Upon impact in a field, two German farmers came to his aid and administered first-aid, which saved his life. At the hospital a piece of one of the fragmentation bombs was removed from his body. All other members of the plane were instantly killed.

1st Lt. Roy V. Stephens was flying *Hairless Joe* that day when a German fighter flying close by was hit by one of the B-17's gunners. The fighter exploded just off the B-17's left wing and tore it off as it went by. The Fortress crashed near Varenesch, Germany, but not before four of the crew members managed to bail out. Stephens and his co-pilot F/O Raymond C. Hines were among the six crew members killed. Another Flying Fortress known as the *Paper Doll*, being flown by 1st Lt. Lascellis W. Yates, Jr., was hit by enemy fighters over Hanover, Germany. The attack left a hole in the wing and set the No. 2 engine on fire, which eventually shook off of the disabled plane. All of the crew safely bailed out and were taken prisoners by the Germans. The plane, which still had its bombs aboard, disintegrated upon impact.

The final plane to receive major damage that day was *Four Freedoms,* whose pilot was 1st Lt. John J. Pesch. Part of the plane's left wing tip was shot off, and the No. 1 and No. 2 engines were knocked out. As the plane desperately tried to return back to England, everything inside the plane was thrown out to lighten the load including the right waist gunner, S/Sgt. James F. Rouse who had been hit in the head by an enemy bullet and was badly bleeding. Members of his crew attached his parachute and dropped him out of the plane, hoping that the Germans would get to him and take him to a nearby hospital. The plan succeeded and Rouse survived. Due to the grave condition of the plane, Pesch subsequently ordered the entire crew to bail out. All crew members safely bailed out except his co-pilot, 2nd Lt. Joyce C. Amley, who refused to leave Pesch alone at the controls. At this point the plane could not be maintained by just one pilot because the control cables had been blown out. The two men were again fired upon as they crossed over the Channel. This attack left about 100 more holes in the plane and one bullet just missed Amley's head. The plane held together as the two pilots barely made the English coast and crash-landed in a meadow. Pesch and Amley returned to active duty, while the rest of the crew, who had bailed out, became prisoners of the Germans. Their plane was salvaged, but later destroyed on the ground when it was flown to Poltava, Russia, by another crew on a June 21, 1944, mission. At the end of the day, sixteen airmen from the Group had given their lives while flying.

Four Freedoms, piloted by John J. Pesch, received major damage on the March 23, 1944, mission. Pesch and his co-pilot miraculously flew the plane back to England after the rest of the crew had been ordered to bail out. - *Collection of the 452nd Bomb Group Association.*

The next two days were a time of relaxation for the crews of the 3rd Air Division. The 8th Air Force did, however, dispatch over 400 planes from the 1st Air Division and the 2nd Air Division to targets in Germany and France during these two days. The airmen from the 452nd Bomb Group all divided into teams and played lots of baseball, which helped them forget about the events of the past few days. Many men took time to organize their possessions inside the quonset huts to try to make it feel more like home. The gunners on the *Sunrise Serenade* all stayed together in a hut named "Tumble Inn" with the gunners of the *Kickapoo Joy*

Juice. Each enlisted man's hut contained 12 men. The gunners of the *Kickapoo Joy Juice* were George Kelly, Earnest Smith, Delbert Fenton, James Clark, William King, and Dan Wilkerson. The officers of the *Sunrise Serenade* stayed in the same hut with the four officers of *The Big Noise*, who were Bill Denham, Bob Krout, George Van Hersett, and Bob McCready. The four officers stayed in huts comprised only of other officers. The walls in their huts were often covered with pin-ups of Betty Grable, Lana Turner, Dorothy Lamour, Rita Hayworth, or the "girl back home".

The radio operator aboard the *Woolf Pack*, Michael A. Barbara, snapped this photo of the **Sunrise Serenade** during its 7th mission. The crew of the *Woolf Pack* were lucky and completed their required 30 missions; however, the plane would be later shot down with another crew. - Collection of Michael A. Barbara.

Sunrise Serenade Mission #8

On March 26th, the Group again took to the skies to bomb targets in Northern France. The initial mission to Liepzig was cancelled; however, secret targets in the Cherbourg peninsula were attacked. The flak was moderately heavy, but accurate. Two separate bomb runs had to be made on the target because it was hard to identify. About five planes from the 452nd Bomb Group received major damage that day. The *Sunrise Serenade* suffered three flak hits in the left wing and one in the right engine. One of those going through the left wing went through a gasoline tank, initially causing much concern, though the plane was able to land safely.

Sunrise Serenade Mission #9

The damage inflicted to the *Sunrise Serenade* was repaired overnight by the excellent ground crews attending the planes. By the morning of March 27th, the crew of the *Sunrise Serenade* participated in a raid to Bordeaux, France. Although the air crews did not fully know what the 8th Air Force leaders had in mind, it was increasingly evident that attacks on close targets in France were becoming more frequent. Over 700 heavy bombers from the 8th Air Force were dispatched that day to many different targets almost entirely in France. Of this total, only 6 planes were lost that day, but none from the 452nd Bomb Group. Harry Shoffner described the events of that day in his diary:

> *"Mission to Bordeaux. An attempt to cripple all Nazi airfields and advanced training schools, repair shops, etc. It was a long trip with no fighters, but pretty accurate flak. Everyone says we did a good job. I laid down on the floor with a carry-around oxygen bottle and watched the bombing and I called it rotten. Shorty will be down shortly with pictures of yesterday's bombing. I could see the target very plainly, and I saw what seemed like a million of those 20 lb. fragmentation bombs go off. Carried 36 large bombs x 6 as there were 6 small to the large. The area was black with those rascals. It proved to be a 'milk run'. We had a little trouble with enemy shipping. Two or three large boats shot flak at us. One was said to be a cruiser, one or two destroyer escorts and a large steamer or cargo. It took them a while to get our range, but they finally did. Griffin dropped two fragmentation bombs at them, as these failed to leave the bomb bay when we salvoed them. Oh yes, two or three flak holes in the ship. (small). Guess the flak was more accurate than I thought."*

Sunrise Serenade Mission #10

On March 28, 1944, the crew of the *Sunrise Serenade* flew as the low squadron leader and their Group was leading the entire 8th Air Force. This was possibly the first time that the crew had experienced being in the lead position in a squadron during a bombing run. The commanding officers showed their trust and faith in the officers of the *Sunrise Serenade*. This was also the first time that the crew of the *Sunrise Serenade* had successfully flown missions on three consecutive days. The airmen would later realize that this constant flying was in preparation for the secret invasion at Normandy, France, a few months away. Since the average number of missions flown by any bomber crew before getting shot down was ten, the crew of the *Sunrise Serenade* were now considered "old-timers" within the Group. The target that day was at Chateaudun, France, to bomb more German airfields. A total of five Groups passed over and dropped their bombs on a very important target. The 8th Air Force dispatched 450 heavy bombers that day, including 127 to the Chateaudun airfield. Only two bombers were lost that day from the entire 8th Air Force, both of which belonged to the 452nd Bomb Group. The loss of life for the Group that day was thirteen men, with the total death toll now at 93 for the Group since their combat missions had begun.

1st Lt. Robert M. Cook was flying his replacement plane, *Passionate Witch II*, which was only eight days old, after losing his first plane on the March 20th mission. His new plane took a direct hit in one of the gas tanks, which caused the plane to explode in mid-air, losing its right wing. The plane immediately went into a steep vertical spin as horrified airmen from other crews watched the plane's centrifugal force pin the crew inside the plane. Three of the crew, including Cook, managed to escape and bail out of the burning wreckage as the plane dove into the ground south of the Chateaudun airfield. Moments later, another plane, whose pilot was 1st Lt. Charles J. Robinson, took a direct hit of flak and exploded at the radio room, breaking the plane apart. The two waist gunners each bailed out, and the radioman was blown out, but luckily he had his parachute attached. The tail gunner somehow managed to attach his parachute and jump to safety, but only after dropping nearly 12,000 feet in the unattached tail section of the plane. Harry Shoffner recorded the days events in his diary:

> "*Mission to Chateaudun. Still after the Nazi airfields. Target not far away, and what I thought was to be a 'milk run' turned out really to be rugged. Lt. 'Pappy' Smedley led the low Squadron, and our Group led the 8th Air Force. Five Groups passed over the target and believe me it ain't what it used to be. We were carrying 500 lb. demolition, and four of the five Group hit, and good. The fifth was too far away to observe. The flak was terrifically accurate. The most accurate I have ever seen. They had our altitude from the very first burst. Two of our bombers failed to return. In fact I saw both of them not 100 yards away burst in flames and explode. I thought that they hit the bombs just at "bombs away" but one of the other fellows said it was direct hits in the gas tanks. The planes were out of the 728th Squadron, 452nd Group (ours), and it was really hitting close to home. Lt. Robinson and Lt. Cook got it. Both old crews flying new silver jobs (2nd bomb mission for both ships). It was a pitiful sight. They were High Group. Lt. Newman of 728th (our friend) has only five of the original crews left. Robbed Tim's barracks again. I feel sorry for him, but I know how he feels. We have lost too. By the good graces of God we are still alive. I pray that we will stay for a long time. Lt. Hess nearly got it. The flak was really after him. Most all of the ships were hit. Bob took pictures today. He will get some of the skirmishes. We had very good fighter escort, but no enemy fighters appeared. I flew tail gunner today for the first time. I was always griping because I had never seen enough, but today I got my fill. I saw plenty and believe me I was scared. All I can remember thinking about is 'let's get the hell out of this hot box'. Stand down for tomorrow, so we should get some sleep. Will write my sweetheart tomorrow. This is on the 'must do' list.*"

The pictures that were taken during missions by airmen were done with Air Force cameras. Most airmen could request a camera, if they were available, and take pictures during the mission. The cameras were then turned in after the mission and the pictures became the property of the Air Force. After airmen were shot down, their personal belongings back at the airbase were sometimes divided among those that were still there even if the airmen were "just missing". It was often difficult for the Air Force to gather all of these personal belongings and send them home to their parents or wives. First priority was to fill out the paperwork describing the circumstances of each airman's disappearance. Many airmen who were shot down never saw their personal belongings again.

The next three days were days of rest for the 452nd Bomb Group with no scheduled missions. Most of the airmen were able to obtain passes to leave the base and get away from the planes and atmosphere of the War. For the month of March the 452nd Bomb Group had lost 24 of their planes, but had also shot down 32 enemy planes with another 13 probable and 6 others damaged. During this time, the Bomber Command of the Royal Air Force was still conducting night bombing missions. One particular mission to Nuremberg, Germany, during the night of March 30/31, 1944, had disastrous results when a total of 96 British aircraft were lost to the Germans. During this single night the British had lost more aircrew than were lost in the entire three months during the Battle of Britain in 1940.

A familiar sight for the bomber crews of the Royal Air Force while bombing Germany at night were the many flashes and streams of fire created by the ground based anti-aircraft guns. - Collection of the author.

On April 1, 1944, the scheduled mission to Ludwigshaven, Germany, was recalled due to bad weather just after the formations comprised of 245 planes had crossed over the enemy coast and were being attacked by flak. The *Sunrise Serenade* did not participate in this recalled mission.

A lecture was given by two officers named 2nd Lt. Robert L. Costello and 2nd Lt. Paul L. Packer who had recently returned to the base. They were the co-pilot and navigator on one of the first planes to go down on the mission to Frankfurt on February 8, 1944. They, along with their pilot, 2nd Lt. Robert O. Lorenzi, and engineer, S/Sgt. Edward J. Sweeney, managed to evade capture by the Germans after they bailed out over France. The lecture presumably gave details about how they were able to avoid becoming prisoners of the Germans so other airmen might also have the same good fortune.

For the next seven days the crews all got a much-needed break as there were no missions flown by the 452nd Bomb Group. It was during this time that Harry Shoffner had received word from home that his wife was ill. The specifics of her condition were not made available, so Harry could only worry about the situation. A scheduled mission for April 6th was cancelled, so Harry met with the chaplain for guidance regarding the situation. The crews were alerted that they should be on standby to possibly fly the next day. The standby stayed in effect until 11:00 p.m. that evening when it was finally announced that there would be no mission on April 7th.

Flying in close formation served two separate purposes: It prevented the German fighters from penetrating into the middle of the formation, and it ensured a denser strike upon the target after the bombs were released. - *Collection of the 452nd Bomb Group Association.*

Sunrise Serenade Mission #11

On April 8th the *Sunrise Serenade* flew with their Group to Achmer, Germany, to bomb another airfield in that vicinity. Other planes from the Group also flew to Rheine, Germany, to bomb the airfield. The 452nd Bomb Group lost no planes that day, although the 8th Air Force sustained a loss of 34 Fortresses, which was mainly from a raid to the Brunswick, Germany, area. Aside from the loss of planes, 340 airmen were also no longer available to fly missions again. Losses for the American fighter escorts was also extremely high, having lost 23 fighters, 14 of which were the valuable P-51 Mustangs. Harry Shoffner gave this account of the mission to Achmer:

"Mission to Achmer Airdrome - Onsnabruck, Germany. The 8th Air Force hit at several airdromes in Germany. Most of the targets were completely demolished. Our target will not be used for quite some time. There were no enemy fighters at all. Our escort was very good (exceptional). Flak was moderately heavy and accurate. No damage was noted to our Group."

The next day, April 9th, turned out to be a bad one for the Group. The mission to Posen, Poland, would be remembered among airmen as one of the worst ones in which they participated. Six planes from the Group failed to return due to German fighter attacks. Francis Smedley and the crew of the *Sunrise Serenade* were leading the low squadron; however, heavy fog and bad weather moved in which broke up the formations to the extent that they lost sight of each other. Smedley eventually flew the *Sunrise Serenade* back to Deopham Green, having lost all contact with the rest of the formation. Unfortunately the mission did not count for the crew, even though they had been flying in dangerous conditions for many hours that day.

As the rest of the disorganized planes continued toward the target at Posen without the *Sunrise Serenade* to lead them, a new Fortress being flown by 2nd Lt. Joseph R. Patterson was badly damaged by flak over the target. Soon German fighters came upon the crippled plane and inflicted further damage, causing the plane to crash-land near Nakskov, Denmark. Upon landing, the crew set the plane on fire and then fled from the area. Six crew members including Patterson were eventually caught and taken prisoner, but four managed to evade capture and eventually return to England.

The Commanding Officer of the Group, Major George Oxrider, flew as the co-pilot in *Iron Bird* which was piloted by 1st Lt. John J. Mayek. The crew flew as group leader on this very long mission in which both fatigue of the airmen and fuel consumption was a major concern. On the return trip, Mayek's plane was seen to have had at least two engines on fire. Mayek then took the plane into a steep dive in an attempt to extinguish the flames. Apparently the dive was too intense for the pilot to recover, and the plane crashed into the Baltic Sea. All crew members were killed and only three bodies, including Major Oxrider's, were ever found.

1st Lt. Clyde T. Boy, Jr. was flying *Dinah Might II* that day and took several hits from German fighters. According to Boy, an estimated 20 fighters came into the formation on their first pass 4 abreast and 5 deep. Direct hits to the No. 2 engine caused a massive fire, and the plane was evacuated by the crew before it crashed near Todendorf, Germany. The copilot with Boy that day was Major Dain E. Wirt, who was the Assistant Group Operation's Officer. Wirt and the bombardier, 2nd Lt. Owen P. Quintana, both struck the open bomb bay doors as they were exiting and were killed. The rest of the crew including Boy were taken prisoner by the Germans.

At nearly the same time *Bar Fly*, being flown by 1st Lt. Carroll G. Boyd, was shot down by German fighters near Meltofte, Denmark. Six crew members including Boyd were killed in the crash, and the other four were taken prisoner. The same fate met the plane known as *Lucky Lady II*, being flown by 1st Lt. Norman G. Bodet, Jr. His plane crashed near Lüngerau, Germany, and killed the navigator, ball turret gunner, and also the right waist gunner who was hit by several 20mm shells in the chest, killing him inside the plane.

Engines on fire also caused the plane known as *Punchboard* to make a forced landing at Vaerlose, Denmark. This plane, being flown by 1st Lt. Earnest L. Racener, was captured nearly intact on the ground by the Germans. Having a salvageable plane in the hands of the German *Luftwaffe* meant that they could use it to better train their fighter pilots against its defenses. In rare instances, the Germans actually flew captured B-17's into formations and tried to join up with a particular Group. After this had been discovered, crews were often reluctant to let straggling planes come into formation unless they could completely identify themselves. Usually radio silence was maintained, so identification was difficult.

Harry Shoffner of the *Sunrise Serenade* noted in his diary that day the loss of several friends on Carroll Boyd's plane, which was one of the six to go down on that mission. He also noted that the ball turret gunner on 1st Lt. James C. "Big Jim" Reynold's crew broke down that day under the intense strain of the War. The crash landing of their plane on March 20th, and also the constant fear caused by flak exploding all around them was just too much for him to bear. The airman was taken to the area hospital for recovery, and S/Sgt. James E. Gallagher, who would later join the crew of the *Sunrise Serenade*, became the replacement ball turret gunner on Reynold's crew. Those airmen suffering from combat fatigue caused by the constant barrage of flak around them were often said to be "flak happy".

Sunrise Serenade   Mission #12

Courcelles, Belgium, was the 452nd Bomb Group's target for April 10, 1944. The Group was led by Col. Archie Olds and Lt. Harold G. Fulmer in the lead plane. Twenty-eight planes were sent out, but only 21 actually bombed the target because seven aborted after take-off. Due to 90% cloud cover, the target was very difficult to see; therefore, about five bomb runs were made on the target until it was visible. The entire bombing run lasted 1 hour and 20 minutes, and luckily there was no flak encountered directly over the target. Flak, however, did appear away from the target area each time the formations were turning around to try another bomb run. After the bombs were released over the intended target, it was soon discovered that the target had been completely missed despite all the Group's efforts. One plane flown by Lt. Bill McKenzie crash-landed at Caister-on-the-Sea, England, on the return to Deopham Green.

Because of sickness, Francis Smedley had stayed back at the base while Lt. Elwood W. Schwenn took over for Smedley at the controls of the *Sunrise Serenade* beside copilot Bill Hewett. This was the first and only mission that Smedley would miss during all of their missions, and it also was the first time that a non-crew member of the *Sunrise Serenade* flew with the plane in combat. Schwenn was also member a member of Francis Smedley's graduating class at the Merced Army Flying School during training in the states.

———

Safely back at his base, the tail gunner of the *Sunrise Serenade*, Raymond E. Dean, demonstrates how he successfully shot down a German fighter coming in at their plane. - *Collection of Robert A. Lalumiere.*

The *Sunrise Serenade* did not fly on the April 11, 1944, mission; however, part of the crew flew with another crew. Bill Hewett flew as the copilot in Jim Reynold's plane known as the *Silver Shed House*. This plane was relatively new since Reynold's original plane known as the *Shed House Mouse* had been severely damaged on the March 20th mission. His newer plane came straight from the factory in its shiny aluminum look, since the Air Force was no longer painting their planes in the old olive drab color. The Air Force, by this time, knew that the German radar could detect them coming, so the unpainted planes were not considered a detriment. Bob Lalumiere also flew in the ball turret position in this new plane that day. Dusty Rhodes had also originally been scheduled to fly with Reynolds that day, but due to frostbite from a previous mission he stayed at the base. The original target was to be Posen, Poland; however, due to cloud cover at Posen the target was changed to Rostock, Germany. The Group was attacked by German FW-190 fighters and also by the Me-210 twin-engined fighters. During the ensuing battle, Bob Lalumiere's ball turret took a direct hit by a bullet from one of the fighters or possibly a stray bullet from another Fortress's .50 caliber guns. The bullet struck part of the frame, sending pieces of the turret into Lalumiere's leg. Waist gunners S/Sgt. Robert E. Hearn and S/Sgt. Sylvester Petri pulled Lalumiere out of the ball turret and administered aid to his wound. Despite his pain, Lalumiere refused any morphine that the men attempted to give him. As the plane approached the airfield, the crew sent up two red flares indicating that their plane carried at least one wounded airman. This alerted the ground crews, who readied themselves to approach the plane with an ambulance and paramedics. All planes that carried wounded crew were always given priority to land first.

Crew members of *Flatbush Floogie*, piloted by Thomas L. Gardner, are taken prisoner by the Germans after crash landing their plane at Jadebusen, Germany on April 11, 1944. - *Collection of Susan Birbeck.*

Upon landing at the base, Bob Lalumiere was removed from the plane on a stretcher and then taken to the hospital to recover. This mission would be the last one that Lalumiere would fly with his regular crew or aboard the *Sunrise Serenade*. Also that day the Fortress known as *Flatbush Floogie* being flown by 1st Lt. Thomas L. Gardner took flak hits in both the No. 1 and No. 2 engines and crash landed on the mud flats in northern Germany at Jadebusen. The entire crew was immediately taken prisoner by the Germans upon landing. Another plane, *Cow Town Boogie* being flown by 1st Lt. Robert C. Schimmel, experienced engine trouble and Schimmel decided to fly the plane to Sweden. Upon arrival at Angelholm, Sweden, the crew was interned for the rest of the War by the neutral forces in Sweden. Schimmel was the pilot who had earlier flown another plane back to Deopham Green alone on the March 6, 1944, mission to Berlin after he had prematurely ordered the rest of his crew to bail out.

The next day, April 12th, the Group took off at 9:30 a.m. for a target at Halle, Germany. Although the crew of the *Sunrise Serenade* was expecting to add one more mission to their quota, Lt. Col. Robert B. Satterwhite decided to abort the mission due to bad weather. The cloud cover over the target was partly due to the dense contrails being created by the hundreds of bombers on their way to various targets. All 455 planes dispatched by the 8th Air Force had been called back. Even though the crews had been in the air for 4 hours, the mission did not count. The 452nd Bomb Group's 2nd Lt. Leland J. Evers was flying *Three Cads and a Lad* that day, and as they were heading out over the North Sea, the plane stalled and then broke up while going into a vertical spin. The plane then crashed into the Sea, killing six of the crew including Evers. The two waist gunners and also the co-pilot, 2nd Lt. Edward M. Kaminski, were able to somehow bail out of the spinning plane. The centrifugal force pinned the remainder of the crew in their seats as it headed down. When the plane broke apart, the engineer, S/Sgt. Robert G. Givens, was catapulted out of the plane. His parachute was dangling above his head, but still attached to the loose straps of his harness. Only by pulling down the parachute hand over hand, was Givens finally able to pull the rip cord after falling nearly 12,000 feet. The British Air-Sea Rescue picked up the four surviving crew members from the cold water.

Even though these near-death adventures took their toll on many of the men, they did occasionally have fun joking around with each other. On one occasion Bill Hewett wanted to see what it was like to be crammed inside the ball turret, so his gunners assisted him into it while it was parked at their airfield. Due to Hewett's height of 6 feet 6 inches, he could not reach behind to open the latch on the door to let himself out. The gunners left Hewett inside the turret until the crew chief finally came along to let him out. Smedley also liked to play tricks on the crew whenever he could get away with it. One of his favorites over friendly territory was to stall an engine and then call on the intercom to Andy Senetsky in the radio compartment to have him look out and see if all the engines were working. Fortunately this trick was only played a couple of times.

Sunrise Serenade Mission #13

On April 13, 1944, the crew of the *Sunrise Serenade* was again airborne for their thirteenth mission. Jim Gallagher was now the full time replacement at the ball turret position until Bob Lalumiere could recover from his leg wound. Gallagher had also flown several missions with Jim Reynold's crew, the same plane in which Lalumiere had been wounded. Had Lalumiere not been taking Gallagher's place that day on Reynold's crew, Gallagher would have been the one wounded. Gallagher was a fine addition to the *Sunrise Serenade* as the entire crew welcomed him aboard. Harry Shoffner stated the events of that day which took them to Augsburg, Germany, and resulted in 26 planes bombing the target:

> "I was rather worried for we had only three flak suits in the plane and I didn't have one of them. Especially when I knew there were 140 guns over the target. We made an exceptional long bomb run and flak all the way. I was down behind the armor plating with my chute on and only looking out occasionally. We were hit twice quite violently and I wasn't sure if we were going to get back or not. Also ran into flak on the way back, but not too bad. When we landed and counted holes, they were all over the ship. We had about a dozen of them."

The nearly 9-hour mission to Augsburg took the formations close to the neutral border of Switzerland. Flying this close to Switzerland tempted many crews to fake mechanical problems with their planes and land them in Switzerland. This would have taken a total commitment from the entire crew to go along with the plan, which fortunately rarely happened.

The crews of the 452nd Bomb Group took the next four days off, and the men all got some much-needed rest. On the evening of April 17th, the crews were alerted that they would fly the next day. Rumor circulated among the airmen that it was probably going to be a big mission.

Sunrise Serenade Mission #14

The April 18, 1944, mission was to bomb a fighter engine facility at Luneberg, Germany, near Berlin. As the formations approached the target area, Francis Smedley lost his supply of oxygen due to a break in the line near the navigator's position. Because of the impending situation, the crew had to regretfully leave formation and return to England. As they were returning alone, the crew spotted a convoy of German ships near the Elbe River and decided to salvage the mission by attacking the ships. The *Sunrise Serenade* positioned itself over the ships and Griffin dropped their bombs, but because they did not carry the Norden bombsight that day, their mark was off, and the ships escaped untouched. The rest of the formation bombed the airdrome at Luneberg and had caught the German *Luftwaffe* off guard and on the ground. The bombs heavily damaged many German planes which did not have a chance to take off to attack the Fortresses. Two main hangars were completely destroyed during the bombing raid. Since the *Sunrise Serenade* had flown nearly all the way to the target and had attempted to bomb the convoy of ships, the mission that day was credited for the crew.

Two gunners aboard the *Sunrise Serenade* pose for the camera. Norbert E. "Dusty" Rhodes, the top turret gunner, (left) stands in front of the plane, while Harry C. Shoffner, the left waist gunner, appears ready for battle. Shoffner is wearing "Tiger Bob" Lalumiere's leather jacket. - *Collections of Esther Rhodes and Mary Lou Shoffner.*

Sunrise Serenade Mission #15

The next day, April 19th, the Group flew to Lippstadt, Germany, and bombed the airfield. The 8th Air Force dispatched 772 heavy bombers that day from 30 different Bomb Groups. The losses that day were a total of five B-17's belonging to the 91st and 381st Bomb Groups. The American fighters fared a little better with only losing two planes out of the 697 that were dispatched. Both American fighter losses were P-51 Mustangs.

Sunrise Serenade Mission #16

April 20th again saw action for the crews as they headed for targets on the coast of France. The target, reported to be secret, was evidently hard to determine as the bombers flew around and attempted to find it. The bombs eventually had to be jettisoned in the English Channel. On the return trip, flak hit the B-17 flown by 2nd Lt. Joseph G. Thomas as it was heading over the French coast. Thomas turned his plane around and headed back toward the enemy coast as all ten crew members were reported to have been seen bailing out. Air-Sea Rescue picked up six of the crew from the water, including Thomas, and then stayed in the area until the next morning searching for the other four who were never found and presumed to have drowned. Thomas, along with the navigator, and two waist gunners continued to fly together and were again shot down on the May 12, 1944, mission to Brux, Czechoslovakia. Thomas was killed during their last mission, but the three others, after having had to parachute twice in three weeks, survived and became prisoners of the Germans.

German ground troops prepare to fire their 20mm anti-aircraft gun at lower flying aircraft. The soldier at the right is determining the altitude of the planes. - *Collection of the author.*

During the next two days the crew of the *Sunrise Serenade* had passes and did not fly. On April 21, 1944, their Group took off to bomb a synthetic oil plant near Lippstadt, Germany. Due to inclement weather the Group had to return to base. The visibility was extremely poor due to very heavy fog. The ceiling was reported to be at 1,000 feet and at 14,000 feet it was still foggy. At this altitude a plane known as *Little Chum* being flown by 1st Lt. Dixon Wands ran into very heavy turbulence and lost control. As the plane spun downward, five crew members were able to bail out of the plane. The engineer, T/Sgt. Leroy George, had cheated death by being one of those to escape from the plane, but he was killed when his chute failed to open. The other five crew members still aboard the plane, including the pilot, also died.

The 452nd Bomb Group flew to Hamm, Germany, on April 22nd to bomb the marshalling yards. No fighters approached the formations during the entire trip. A mission to Friedrichshafen, Germany, provided the target on April 24th. This entire mission lasted 10 hours. The crews had to be on oxygen for 7 of those hours. These two missions were #34 and #35 for the Group with no losses of planes or crew, although the 8th Air Force did have 55 bombers and 524 crew members missing from other Groups during those two days.

Sunrise Serenade Mission #17

The April 25, 1944, mission was a 7-hour trip to Dijon, France, and would be the seventeenth mission for the crew of the *Sunrise Serenade*. Because of excellent navigation, the formations encountered no flak, and were not attacked by any enemy fighters although at least two Me-109's were seen. The fighter escorts, or "Little Friends" as the bomber crews called them, were with the Fortresses the entire trip. A total of 554 B-17's and B-24's were dispatched that day by the 8th Air Force, with 7 becoming casualties. Three B-24's also flew to Switzerland that day and were interned.

The next day, April 26th, the Group flew to the Brunswick and Hildesheim, Germany areas while the crew of the *Sunrise Serenade* rested. The targets were factories that produced aircraft parts and components. On this mission the Group utilized a type of system for locating the target called Pathfinder Force (PFF). PFF bombing used a radar device suspended from the lead plane where the ball turret would normally be located. The use of this system was intended to enable the crews to bomb the intended target through cloud cover, which would have normally caused the mission to be aborted. The *Sunrise Serenade* attempted to fly on this mission, but had to abort just after takeoff due to problems with the engines. The *Sunrise Serenade* was beginning to show the tremendous amount of wear upon it.

Railroad marshalling yards were prime targets for Allied bombers since the damage inflicted disrupted the Germans' ability to move equipment on the ground. - *Collection of the author.*

Also just after take-off a plane from the Group, known as *Tangerine* being flown by Lt. Hugh Wilson, crashed into several fences and trees in an open field. The mission by the Group was considered a complete failure since no target had been bombed even with the PFF device. The bombs were released onto the German homeland in the general area of Hildesheim without any visual observation of what they actually might have hit.

Sunrise Serenade Mission #18
On April 27, 1944, Smedley's crew participated in the mission to secret targets in Northern France, which were thought to have been German V-2 Rocket installations or launching pads. Some flak was encountered, which resulted in having three holes tear through the *Sunrise Serenade*. One piece of flak went through the tail, which cut the intercom wires to tail gunner Raymond Dean's position. Another piece of flak went through the rear elevator, and one went through the nose of the plane, just missing co-pilot Bill Hewett.

After a day of rest, the Group flew to Berlin on April 29, 1944, which was called a "routine mission". The *Sunrise Serenade* was a scheduled spare that day in case another crew's plane could not be made ready for the mission. There was no need for a spare, so the crew stayed on the ground. Since most of the bombing had been concentrated on the airfields and railroads in the France area, the Air Force decided to let Hitler know they were still around by once again selecting Berlin as its target.

The 452nd Bomb Group was leading the entire Air Force that day during the 9-hour flight. Over the target, a plane named the *Karen B.* being flown by 2nd Lt. Hal J. Nelson, was damaged by flak and then became a straggler away from the safety of the formation. All crew members eventually bailed out before the plane crashed near Ruurlo, The Netherlands. Six of the crew, including the pilot, were able to evade capture. The other four members were eventually caught and taken prisoner. Most of the men who evaded capture were eventually liberated at the end of the War. The ball turret gunner, S/Sgt. Robert W. Zercher, however was caught hiding with the Dutch Resistance in late September of 1944. The Germans murdered Zercher, along with a British flight sergeant and six Dutchmen from the Resistance. Their bodies were placed at the main intersections in Apeldoorn, The Netherlands, and each had a sign attached that read "Terrorist".

Another plane that day named *Rugged but Right*, which was being flown by 2nd Lt. George A. Haakenson, was also hit by flak over the target. This plane was soon shot down by German fighters and crashed near Burg, Germany. All of the crew safely bailed out and were taken prisoner. This plane was assigned to a pilot named Hugh Atkinson whose crew had stayed at the base that day and escaped this fate. Less than two weeks later on the May 12, 1944, mission to Brux, Czechoslovakia, Atkinson and his crew were shot down by German fighters and taken prisoner.

The photographer caught plane #297130 directly below other bomber formations many miles in the distance. The column of smoke below and left of the plane may be from an earlier bomber which was shot down - *Collection of Sylvester Petri.*

Sunrise Serenade Mission #19
The last successful mission flown by the crew of the *Sunrise Serenade* would be their nineteenth and occurred on April 30, 1944. (Some of the crew members may have actually already completed 19 missions since they had substituted on other planes, and Smedley was believed to have had only 18 since he was ill during the *Sunrise Serenade's* 12th mission).

The mission, which was the 40th for the Group, was to an airdrome at Clermont-Ferrand, France. The mission over France was a long and tiring one, but the Group encountered no flak or German fighters the entire trip. Upon arrival back at Deopham Green the crews were alerted that they might fly again the next day, although this was not definite.

Through the end of April 1944, the 452nd Bomb Group lost nearly 40 planes and 131 men had died. Many other planes had been badly damaged, and several airmen had also been wounded. These first 40 missions in just less than 3 months had claimed 30% of the total men that would eventually die in the 452nd Bomb Group. The Group would continue to fly for another year and add 210 more missions and have 310 more men die. Of the four squadrons of the Group, the 728th Squadron was affected the most since 49% of the 131 men that died during the first 40 missions were from that squadron. The 730th Squadron, which included the *Sunrise Serenade*, had 20% of these deaths. The worst position on the plane during this time was the bombardier, since 22 men had given their lives at this position, which was more than any other position. The two waist gunner's positions had lost a combined total of 20 men, while 15 copilots and 12 pilots had also died. All other positions on the plane had lost between 11 and 13 men, which indicated that there was no safe position on the plane. The total number of 8th Air Force bombers lost during these three months was approximately 880 planes, while the number of lost 8th Air Force fighters numbered approximately 440 planes. The British suffered losses of over 700 bombers during this same period, which mostly came from night bombing missions. The American 9th and 15th Air Forces, who were also operational at this time, had lost many planes as well in England and Italy.

The Germans captured 244 airmen from the 452nd Bomb Group in the first three months of their combat missions. Twenty-two airmen from the Group managed to evade capture. Also, some airmen were interned in Sweden, and some were in hospitals recovering from wounds. If an original crew had been lucky enough to still be flying by the end of April 1944, the majority of men that they had trained with were now gone. The barracks at the airfield, which in the beginning housed men of similar circumstances, now exhibited a mixture of war-hardened faces and fearful faces of the replacement crews.

With nearly two-thirds of their mission quota now complete, the crew of the *Sunrise Serenade* was feeling confident about having a good chance to complete their tour, and possibly prepare to return home in a few weeks. The missions were getting easier, but none of the crew could have predicted that less than 24 hours later their own fate would be changed forever.

The view aboard a B-17 Flying Fortress was breathtaking as the crews flew over the European countryside; however, the airmen usually had little time to actually enjoy it. Soon squadrons of German Me-109 and FW-190 fighter planes firing their 20mm guns upon the formations would disrupt the serenity of the moment, and later huge barrages of flak would erupt on all sides of their planes sounding like hail hitting a tin roof. - *Collection of the author.*

The Final Mission

On the morning of May 1, 1944, the crew of the *Sunrise Serenade* still had the events of the previous day's mission to Clermont-Ferrand, France, on their minds. There was no particular hurry that morning as they watched other planes from their own Bomb Group assemble and take-off for a mission to bomb German V-2 Rocket sites across the Channel. Weather was an important factor that day for the 8th Air Force, having obscured all but three of that morning's 23 targets.

Later that same morning the crew of the *Sunrise Serenade* was alerted that they would also fly that day on an unprecedented second mission to bomb targets in France and possibly Belgium. This was the first time that the 452nd Bomb Group had attempted to fly more than one mission during a single day. May 1, 1944, also marked the beginning of the bombing campaign specifically targeted to disrupt the German rail network in France and Belgium in preparation for D-Day. The primary target was the railroad marshalling yards at Metz, France. The mission would be a round trip of about 5 hours to a target that would hopefully be lightly fortified by the Germans. Such a mission was often referred to as a "milk run" by airmen, knowing that they would encounter only light flak and probably only a few enemy fighters.

Coordination to mobilize early in the afternoon for this second mission was weak, and the first plane to take off from the runway at Deopham Green did so at 2:44 p.m., which was 12 minutes behind the scheduled time. Other planes were still trying to taxi into position, while others were still doing their pre-flight checklist. After the lead plane had traveled eight miles, only one other plane was following. At the time the first planes had reached their assembly point, only 5 of the scheduled 24 planes were in formation. Finally, after cutting short the first two control points, and proceeding to other assembly points, nine more ships had joined the formation before reaching the English coast at Felixstowe. Eventually 19 of the scheduled 24 planes from the 452nd Bomb Group came into the formation, having left the English coast 3 minutes late. The five planes that did not join the formation consisted of one spare plane returning to base, one plane aborted the mission just prior to being dispatched, and three planes aborted after being dispatched. Soon after leaving the coast, the planes from the 452nd Bomb Group had made contact with the other two groups of their 45th Combat Wing that they believed were behind them. The 452nd's formation turned around in an attempt to await the other groups who were supposed to be flying seven minutes behind them. However, these other groups were not seen, so the *Sunrise Serenade*, flying as the High Squadron Leader, and the rest of the Group turned back around and proceeded across the English coast for the second time. The Group was now 15 minutes late and charted a magnetic heading of 145°, and an altitude of 18,750 feet as they crossed the North Sea.

The intended course over the North Sea was reached at 5:07 p.m., which was 2 hours and 23 minutes after the *Sunrise Serenade* had initially taken off from the airfield. The gunners tested their .50 caliber machine guns just as they had done on nineteen previous missions over the sea. Smedley and his crew tried to settle in for the rest of flight, while hoping that the confusion caused during this mission was now behind them. They crossed the enemy coast of Belgium at an altitude of 18,000 feet encountering light flak. At this time the group commander decided to try to catch up with a formation of other B-17's that had been spotted ahead of them. Keeping to the inside on all turns, the planes from the 452nd Bomb Group eventually caught up with the other formation near Namur, Belgium. A triangle insignia on the tail identified these planes as being from the 1st Division. Since they seemed to be heading in the same general direction of Metz, France, the 452nd Bomb Group's planes attached themselves to the rear of the 1st Division's formation. While crossing into France it became obvious that these planes were not heading for Metz, but were instead continuing south. The 452nd's group commander then decided to stay attached to this formation since the 452nd Bomb Group's formation was relatively small.

Near the town of St. Menehould, France, they turned southwest toward Chalons, and then made a sweeping turn north toward Reims, France. The planes of the 1st Division bombed the railroad yards at Reims, but the 452nd planes were never sure of the intended target, so their bombs were held at the command of their group leader, Lt. Col. Jack W. Hayes, Jr. After leaving Reims, the entire formation continued north over Rethel and then into Belgium. At Charleroi, Belgium, the planes from the 1st Division made a left turn and headed back to their respective bases in England. With their bombs still aboard, the 452nd planes decided to proceed north to bomb the Schaerbeek railroad marshalling yards at Brussels, which was their target of last resort. It was hoped that something good could still be made of this mission which had been one of confusion from the very beginning.

The cameras aboard the 452nd Bomb Group's planes recorded the bombs making a direct hit upon the Schaerbeek marshalling yards in Brussels, Belgium. The long trails of smoke are the result of the Germans' meager attempt to obscure the target before the bombers arrived. Moments later the *Sunrise Serenade*, flying as high squadron leader, would have its 20-mission bombing streak come to an end as a result of several hits of flak. The direction of North is to the top right corner of the photo. - *Collection of Irwin Math.*

As the sun was setting lower on the horizon, the planes from the 452nd Bomb Group arrived over the eastern limits of Brussels and turned their planes westward to began their bombing run on the marshalling yards located in the northern part of Brussels. Just prior to their arrival the Germans had estimated that the railroad yard might be the target and tried to set up a smoke screen to obscure the target. The Germans were also placing the final altitude adjustments on their anti-aircraft guns located in the area. Four German batteries from the 402nd and 553rd Air Defense flak units fired their 88mm and 105mm guns upon the formation. A barrage of flak soon erupted in front of the formation as the planes remained on their steady bomb course. By this time the bombardier of the *Sunrise Serenade*, George D. Griffin, had already taken control of the final moments of the bomb run and was zeroing in on the target through the plane's Norden bombsight. The delayed bursts of flak tracked right along with the formation, exploding on every side as well as overhead and underneath the planes. As the target came into view, Griffin replied over the intercom "Bombs away".

The bombs were released from the bomb bay of the *Sunrise Serenade* at 6:57 p.m. Upon seeing their High Squadron Leader release its bombs, the rest of the planes in the high squadron did also. Almost simultaneously all 19 planes had released their loads as every plane surged upward from the absence of the heavy weight.

Just as they were starting to think about plotting a course for home, the crew of the *Sunrise Serenade* was suddenly jolted as four to five direct or near direct hits of flak struck their plane. One hit went through the No. 3 fuel tank, resulting in a hole blown through the entire wing and into the bomb bay area. Flaming gasoline spilled into the body of the plane. The fire was not immediately noticed until the plane's radio operator, Andy Senetsky, saw the wing on fire while looking back out of the door to the bomb bay area. Normally Senetsky had always kept this door closed, but that day for some unexplained reason, he had left it open. Senetsky immediately called out over the intercom to Smedley to alert him of the fire. At the same time John

Brown was reaching for a fire extinguisher in an attempt to extinguish the flames, but it was useless. A piece of flak had also struck the nose of the plane hitting the Norden bombsight which had possibly saved the lives of both George Griffin and John McGrath who were seated behind it. Other pieces of flak may have entered the cockpit around Smedley and Hewett. In a brief cry over the intercom, Smedley may have indicated that he had been hit in the stomach by a piece of flak. Confusion was starting to become evident as the men scrambled to locate and attach their parachutes. Almost simultaneously Smedley rang the bell and gave the order to bail out as he tried to maintain control of the plane to take it away from Brussels and an entire population of civilian people. Griffin, McGrath and Rhodes all went out of the door in the nose of the plane. Shoffner, Gallagher, Senetsky, and Brown went out the side door near the waist guns. Dean went out his door near the tail gunner's position. He was seen hanging onto the door with his legs dangling in the air by the crew of the *Kickapoo Joy Juice* as if he was not sure he wanted to jump. After free-falling for nearly 15,000 feet, Dean pulled his rip cord as his chute blossomed out above him. In his memoirs, Ray Dean later wrote of the experience:

> *"As I fell away from the airplane, I was in a head down position on my back. I still had on my oxygen mask and the short flexible hose was beating my head. I could have easily unsnapped it and removed it, but in the excitement I just grabbed the hose and tried to pull it off. The hose broke and the mask snapped back into my face. I finally got it removed and when I released it, it seemed to go up. Of course I was falling faster and was really falling away from it. I also had a pair of binoculars around my neck. I removed these and released them. I was quite startled to look back later and find them floating beside me. My arms and legs flopped around, and I felt like I was supported on a blast of air. I never did have the sensation of falling and found no difficulty in breathing; my senses were completely clear. My main concern was I wanted my Mother."*

Jumping out of their home in the sky took a lot of courage, since none of the crew had ever experienced jumping before. Just a brief lesson on the ground regarding the basics of how to properly jump and open their chutes was all the knowledge on which the men had to rely. If a parachute had not been properly packed by a member of the ground crew, their chute could easily become a "streamer" and fail to open. There were no backup parachutes in the event this happened, and streamers were not an uncommon occurrence. The ground crews did everything they possibly could to ensure that these parachutes would open properly, but conditions beyond their control such as having the wind tangle the cords could not be helped. When crew members picked up their chutes, they would sometimes make remarks about hoping they opened up right. The ground crew members would jokingly tell them to bring it back if it didn't.

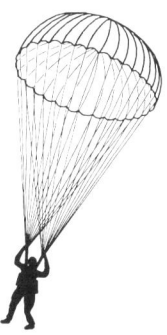

Jumping out of a bomber that was usually over 20,000 feet above the ground took courage since the airmen had never practiced it in real life.

The fire on the *Sunrise Serenade* rapidly began spreading into the cockpit as the pilots were preparing for their own escape. The co-pilot, Hewett, was severely burned as he went back through the flames to exit out the door in the nose of the plane. At the same time Smedley was trying to determine the best way to exit the plane, which had its cockpit now nearly engulfed by the fire. Exiting out the nose of the plane as Hewett had done was no longer an option for Smedley due to the intense fire. With the rest of the plane almost completely engulfed in fire, Smedley slid back the small window next to the co-pilot's seat on the right side of the plane. He then climbed outside of the small window one leg at a time, and managed to stretch his long legs backward and onto the wing of the plane as the air stream strained against his body. He then reached back inside the window for his parachute while hanging onto the edge of the window with his other hand. He began to attach the parachute to his chest harness as the fire from the wing was luckily being swept back by the air current. After succeeding in attaching one D-ring to the harness and then attempting to attach the other, the parachute somehow prematurely opened up. The force of the air stream catching the parachute pulled Smedley off the wing. As his chute went over the rear stabilizer wing, the weight of Smedley's body pulled him under the bar. As the plane plummeted the fire swept back and burned up Smedley's parachute that was caught on the wing.

After the *Sunrise Serenade* had continued a little farther west, it exploded and then finally struck the ground near a castle known as Sint-Ulriks-Kapelle. The area was soft and marshy so the parts of the plane that were embedded sunk into the ground, but other pieces were strewn across the general area. Most of the wreckage above the surface would later be salvaged since aluminum was in high demand for the War effort.

The *Sunrise Serenade* struck the ground and disintegrated near the castle known as Sint-Ulriks-Kapelle. The crash site was approximately 7 miles west of the railroad yard where the bombs had been dropped. - *Collection of Gwendolyn Dean.*

The rest of the crew survived their jump from the disabled plane and were scattered over small villages and the suburbs of Brussels. John Brown landed on the top of a city gymnasium. The impact of his stiff legs hitting the roof drove his knees up under his chin, and he lay stunned for a few seconds. George Griffin landed on a slate roof of a school gymnasium, where upon impact his legs broke through. As a result he became stuck, though the Germans soon arrived with a ladder to get him down off the roof. Ray Dean realized that he, too, was going to land upon some buildings, so he pulled down on the risers in an attempt to direct his chute away from the buildings. This maneuver, which had never been practiced, resulted in collapsing the parachute. The chute popped back open and Dean decided against trying it again. He landed on top of a four-story building, but the wind caught his chute and pulled him off and into a lot at the rear of the building. The impact knocked him unconscious, and when he woke up many Belgian people had come over to him. Two German soldiers parted the onlookers and grabbed him before anyone could try to hide him.

Andy Senetsky and Bill Hewett landed in open fields, where they, too, were quickly apprehended by the Germans since there was little time to escape. John McGrath drifted toward the faces of some high buildings, but was lucky enough to stay airborne long enough to land upon the roof of a four-story schoolhouse in the center of town. Since the building was too high to jump off, McGrath was soon captured by the Germans, who had found their way into the building and through a door in the roof. McGrath was put into the sidecar of a German motorcycle and taken to a nearby jail in Brussels. While being transported to the jail, a Belgian woman threw flowers into his lap. At the jail, McGrath saw that most of the crew of the *Sunrise Serenade* had already arrived. Most, if not all, of the crew members were put into solitary confinement in Brussels at a place known as St. Gilles Prison. It was here that some brief interrogation was done by the local German police who had apprehended the men.

Within a short time after their exit from the plane, eight of the crew members were in the custody of the Germans. Harry Shoffner had successfully escaped with the help of the Belgians, and their pilot unbeknownst to any of them was already dead. Bill Hewett was taken to a nearby St. Gilles Hospital to receive treatment for severe burns.

The *Sunrise Serenade* was only one of three B-17's to be shot down that day from the entire 8th Air Force. The other two planes were from the 91st and 96th Bomb Groups. The plane from the 91st Bomb Group was named *Cool Papa* and was shot down by flak over Bavereyde, France, killing two aboard. The other eight were taken prisoner. The plane from the 96th Bomb Group was also shot down by flak and crashed near the town of Chivres, Belgium. One crew member was killed, one escaped, and eight were taken prisoner; the same fate as the *Sunrise Serenade's* crew.

History would later prove that the loss of the *Sunrise Serenade* and crew was just the beginning of the costliest month for B-17 losses in 8th Air Force history. The 8th Air Force lost 237 B-17's during May of 1944 which was the highest monthly total during the entire War. April had been the second highest total preceded by the third highest in March and the fourth highest in February 1944. The crew of the *Sunrise Serenade* had been required to fly their combat missions during the four deadliest months of the War. During this four month period over 500 mothers of sons flying aboard 8th Air Force bombers would never receive letters from their sons again while nearly 8,500 other mothers would only receive telegrams stating that their sons were missing.

The 452nd Bombardment Group's Mission #42 on May 1, 1944.
The Final Mission of the *Sunrise Serenade*.

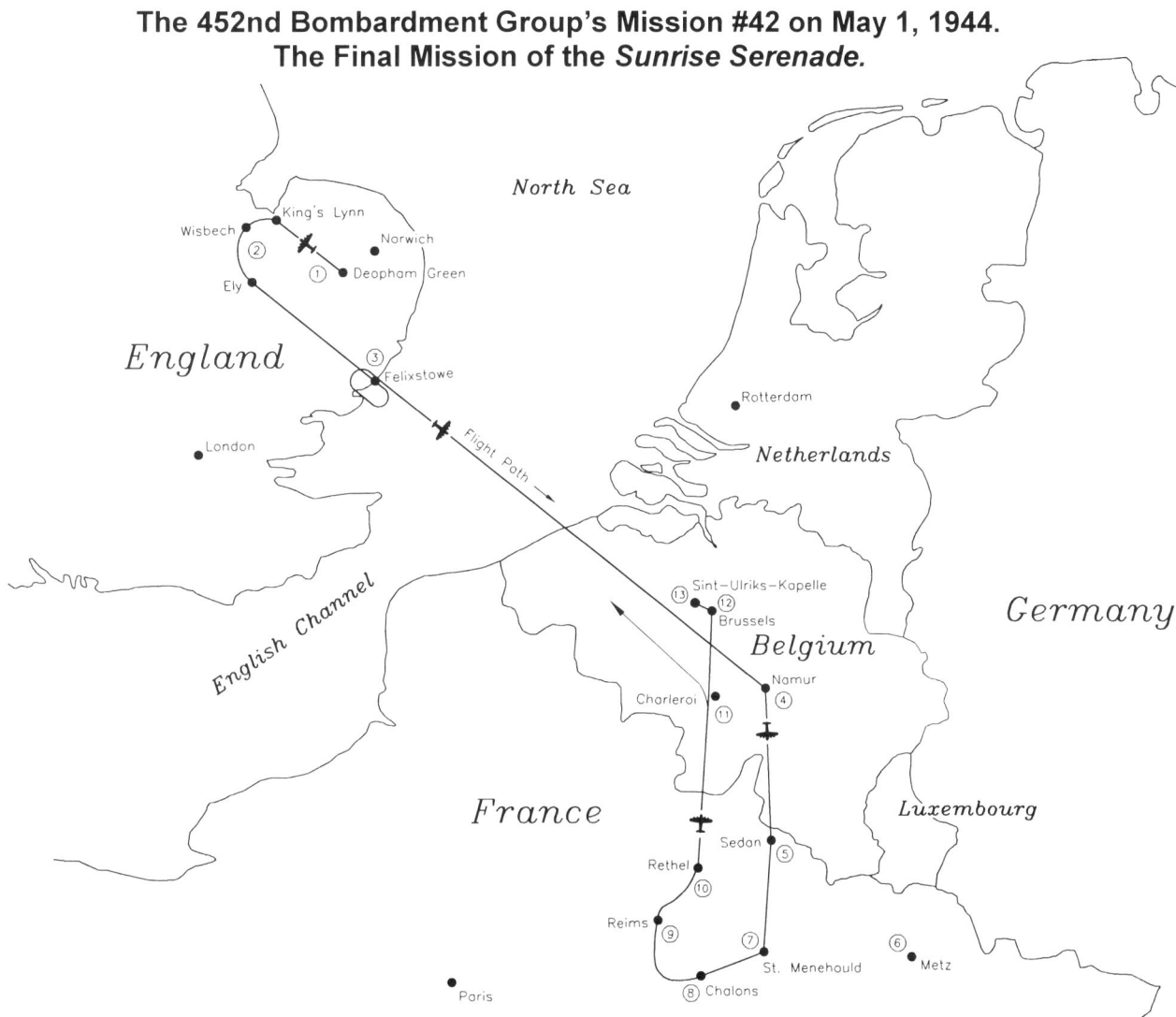

1. The initial planes from the 452nd Bomb Group began to take off from their base at Deopham Green, England, at 2:44 p.m. After the lead plane was out 8 miles from the airfield, only one other plane was following.
2. While assembling into formation over the check points of King's Lynn, Wisbech, and Ely, eleven more planes attached themselves to the formation during these turns.
3. The formation reached the coast of England at Felixstowe three minutes late with 13 planes now in formation. The Group Leader decided to turn around and wait for two other Groups that were supposedly seven minutes behind them. These planes were not seen, so the group passed over the English coast the second time fifteen minutes late at an altitude of 18,750 feet.
4. After crossing the North Sea, the group commander attempted to catch up with another formation of bombers ahead of them. At Namur, Belgium, these bombers were caught and identified as being from the 1st Air Division. Since they appeared to be heading for the same target, the planes from the 452nd Bomb Group attached themselves onto the 1st Air Division's formation.
5. While passing over Sedan, France, it became obvious that the planes of the 1st Air Division were not heading for the same target. The 452nd Bomb Group's commander decided to stay attached to this larger formation due to the small number of planes in their own formation.
6. The original briefed target for the planes of the 452nd Bomb Group was Metz, France, but was never reached.
7. The 452nd Bomb Group's planes passed over St. Menehould, France, with the planes of the 1st Air Division.
8. The 452nd Bomb Group's planes passed over Chalons, France, with the planes of the 1st Air Division.
9. The marshalling yard at Reims, France, was bombed by the planes of the 1st Division; however, the planes from the 452nd Bomb Group held their bombs at the command of their group leader.
10. The 452nd Bomb Group's planes passed over Rethel, France, with the planes of the 1st Air Division.
11. The planes from the 1st Air Division returned to their respective bases in England after passing near Charleroi, Belgium, while the planes from the 452nd Bomb Group continued north to their target of last resort at Brussels, Belgium.
12. The Schaerbeek Marshalling Yard at Brussels, Belgium, was bombed by the 452nd Bomb Group at 6:57 p.m. at an altitude of 18,000 feet. The *Sunrise Serenade*, while flying as the high squadron leader, took several direct hits of anti-aircraft fire. The crew began to bail out as the pilot, Francis C. Smedley, guided the plane away from the city.
13. After exploding in the air, the main part of the *Sunrise Serenade* struck the ground at Sint-Ulriks-Kapelle. The rest of the planes from the 452nd Bomb group began arriving back at Deopham Green, England, at 8:31 p.m.

Local Belgian women search for relics around the massive hole created by the crash of the *Sunrise Serenade* soon after the incident occurred. Since the area was soft and marshy, the hole had already begun to fill with water (top photo). The main portions of the plane that were not embedded into the ground had already been removed when the photos were taken. - *Collection of Mary Lou Shoffner.*

A Mother's Worry

Receiving mail from her son in Europe was comforting to a mother, and assured her that he was still safe. It was the mother who generally took the time to write to her son, while the father continued to provide for his family. The one message that a mother never wanted to receive was a Western Union telegram concerning her son. A short message in the form of a telegram was usually the first item that parents or spouses received to inform them that something was wrong with their loved one. This message generally contained no details even if the Armed Forces knew that a soldier had been killed or taken prisoner. Those doing the paperwork never wanted to wrongly name a person as being dead unless the details had been thoroughly verified. The following was the telegram that the mother of First Lieutenant Francis C. Smedley had received soon after the *Sunrise Serenade* had been shot down.

> THE SECRETARY OF WAR DESIRES ME TO EXPRESS HIS DEEP REGRET THAT YOUR SON FIRST LIEUTENANT FRANCIS C. SMEDLEY HAS BEEN REPORTED MISSING IN ACTION SINCE ONE MAY OVER GERMANY. IF FURTHER DETAILS OR OTHER INFORMATION ARE RECEIVED YOU WILL BE PROMPTLY NOTIFIED.

The majority of the information that follows centers around the pilot's mother, Clara W. Smedley, and the letters she received from the other mothers of the crew. Although it is believed that all of the mothers had corresponded with each other after the *Sunrise Serenade* had been shot down, the best collection of letters still available were from those sent to Mrs. Smedley. The general worry and sorrow expressed in the excerpts taken from these letters represents the concerns of the mothers for the crew as a whole. After the telegram, the first official letter received by the parents was dated on or near May 19, 1944.

> *This letter is to confirm my recent telegram in which you were regretfully informed that your son, First Lieutenant Francis C. Smedley, 0747347, Air Corps, has been reported missing in action since 1 May 1944 over Germany. I know that added distress is caused by failure to receive more information or details. Therefore, I wish to assure you that at any time additional information is received, it will be transmitted to you without delay, and, if in the meantime no additional information is received, I will again communicate with you at the expiration of three months. Also, it is the policy of the Commanding General of the Army Air Forces upon receipt of the "Missing Air Crew Report" to convey to you any details that might be contained in that report. The term "missing in action" is used only to indicate that the whereabouts or status of an individual is not immediately known. It is not intended to convey the impression that the case is closed. I wish to emphasize that every effort is exerted continuously to clear up the status of our personnel. Under war conditions this is a difficult task as you must readily realize. Experience has shown that many persons reported as missing in action are subsequently reported as prisoners of war, but as this information is furnished by countries with which we are at war, the War Department is helpless to expedite such reports. However, in order to relieve financial worry, Congress has enacted legislation which continues in force the pay, allowances and allotments to dependents or personnel being carried in a missing status.*
> *Permit me to extend to you my heartfelt sympathy during this period of uncertainty.*
> *Sincerely yours,*
> *Robert H. Dunlop*
> *Brigadier General*
> *Acting The Adjutant General*

For the most part, this follow-up letter was just a form letter which only varied with the soldier's name, serial number, and the person to whom it was being sent. The Army Air Forces literally had rooms full of people typing away at individual typewriters who had these form letters memorized. The indication that the next letter might not be received until the end of the next three months was little comfort to the mothers. This prompted many mothers to write to the War Department in hopes that their persistent letters would receive a quicker response.

A letter written to the War Department by Clara Smedley on June 5, 1944, was answered two weeks later on June 19th by a personal letter signed by Adjutant General, Major General J. A. Ulio. In this letter was the assurance that everything was being done to learn the fate of her son. The letter also contained the names and addresses that Clara had requested of the parents of the other nine crew members. The War Department letter also indicated that they could find no record of a crew member named Robert Lalumiere being in the casualty records of their office. They did, however, provide the name of James E. Gallagher and his mother's address. Since Francis Smedley's last letter written to his mother had been on April 10, 1944, she was not aware that Robert Lalumiere had been wounded on April 11th, nor did she know that Jim Gallagher was now the ball turret gunner on the plane. The War Department letter further stated that everyone listed except Harry Shoffner had now been reported as being a prisoner of war.

The following day, June 20, 1944, a letter from Major E. A. Bradunas from the Headquarters of the Army Air Forces provided Clara Smedley with the first details as to what may have happened during the last mission flown by the *Sunrise Serenade*.

> *"Further information has been received indicating that Lieutenant Smedley was a crew member of a B-17 (Flying Fortress) which departed from England on a bombardment mission to Metz, France, on May 1st. Full details are not available, but the report indicates that during this mission, over the target area, your son's plane was seen to sustain damage from enemy antiaircraft fire, and subsequently it was observed to go down at about 7:00 p.m., in the vicinity of Brussels, Belgium. The report further states that nine parachutes were seen to leave the damaged Fortress. The crew members of accompanying planes were unable to furnish any other details with reference to the disappearance of this bomber, therefore the above constitutes all the information presently available."*

The letter was disheartening to Clara since only nine parachutes had been seen to open, and also since her son was not listed as being a prisoner of war. Her worst fear began to materialize with the realization that her son may very well have died during the crash. Mrs. Smedley began writing letters to the other mothers to help lessen her pain, and she, in turn, began to receive letters from each of them. On June 26th, Clara received her first letters from the mothers of the tailgunner, Ray Dean, the upper turret gunner, Norbert Rhodes, and the co-pilot, Bill Hewett.

> *Valier, Montana*
> *June 26, 1944*
> *Dear Mrs. Smedley,*
> *We received your letter today and were glad to hear from someone who also had boys in Raymie's plane. You see we didn't know any of the boys' names or addresses at all. Our telegram from the government said our son was missing over Germany since May 1. We immediately contacted our local Red Cross and asked them to write the International Red Cross to get us what information they could. On Sunday, June 11, we got another telegram from the U.S. Government saying the International Red Cross reported to them that Raymie was a prisoner of war of the German government, and that a letter of information was following. When it came it didn't have any more information as his prison camp was not stated, and it would probably be about three months before that would be known. As yet we have received nothing direct from Ray.*
> *I know how terrible the suspense is and how hard it is to carry, and while we were greatly relieved to hear he was safe, we know that won't be too pleasant for him but at least he is alive and we have hopes of having him home again sometime. I am very sorry that you haven't received even that encouraging news and hope and pray you learn soon your boy is O.K. Raymond thought a great deal of his "pilot" and we were very pleased he had such a good one. Would you please send me the names of the rest of the crew. Maybe your son could be in the Underground working his way out and in this case you wouldn't hear for some time, but I sincerely hope he is safe somewhere. We are farmers and were very grateful for the work that must be done, as when we were busy we didn't think as much, but I know what a terrible worry it is on us mothers. If I get any more information or anything I will write you at once, in the meantime I hope to hear from you again.*
> *Yours sincerely,*
> *Mrs. Freda Dean*

> *Williamsburg, Pennsylvania*
> *June 26, 1944*
> *Dear Mrs. Smedley,*
> *Was very glad to receive your letter today. I did want to write you, but did not know where to write. I only knew your son's last name. I am sending you a copy of both telegrams and the dates that I received them. This is all I have as yet. Sure hope to hear something more soon. This suspense is awful. I sure hope your son is with Norbert, also the rest of the crew, and that they are all O.K. I will let you know at once if and when I hear more, which I hope and pray will be soon. Norbert spoke so well of your son, and I am glad they were pals. Have you heard from any of the other boys' parents that were in the crew? I do not have any of their names, or I would have written them. Thanks for writing me and feel free to do so at any time. I will be glad to hear from you if you get any news or not.*
> *Very sincerely,*
> *Mrs. Lola Rhodes*

The postage stamps being used during the War carried "WIN THE WAR" and "V" for Victory slogans as evidenced by this letter mailed by Clara Smedley to one of the other mothers. - *Collection of the author.*

Shaker Heights, Ohio
June 26, 1944
Dear Mrs. Smedley,
We received your letter this morning and fully realize how you feel. The following are copies of the telegrams and letter we received from the government. May 18, 1944: "The Secretary of War desires me to express his deep regret that your son Second Lt. William J. Hewett has been reported missing in action over Germany since May 1st. If further details or other information are received you will be promptly notified". June 14, 1944: "Report through the International Red Cross states that your son is a prisoner of war of the German government. Report further states wounded. Letter of information follows from Provost Marshall General". June 17, 1944: The Provost Marshall General has directed me to supplement the information you received recently concerning the above named prisoner of war. Information has been received, which indicates he is now interned as a prisoner of war. Camp unstated, Germany. The report received did not give the place of his internment. Past experience indicates that one to three months is the normal time required for this office to receive that information. Until the exact place of his internment is known it is impossible to direct letters or parcels to him. Mailing instructions and parcel labels will be forwarded without application on your part, when his internment address is received. Sincerely yours, Howard F. Bresee, Colonel CMP, Assistant Director Prisoner of War Division."

This is all the information we have received so we are now wondering how bad he is wounded. All we can do is wait and that is hard. The last letter we received from Bill had a picture of the "Sunrise Serenade" with all the crew. He spoke particularly of your son and said people thought they were brothers and could wear each others' clothes. Bill sent the names of each one, but not their addresses so we are mailing you the list hoping you will fill in the address of each one so we can write their folks. Any news you get we will be glad to receive and we will be sure to send you all we hear. We pray that they are all safe and that their folks will all hear that they also are well. Please write us again.
Yours sincerely,
George and Jane Hewett

The next day, Clara received a letter from the mother of the navigator, John McGrath. This letter would strengthened Clara's hope that her son, Francis, may have survived the crash since she now had confirmation that at least three of the crew members were now prisoners of the Germans.

Langhorne, Pennsylvania
June 27, 1944
Dear Mrs. Smedley,
It was so nice to receive your letter. I would have gotten in touch with all the crew mothers, but John sent me a picture of the plane and crew and put the names on the back in order, but not addresses. I thought at the time he had a reason. He said in his letter if you receive these pictures mother, you will be looking at a fine loyal bunch of fellows and that is more than some crews can say. The first telegram we received was at 7:37 a.m. on 5/17/44. The shock left me speechless. I am just getting back gradually. We received a second one dated 6/5/44. It stated that a report just received through the International Red Cross states that your son John is a prisoner of war of the German government. This was good news as it gave us hope of seeing our boy again. Our neighbors were surprised we got the news so soon because ten of the boys in our community have been missing for five or six months. They say when they parachute down they can direct them, and they are picked up at different points and it would take longer for the news to get through so don't give up hope. I feel sure your boy is safe and maybe much better off than John. It will be a great day when we hear direct from my boy. The War Department sent us some forms to send a package and letters to him. This is it: 2nd Lt. John J. McGrath, United States Prisoner of War, Stalag Luft 3, Germany, G-15216. We have sent him several letters and are getting a package off to him. You can't ask him any questions about the War or what happened. We will certainly get in touch with you when we get any word from John, which we hope and pray to God will be soon. We have another son Harry somewhere in "New Guinea" we have not heard from him since April 19th. He enlisted in the Air Corps engineer dept. He was writing every day and all at once his letters stopped, so I can certainly sympathize with you. The suspense of waiting word of their safety is beyond words. If you can send me the addresses of the other crew members, I would certainly like to have them. We sincerely hope to get some good news soon.
Very sincerely,
Mrs. Henry A. McGrath

The following day Clara received a letter from the mother of the right waist gunner, John Brown. The letter from John's mother would also indicate that she had received word that her son was now a prisoner. Clara began to realize that many of the families of the crew members that had survived the crash had already been told that their sons were alive. She had not yet received these positive words, so her hope began to fade.

Abingdon, Virginia
June 28, 1944
Dear Mrs. Smedley,
Your letter of recent date received promptly asking for information as to S/Sgt. John G. Brown. I have received a telegram from the Adjutant General in Washington that they had received word through the International Red Cross that he, John Brown, is a prisoner of war of the German government. I also received a letter from Howard F. Bresee, Assistant Director Prisoner of War division, stating that until the place of his internment is known it is impossible to direct letters or packages to him, and that it takes from one to three months for this office to receive that information as to the prison camp he is in. So if you receive any message as to your son or any members of the crew of the Sunrise Serenade please let me hear from you. I do hope that you have received more information about your son by now. Any news that I may receive will be forwarded to you at once. I was glad to hear from you, and do write again and again.
Very sincerely,
Mrs. Mary Brown

Over the next six days Clara Smedley would receive letters from the mothers of the ball turret gunner, Jim Gallagher, the bombardier, George Griffin, and the radioman, Andy Senetsky. Clara never reached the wife or the mother of Harry Shoffner since the military had supplied her with an incorrect address for Harry's mother. The letters from the mothers of Jim Gallagher and George Griffin also indicated that they had received word that their sons were being held as prisoners of war. Eventually Clara would receive follow-up letters from the mothers of Dusty Rhodes and Andy Senetsky stating they too had received letters indicating that their sons were being held prisoner as well.

Pittsburgh, Pennsylvania
June 30, 1944
Dear Mrs. Smedley,
I received your letter and was very glad to hear from you. I know how you feel about your son and my heart aches for you and all the other mothers of the Boys that are over there. I have been under the doctor's care since I received the first telegram. But am much better. I received a telegram from the War Department Thursday June 29th stating that my son is a prisoner of the German government. I hope you have had some word about your son. The waiting is terrible not knowing what happened to them. But try to bear up. I am sure you will hear good news if you haven't so far. I light a candle for the Boys every week in church. And have had Masses for them, so I feel sure they are all safe. Please let me know if you have heard anything of your son. And if I hear anything at all I will let you know at once.
Sincerely yours,
Beatrice Gallagher

Roxbury, New York
July 2, 1944
My dear Mrs. Smedley,
Your letter of inquiry was received. You seem to have some information that we haven't and on the other hand we seem to have some that you haven't. We didn't know they were found down near Brussels, Belgium. On the other hand we have Donald's address. We always called him Donald as his name is George Donald. Whether or not your son is in the same camp, I don't know. We have had no letter from Donald himself. I will enclose his address so if you want to write and ask him about your son you may. It is a very anxious time for us all. May the Master of it all allow it soon to be over. If we hear anything definite we will let you know. Meantime do not get too discouraged it will work out for the best. Here's hoping you get some news soon.
Sincerely yours,
Mrs. O. J. Griffin
    Donald's address.
    2nd Lt. George D. Griffin
    United States Prisoner of War
    Stalag Luft 3
    Germany

Dickson City, Pennsylvania
July 4, 1944
Dear Mrs. Smedley,
I appreciate your writing to me. I have nothing to add to what you have received except to state that my son was missing May 1st over Germany. A letter which we received from the War Department added nothing to the telegram. So far we know nothing except that he is missing over Germany May 1st. That letter also stated that any definite information would be relayed to us immediately. I am enclosing the clipping of Andy. When we hear anything more I will gladly write and tell you. Will be waiting to hear from you.
Sincerely,
Anna Senetsky

The letters obtained from the other mothers brought them closer together. Clara Smedley was alone in her sorrow since her husband had left the family twenty years earlier, and also since her other child, Vincent, was stationed somewhere in the newly liberated country of France. The crew had been together for nearly nine months, but none of the parents of the crew had ever corresponded with each other before. The worried and mixed thoughts of Clara Smedley were well evident in her letter to Mrs. McGrath. She was beginning to accept the fact that her youngest son was dead, yet she still wanted to have hope that he was alive.

Oconto Falls, Wisconsin
July 4, 1944
My dear Mrs. McGrath,
So glad and thankful that you answered my letter so promptly. I am happy with you, knowing that John is a prisoner because you can get word to him and he will write. If it's possible could you be so kind to ask him what happened to "Pappy", that is what they called my son the pilot – or "Skipper" was another nickname. I learned that Francis was killed in the message I read on June 30. He always wrote in his letters that his family of 9 boys caused him no trouble, and was always proud of his crew. The War Department claims the observer saw 9 parachutes leave the plane after it sustained damage from anti-aircraft fire, but no one saw what happened to the plane. So whether Francis stayed with his plane until his crew bailed out and flew a distance farther, or perhaps he was hit fatally, since the co-pilot's mother writes me her son was reported wounded. That sounds as if the damage was done up front. But I shall not give up hope as yet. I only feel badly that Francis knows he can't write me to tell me he is all right. He always was so concerned of my welfare. He suffers because he knows I am in suspense. I am enclosing the crew home addresses. The War Department also informed me that nine were accounted for and all were prisoners. So keep faith with me. I'm sure your son will knock on your back door again some time soon and say "Hi Mom". That's what I hope to experience at my house.
Sincerely,
Clara Smedley

The letters continued to be written among the mothers for the next year. One by one each mother wrote to Clara with positive news about her own son, and also sent words of encouragement to her. Clara began also to feel closer to the other crew members who were now prisoners. The positive news coming from the other mothers kept the spirit of her son alive knowing that he had shared so much with their sons. Each mother tried to console Clara with words of condolences and hope. Over the next year Clara Smedley would receive over 50 letters from the other mothers telling how they had heard from their sons and the joy they felt. Clara would also receive personal letters from at least two of the crew members in the form of postcards originating from the POW camps. Eventually news was received that Bill Hewett had escaped and returned home, and also letters from Harry Shoffner stating that he had been in the Belgian Underground and had come home early. These reports were beacons of hope for the other mothers of the seven boys who were still being held as prisoners.

One of the closest bonds formed among the mothers was that between Mrs. Smedley and Mrs. McGrath. Both could relate to each other, having one of their sons presumably dead with few details. The circumstances surrounding the death of Mrs. McGrath's other son, Harry, were never fully learned nor was his body ever recovered. The most that the War Department could ever provide was that her son Harry and several other soldiers stationed in New Guinea never returned from a special detail. Since Harry McGrath was married, he also left behind a grieving wife in Pennsylvania. Mrs. McGrath wrote to Clara Smedley on the day that she received word that the War Department had officially declared her son to be dead.

Langhorne, Pennsylvania
April 18, 1945
Dear Mrs. Smedley
I received word today from the War Department claiming that my son Harry is officially dead. He is missing now for over a year. I still hope and pray he is still with us. This awful war has certainly changed things. How happy we were a short time ago. I have not had any word from John since November 29th. I hope and pray to God he is spared to us. I know what you are going through. I can't think or write any more. I will certainly be at mass on May 1st for that wonderful son of yours and will always remember him and you in our prayers, and pray to God that you will have strength to accept this trial in perfect submission to His will. Many thanks for the picture. Write to me when you can.
Sincerely,
Frances McGrath
P.S. – Excuse this letter writing. I am not myself. I will remember your other son in our prayers. My sister's son was shot down March 9th over Austria, and just received a letter from him in a hospital in Italy. He broke his leg landing. Thank God, that is bad enough.

Clara Smedley never felt that she had really been able to say goodbye to her son. Many American families were desperately trying to put their lives back in order as they dealt with the loss of their loved ones. On March 2, 1945, Clara Smedley received a letter from the Internal Revenue Service (IRS) indicating that she must file an income tax form on the behalf of her deceased son for the years that he was on the Government's payroll. The letter caught the grieving mother by complete surprise, since her government seemingly wanted her to pay in addition to the price that had already been paid with the life of her son. What more could she sacrifice? Clara quickly contacted the Adjutant General's Office of the United States Army for details pertaining to Francis's exact pay for the years of his enlistment in 1942 to the time of his death in 1944. She also contacted the IRS to request a 90-day extension to the March 15th filing deadline. Two weeks later she received another letter from the IRS indicating that the previous letter had been mailed to her in error since they had not known that Francis was a casualty of War. Section 421 of the Internal Revenue Code was attached in this follow-up letter which explained that any individual who had died after December 7, 1941, while in the active service of the United States Armed Forces was exempt from having to pay federal income taxes. Another similar battle with the Social Security Administration lasted until 1951 when Clara could finally prove that she had been financially supported by Francis, therefore being entitled to his benefits. The coldness of bureaucracy brought forth by these organizations indicated that many in the United States government offices may have never had the same first-hand experience with the loss of a loved one due to the War. After the other seven crew members were finally liberated from the prison camps on April 30, 1944, most of them took the time to write to Clara Smedley expressing their sorrow for the loss of their pilot and friend. Most of the men never fully realized that Francis Smedley was dead until after they had been released. Clara's other son, Vincent, was still in Europe, and it would be several more months before he could finally return home to see his mother. When Vincent returned home in the summer of 1945, he found his mother had changed from the way he remembered her. She was broken from the constant strain placed upon her during the previous year having to cope, mostly alone, with Francis's death. The War had changed Clara so much that she was never truly happy again, which often brought conflict between her and Vincent. The mother and son would spend the majority of their lives apart from each other. Even though the war in Europe and the Pacific had come to an end, the battle continued for many years in the changed lives of thousands of families all across the world, especially those who had been asked to sacrifice loved ones for the War.

Clara Smedley and her son Francis were able to spend a few days together in August of 1943 when he was still training in the States. The meeting would prove to be the last time the two would ever see each other again. – *Collection of the author.*

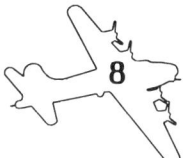

The Ultimate Sacrifice

Families who lost loved ones in the War sometimes never knew the circumstances surrounding their deaths, which made the deaths even more difficult to accept. This was the case for Francis Smedley's mother. Clara Smedley tried to learn how her son had died but few details were ever made available.

According to several eye-witness accounts from airmen aboard other B-17's that day, they all agree that his parachute became entangled on the rear horizontal stabilizer bar of the *Sunrise Serenade*. Since the plane had left the formation and was also going down, those in the air only had a short time to observe what was happening before all visible contact was lost. The transition quickly changed from fellow airmen observing from the air to the Belgian citizens observing from the ground. The *Sunrise Serenade* had been directed by Smedley, and the co-pilot, Bill Hewett, away from the city of Brussels in an attempt to have the plane crash outside of a heavily populated area. Many of the eye-witnesses on the ground in the less-populated area west of Brussels were not close to the plane, but because the events happened on a clear day high above the ground, the situation in the sky could be clearly seen from a long distance and over a wide area. One man observing from the ground, Jef Vermeiren from Asse, Belgium, saw one of the planes leave the formation and then he saw four little white balls. He later realized that these little balls were the parachutes from the members of the crew bailing out. The plane then dove downward leaving a trail of smoke. Soon a total of nine parachutes were seen in the sky at various altitudes by Vermeiren. At the same time, a Belgian man named Frans Esselens was standing at the gate outside his house at St. Godardusstraat when he noticed the *Sunrise Serenade* make a turn and head in his direction. After directing his wife and little son into a nearby ditch, he joined them as the plane made two full circles above the village of Bekkerzeel at a lower altitude.

This circling of the plane caused the people on the ground to assume that the plane was attempting to make a crash landing. In reality, the action of the plane had been caused by Smedley placing the plane on automatic pilot just before he had left the plane. The circling motion of the plane was similar to what other airmen have reported seeing their own aircraft do after it was abandoned and set on automatic pilot. During this circling, the *Sunrise Serenade* exploded and broke into two main pieces. The rear part of the plane, which included part of the fuselage and the tail, crashed at a place known as De Meil near the pub of Cooman. The front part of the plane, with the engines and wings, crashed into the ground at the garden of Count De Ghellinck at Sint-Ulriks-Kapelle.

Francis C. Smedley became the pilot of the *Sunrise Serenade* when he was just 20 years old. Known as "Smed", "Pappy", or "Skipper" to his crew, he always had a smile and positive outlook on life. He gave his life so that others could live in freedom. - *Collection of the author.*

After the explosion, witnesses observed many pieces of the plane coming loose as the burning wreckage of the *Sunrise Serenade* made its final descent. Frans Esselens observed an object that appeared to be larger than the rest of the pieces coming off the plane. This piece quickly fell and landed about 100 meters from him on land owned by Jozef Tirry. As the local citizens arrived at this location they were astonished to learn that what originally had appeared to be a large piece of the airplane was the body of an airman. The body was lying face up and he was wearing his leather jacket and flying helmet. Attached to him was his chest pack parachute and harness, although the deployed parachute had been completely burned up. Smedley's name and rank were clearly marked upon the pack, which in addition to his dog tags, identified him as the person to whom they belonged. Other witnesses on the ground further claimed to have seen a parachute on fire as it came down, indicating that Smedley may have somehow been able to free himself from the plane after it broke apart. The intense fire consuming the *Sunrise Serenade* would have quickly burned up the parachute, which was not fire resistant. The main crash site at Sint-Ulriks-Kapelle and the location of Smedley's body were approximately three kilometers apart.

Smedley's body was carried away by men of the local fire brigade toward the village hall of Bekkerzeel. Louis Catoir of Asse remembers seeing the contents of Smedley's pockets which consisted of cigarettes, a lighter, a few coins and his dog tags. These items were later transferred to a hall in Asse for display, but were misplaced when the Belgian government consolidated the smaller villages together in 1978. At Bekkerzeel the Germans immediately arrived to take possession of Smedley's body from the local men. Smedley's body was then loaded into the back of a truck and the Germans drove away toward the site of another airman who had been apprehended after landing in a field. This airman was the co-pilot of the *Sunrise Serenade*, William J. Hewett, who was badly burned and disoriented. The Germans took Hewett, who was now temporarily blinded, and placed him into the back of the truck on top of Smedley's lifeless body.

Francis Smedley was given a military funeral at his first burial site by the Germans who recognized his display of courage and valor while staying with the plane to take it away from the city of Brussels. - *Collection of the author.*

A few days later the Germans took Smedley's body to the Evere Cemetery in nearby Brussels, which was designated as an English memorial cemetery. Among those who witnessed the funeral were members of the Belgian Underground who would soon come to the assistance of Harry C. Shoffner, the left waist gunner of the *Sunrise Serenade,* who had escaped from the Germans. They later reported details to Shoffner regarding comments made by a German officer about Smedley and how the Germans had given Smedley a wonderful military funeral rite. One German officer had taken a pair of scissors and proceeded to cut several pieces out of Smedley's flying coveralls as the Belgians watched in disbelief not realizing what he was doing. The officer then took the strips of material and gave some to the local people and said "*You must keep this as a souvenir of the pilot who guided his plane from the city so that it would not fall destroying property and killing citizens of Brussels.*" The Germans recognized the bravery that had been displayed by the airman officer when he stayed with the plane to direct it away from the city of Brussels. Although Smedley was an enemy of the Germans by association with the Allied forces, they recognized the ultimate sacrifice that had been made by this young man to avoid injuring those who were on the ground. Francis Smedley could have saved his own life by quickly exiting the plane and letting it crash over the populated city. The many lives he may have saved by guiding his plane away from the city will never be known, but he made a decision to do what he thought was right. This decision was based upon an ideal of valuing human life, even if it meant sacrificing his own life.

The word of Francis Smedley's death did not reach his brother Vincent until over a month later. Twenty-eight days after Francis had died, Vincent wrote a letter addressed to him at Deopham Green, England, believing that he was still alive. The letter returned to Vincent with the word "MISSING" stamped upon the envelope in bold red letters. Vincent immediately assumed the worst since there was no reason for his brother to be missing from his base unless he had been shot down. There was also no way for Vincent's mother to quickly contact him since his 142nd Armored Signal Company was constantly moving, which further delayed the arrival of mail. The returned letter that Vincent had mailed to his brother would remain folded up in his wallet for the next fifty years. He reread it a thousand times until the letter became very tattered.

During the next year Vincent traveled across France and Germany with his signal company that was part of the 2nd Armored Division and helped to push the German army back toward Berlin. In early 1945, Vincent obtained a pass to go to Brussels in an attempt to find his brother's grave. He had been sent a picture of the grave marker by his mother who had received it from Harry Shoffner after Belgium was liberated. After arriving in Brussels, the American Red Cross was unable to direct Vincent to the cemetery, but the Belgian Red Cross provided a woman who escorted him there. Francis Smedley's burial location at the Evere Cemetery was Plot 10, Row 20, Grave 10; the first of three burial locations.

His body was exhumed on March 17, 1945, and taken to the United States Military Cemetery at the southeast edge of Neuville-en-Condros (Neupre), Belgium, which is located 12 miles southwest of Liege. This cemetery had been established on February 8, 1945, by the American government. The land occupying the cemetery had been liberated on September 6, 1944, by members of the American 3rd Armored Division and the 47th Infantry Regiment of the 9th Division. In acknowledgement of gratitude for the liberation of their country the people of Belgium had given the land to the United States. Once the cemetery was opened, the United States government began the process of removing the thousands of American servicemen from their local burial places and then joining them together in one location to be next to each other. Francis Smedley's initial burial location at this cemetery was Plot B, Row 5, Grave 111.

Francis Smedley's mother, Clara, was sent a letter from the Office of the Quartermaster General of the Department of the Army. The letter explained that the citizens of the United States, through Congress, had authorized the disinterment and final burial of the heroic dead of World War II. This meant that Francis could finally come home from the War. Documents attached to the letter provided a choice of burial locations in 63 national cemeteries located in the United States where American soldiers have been buried throughout the history of our country. The closest military cemeteries to Wisconsin were at Fort Snelling, Minnesota, or Rock Island, Illinois. Both places were still a considerable distance from Oconto Falls, Wisconsin, where Clara Smedley was living. Another option was to bring Francis's body back to Oconto Falls to be buried in a local cemetery. Even though Oconto Falls had been the town where Francis was living when he had left to join the armed forces, he had spent most of his life growing up in Winnetka, Illinois. He and his mother had only lived in Oconto Falls for a couple of years prior to his death, and his brother Vincent had left for the service before ever having actually lived there. Both boys did consider Oconto Falls as "home" since that is where their mother, uncle, and cousins lived. Clara wanted to bring Francis close to her side and have his grave be near her at Oconto Falls. There would be added expenses involved with buying a plot and there would be other expenses that would be associated with not having him buried elsewhere in a military cemetery. Vincent finally persuaded his mother to leave Francis overseas and have him permanently buried along with his comrades in Belgium. The decision was wise since circumstances in Clara's life some years later would eventually have her move away from Oconto Falls to the state of Michigan.

Many American families did choose to have their loved ones exhumed and brought back to the United States to be reburied in the family plot or in one of the national military cemeteries. This mass transfer of American servicemen created gaps everywhere in the military cemeteries located in Europe. As the last of the American dead who had been requested a transfer home were removed from the European cemeteries, the American government began a process of rebuilding the overseas cemeteries into national memorials. Nearly every grave left in these European cemeteries had to be exhumed one last time to bring them all together into one area of each individual cemetery that formed perfect rows. Francis Smedley's body was exhumed one final time in 1949 and moved to his final resting place at Plot D, Row 33, Grave 21 in the United States Military Cemetery at Neuville-en-Condroz, Belgium. After the completion of the cemetery it became known as the Ardennes American Military Cemetery and Memorial.

The final resting place for Francis Smedley is at the Ardennes American Military Cemetery and Memorial located southwest of Liege, Belgium. - *Collection of the author.*

In the 90 acre cemetery are also the remains of approximately 5,300 other American servicemen whose families also decided to memorialize them there. Most of the graves are from those who had fought the Germans during the nearby counteroffensive known as the "Battle of the Bulge" in December 1944. There are 746 headstones marking the graves of "Unknowns". A memorial in the cemetery depicts the names of 462 Americans whose bodies were either never found or identified. These numbers are subject to change due to the fact that this cemetery is the only one remaining open today for additional burials of remains that still might be recovered in Europe.

At the end of World War II, seventeen military cemeteries were established to serve as the final resting place, and as a memorial for the American dead. Of all the Americans who were originally buried in foreign land, only 39% remained overseas; the rest were brought back to the United States for reburial. At the Ardennes American Military Cemetery and Memorial 5,400 of the soldiers originally buried there were repatriated to the United States. The final construction of this cemetery was completed with the dedication ceremony on July 11, 1960.

In the summer of 1945, Francis C. Smedley was posthumously awarded the Air Medal and two Oak Leaf Clusters to replace the medals that had been lost after his death. These medals were presented to Clara Smedley, which she placed alongside the Purple Heart Medal that Francis had been posthumously awarded on August 7, 1944. Four years later Clara petitioned the military for replacements of Francis's other medals that had never been returned with his personal belongings. In September of 1949, Clara received, on behalf of her son, the American Campaign Medal, World War II Victory Medal, Good Conduct Medal, Aviation Badge, and the European-African-Middle Eastern Campaign Medal with one bronze service star for his participation in the Air Offensive Europe Campaign. With the arrival of these additional medals Clara could now proudly display the achievements made by her son while serving his country. Francis Smedley's name was placed on a memorial in Oconto Falls, Wisconsin, along with the other fallen soldiers originating from that area. Oconto Falls had a wartime population of around 1,500 residents. Ten young men from that community had given their lives during World War II. Every town or city across the entire United States, regardless of size, had seen their young men and women go off to war and many of them never returned.

The Ardennes American Military Cemetery and Memorial was established on February 8, 1945, and contains the remains of approximately 5,300 American servicemen who gave their lives during World War II. Approximately 56 men from the 452nd Bomb Group, including Francis C. Smedley, are buried at this site. - *Collection of the author.*

An Eagle in a Sparrow's Nest

Though the exact details surrounding the death of the pilot, Francis C. Smedley, may never be known, much more is known about the fate of the rest of the crew after the crash. After the other eight crew members had exited the *Sunrise Serenade,* which by then was ablaze, co-pilot Bill Hewett and pilot Francis Smedley prepared for their own escape. Hewett had his chute with him, as he was sitting on a fanny-pack type, which was larger than the standard U.S. Army Air Corps issue. His parachute was 28' in diameter instead of the one issued by the Air Corps which was 24'. The larger parachute was needed due to Hewett's size of 6'6" and 220 pounds. Having his parachute, Hewett was ready to dive through the fire, which had already consumed the nose of the plane. On this particular day, Smedley had chosen to fly the plane from the right hand position, which was normally where the copilot was seated. Smedley, without another option, chose to go out the copilot's window since the fire had become too intense to his left side. Hewett, after clearing the plane by a short distance, felt the massive concussion of the plane exploding above him. As he began his free-fall toward the ground, he remembered the instructions learned in training about how not to pull the rip cord prematurely. Many airmen had become easy targets for German rifle fire because they had allowed themselves to slowly float to the earth from a higher altitude. After falling for nearly 18,000 feet, Hewett finally pulled the rip cord as the ground rushed nearer. The sudden jolt of the parachute catching the air pulled heavily upon his harness, but it opened and worked without any problems.

Hewett landed in a farmer's pasture near the suburb of Zellik along the western perimeter of Brussels. A Belgian farmer had witnessed the events of the plane being shot down, including Hewett drifting toward his field. The farmer tried to pull Hewett away from his parachute harness after seeing his vain struggles to use a burned hand to open the clips. Seeing a German command car with three occupants approaching at high speed across the field, Hewett urged the farmer to get away and save himself. With the harness now undone, Hewett held his hands high and yelled "Kamerad" at the top of his lungs to the armed Germans now exiting the car. This was one of the German words that Hewett had known and its American translation meant "friend". This quick thinking immediately let the approaching Germans know that Hewett was not going to put up a struggle against them.

Only after the initial sequence of events did Hewett notice that he had been severely burned on his left hand and also on the left side of his face. During the mission, Hewett had taken off his flight gloves which allowed him to have a better feel for the controls, but unfortunately resulted in severe burns to his hand. The swelling as a result of the burns on his face caused a gradual loss of sight, which for a few days left him temporarily blind. As he was realizing the severity of his injuries, the German soldiers hustled him into the back of a truck as they drove to the edge of town. The pain in his face and hand was becoming more intense, and Hewett did not immediately realize until some distance down the road that he had been lying on top of the dead body of another flyer. Hewett later realized that this was the body of his friend and pilot of the *Sunrise Serenade*, Francis Smedley.

The copilot of the *Sunrise Serenade*, William J. Hewett, was badly burned upon his exit from the plane and spent several months in a POW hospital. - *Collection of William J. Hewett.*

They arrived at a Brussels police station where Hewett was then placed into a cell. Alone without any medication or painkiller for his injuries, Hewett had to endure the pain the entire night inside the jail. The intense pain from his burns blocked out any memory of the events that took place that night, as the Germans had most certainly tried to interrogate him. The next morning Hewett was taken to the St. Gilles Hospital, which was designated Luftwaffen Lazarett, and was a subsidiary camp of Stalag Luft III. Hewett became prisoner No. G-19270 during his stay at this hospital in the St. Gilles area of Brussels. Those of his crew who had also been captured by the Germans were being held temporarily in the same area of town at the St. Gilles Prison. Since Hewett had been the only captured member of his crew who had sustained injuries, he never saw his crew while he was alone at the hospital. The German doctors who initially attended Hewett told him that they were going to have to amputate his left hand. Luckily, Hewett had learned enough of the German language from his grandmother to talk them out of amputating. He later underwent skin grafts on his hand at the same hospital.

The treatment at the hospital was excellent at the hands of Hewett's physician/surgeon Dr. Hans Von Brucke of Vienna, Austria, and his nurse Sister Frieda. Despite the fact that he was being well taken care of, Hewett attempted to escape from the hospital at least four or five times without success. No intricate escape plans had been laid out, but rather Hewett just simply walked out of the hospital each time and headed for the front gate. A 6' 6" inch pilot in pajamas with facial and hand bandages quickly caught the attention of the guards each time, and he was taken back within the confines of the hospital. The boredom of being confined to the hospital gave Hewett plenty of time to think about new escape attempts.

As a pilot in the mighty 8th Air Force, Hewett saw himself as an eagle having to stay in a sparrow's nest of the hospital. As Hewett's hand improved, he was able to help a few other prisoners at the hospital saw through their window bars. The total number of officers and air crew at the hospital with Hewett was about 20, mostly British men. One day at the hospital a well-known German propagandist known as Axis Sally visited the prisoners and personally spoke with Hewett. Over her frequent radio broadcasts called "Home Sweet Home" she reported that she had met an American airman named Bill Hewett at the hospital, and that he was blind. Hewett's parents back in Cleveland, Ohio, got word of the broadcast and believed that he was indeed blind. His parents held this mistaken belief until he was able to call them after his release.

Axis Sally's real name was Mildred E. Gillars and she was in fact born as an American citizen. She preferred the name "Midge at the mike" during her radio broadcasts in which she spoke in a sensual tone in English to Allied servicemen in an attempt to make them homesick for their wives and girlfriends back home. After the War, Gillars was apprehended and then tried and convicted for treason. All of her radio broadcasts had been recorded during the War and were used as evidence against her. Axis Sally spent 12 years in prison for her efforts to aid the Germans during the War.

Bill Hewett met the infamous German female propagandist Axis Sally while recovering in the St. Gilles prison hospital. She wrongly stated that he was blind over one of her Radio Berlin broadcasts. - *U.S. Army photo.*

On July 15, 1944, Bill Hewett wrote a letter home to his parents for the first time from his hospital room. The letter would take several months to reach them.

Dear Folks,
　Two days until another birthday and I wish I could spend it with you. You'll be in my thoughts and maybe next year we will all be together. I've been in a hospital since our ship went down. I didn't want to tell you until I was O.K. My face was slightly burned and my left hand also. The face was not severely burned and healed in three weeks. You can't notice it now. My hand was burned a little deeper - skin was taken from my leg and grafted on the back of it. It is as good as new. The care has been excellent. They did a swell job on me. I do hope you people are well, and please don't worry about me and my being in the hospital. I get 11 hours of sleep each night, nothing to drink and good eats. I am in better shape now than before we were shot down. I even have fat cheeks. I am counting the days until we are all together.
All my love,
Bill

Hewett's parents received a telegram on August 12, 1944, stating that an unofficial short-wave broadcast from Germany had been intercepted stating that their son had suffered burns on his face and hands, but the injuries were healing fairly well without complications. They were comforted to know that their son was still doing fine fifteen weeks after the crash of the plane, and that the military was providing every new bit of information they had learned.

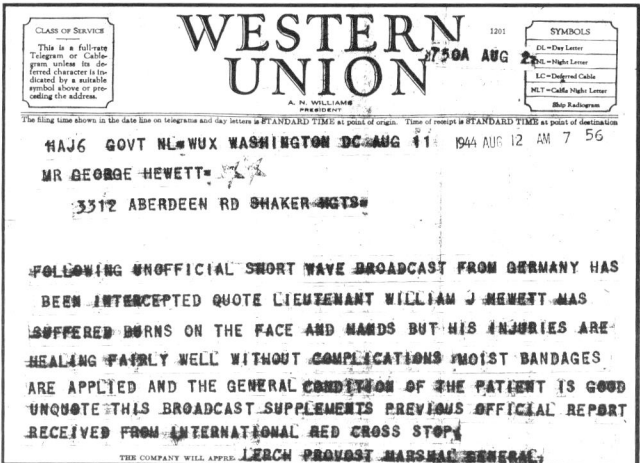

A short wave radio broadcast intercepted from Germany was relayed to Hewett's parents in the form of a telegram on August 12, 1944. - *Collection of William J. Hewett.*

Near the end of August 1944, the Allies were close to capturing the city of Brussels from the Germans. With the capture of the city seemingly imminent, the responsibility of the hospital was given to the elite Nazi German SS troops. They planned to move the hospital staff and patients to new locations away from the advancing Allied forces. On September 4, 1944, just as Brussels was about to be liberated, a convoy of German vehicles was assembled to evacuate the St. Gilles Hospital. The steel bars, which the men had painstakingly sawed, were now parted and the men were merely waiting for a break in the weather to escape. Their chance to escape through the bars at the hospital never came. Bill Hewett and the rest of the hospital patients were put aboard a bus at the rear of the convoy, and also into an ambulance at the front. The Allied fighter planes had developed a tactic where they would strafe the German convoys in such a manner as to disable the front and rear vehicles. This left no escape for the vehicles in the middle of the convoy, which could then be destroyed. Placing the patients in the front and back locations ensured that if a fighter plane would attack, the patients would be the first ones to get hit. The prisoners aboard the bus and ambulance hoped that such an attack would not occur while they were being moved toward the German homeland as human shields.

As the convoy began its movement northeast toward the town of Diest, Belgium, American P-47 Thunderbolt fighter planes suddenly appeared and dove down upon the column of vehicles. As the guns began to blaze from the Thunderbolts, the column came to an abrupt halt as everyone in the vehicles quickly exited to find safety in the roadside ditches. As soon as the ambulance at the front of the column came to a stop, Hewett and two other prisoners leaped out of the back of the bus at the rear of the convoy. The other two men with Bill Hewett were U.S. Air Corps 2nd Lt. Bill Stein and Royal Air Force Gunnery Sgt. Ellis Durland. Another acquaintance of Hewett aboard the bus was Joe Wright who had been a B-26 bomber pilot before coming to the St. Gilles Hospital. One of Wright's legs had been amputated due to the injuries he sustained during the crash of his own plane. As Hewett and the two other men were escaping, Wright yelled out that he would go with them if he could. Instead of lying in the ditches and culverts as their guards had done, Hewett and the two other men kept running as fast as they could as the planes continued to destroy the convoy. As the Germans dove for cover every time the bullets from the planes came at them, Hewett and the other two men would get up and run to escape from the Germans.

Bill Hewett (center) and two other POW's, Ellis Durland (left) and Bill Stein, escaped from the Germans while being evacuated out of Belgium. - *Collection of William J. Hewett.*

As the three fugitives neared the first farm house down the road, something instinctively told Hewett not to stop, but rather to keep going until the next farm house. He later found out that the owner of the first farmhouse was a member of the "Black Brigade", Nazi sympathizers, and who would have immediately turned them over to the Germans. Fortunately for the three airmen, the second farmhouse contained members of the "White Brigade", who were part of the Belgian Underground. The occupants of the house were Basile and Filomene Croes, young farmers who lived near the town of Bekkevoort, Belgium, and had recently been married. As the three men approached, one of them began to speak in broken German, and then the Croes noticed the lone RAF insignia on Ellis Durland's uniform. Without any hesitation, the Croes quickly placed the three men in the hayloft of their barn, despite the reasoning from the airmen that they would be safer hidden in the woods. Basil and Filomene had previously helped at least eight other servicemen, so taking in the three airmen was done without hesitation. For five days the couple provided the men with corned beef sandwiches made from horsemeat. The food supply available to the Croes was very limited due to war rationing and also because the Germans collected a portion of what they grew on their farm. The Croes nervously tried to maintain their usual way of life without giving any hint that they were hiding the three men. If they had been caught, the Germans would have quickly executed them.

The night of their arrival at the Croes, the three men were questioned by members of the Belgian Underground to determine if they were German spies trying to infiltrate their system. The Underground asked the men their mother's maiden names so that this information could be verified. If the information provided by the three men turned out to be incorrect, they were told that they would be shot as spies the next morning. While waiting for the names to be verified through United States underground contacts, the men remained inside the hayloft. German squads had been searching for the three men soon after the fighter planes had ceased to fire upon the convoy. As the Germans searched around the barn and periodically checked inside, the men could hear them talking. The intense search for the three men lasted for two or three days without success. One of the men with Hewett, Sgt. Ellis Durland, was a chain smoker and wanted to light up a cigarette in the hayloft, but Hewett stopped him by threatening him with his life if he dared to do so. The area that the three men had to share for those five days of hiding was approximately ten square feet and was actually a false wall made from hay bales.

No one from the Belgian Underground returned, so evidently the information they had provided about their mothers' names had been successfully verified. On September 9, 1944, the men heard the sound of approaching tanks outside the barn. Thinking that they were American or British tanks, the men quickly left the barn and ran to the road only to discover that they were retreating German "Tiger" tanks. The men just barely dove for cover in time as the tanks rolled past them. Soon another vehicle approached their hiding spot along the road, and it turned out to be a British jeep leading a British tank column with the Commander standing at attention. The Commander held one hand on the top of the windshield and a parade baton firmly held in the other - quite a sight for sore eyes! The three men quickly hailed it with great shouts as the driver approached. Having said their good-byes to the brave Croes, the three airmen were taken to a British hospital in Brussels where Hewett was able to obtain medical attention and fresh bandages for his wounds. It would be fifty years before Hewett would speak again with the two men who had shared this harrowing experience in the hayloft.

Many brave Belgian citizens risked their own lives to save American and British airmen who were shot down over their country. Basil and Filomene Croes-Caubergs (front center) pose with Durland, Stein and Hewett (back). Seated in front, Louie Croes (left) and Manil Croes are Basil's brothers.
- *Collection of William J. Hewett.*

While waiting in Brussels, Hewett tried to hitch a ride back to England by attempting to board a C-47 cargo plane on a runway. The pilot of the plane informed Hewett that the plane was reserved for English "ministers", and refused to let him board the plane. Hewett, rationalizing in American thinking, wondered what these religious "men of cloth" were doing on the plane and what the importance of their mission might be. He found out shortly thereafter that these "ministers" were actually members of the British Parliament, more specifically, the Right Honorable Sir Oliver Lyttelton, the minister of war supply, and Sir Archibald Sinclair, the air minister. Lyttelton and Sinclair soon learned of Hewett's predicament and let him board their plane for the trip back to England. After arriving in England, but before deplaning, Lyttelton and Sinclair ordered the pilot to fly Hewett back to his base at Deopham Green after they had departed. Sir Oliver immediately called Hewett's parents in the United States to assure them that their son was free and safe. As Sir Oliver told Bill's father, "Good news shouldn't wait…Your son is alive!"

Upon arrival at his former base at Deopham Green, Hewett was surprised to find a great party celebration was in full swing. It had been over four months since he had been at his base, and he wondered if he would recognize anyone. A friend of Hewett's noticed him walk in the party at the Officer's Club, and as the room grew silent his friend exclaimed "Hewett! What took you so long?!"

Because Bill Hewett had returned to his base without his plane, he joined an exclusive club whose members were given a silver lapel pin shaped like a boot, inscribed with the words "Late Arrival Club". He also earned the right to wear a silver caterpillar pin and induction into the "Caterpillar Club" signifying that he had saved his life with a parachute. The burns to his left hand later required extensive plastic surgery. Upon arrival back in the States, he was admitted to Wakeman General Hospital at Camp Atterbury, Indiana, on September 30, 1944, to have surgery performed on his hand. Camp Atterbury was located near Indianapolis, Indiana, so Hewett was now very close to his home state of Ohio. Hewett would spend two years under a doctor's care concerning his hand. By undergoing a variety of surgeries, Hewett's ability to use his thumb and index finger for grasping was somewhat restored, but his other three fingers were to remain permanently clenched. Since these injuries were received during combat, Hewett was later awarded with the prestigious Purple Heart Medal.

On February 7, 1993, the United States government also belatedly awarded Hewett the Prisoner of War Medal for his time spent as a prisoner in the St. Gilles Hospital in Belgium. Many servicemen did not properly receive the medals that they were due immediately after the War because different criteria had been used to award them. Those airmen and other servicemen who went to Stalags were obvious recipients for getting the POW Medal. Only later did the United States government fully recognize that hospital patients such as Hewett were indeed prisoners of the Germans. The presentation of the Prisoner of War Medal to Hewett in Florida was by Major General John Roth, commander of the 81st Army Reserve Command.

During his farewells at the time of the St. Gilles Hospital evacuation in Brussels, Bill Hewett and Dr. VonBrucke exchanged addresses and telephone information in the hope of a peacetime reunion. In the 1950's Hewett and Dr. VonBrucke met in Vienna; one of three such meetings that would eventually take place. As they sat on an Alpine Hotel veranda overlooking a mountain lake at sunset, a string quartet played Mozart while the two men enjoyed after-dinner cognacs and cigars. At this moment both men reflected back and pondered, in Hewett's words "Just what the hell had it all been about...?"

Bill Hewett also kept in contact with the Belgian couple who had saved him. After the War, he made three trips to Belgium to visit them. On one of the visits Hewett gave them his Purple Heart Medal. To commemorate the 50th anniversary of his rescue, Hewett arranged for Basile Croes and his wife Filomene Cauberg-Croes to fly to Florida and stay as his guests in Palm Beach County. Hewett was also able to track down both of the men that he had escaped and hidden with in the barn. Bill Stein joined the Hewett's and Cauberg-Croes for the gathering in Florida. Ellis Durland in England was contacted through letters and telephone calls. The reunions served as a reminder to Bill Hewett of the grace of God and the way He orchestrated the circumstances which occurred during the War that allowed him to return home safely.

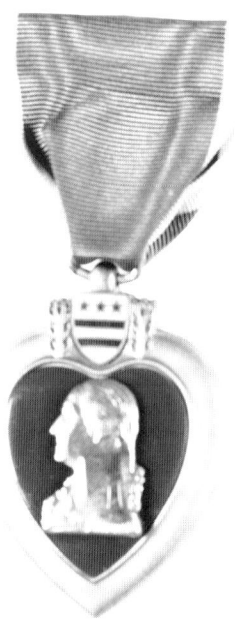

The Purple Heart Medal was awarded to soldiers who were wounded during combat. Among those airmen flying aboard the *Sunrise Serenade* to receive this prestigious award were Francis C. Smedley, - posthumously for giving his life for his country; Robert A. Lalumiere for the injury to his leg on the April 11, 1944, mission; Harry C. Shoffner for wounds received after leaving the plane; and William J. Hewett for burns to his hand and face while leaving the plane. John J. McGrath had received a slight wound to his forehead after a piece of flak came through the nosecone during a combat mission, but he never pursued obtaining the medal.
- *Collection of the author.*

The Caterpillar Club

Airmen aboard combat planes in World War I did not carry parachutes because the idea of saving one's life by using a parachute had never been considered. Once an aircraft had become disabled, it almost always meant certain death for the pilot or passengers. In 1922, four years after World War I, a 27-year-old United States Air Corps test pilot named Lt. Harold Harris strapped on his parachute as he prepared for a flight over Dayton, Ohio. It was widely thought that an airman would have insufficient control over his arms and would not be able to pull the ripcord. After Harris's plane developed mechanical problems, he stood up in the cockpit and was pulled out of his disabled aircraft by the passing air. Approximately 500 feet above the ground he activated his parachute, and it worked without fail. Harris became the first verified person to save his life by using a parachute on October 20, 1922. It seemed only natural that a brotherhood would soon form whenever airmen survived because of their parachutes. Thus the Caterpillar Club came into existence.

By World War II, parachutes had become standard issue for all airmen because they were proven to save lives. During the period that the crew of the *Sunrise Serenade* were flying combat missions over Europe in the spring of 1944, over 10,000 airmen had already reported that they had saved their lives by using a parachute. By the end of the War that number had increased to nearly 34,000.

Induction into the Caterpillar Club required that an airman had saved his life by using a parachute after bailing out of a disabled aircraft. The name of the organization is derived from the silkworm caterpillar that produced the silk from which the parachutes were made. At least three companies sponsored Caterpillar Clubs - Irvin, Switlik, and Pioneer. Irvin was a company based in England while Switlik and Pioneer operated in the United States. Only the Irvin and Switlik companies continue to operate today. During World War II there were as many as 21 companies making parachutes for the War. For many men the parachute symbolized a second chance at life, and induction into one of the Caterpillar Clubs served as a reminder of their gratefulness to its maker. Many airmen deemed it the most valuable piece of equipment they had and knew where to quickly find it in an emergency.

Any airman desiring to be inducted into the Caterpillar Club had to contact one of the companies and furnish documented proof that his life had been saved by using a parachute. In all truthfulness, most airmen had no idea which company had produced the parachute that they had used. Neither the Irvin nor the Switlik parachute companies required this information. For the most part an airman's statement detailing his life-saving experience was taken to be true and rarely investigated by either of the parachute companies. Each company provided a small lapel pin resembling a caterpillar, a certificate and a membership card. Unfortunately many airmen never heard of the Caterpillar Club's existence and never applied for membership. Both the Irvin and Switlik parachute companies still award membership into their clubs and issue replacement pins and certificates. The Pioneer Parachute Company went out of business, and their Caterpillar Club records were given to Switlik.

Among those airmen flying aboard the *Sunrise Serenade* who applied for membership into the Switlik Caterpillar Club were John J. McGrath, Raymond E. Dean, and William J. Hewett. Andrew Senetsky became a member of the Irvin Caterpillar Club.

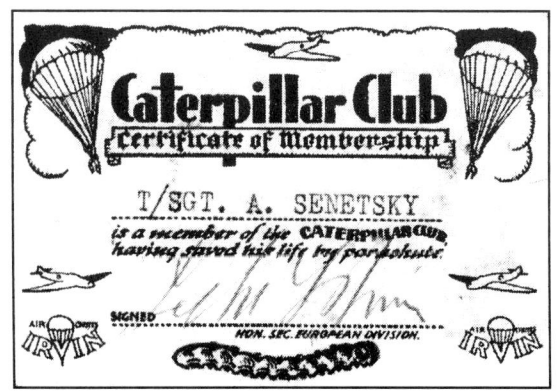

The radioman of the *Sunrise Serenade*, Andrew Senetsky, became a member of the Irvin Caterpillar Club while the navigator, John J. McGrath, became a member of the Switlik Caterpillar Club. - *Membership cards are the collection of Andrew Senetsky and John J. McGrath.*

In The Belgian Underground

Like his copilot, Harry Shoffner probably recognized the hand of God in the events surrounding his last mission aboard the *Sunrise Serenade*. He escaped being captured even though at one time, he probably thought he should have managed to avoid being aboard the plane completely if the Air Force had moved a little more quickly in dealing with a personal matter.

It all began on April 5, 1944, while he was at the base in Deopham Green, England. Shoffner received a letter from his wife's mother, informing him that his beloved Mary Lou was very ill. She also advised Harry to see his commanding officer to request a furlough home. For whatever reasons, possibly security, her letter did not disclose Mary Lou's illness. The illness must have been serious enough to need him to return home as soon as possible to see his wife whom he had been married to for only two years. Shoffner became worried, his mind filled with many thoughts, none of which could be easily sorted. The following day brought some temporary relief to his anxiety when a planned bombing mission that the crew of the *Sunrise Serenade* was to be part of was scrubbed. Shoffner, now having some time to himself, sought the counsel of the Bomb Group's chaplain regarding the letter from home. His diary that day detailed his thoughts:

> "I saw chaplain Gosnell this morning concerning Mom's letter and he advised me to seek more information before I do anything. He could not promise me a thing even if the most tragic thing had happened. I also saw the Red Cross director so he is trying to find out more for me. I'm still worried, for Mom isn't one who would be excited about anything. Hope to hear soon. In the meantime I'll pray that everything is O.K."

Back in Kansas, Mary Lou had undergone surgery on her throat to remove a goiter that had begun to form when she was a child. The doctors doing the surgery diagnosed Mary Lou with thyroid cancer, and as a result she was given powerful radiation treatments. By April 7th, Shoffner had still not received any news from home, and he felt helpless given his circumstances. Shoffner continued to fly missions, and finally the Red Cross vaguely informed him of the condition of his wife, and arrangements were made through the Air Force to have him return to the United States. The exact details of his wife's condition were still uncertain, and it was undoubtedly on his mind while attending his waist gunner's position during the bombing missions. From the time that Shoffner first learned of his wife's condition on April 5th, until he was shot down, he flew nine more missions, which brought his total to twenty.

With only ten more missions to complete before his quota was complete, a decision may have been made to have him stay until he was finished. An early trip home to the States would have probably meant having to return to England later to fulfill his duty. His position on the crew would have been replaced, and he wouldn't have shared the excitement of returning with his crew on their last mission together. The crew of the *Sunrise Serenade* had gone through a lot together since training, and they had become as close as brothers. If Shoffner was given a choice to return home, or stay just a little longer, it couldn't have been an easy decision to make. The mission on May 1, 1944, put an abrupt end to any chances of him returning home or even receiving any more letters to update him on his wife's condition.

It did not take long for Shoffner to realize that the *Sunrise Serenade* was in serious trouble before he bailed out of the plane. By his own account, as recorded in the Air Force Missing Air Crew Report, he was the first crew member to bail out. Since Shoffner was a waist gunner, which made him closer to an exit door on the side of the plane, he was in an excellent position to make a quicker exit than some of the other crew members. This alert action by Shoffner to leave the plane immediately was probably the defining factor that let him evade the Germans rather than be captured and taken prisoner. Shoffner's personal experience with flak, recorded in his diary dated March 23, 1944, indicated that the thought of having to bail out of the plane had crossed his mind.

> "...I've gotten over my fear of flak after the second mission. Occasionally I duck when those big ones go off and splatter the ships. There is no telling how many missions we will have to make. I just hope I have a chance to bail out when the time comes."

Shoffner's readiness to bail out of the plane was also due to his constant thoughts about home and being able to once again see his wife, Mary Lou, and his new son, Larry. His son had been born in October of 1942 at the same time he had been drafted into the Air Force. Since Shoffner had previously spent two years in the Kansas National Guard, he was called to duty earlier than others. As a constant reminder of the son he had barely seen, he pinned a pair of baby booties to his flight suit during every mission. Not being there to see his son grow became just one of the many hardships that Shoffner was to encounter. During his absence, Mary Lou and young Larry had returned to Lawrence, Kansas, her hometown, to be closer to family members.

The entire bombing run over Brussels had only lasted two minutes, so it took the Germans a little more time to react and reach each location of the downed airmen as they drifted to the ground in their parachutes. The Belgian people, however, were already in many of the areas that the Germans were not. It is very likely that Shoffner was the first crew member to reach the ground. He was immediately picked up by a member of the Belgian Underground named Marcus Van Buggenhout, who had raced to the scene before the Germans arrived. The Germans knew that the B-17 bombers carried a crew of ten men, so they used all means available to account for every man.

When Harry Shoffner was picked up by the Belgian Underground all communication with the outside world was severed to protect and hide his identity. Mary Lou was sent a telegram from the Air Force dated May 16, 1944, informing her of the "Missing" status of her husband. This began a five-month ordeal for both Mary Lou and Harry, each one not knowing of the other's fate. Harry could do nothing to contact his wife, and she did not know whether he was a prisoner of war or dead. Since the planned D-Day invasion of France by the Allies was only a month away, the Belgian Resistance workers were notified from England to hold all downed airmen until further notice. Typically the Underground workers would be arranging to provide a safe passage back to England for downed airmen, but the planned invasion of France changed everything. Any airman trying to make his way back to England would have little chance of survival once the invasion was underway. The families of the other crew members had actually received word about the fate of their sons long before Mary Lou had learned of her husband. At least being a POW meant that the military eventually had some record of where a downed airman might be located, and that he was alive.

The Belgian Red Cross had secretly attempted to communicate with Mary Lou at least two times through letters during Harry's stay in Belgium but were unsuccessful. The letters were sent from a woman who was posing to be an old friend of Mary Lou's. The intent was to let Mary Lou know that her husband was safe through the use of coded words such as "Harryette". The first letter to Mary Lou dated June 23, 1944, read:

> "My dear Mary, I am always in good health, and I hope the same of you and the little Leary. Answer quickly please. Harryette."

The second letter dated July 10, 1944, read:

> "How do you do my dear Mary. I hope that your health is better. With me always good. Answer quickly please. Many kisses from Harryette."

Any mail, regardless of its origin, even the Red Cross, was checked very thoroughly by the Germans to hopefully catch suspicious activity. Wartime mail was routed many places and even held for long periods before being delivered. Both letters had various Red Cross stamps upon them, with an American Red Cross stamp on the first letter bearing the date October 19, 1944, and a date of December 8, 1944, on the second letter. Both dates were after the time Harry Shoffner had finally arrived back home, meaning that Mary Lou never knew about her husband's situation, and he feared the worst since both letters went unanswered.

At least two secret attempts were made by the Belgian Red Cross to contact Harry Shoffner's wife in the United States. Both letters finally arrived after Harry had actually returned home. - *Collection of Mary Lou Shoffner.*

Since the Belgian Underground had stopped moving downed airmen back to England, Shoffner began to think about escaping on his own. His plan was to try to somehow cross the German front lines himself and make it back to England. Contemplating how he would accomplish this was more comforting than doing nothing. His thoughts were constantly on his wife and son, and he had safely kept his pair of baby booties in his pocket as a reminder. The pain in his heart was unbearable, and intruding thoughts about the unknown situation at home gave him little rest. He struggled to remember what his wife and son looked like, since his pictures and personal belongings were back at the airfield in England. His Belgian helpers repeatedly talked him out of trying to cross the German lines, and explained that he would be reducing the chances of ever seeing his family by doing this. They were likewise in pain just to see Shoffner in anguish over what he was thinking of doing.

Shoffner did not realize how safe he was in German-occupied Belgium. Being shot down over German-occupied countries was generally safer than being shot down over the German motherland. Many airmen had become victims of angry German citizens while having to bail out and land over German soil. Residents of the occupied countries such as Belgium were, in a sense, prisoners themselves in their own country. They did not like to take orders from an enemy and only a few Belgians ever closed a door to an airman in trouble. The Germans had strongly warned any citizen against helping downed airmen, as this would be seen as a high crime. Belgium had already been under German control for nearly four years since the invasion of that country had taken place on May 10, 1940. Most of the assistance in Belgium at the time the *Sunrise Serenade* was shot down was now, however, only through the well-trained Resistance groups.

Harry Shoffner rarely saw the outside world while hiding in the Belgian Underground for 126 days. As he stares out the window he ponders what the fate of his wife and former crew members might be. - *Collection of Mary Lou Shoffner*.

While Shoffner was being hidden by the Belgian Underground, he faced a whole new set of worrisome situations. Not only could he not receive mail from home informing him of his wife's medical condition, he was also separated from the rest of his crew and had no idea how long it would be before he would be passed through the Underground back to England. To make matters worse, Shoffner soon learned of the fate of his pilot and very close friend, Francis Smedley, after the crash. Other downed airmen who had been taken in by the Underground had informed Shoffner that the Germans had buried Smedley in a small cemetery near the home in which they were staying.

Each airman taken into hiding was thoroughly questioned and instructed to fill out a form stating personal facts about himself and also details about his crew and Bomb Group. This was done to hopefully reveal any Germans who were trying to infiltrate the Underground as Allied airmen. Reports were being passed around that Germans who could speak perfect English, and who were also well rehearsed in Air Force operations, were impersonating airmen to expose the Underground movements. One simple test applied to the airmen was to have them print out their entire names and also write down the numbers from 1 to 9. Details in the way that certain letters and numbers were written, such as the number "7" with a bar across the downward stroke would reveal a European background. On the form that Harry Shoffner filled out, he must have seen or heard something that gave him the impression that both his pilot and copilot had been killed and that one crew member was wounded since he indicated on the form this information. In reality only the pilot had died, but the copilot, Bill Hewett, had been severely burned and was being cared for at a local hospital under German guard.

When Shoffner was taken into hiding by the Resistance workers he was still wearing his highly recognizable flight suit. He was soon given civilian clothes. His dog tags were then sewn into the cuffs of his trousers. In the event that Shoffner might later be captured by the Germans, his dog tags would identify him as an allied airman which would have hopefully landed him in a POW camp rather than a concentration camp. Difficulties arose when an airmen landed and needed medical assistance. The Germans would arrive at the hospitals every morning and make note of any new patients. Injuries would, therefore, have to be treated during the night, with the airman needing to be back into hiding before morning.

One member of the Resistance group was a woman in her mid-thirties from Brussels named Anne Brusselmans who was just a small child when the Germans violently attacked Belgium in the fall of 1914, ushering in World War I. Her career in the Belgian resistance movement began early in World War II.

Anne, being half English and also very fluent in that language, was approached by Pastor Schyns to translate British Broadcasting Company (BBC) news broadcasts from London. The translations would then be distributed clandestinely among the Belgian patriots. The Germans, who were in complete control of the Belgian Radio Station broadcasts, censored and biased the news. The BBC news coming from London was a great morale booster to the Belgian patriots for factual representations of the War, and also for information needed to conduct their secret operations to help the Allies.

Anne Brusselmans and her husband, Julien, were clearly made aware of what could happen to them if they were caught assisting the Allies. If Resistance workers were caught, they and their families would be arrested, tortured and probably shot. Belgian people were duly warned not to come to the aid of downed airmen, and posters could be seen virtually everywhere indicating that such activity would result in the death penalty. The Brusselmans' apartment was selected as a suitable site for hiding airmen during their interim before they could be returned to England. Finding safe houses for airmen was extremely difficult. The houses had to be well away from any military installation, airport, or railroad junction. Families with children often were a bad choice since the children were prone to talk, and a couple without children was equally awkward since the husband might become jealous with young airmen around his wife. Families which had grown daughters still living at home were also bad choices for obvious reasons.

Somehow, Anne Brusselmans had evaded the German authorities time after time while other Resistance workers were caught. The Gestapo had heard of a woman nicknamed "Madame Anne", but because she was known to speak fluent English, they were looking for a British woman. Because of the persistent searches being conducted by the Germans to find Resistance workers, one incident greatly hampered the Resistance fighters when in October of 1943 eleven members were caught by the Germans. The members were taken to an area and killed by a firing squad. A notice then appeared in the newspaper reporting the executions, and also stating that anyone who gave help in any way to enemy (Allied) airmen, or failed to report airmen to the nearest German headquarters, would realize the consequences of their action. A small memorial church service was held for the victims in which Pastor Schyns gave a sermon and quoted from the book of Mark, Chapter 8, Verse 35: *"For whoever will save his life shall lose it, but whoever shall lose his life for my sake and the Gospel, the same shall save it"*. While attending the service, Anne Brusselmans glanced around the room and noticed that she was not the only person who had regained her courage after listening to Pastor Schyn's words. The Brusselmans' family resumed their daily activities with the father going to work and the children going to school every day, never disclosing their secrets at home.

The pay for the Belgian resistance workers was 70 Belgian francs per day and was usually paid once a week. This amounted to very little since everything available in the war-torn country was highly inflated, if it could be obtained at all. The pay did, however, help to offset a little of the extra costs incurred by having the airmen in their homes. Most airmen were used to having full-sized meals back at their bases, but now their present situation had changed. The airmen in hiding did, however, fair much better than their comrades held in the German prison camps.

A typical scene in Brussels during the War was the German soldiers checking identification papers of people using the local trams. At least thirteen German soldiers are in this photo. - *Collection of Mary Lou Shoffner.*

While living in and near Brussels, Harry Shoffner had to endure many long days of seclusion while not being able to venture outside unless he had proper papers and an escort. The German Gestapo was actively looking for downed airmen and they knew that many were being hidden in the Brussels area. All of the other surviving crew members of the *Sunrise Serenade* had been thoroughly questioned by the Germans before being taken to the POW camps. The Germans often knew more about a particular crew's bomb group and squadron than the crew members themselves. It was reported that one downed airmen once had even been presented with a picture of his entire crew posing by their plane. The German intelligence system was very thorough, and they knew they were looking for an airman named Harry Shoffner. German sympathizers would often tip off the Gestapo to the locations of these airmen, so even close neighbors could not be trusted. During his stay in Brussels, Shoffner had been given at least three fake identities. Among these were Henri Jean Blochman, Gaston Paul Dumont, and Ministere de L'ulntirieur.

Enduring similar circumstances, Allied airmen in the Belgian Underground pose together in Brussels. (Back L. to R.) Tommy Mikulka, Elmer Loveland, Harry Shoffner, (Front) John Brown, and William Grosvenor. (The John Brown in the photo is not the same person that flew aboard the *Sunrise Serenade*). - Collection of Mary Lou Shoffner.

The occupied countries were sensing something big was about to happen from the Allied fighting forces. Targets that had been missed on daytime raids were scheduled for the following nights. Bombing missions to railroad yards such as the one at Brussels were increasing and also sabotage missions were on the rise. The Allied invasion of France was in the final preparation stages. News from England again advised the Underground not to evacuate airmen back to England until further notice. While this news was well received by the Belgians because it signaled a possible end to being under German control, it was disheartening to the airmen like Harry Shoffner who now knew that they would have to endure many more days in seclusion before they could return. At this time there were 54 airmen in the Underground who were scattered in various houses in the Brussels vicinity. With the increased bombings of military and railroad installations, it resulted in civilian houses inevitably being hit. To many Belgians, losing their possessions from Allied attacks seemed worse than having to live in an environment with Germans. Most of the Belgian people were not connected with the Underground so they knew very little about the effect the Allied bombings were having upon the German war effort.

The invasion of France eventually took place on the beaches of Normandy on June 6, 1944. At this point Shoffner knew that the end of his seclusion was near, but it would still take time for the Germans to be pushed back to their homeland.

By late August of 1944, the Germans were retreating from the Brussels area, but were not going without committing some last acts of violence against the citizens. The Gestapo rounded up any one they thought might be collaborating with the Allies and shot them in cold blood, instead of first taking them prisoner. On the evening of September 1, 1944, the Brusselmans' apartment was stormed by the German police looking for evidence of collaboration. Anne and her husband had quickly hidden some incriminating documents, but a member of the Belgian Secret Army was still hiding in their son's room. Only quick thinking saved them from the Germans when Anne told them that their son had typhoid, and that they had better not open the door. The German police, fearing for their own health, never opened the door and left.

On September 3, 1944, the Allied fighting forces, with the assistance of the Belgian Patriots, finally pushed the rest of the Germans out of the area as they retreated back to Germany. Harry Shoffner and the rest of the airmen still in hiding were now free to walk around by themselves without fear. The British set up headquarters at the Hotel Metropole in downtown Brussels. Anne Brusselmans immediately went to the hotel to give the Intelligence Service the list of the 54 airmen housed in various parts of the city. Upon meeting a young lieutenant, Anne asked "*I have 54 downed airmen scattered all over this city. What do you want me to do with them?*" The lieutenant in disbelief replied "*I suggest that you round them up and bring them here*". Some of the airmen had been hidden in Brussels for nine months. For Harry Shoffner it had been four months and three days (126 days). While leaving the hotel, Anne Brusselmans was called by a familiar voice. She barely recognized the very thin and emancipated body of her fellow compatriot Marcus, who had been the one to rescue Shoffner. Marcus and his wife had been arrested on August 1, 1944, and were badly beaten, imprisoned, and starved by the Germans. As a last effort to keep their prisoners from being liberated by the Allies, the Germans had put Marcus and many other political prisoners aboard a train for Germany. Efforts to have the train leave Brussels were continually delayed by Belgian patriots until a last minute diplomatic agreement was made with the help of the Swiss Consul and the Red Cross, freeing Marcus and others.

The airmen were all rounded up and brought to the hotel where they were debriefed until transportation was finalized. The scene was overwhelming for many of the airmen and Resistance workers alike who knew that they would soon be parting company. Many hugs and expressions of gratitude, amidst bottles of overflowing champagne, were shown to the Belgians who had risked their lives to save them. The Belgian people who had kept them had grown to think of them as their own boys, and saying goodbye was very hard. The airmen were eventually all loaded onto trucks and were taken to the newly liberated city of Paris, France, accompanied by Marcus and Julien Brusselmans. From Paris they were taken by planes back to England. Many of the Belgian Resistance workers were later recognized by various governments for their heroic deeds associated with hiding the downed airmen.

Shoffner's wife, Mary Lou, received a telegram from France stating that Harry was alive and now free. On October 19, 1944, Shoffner boarded a military plane and headed back toward the United States arriving the next day. All communication between Shoffner and his wife had been crossed up so badly that his wife was surprised when he walked into their house in Lawrence, Kansas. Shoffner was now home with his family, but the War had taken its toll on him. The emotional stress placed upon him while overseas was just too much for a young family man to endure. Shoffner refused to ever discuss the War, even with his family, in the years after he came home. He was officially separated from the military on August 26, 1945.

The full extent of Harry Shoffner's war-related injuries are unknown, although he later received the Purple Heart Medal. By the time Shoffner arrived back home his injuries had healed, and he never discussed them. One Belgian citizen later told Shoffner's wife that "Harry was pretty beat up when they got to him" indicating he may have gotten his injuries while landing on the ground. Harry Shoffner never knew exactly what had happened to the rest of his crew, and he never attempted to reunite with them after the War.

Harry Shoffner died in 1972, and was the first crew member of the *Sunrise Serenade* to die after the War. The diagnosis of cancer for Mary Lou in 1944 turned out to be wrong, even though she had to undergo the massive radiation treatments. The effects of the earlier radiation treatments had ironically caused her to have multiple cases of cancer in later years.

Anne Brusselmans eventually moved to the United States and settled in Florida to be with her daughter. Anne died in 1993, but not before having her daughter, Yvonne, write her complete story of the War and her efforts. These memoirs were compiled into a book, "*Anne Brusselmans – Mission Accomplished*" in 1993 by her daughter. Anne Brusselmans was credited with helping over 100 Allied airmen escape from being captured by the Germans during World War II. For her bravery under life-threatening circumstances, she was awarded many medals and citations from several governments and organizations after the War had ended.

Each airmen who was picked up by the Belgian Underground was required to fill out a sheet stating their personal data as well as any details regarding their crew. In Harry Shoffner's report he indicated that he thought that two members of his crew were killed. - *Collection of the author.*

Two Officers Stay Together

Although there were many Europeans willing to help the Allies, such as the members of the Belgian Underground, many of the downed airmen never had a chance to meet them. Instead, they were captured by the Germans and taken to various prison camps scattered across Germany. Several of the crew members from the *Sunrise Serenade* suffered this fate. They included five enlisted men and two officers, bombardier George D. Griffin and navigator John J. McGrath. These men were immediately interrogated by the Germans at Brussels. Any personal items that the airmen had were quickly taken, especially the valuable watches that Griffin, McGrath and Senetsky had been required to wear because of their positions on the crew. After a few days in Brussels, Griffin and McGrath were then taken by train to an interrogation center at Oberursel, Germany, which was located just north of Frankfurt.

At Oberursel the men were photographed, fingerprinted, and again placed in solitary confinement. Each man was ordered to fill out a Red Cross form. The official purpose of this form was to obtain the name, rank, and serial number of each crew member, but the Germans often added other questions to the form in an attempt to gain further information. Under solitary confinement for a few days, the men were each repeatedly questioned and threatened if they did not provide answers to the German's questions. The interrogators were specialists in the area of obtaining information from downed airmen. They had a massive library of information on every aspect of the United States 8th Air Force. Every new airman that was questioned often added just one small piece of information even though they were told to state only their name, rank, and serial number no matter the threats. John McGrath was surprised when one of his German interrogators spoke perfect English and had in fact worked for the same Fuller Brush Company in the United States where John had once been employed.

Oberursel was located within 1,600 yards of the main railroad station at Frankfurt; a direct violation of the Geneva Convention which dictated the placement of POW camps away from potential military targets. In November of 1943, the Swiss made an inspection of the camp and noted that the proximity of the camp to the railroad station left it vulnerable to Allied air attacks which might target the railroad yards. This, of course, made no difference to the Germans who wouldn't have minded if the Allies accidentally bombed their own men. Later in the War, the inevitable happened when the interrogation center was destroyed by an air raid.

The Germans would use knowledge that they already had obtained to try to trick airmen into revealing more. From the remaining wreckage of the *Sunrise Serenade,* information was relayed to Frankfurt that the men were from the 452nd Bomb Group located at Deopham Green, England. Since the tail of the plane had crashed separately from the main wreckage, the information on it was still legible. This information included the plane number, call letter, and bomb group designation. Often the Germans would say that one of the other crewmen had already revealed this information in an attempt to get the others to talk. Very rarely did this work since the airmen had been warned of this tactic beforehand by their commanding officers, and were repeatedly told to only give their name, rank, and serial number. However, one famous German *Luftwaffe* interrogator named Hanns Scharff gained the reputation as the man who could magically obtain all the answers he needed from the prisoners of war. In most cases the POW's being interrogated by Scharff never realized that their words, small talk or otherwise, were important pieces of a vast system of information being gathered for the German war effort.

After being interrogated the airmen were sent to a transit camp named Dulag Luft near the town of Wetzlar. This large camp became the new processing location for many new airmen taken prisoner before being shipped off to various other POW camps. Prior to the use as a transit camp, it had housed German army troops from flak battalions.

Stalag Luft III - Sagan

After a short stay at Dulag Luft, George D. Griffin and John J. McGrath were then taken to Stalag Luft III, which was located in the Province of Silesia at Sagan, Germany. The literal translation of Stalag Luft III is "Camp Air Three". The prisoners being held there were almost entirely airmen officers. The camp was approximately 80 miles southeast of Berlin, Germany, near the border of Poland. The Bober River, which was a tributary of the mighty Oder River, ran through the wooded terrain nearby. In later years after the War, this area was to be located completely inside the borders of Poland, with the name of the city changed to Zagan. All incoming airmen soon became known as "Kriegies", a contraction of the German word "Kriegsgefangenen", meaning prisoners of war. The camp had six compounds, three being occupied by American officers, and three by British officers. The prison camp was rectangular in shape with a double barbed wire fence

This aerial view of part of Stalag Luft III at Sagan was taken by an American reconnaissance airplane while the camp was still in operation. Only the West Compound of this massive POW camp where George D. Griffin and John J. McGrath were held is shown. Barrack #165 in which they were housed is located in the third row down and the third column from the right. The direction of North is to the left of the photo. - *Collection of Robert F. Yeager.*

around the perimeter. Inside the barbed wire and about 50 feet back, was a small railing signifying the closest that POW's could venture near the fence. The area inside the railing and the fence was designated as "no man's land", and anyone breaching this area would be shot by the guards who were in the watch towers. Each compound was divided into 15 buildings, each containing 12 rooms. Each room housed from 10 to 14 men. The West Compound, one of those assigned to American airmen, was opened on April 27, 1944, so George Griffin and John McGrath arrived as some of its newest inhabitants. Eventually the camp had 10,000 prisoners confined there; 75% being American Air Corp officers.

One of the British compounds at Stalag Luft III had been the site of a major escape attempt in March of 1944. The British POW's had dug three very long tunnels named "Tom", "Dick", and "Harry", which went under the perimeter fence and into the woods. The tunnel named "Tom" had been discovered and destroyed in the summer of 1943, but work on "Harry" progressed with "Dick" as the backup. Since many of the British prisoners had already been confined for several years, they were more than ready to make their escape. During the night of March 24th, and the early morning of March 25, 1944, the British had successfully freed 76 of their comrades before the tunnel was discovered. The planned exit of the tunnel had been miscalculated and came up well short of the tree line and within 30 yards of a watch tower. The original plan was to free 250 British prisoners. A massive hunt for the escapees was undertaken. Hitler himself was actively involved. Fifty of the caught escapers were shot and killed by the German gestapo as a deterrent for future escape attempts. Only three British airmen eventually made it safely back to England. At least two major motion pictures were later made which detailed this escape at Stalag Luft III, including the American version titled "The Great Escape".

Since this escape attempt had only been less than two months before George Griffin and John McGrath arrived, the tension in the camps was still very high. Some guards had been executed for failing to report missing items that were later found in the tunnels, so every guard was now very alert. To the recollections of Griffin and McGrath, no major escape attempts had ever been planned in the American compound during their stay.

When it rained, some of the barracks were converted into miniature ponds when the poorly constructed roofs failed. The German guards made their rounds every night at ten o'clock and would barricade the barracks doors with wooden bars. Lights were to be completely extinguished at midnight, otherwise the German guards would shoot into the barracks to impress upon the prisoners that the rules were to be observed without exception.

Food was primarily sent into the camps through the Red Cross who also made inspection visits regarding camp conditions. Parcels sent from family members back in the United States was also a main source of food. Often very little was left of a food parcel after it had been exchanged through many different hands before arriving to its intended person. The German guards were also poorly fed, so they enjoyed whatever they could get their hands on. Generally everything that came into the camps was shared among the prisoners so no one would go without food. The initial problem was the hunger pains and other health-related problems the body experienced from lack of a proper diet. Eventually the prisoners became accustomed to little food; however, illness due to the lack of food was inevitable. Initially each man received one food parcel per week, but as the War dragged on this was reduced to one parcel for two men, then one parcel for 4 men and so forth. An American food parcel consisted of the following items: 12 oz. of Spam; 1 lb. of Klim (powdered milk); 12 oz. of corned beef; 7 oz. of salmon; 6 oz. of jam; ½ lb. of cheese; 11 crackers; 4 oz. of coffee; ½ lb. of sugar; 4 oz. of D-bar (chocolate); 6 oz. of pate; 1 lb. of oleo; 12 oz. of prunes; 12 oz. of raisins; 1 bar of soap; 5 packs of cigarettes; and 6 oz. of orange concentrate.

The German rations which supplemented the food parcels consisted of daily potatoes; sugar once a week; daily bread; jam once a week; dried oatmeal twice a month; cabbage in season; soup three times a week; cheese once a week; and margarine once a week. Vegetables were seldom available and when they were, they had to be screened to remove the maggots, and other inedible items. With barley soup it was especially hard to sort out the maggots from the actual pieces of barley. Blood sausage was made available once a month which was never popular inside the camp. It was nothing more than congealed blood with a few slices of onion added. Another type of meat that was sometimes provided was horsemeat, and it was mostly gristle. In the morning for breakfast, the main source of food consisted of coffee and a few slices of toast coated with a thin layer of margarine or jelly if available. John McGrath remembered that the German black bread weighed over 4 pounds. He once cut 80 slices of bread per loaf, so each man could get 2 or 3 slices. These slices were only 1/8" thick. The German coffee was described as terrible, and the usual way in which it was prepared was to take two spoons of instant coffee and mix it with 24 cups of water. For special days such as Thanksgiving and Christmas, the men saved extra food from the Red Cross parcels for a few weeks so they would have a real "feast" those days.

Clothing was another problem for the men since items of civilian nature were strictly forbidden, due to their usefulness if a successful escape was made. Such civilian clothing, if obtained, was carefully hidden for possible escape uses. The Red Cross furnished much of the clothing in the camp. For the most part, the officers tried to maintain some sort of clothing or insignia to determine their rank, although it was not uncommon to see men wearing whatever they could find. The shortage of adequate clothing was not initially a problem for George Griffin and John McGrath who had arrived in the spring when the weather was becoming warmer. The shortage of clothing at Stalag Luft III, however, became much more apparent when colder weather began to set in. Conditions at night inside the cheaply constructed barracks reached below the freezing level without adequate blankets or heat.

Red Cross food parcels were generally the only food that was obtainable at German POW camps. As the War progressed, even these parcels became scarce, making the living conditions much worse. - *Collection of Andrew Senetsky.*

Religious activities were held with complete freedom of choice without persecution. Church services were held in specially constructed chapels. Available inside the camp were 7 Protestant chaplains and 2 Catholic chaplains. The only English newspaper allowed inside the camp was the German-printed "O.K." (Overseas Kid). The Berlin newspapers Deutche Allgemeine Zeitung and Volkischer Beobachter were popular among the Kriegies as crack filler in the walls of their barracks. Another form of entertainment was watching the German air shows. The German Me-109 and FW-190 pilots regularly practiced over the camp to show the thousands of Allied airmen that they were still ruling the skies in that area.

Activities at Sagan consisted of various sporting events for which the Red Cross supplied the equipment. The YMCA was also active alongside the Red Cross to deliver sporting equipment, books, food, and other items into the camp. Since the Germans were signers of the Geneva Convention, they were required to allow these items into the camps. Many of these items came from the neutral country of Switzerland. A concrete fire pool located inside the compound was six feet deep and was used for fire protection. In mid-summer this pond provided relief from the heat in the form of swimming, but soon the water became stagnant and the practice was stopped.

During the last five months that Griffin and McGrath spent at Sagan, the Red Cross parcels became fewer and fewer. Possibly the Allied bombing of roads and other installations was a contributor to this, but generally it was just the strain that the lingering War had put on these resources. The Germans sent food and other items to many of their own POW's being held in the United States. These POW's were already being well taken care of, but it may have been an excuse by the Germans to divert food away from Allied prisoners.

During the summer of 1944, the men from the camp organized themselves into baseball teams. The baseball teams gave the men something to keep their mind off the War, while also giving them exercise and good spirits. Since each barracks housed from 10 to 14 men, many teams were made up entirely of men in the same barracks. George Griffin and John McGrath played on a team known as the "All Stars" from barrack 165. Griffin played shortstop while McGrath held the 3rd base position. The team to beat that year was the Cardinals from barrack 163, who went undefeated with 21 wins. The All Stars and the Cardinals met at 2:00 p.m. on Sunday, August 26, 1944, for one of the best games of the season. The following story obtained from "A Wartime Log", by Clyde W. Bradley, describes the play of the game:

> "An alert 163 Cardinal outfit took advantage of a break and made the All Stars their 20th victim in a row winning by a score of 2-0 before a crowd of 1,113 Kriegies yesterday on the old field. The game was outstanding. The fourth inning was the turning point: Bausano led off with a walk, Bowles tossed away O'Donnel's bunt and the runners went to second and third. Esau, an All Star second baseman, made a stop of Leaser's line drive, but Bausano scored. O'Donnell also scored when Bowles threw hurriedly to second trying to get Leaser."

John McGrath broke his nose after running into the 1st baseman. The Germans set it incorrectly, and McGrath had to later have it reset. The "All Stars" team lost 82 D-Bars and 120 packs of cigarettes to the opposing team. After the War, George Griffin went on to play major league baseball.

Stalag Luft III also had a library for the POW's. This, combined with many talented singers, actors, and musicians gave the prisoners various things to do for entertainment when not involved with physical activities. The food shortage was, however, still a major problem and many men did not have sufficient energy to take part in the physical activities. Some prisoners occasionally blacked out due to the increasing shortage of nutrients being supplied to their bodies. The food shortage in the winter months made the situation even more difficult since the calorie intake was not sufficient to keep the body warm.

Heat became a major problem for the prisoners for both warmth and cooking. Many stumps located inside the camp had to be dug up and used for firewood. Often even parts of the barracks themselves, such as bed boards, flooring, and siding had to be utilized for fuel.

Often men in the same barracks would find themselves incompatible with a fellow POW. Friction would develop from a variety of causes, including the want for privacy, or a need to vent their frustrations at being a POW. As time progressed, more and more airmen were brought into the camp creating overcrowding. Usually disputes among fellow POW's did not have a lasting impact upon those involved, and they usually apologized and resolved to get along with each other.

Mail from family members was difficult to obtain, and it often took well over a month to arrive. The POW's could also send out mail in the form of a postcard, so messages had to be brief. While in Stalag Luft III, Griffin and McGrath received a letter from their pilot's mother informing them of Francis Smedley's death. Other airmen who had arrived at the POW camp after Griffin and McGrath had earlier given them some details of the crash, so the news was not a total shock to them, although the confirmation of Smedley's death was. On November 29, 1944, John McGrath sat down to write Clara Smedley a short note concerning his pilot and friend.

> "Dear Mrs. Smedley, I received your letter. It sure was nice of you to write to me. My mother has mentioned your letters in her letters to me. Smed was one of the best friends I've ever had. I haven't heard from him, but I'm still hoping for the best. I'll try to see you. Give my regards to Vince. - John."

Even though John had heard from various sources about Francis's death, he still held out hope that he would be alive. In some circumstances wrong information had been given about a particular serviceman, and he later showed up alive. Also, those servicemen, being held in various Underground networks were very hard to track down.

The bombardier, George D. Griffin (left), and the navigator, John J. McGrath, were both officers on the *Sunrise Serenade*. They were also the only two crew members to stay together after the plane was shot down. - *Collection of the author.*

Upon confirmation that an American soldier was indeed a prisoner of the Germans, the Red Cross sent the parents, or next of kin of the POW, a newsletter. John McGrath's mother received the June 1944 issue of "*Prisoner Of War Bulletin*" which contained 12 pages of information. This issue just happened to be the one-year anniversary of the newsletter. The newsletter gave those back in the United States an account of the living conditions and lifestyle that their sons or husbands were having to endure. Descriptions of the camps, a map showing where the camps were located, pictures, and also personal letters that had been received from actual POW's were printed in the newsletter. It was also a reference tool to help loved ones understand how to correctly package items to be sent, and also what sort of things not to send. Stalag Luft III was special in the sense that all letters sent to airmen POW's were routed to this camp first regardless of the camp where the POW was actually being held. These letters sent from home needed to carry the Stalag Luft III address first to ensure that it would not get lost. The Germans had a staff of 60 censors working daily to sort and inspect every letter that arrived. Next of kin packages, however, could be sent directly to the camp where the POW was being held once the location had been identified. These packages were opened in front of the receiving POW, with the Germans quickly confiscating anything they deemed a possible tool to use for an escape attempt.

On Christmas Eve 1944, the men were waiting for dismissal from the evening roll call when a small wagon with sleigh bells arrived carrying Santa Claus. The wagon was pulled by two men dressed as reindeer and huge bundles of mail were thrown out. The mail had been secretly allowed to accumulate so that everyone would receive a letter from home. On Christmas Day the men all had something to be cheerful about as they laid around in their barracks rereading the letters from home.

As the winter months arrived, it was rumored that the Russian Army was advancing toward the camp. The Germans were very worried that if the Russians liberated the camp they would use the prisoners in combat against them. The senior American officers at Sagan were aware of what the situation could become if the Germans decided to abandon the camp and make the POW's march to a different location. Near the end of December 1944, an order by an American officer was made stating all men should walk at least 10 kilometers per day to gain strength for a possible march. The order did not come without some moans and griping from a few prisoners, since most of the them had never been on a forced march before. Stalag Luft III was the only home they had known since being shot down. Some POW's rationalized that there was no way the Germans could manage such a move, and thought that the practice walking was a waste of time.

Most, however, complied with the order, and it turned out to be well worth the effort.

On the evening of January 27, 1945, the Russian Army advanced within 20 miles of the camp, so the Germans decided it was time to leave. The decision to abandon the camp should have been made sooner giving everyone more time to organize. As it was, the Germans only gave between 30 to 45 minutes for everyone to be ready to march out of the camp. This lack of time created a panic, especially among those who had not taken the prior warnings seriously. Men were hurriedly trying to assemble food and other necessary items into makeshift backpacks for the trip, while the German guards were ordering them to get moving. Many men tried to tie a shirt together over their back while others tried to construct packs out of blankets tied together. The grouping of men outside of the camp was in a blizzard with -40° wind chill. The POW's were then ordered back into the compound and told to reassemble in one hour. This proved to be even worse for many of the prisoners, as they now tried to construct even larger packs of food and belongings. Some men stayed around so long in the camp that the main column was well ahead of them. The guards through numerous threats that they would be shot, forced these men to catch up with the main group. In their hurry to catch up with the rest of the group, the men began to sweat in the frigid air, which soon led to sickness for many of them.

Most men began to toss their excess food and other articles alongside the roads to lighten their load. The road resembled a junkyard from all of the articles tossed aside from the estimated 10,000 to 12,000 marching prisoners. Constant warnings were issued by the German guards to those who were starting to lag behind. Inadequate clothing and especially the lack of winter shoes resulted in wet feet for nearly everyone as they marched through the snow in frigid temperatures. The POW's had been told that they would march for 50 minutes and then rest for ten minutes, but rest breaks were rarely given as they continued on both day and night.

George Griffin and John McGrath were assigned by the captain of their barracks to be part of a group known as Commandos. This group was involved with assignments along the marching lines, such as helping people who were falling behind or issuing any food obtained from local town people. Griffin held this title for the entire march, while McGrath helped on the last part.

During the march, the Germans seemed to be confused as to their intended destination. On one particular day, a wrong road was taken. This resulted in going the wrong direction for nearly 5 miles before the problem was discovered and their route back had to be retraced.

THE OFFICERS' POW CAMPS
Griffin & McGrath

After being interrogated at the temporary holding site of Dulag Luft in southwest Germany, George D. Griffin and John J. McGrath were then taken to the large officer POW camp at Sagan. Later they either were forced to march or were taken by railroad to two other camps at Nuremberg and Moosburg. The initial route by railroad from Dulag Luft to Stalag Luft III at Sagan is not shown on this map.

The roads were also filled with German refugees either walking or with horse drawn wagons fleeing their bombed out cities. Constant commands were yelled out to move to the right to let the refugees by the column. Many Germans were basically wandering without knowing their intended destinations either. They knew that the Russians were advancing from the north and east while the British and Americans were coming from the south and west. By this stage of the War most German civilians had heard of the terrible atrocities being inflicted by the advancing Russian Army upon the German towns.

By the end of the first day, the men had marched southwest reaching the German town of Halbau, (later to be known as Iłowa, Poland), and by noon two days later on January 29, the men had reached the German town of Freiwaldau (later to be known as Gozdnica, Poland). The local citizens in Freiwaldau yelled and cursed as the prisoners came through the town. After reaching the outskirts of town, the men were given several hours to rest. It soon became apparent that the rest periods were given only because the guards themselves were too tired to continue.

The marching through the snow and bitter cold continued to the German town of Priebus (later to be known as Przewóz, Poland). All indications were that their short-term destination would be Muskau, Germany. On January 30, the prisoners did indeed arrive in Muskau. Most were completely exhausted, sick, and many had frostbite. John McGrath temporarily went blind from exhaustion, but was relieved of this condition when he was able to take a small amount of sugar. While in Muskau, the POW's were left standing in the road for several hours while the Germans debated about their next course of action. Finally the Germans decided to find whatever shelter was available for the men, and plan their next move. Many prisoners, including Griffin and McGrath, found much-needed relief inside a large brick factory that provided heat and a place to sleep. German Red Cross units were also available to provide whatever they could in the form of food. On January 31, 1945, the POW's rested the entire day while they stayed in Muskau.

The next day the prisoners were all rounded up, and again made to mill around in the streets as the Germans decided which direction to take. It was finally decided to go in a westerly direction toward Spremberg, Germany. Along the route to Spremberg were many barns, which the Germans utilized to temporarily house their prisoners for the nights. The German guards were becoming afraid that more prisoners would try to escape, since they were now becoming scattered in many different locations. The guards kept a finger close to the trigger on their rifles. The barns were all intensely filthy and had not been cleaned out in quite a long time. While in one barn, John McGrath and some other men came across an old loaf of bread that had holes chewed through it by rats. After scraping around the holes, the men enjoyed a good meal of stale bread. The towns that the POW's passed through after leaving Muskau included Wolfshain and Graustein. Overnight stays in barns well outside the towns were now the normal procedure.

After arriving at Spremberg on February 2, 1945, the men marched to the railroad station where they were loaded into railroad boxcars. Each car contained about fifty men, one guard and about 40 Red Cross parcels. The men were divided up with the South and Center Camps from Stalag Luft III going directly to Stalag VIIA at Moosburg, Germany. The North and East Camps went to one of the camps near Bremen, and the West Camp went to Stalag XIIID at Nuremberg, Germany. Both George Griffin and John McGrath were loaded into the boxcars that were destined for Stalag XIIID at Nuremberg.

The trip to Nuremberg by rail was equally stressful for the POW's. The boxcars were dark, filthy, and had no heat, water, or restroom facilities. Since the German Army was desperately trying to move more men and equipment to the front lines of the War, the trains carrying the POW's were constantly being moved onto sidetracks. While the passing military trains went by the POW trains, the prisoners were allowed to temporarily come out of the cars and relieve themselves.

Air raids by Allied bombers was another constant problem while the POW trains moved south toward Nuremberg. Many railroad marshalling yards had been completely bombed, and constant rerouting was necessary in order to continue by rail. Since the boxcars were so crowded, most POW's did not even have a chance to sit down, and sleeping was often done in a standing position. The route by rail between Spremberg and Nuremberg first went north to Cottbus, then south and west through the towns and cities of Grossenhain, Chemnitz, Zwickau, Plauen, Hof, and Bayreuth. Finally on February 6, 1945, the POW's arrived in Nuremberg on a cold and rainy day after being on the train for nearly four days.

Stalag XIIID – Nuremberg

After unloading at the railroad yards in Nuremberg, the first thing most POW's noticed was the large swastika which was atop the Nuremberg Fair Grounds. This had been the site where Hitler had given many of his speeches to thousands of Germans to give them propaganda messages about the Third Reich. Stalag XIIID had been previously occupied by Italian prisoners who had failed to go along with the Italian government in siding with Hitler and the Germans.

The camp was absolutely filthy, with the barracks full of trash, overflowing outdoor toilets, and rotted food and waste everywhere. These were the initial visible signs of the filthy camp while the discovery of fleas, lice, bed bugs, rats and other vermin that had completely infested the camp was soon to follow. No cleaning supplies were available to clean up the mess, so the POW's had to make the best of what was there. In most areas the outdoors was much cleaner than anything indoors. The camp had no heat and the water supply was a single water fountain for hundreds of men to share. The daily meals consisted of ½ cup of soup, a single slice of bread, and one small potato.

During the night the lice and bedbugs would attack every prisoner so severely so that they could not even sleep. The itching and burning sensations of the bites drained even more strength from the men. The lice were so prevalent that they even got into the POW's eyebrows. John McGrath recalled that the normal procedure every morning was for the POW's to hang their mattresses and blankets on the fence outside and kill as many lice as possible between their fingernails. The mattresses were usually filled with wood shavings, which provided very little comfort. No powder or delousing chemicals were available at the camp. Often men had their hair full of eggs and even larvae. The lice upon biting a victim would leave a large red itchy welt, so many men wore hoods and gloves during the night. George Griffin got a severe case of dysentery while at Nuremberg and became too weak to even leave his bunk. As a result, his body was completely covered with welts. Many men refused to wash even their hands because the lice and fleas preferred to attack areas of the body that were clean. Soap and warm water were non-existent at the camp anyway.

The dehydrated vegetables used to make soup were always wormy and the total amount of calories consumed on a daily basis was not enough to warm the body. Coffee referred to as "ersatz" was thought to have been made from acorns. Coffee made from shavings of charred German black bread was considered a delicacy among the POW's. Extra clothing was non-existent; the men only had the clothes on their back. The barracks were so crowded that only 10 square feet per man was available. This was just about the area needed to lay down side by side with all the other POW's. The constant itching and coughing throughout the night by the many weak and sickened men made sleep nearly impossible for those who were not sick. The available air space for each man was so small that the air was full of respiratory viruses. Since no coal or wood was available for heat, the men resorted to tearing off pieces of the siding on the barracks while risking being shot by the guards. No lights were available during the period between dusk and dawn. No recreation, reading, or other facilities existed at the camp for the men to pass the time.

The dysentery problem was rampant among all of the men. To make matters worse, only 50 rolls of toilet paper per month were available for 5,000 men, yet most of the men had chronic cases of diarrhea. Medical supplies in any form were also non-existent at the camp. Men often had to suffer greatly from massive headaches or stomach problems which resulted from the conditions of their confinement. Garbage was disposed wherever it could be thrown and there was no garbage removal. Mosquitoes came in through the broken windows at night making conditions even harder to sleep. The problem of flies was also widespread, particularly near garbage piles and the latrines. Many men vomited upon entering the toilet facilities due to the stench. For those that were dying or near death, spiritual guidance or assurance was not available. Ground space was not even available for doing daily calisthenics. Supplies such as toothpaste, razors, combs or other bare essentials were not available.

Nuremberg was the prized city of the Nazi's where many mass rallies were held to build up support for the Third Reich. Unfortunately for the nearby POW's in Stalag XIIID, the large city also became a favorite target of Allied bombers who continually pounded the area both day and night. - *Collection of the author.*

Since the camp was located just outside of Nuremberg, which had a population of over 410,000 citizens, and many industrial sites, the Allied bombers continually bombed the city both day and night. The only refuge were old bomb craters or small slit trenches which often did little to stop flying debris. Some men removed window shutters to cover the trenches, while others covered their heads with blankets or clothing. The concussions from the bombs shattered windows and threw others out of bed if warnings had not been announced of the coming attacks. While in the trenches, pieces of falling flak from the German anti-aircraft guns would often fall onto the POW's, causing injuries to some. Often the guards ordered the prisoners to stay inside the barracks at gun-point until the raids were over. The night raids by the British were full of tense moments since the fallout from bombs or flak could not be seen if it came near the camp. Usually a night raid was announced over the intercom speaker, stating that large numbers of bombers were entering the German fatherland. When the bombers came within 50 miles of the target, and it was determined to be Nuremberg, the siren would sound. Men who were not already in the trenches were soon trying to find whatever available spot not already taken. A very low and barely audible sound of the bomber engines could then be detected as the men huddled together in the darkness. The lead plane would drop flares suspended on small parachutes to illuminate the target area as German flak batteries opened fire at the planes. The roar of the planes combined with the tremendous noise of the flak guns created a sense of terror throughout the camp. POW's prayed that the bombs would not miss the targets in the city and fall near the camp. Next came the exploding bombs which shook the camp and deafened the ears. Huge German searchlights swung back and forth in the darkness trying to find a target for the guns. The explosion or fire that followed a damaged plane resembled a fireball streaking like a comet as it plunged toward earth. After a bombing raid, Nuremberg would burn throughout the night and into the next day. Many times the Germans would order some POW's from the camp go into town and assist with the removal and burial of the bodies of German civilians killed during the raids.

These conditions at the Camp continued on a daily basis and many POW's invariably thought about the "better" days back at Stalag Luft III. Finally on April 3, 1945, the German Commandant said that Stalag XIIID would be evacuated the next day. Through secret radio broadcasts the prisoners had learned that the Allies were only 65 miles from the Camp, so they had been hoping for a move. The American Seventh and Third Armies were spearheading the drive into the German homeland near the camp. On April 4th, absolutely no one objected to leaving the Camp. Unbeknownst to them, over half of the crew of the *Sunrise Serenade* had been together in the same camp. Griffin and McGrath had always been together, with Senetsky, Dean, Rhodes and Gallagher having arrived at this camp under different circumstances during the preceding two months.

The men began moving out of the camp at 11:00 a.m. in groups of 150 men each. Getting away from the filth and stench of Stalag XIIID was more than enough reason to rejoice, even though yet another long march was underway. Near the town of Feucht, an American P-47 fighter plane swung down upon the marching column and fired upon them thinking that they were marching German soldiers. The incident left two American POW's and one British POW dead, with three other POW's seriously wounded. John McGrath remembered that the bullets had just narrowly missed him. The following day the column laid out a large replica of an American Air Corps insignia on the road with an arrow pointing in the direction of the marching columns. After seeing the insignia, the fighters ceased to fire upon their own comrades.

By the spring of 1945 the roads around Nuremberg that were once used by thousands of prideful Germans displaying their national symbol, were now filled with Allied POW's being marched away from Stalag XIIID as the city was now in virtual ruins. - *Collection of the author.*

Marching continued to the towns of Postbauer where the men were all divided up, and were then placed into barns for the evening. Conditions were better on this march since the weather was warmer, and the hope that the War was coming to an end was prevalent among the men. More and more planes were being spotted in the skies, none of which were German. The Allies clearly controlled the skies over Germany, so it was just a matter of time until the German ground forces could be brought to submission.

The next day the columns of marching POW's went through the town of Neumarkt, and then near Berching the weather turned into a heavy rain. The prisoners were placed into whatever available buildings could be found. Some were put into barns while others were put into other town buildings or churches until the next day. George Griffin and John McGrath had stayed together during the march, and at Berching they and a few others hid out inside a barn located near a church for a short time. They had hoped to escape, but German guards with dogs uncovered their hiding place. The men were ordered out and into the columns of marching POW's, who were now marching in the rain. Fortunately, no harm came to the men by the guards who had discovered them.

On April 7th, the men passed through Beilngries and then Paulushofen where they again found whatever shelter was available for the night. The German guards were becoming more and more relaxed with the rules about staying together. Many men lagged behind at their own leisure without much threat from the guards. Many men were dropping out of the columns since the guards were no longer watching as closely. Most chose just to stay with the main groups since there was safety in numbers. The German Army was now in a desperate situation, with many soldiers, and especially men of the SS or Gestapo, inflicting last acts of violence wherever they could. Unarmed POW's who had escaped from the columns became easy targets for incensed Germans. The once thorough procedure of capturing, beating, and interrogating the enemy no longer mattered since the War was essentially already lost for the Germans. It is very unfortunate that some POW's who had struggled during years of starvation and confinement by the Germans lost their lives in the last remaining weeks of the War because they had left the safety of the columns.

The main source of food between Nuremberg and Moosburg came from bartering. The prisoners had carefully kept items such as coffee, tea, and cigarettes stashed away for just this occasion. These items were used to trade for bread, eggs, and occasionally meat or cheese from the German people who did not have the much-wanted cigarettes and coffee. The Red Cross had supplied the cigarettes to the POW's in the food parcels throughout their entire time in captivity. Since most of these parcels were originating from the United States, this was the only supply of cigarettes coming into the entire country.

The POW's passed through the towns of Schamhaupten, Sandersdorf, Mindelstetten, and Forchheim on April 8th, with some groups of the POW's crossing the Danube River at Neustadt. The next few days they passed through Mülhausen, Schweinbach, Gammelsdorf and various other towns until they finally reached Stalag VIIA at Moosburg, Germany, on April 13, 1945.

Stalag VIIA - Moosburg

At Stalag VIIA the men were searched and given a hot shower before they were put up in tents or available barracks. Upon their arrival at Moosburg, most of the men were shocked to hear that President Roosevelt had died. The men spent two weeks at Stalag VIIA where there were by some estimates up to 60,000 POW's of different nationalities. John McGrath was finally able to locate two friends from his hometown, Joe Downing and Bill Newbold, who had also been at Stalag Luft III, but in different compounds. The conditions were dirty, but not to the extent of being overridden with lice and fleas like at Nuremberg. During their stay at Moosburg, the men could hear the constant artillery fire which was coming closer every day. The necessity of having to leave yet another camp was eminent. More and more American fighter planes began to buzz the camp to let the POW's know of their presence in the area. The men in the camp would all wildly wave their arms at the planes as the pilot would wiggle his wings back in response. The planes were cleaning up any remaining German defenses and also directing the American artillery.

John J. McGrath (center) poses for the camera while he and other fellow POW's try to make the best of their situation at Stalag VIIA. Their arrival at Moosburg would only be about two weeks before liberation. - *Collection of Andrew Senetsky.*

On the morning of April 29, 1945, the artillery was especially close and the absence of the German guards in the camp was also apparent. Word started to spread quickly that this might indeed be the day that they would be liberated. Early in the morning an American B-26 bomber flew low over the camp and dropped a weighted message informing the men of their upcoming liberation. Not long after, a barrage of bullets began to fly through the camp in opposite directions. The men immediately hit the ground as the American forces and the retreating Germans were now within rifle or machine gun range of each other. The battle around Stalag VIIA continued until around noon. Soon the skirmish moved on, and a Sherman tank of the 14th

Armored Division of the United States 3rd Army appeared and rolled into the camp. The flag bearing the German swastika was immediately replaced with the American Stars and Stripes. A couple of hours later, General George S. Patton came into the camp with his pearl-gripped pistols boldly showing on his hips to a jubilant crowd of now ex-POW's. The prisoners crowded around the tank as it came to a stop inside the camp amidst loud cries of joy. After the initial commotion and excitement were over, many ex-POW's still remaining inside the barracks and trenches continued to cautiously come out of hiding. The scene was filled with handshakes, hugs, and laughs for many men, but for others it was just too much, and they broke down and wept uncontrollably. Some, especially the British, had been held as prisoners for as long as five years. Of the American forces liberating the camp, one just happened to be a friend of John McGrath named Ray Lawrence who was from his hometown of Langhorne, Pennsylvania. He gave McGrath and Griffin, as well as a few others nearby, some "K-Rations" which tasted unbelievably good to the men. They offered him a little of their own food from the camp, which he declined to even taste.

The liberated men remained at the camp for a couple of days until the appropriate transportation vehicles or planes could be brought in to evacuate them. John McGrath, George Griffin, and two other men decided not to wait any longer and cut a hole through the camp fence to expedite their formal release. The four men obtained a Volkswagon car with the help of some American soldiers and headed east. As they were traveling down a local road, they suddenly were fired upon by German soldiers who were still hiding in the woods, but luckily their shots were off the mark. The car later ran out of gas, so the men found an abandoned German truck which they had to eventually also abandon when it too ran out of gas. Near Nuremberg the men met up with some American officers of a transportation outfit. After spending the night with the officers, the four former POW's were given a ride to a nearby airfield at Weisbaden that had recently been taken over by the Americans. A plane trip brought the men into Paris on V.E. (Victory in Europe) Day, May 7, 1945, where they celebrated with the local citizens. While staying in Paris for the next few days, John McGrath and George Griffin obtained some fresh clothing and also some money from other Americans. Soon they boarded a train that took them to La Havre, France, to be loaded onto ships for the trip home. The majority of the men still waiting at Stalag VIIA were transported ten miles to the northeast of Moosburg to the town of Landshut where an air strip lined with C-47 cargo planes waited to fly them out a few days after they had been liberated.

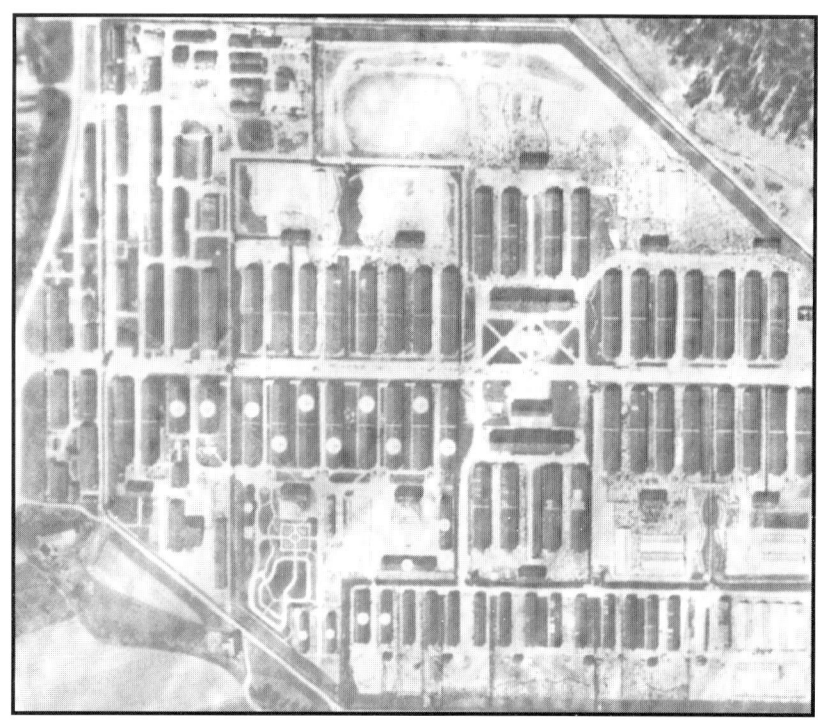

One of the last strongholds for the Germans was Stalag VIIA at Moosburg in southeast Germany. Allied prisoners had been evacuated from many other POW camps all across Germany to keep them away from the advancing British and Americans from the west and the advancing Russians from the north and east. The camp was a melting pot of men and became a temporary home for virtually every nationality that fought on the Allied side. The camp containing an estimated 60,000 prisoners was liberated by the 14th Armored Division of the United States 3rd Army on April 29, 1945. - *Collection of Robert F. Yeager.*

The Prisoner of War Medal

The POW Medal is authorized by Public Law 99-145, section 1128, title 10, United States Code (10 USC 1128), 8 November 1985, and is authorized for any person who, while serving in any capacity with the U.S. Armed Forces, was taken prisoner and held captive after 5 April 1917. The POW Medal is to be issued only to those U.S. military personnel and other personnel granted credible U.S. military service who were taken prisoner and held captive.

(1) While engaged in an action against an enemy of the United States.
(2) While engaged in military operations involving conflict with an opposing foreign force.
(3) While serving with friendly forces engaged in an armed conflict against an opposing force in which the United States is not a belligerent party.

Away From the Battle Fronts

The five captured enlisted men of the *Sunrise Serenade*, all staff or technical sergeants in rank, were also taken to Oberursel for interrogation and then to the transit camp at Wetzlar to be processed and sent to the various permanent POW camps. The five men included the right waist gunner John G. Brown, the tail gunner Raymond E. Dean, the ball turret gunner James E. Gallagher, the engineer Norbert E. "Dusty" Rhodes, and the radioman Andrew Senetsky. (The left waist gunner, Harry C. Shoffner, had escaped into the Belgian Underground.)

These five men did not know what to expect upon being captured so most were very concerned about what may lay ahead. John Brown remembered being ordered to reveal the station number of the 452nd Bomb Group's Deopham Green airfield. Though the station number at Deopham Green was 142, this was something he did not know, but was told he would be shot at sunrise if he did not answer the interrogator's questions. He remembered hearing every little noise and footstep outside his cell wondering if they were coming in to execute him. Raymond Dean was accused of being a spy and was likewise threatened. Needless to say the interrogated airmen got very little sleep those nights spent in solitary confinement after their lives were threatened. Various forms of treatment after interrogation included withholding food, cigarettes, or reading material. This was done for the purpose of breaking the will of the airmen, and inducing them to start revealing information. Other forms of mistreatment included the use of a sweat box and the constant disruption of much-needed sleep. After surviving a few days in solitary confinement, the five men were released into a compound with other downed airmen who were waiting to be shipped to various POW camps.

Although the two captured officers of the *Sunrise Serenade*, George D. Griffin and John J. McGrath, had been taken to Stalag Luft III at Sagan, Germany, the remaining five crewmen were taken to various other POW camps for non-commissioned officers. Four of them, John Brown, Raymond Dean, Jim Gallagher, and Dusty Rhodes were all initially taken to Stalag Luft VI near Hydekrug, East Prussia, (later to be known as Barzdūnai, Lithuania). The fifth, Andy Senetsky, was taken straight to Stalag Luft IV at Grosstychow, Germany, (later to be known as Tychowo, Poland). The initial shuffling of men at Dulag Luft separated the men from each other, and they were not to see each other for a long time, even though some went to the same camps.

On May 10, 1944, Brown, Dean, Gallagher, and Rhodes all arrived at Stalag Luft VI after a long train ride inside boxcars with many other new POW's from Dulag Luft. The camp was very isolated and just a few miles off the southeastern coast of the Baltic Sea in East Prussia. The area was primarily flat with many trees and also swampy areas. The camp itself was located approximately 2 miles southeast of the town of Heydekrug. Access to the camp was by way of an unpaved road that meandered through the woods. The town of Heydekrug was located on a spur track of a railroad that ran between the towns of Tilset and Memel.

Many Allied airmen who were once the hunters searching for German targets to bomb, now found themselves playing the precarious role as the hunted under the watchful eyes of the German guard towers. - *Collection of Andrew Senetsky.*

The first POW's to arrive at Stalag Luft VI in June of 1943 were British who were being transferred from various other POW camps. The first American POW's arrived in February of 1944, and Lagar E was their home inside the Camp. Conditions at Stalag Luft VI were no different from any other German POW Camp. Poor facilities combined with inadequate food, shelter, and clothing was to become the normal way of existence. The situation never improved; it only got worse. The escape and subsequent murder of the 50 British POW's from Stalag Luft III at Sagan in March of 1944, sent shock waves throughout the entire POW Camp system. The German high command made it a point to inform every Camp that methods of escape, such as tunnel digging, would now be met with the strictest of consequences. Prior to that point some crude tunnels had been attempted at Stalag Luft VI, but none successfully breached the outside perimeter of the Camp. The incident at Sagan also brought about a more routine presence of the Gestapo to make sure that the guards fully understood how the Camps should be run. Raymond Dean remembered one fellow prisoner who could speak fluent German. He somehow acquired a German uniform and walked right out of the front gate. He also remembered one tunnel that was doing well until a Russian POW driving the "honey wagon" (a wagon used to empty the latrines) ran over the tunnel and caved it in. This brought much excitement to the guards and the usual lockdown was in place for a short time as they investigated.

Raymond Dean recalled many other things about the POW camp. His description of the meals served at the camps showed some of the hardships the prisoners suffered.

> "Our food in prison was hot water in the morning which we used to make tea or coffee which was obtained from the Red Cross parcels. A type of stew was given for dinner made with horse meat and vegetables. In the vegetables was a small dried round pea or bean, which had a little black bug in it. When you finished your stew, you had nearly two spoonfuls of little bugs. It was a standing joke in the Camp that you could tell how long a man had been a prisoner by the way he ate his stew. A newcomer would see a bug and shove his stew away, but after a few months in prison, he would neatly dip out the bugs and eat his stew. An old timer would scrape the bugs back in his stew if they tried to climb out. At night we received a potato and a ration of black bread, which was sour, but after a time we developed a taste for it."

The sports program at Stalag Luft VI was well developed, similar to that of the officer's camp at Stalag Luft III. There were many boxers originating from England, but baseball was the preferred sport for the American prisoners. The Red Cross or YMCA was able to make sports equipment available to the Camps. The German guards also welcomed this kind of activity since it gave the POW's something to do instead of thinking about how they might try to escape. A radio had been secretly packed inside one package of baseball equipment, which some POW's had quickly hidden. This radio became the lifeline to the outside world, and it was the only way that the prisoners could distinguish between the German propaganda and the true events of the War.

While Brown, Dean, Gallagher, and Rhodes were adjusting to prison life at Stalag Luft VI, Andy Senetsky was attempting to do the same at Stalag Luft IV at Grosstychow. On June 2, 1944, Senetsky decided to attempt making contact with the parents of his friend and former crew member, Bob Lalumiere, who had been wounded on April 11, 1944, and replaced by Jim Gallagher in the Sunrise Serenade's ball turret position. The POW's were allowed to write letters, but only on a postcard that could be easily read and screened by the Germans before it was sent.

> *Dear Sir - Tell Bob I am O.K. I am a prisoner of war and am treated O.K. and not wounded. Also tell him the rest of the crew is O.K. and tell him to write to me through you. Tell him to give my regards to all of the boys. I will kindly appreciate it. - Andrew Senetsky.*

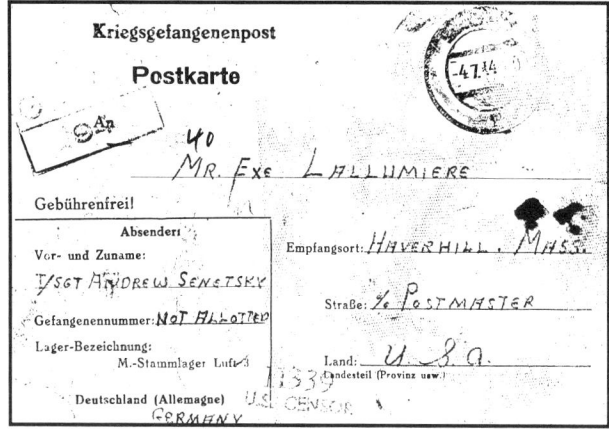

Andy Senetsky wanted to somehow let his former crew member and friend, Bob Lalumiere, know the crew was okay. The above postcard was mailed to Bob's parents from Stalag Luft IV. - Collection of Rita Lalumiere.

This letter would not reach the Lalumiere's in Massachusetts until nearly three months later on August 29, 1944. Even though Senetsky had no current knowledge of the condition of the rest of his crew at Stalag Luft III and Stalag Luft VI, he wanted Bob Lalumiere to feel that everyone from his former crew was doing fine.

In June of 1944, the POW's at Stalag Luft VI at Heydekrug became aware of the Allied invasion of France on D-Day before their guards were. When the Germans finally made an announcement on the loud speaker regarding the invasion, it was reported that the Germans had hurled the Allies back into the sea. Word of the invasion quickly spread inside the camp, and hope and excitement could be seen in everyone's eyes. The more realistic men reminded those who thought that the War was about over, that this was really just the beginning; the Germans would surely fight until the bitter end.

While the American, British, and Canadian forces were now penetrating deep into France, the Russian Army was also reclaiming lost ground that had earlier been taken by the Germans. The threat of the Russians advancing from the East sent panic throughout the entire POW Camp system since many of them were located in eastern Germany. On the one hand, the German pride refused to let themselves believe that they could be defeated by the Russians, yet on the other hand the Russian Army was coming closer and closer to the eastern-most POW camps. Finally as the noise from the Russian artillery was within range of the German POW camps, the Germans decided it was time to leave.

The evacuation of Stalag Luft VI began on July 14, 1944. Several groups left in different phases with about 2,000 American and British POW's going first. They were marched to the railroad station at Heydekrug where they were loaded into boxcars and taken north to the port city of Memel, East Prussia, (later to be known as Klaipeda, Lithuania). At Memel, the POW's were loaded into the bottom of a captured Russian ship known as the *Masuren*. The four crew members from the *Sunrise Serenade* were among those that boarded this ship that day. The *Masuren* had been used as a carrier of everything from garbage to coal; the hold was dark and filthy. The next day another group left the Camp which was comprised mostly of British POW's and approximately 100 Americans. They were likewise taken by train to Memel where they boarded another captured Russian ship known as the *Insterburg*. Another estimated 3,000 POW's from Stalag Luft VI were transported by rail to Thorn where they eventually ended up at Stalag 357 near Fallingbostel, Germany.

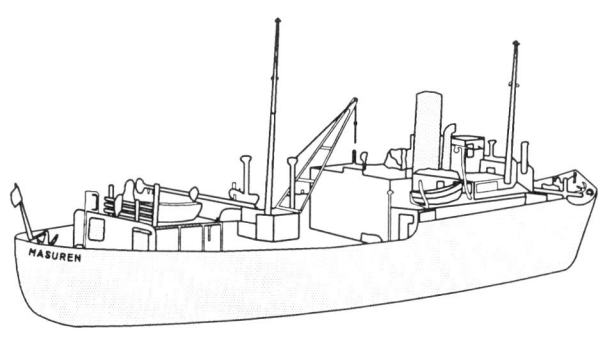

The German ship known as the *Masuren* was one of the methods of transportation used by the Germans to move Allied POW's away from the Russians. The men were locked inside the dark hold of the ship during the 56-hour journey.

The travel across the Baltic Sea inside the *Masuren* was beyond comprehension. The heat of the summer in July was unbearable as the men were crammed inside the bottom of the ship. At first there was not even room to stand up, and men began to panic for fear of suffocation. The personal belongings such as backpacks that had earlier been confiscated were now thrown down into the hold with the POW's. Trying to sort out the personal belongings in the dark was not very productive. Order was eventually established inside the ship as men began to arrange themselves so that an isle could be made. The toilet facility consisted of a bucket that was attached to a rope and continuously lowered into the hold. The movement of the sea caused many men to become sea-sick. What little food they did have inside their stomachs was vomited amidst their fellow prisoners, adding to their distress. There was no room to lie down, and any sleeping had to be done while standing. During the first day, the POW's had some limited time to go onto the deck for fresh air. One POW jumped overboard and was quickly shot by the German guards before the other POW's near him could react to possibly save him. Time outside of the hold was strictly limited from that time on. One of the British POW's who was familiar with that area of the Baltic Sea had remembered dropping hundreds of mines in the area that they were now crossing. Every scrape or banging that was heard alongside the outside of the ship was met with horror, fearing it was one of these mines. Had one of these mines been hit, every man would have drowned since they had no life jackets, and also because there wouldn't have been time to climb out of the small door to the deck. Another real threat was being attacked by Allied fighters or bombers who knew nothing about what the cargo of the ship contained. Luckily the ships did not come under fire from planes as they traveled across the Baltic Sea.

After nearly 56 hours, the *Masuren* finally docked at the city of Swinemünde, Germany, (later to be known as Świnoujście, Poland), in the early morning of July 17, 1944. The men were unloaded from the ship and placed inside railroad boxcars in the heat of the day while they waited for the other ship, the *Insterburg*, to arrive with the other POW's. The *Insterburg* finally arrived in the late afternoon of July 17th, and the men from this ship were also loaded into nearby boxcars.

The *Masuren* was renamed *Empire Anna* after the War and was possibly held under British control since the size of this ship was denied to the German navy through post-war Allied regulations until 1950. Years later it again became a German trading vessel under the name of *Fühlsbuttel*. In 1964 it was finally scrapped at Hamburg, Germany. The *Insterburg* was sunk on May 3, 1945, after running into a mine in the Kiel bay. Ironically that same day another German ship named the *Inster* was attacked by British fighter/bombers and sunk while on a voyage between Lubeck and Flensburg close to where the *Insterburg* had sunk. The attack had killed many German refugees who were fleeing the Russians.

The POW's inside the many boxcars at Swinemünde were put into shackles in pairs. These shackles were very burdensome to the already weaken prisoners. Luckily, a few of the POW's knew how to pick the locks and many shackles were removed during the train trip, and then reattached before getting out again. The trip by train was approximately 100 miles between the city of Swinemünde and a whistle stop station known as Kiefeheide. Upon arriving at Kiefeheide, the estimated 2,000 airmen soon became acquainted with their new German guards at Stalag Luft IV. Captain Walther Pickhardt and Lt. Colonel Otto Bombach were the main leaders while T/Sgt. Reinhard Fahnert was in charge of the German Security System within Stalag Luft IV. Pickhardt was a red-haired tyrannical man who had absolutely no regard for the welfare of the POW's nor the rules governing the POW Camps as spelled out in the rules of the Geneva Convention.

Travel by railroad was less than accommodating with very little light, no fresh air, and no toilet facilities. The German boxcars were commonly known as 40 & 8 cars since they were used to haul 40 men or 8 horses. Up to 60 POW's would be crammed into each car for several days. - *Collection of the author.*

The men began to unload from the boxcars on July 18, 1944, after the 24-hour ride that left them very weak, tired, and hungry. The unpaved road through the trees to Stalag Luft IV was an estimated 2 miles to an area near the town of Grosstychow, located north of the railway station. As the men began to move down the path, the string of POW's stretched to nearly the entire length. An incensed Pickhardt began screaming at the POW's to run to the camp. At first many POW's refused to listen to his orders, but soon guards along the road began to physically abuse the prisoners. Young German sailors of about 13 to 16 years of age had lined both sides of the road and affixed their bayonets to their rifles. Soon men were being stabbed in the buttocks and backs in an attempt to make them run. Mass confusion broke out among the POW's as they began to run as best they could while still being shackled to each other. Backpacks and Red Cross food packages were soon discarded as the men tried to lighten their burden. The scattered packages caused many to fall and the guards struck the POW's in the backs with their rifle butts or stabbed them with the bayonets. German Shepherd guard dogs were also unleashed upon the POW's, biting and chewing at their arms and legs. Those that fell were quickly assisted by other POW's in an attempt to rescue them before the guards came upon them. Some men lay helplessly on the ground as the dogs viciously attacked them at the orders of their young guards. The guards would yell out phrases like "This is for Frankfurt", "This is for Hamburg" and so on, as they stabbed the POW's in the back. These references were to the bombing of these German cities by the Allies. Some men later heard that Pickhardt's wife and daughter might have been killed during one of the bombing raids to Berlin. One POW had managed during the run to keep hold of a banjo that he had acquired back at Stalag Luft VI. As a German dog lunged at him, he swung the banjo, causing the dog's head to go through it breaking its neck. Luckily, the POW was able to get away from the area before any guards could determine who had done it. Raymond Dean was handcuffed to a man named Warren Wright, who had crushed his chest when he parachuted from his plane a few months earlier. He was so short of breath that Dean had to carry him part of the way, even though they were still handcuffed together. Many men suffered permanent damage to their legs and backs due to the many blows from rifle butts, bites from dogs, and bayonet stabs. The entire run up the road lasted about an hour, and the guards were relentless the entire trip. The Germans had hoped that the POW's would panic and try to run into the trees in an attempt to escape the beating of the guards and dogs. Hidden just inside the cover of the trees were German soldiers with machine guns waiting to shoot any POW's trying to escape. All of the POW's held together, and none tried to escape. This same routine of beating the POW's as they ran up the road occurred with every group of POW's coming up from the train station at Kiefeheide.

Once at the Camp, several hundred men were now bleeding and crippled from the attacks of the guards and dogs. No medical treatment was available, and the fear of getting tetanus or rabies was prevalent. The only relief the men could get was to lay out in the sun, hoping that their own weakened immune system would heal their wounds. Many men could be seen lying around inside the camp of Stalag Luft IV with their buttocks, legs, and backs exposed to the sun.

Stalag Luft IV had been opened to American airmen on May 12, 1944. Among those already being held at this camp was Andrew Senetsky who was one of the first POW's to initially be sent there. His arrival at the camp was also by way of railroad boxcars direct from the transit camp at Wetzlar. All five enlisted men of the *Sunrise Serenade* who were taken prisoner by the Germans were now all at the same camp. The camp consisted of 4 compounds with each compound having 10 large single-floor barracks. Each barrack was supposed to house up to 250 prisoners, but by December of 1944, there were at least 300 men in each barrack. The barracks each had 10 rooms with a

STALAG LUFT IV
Grosstychow

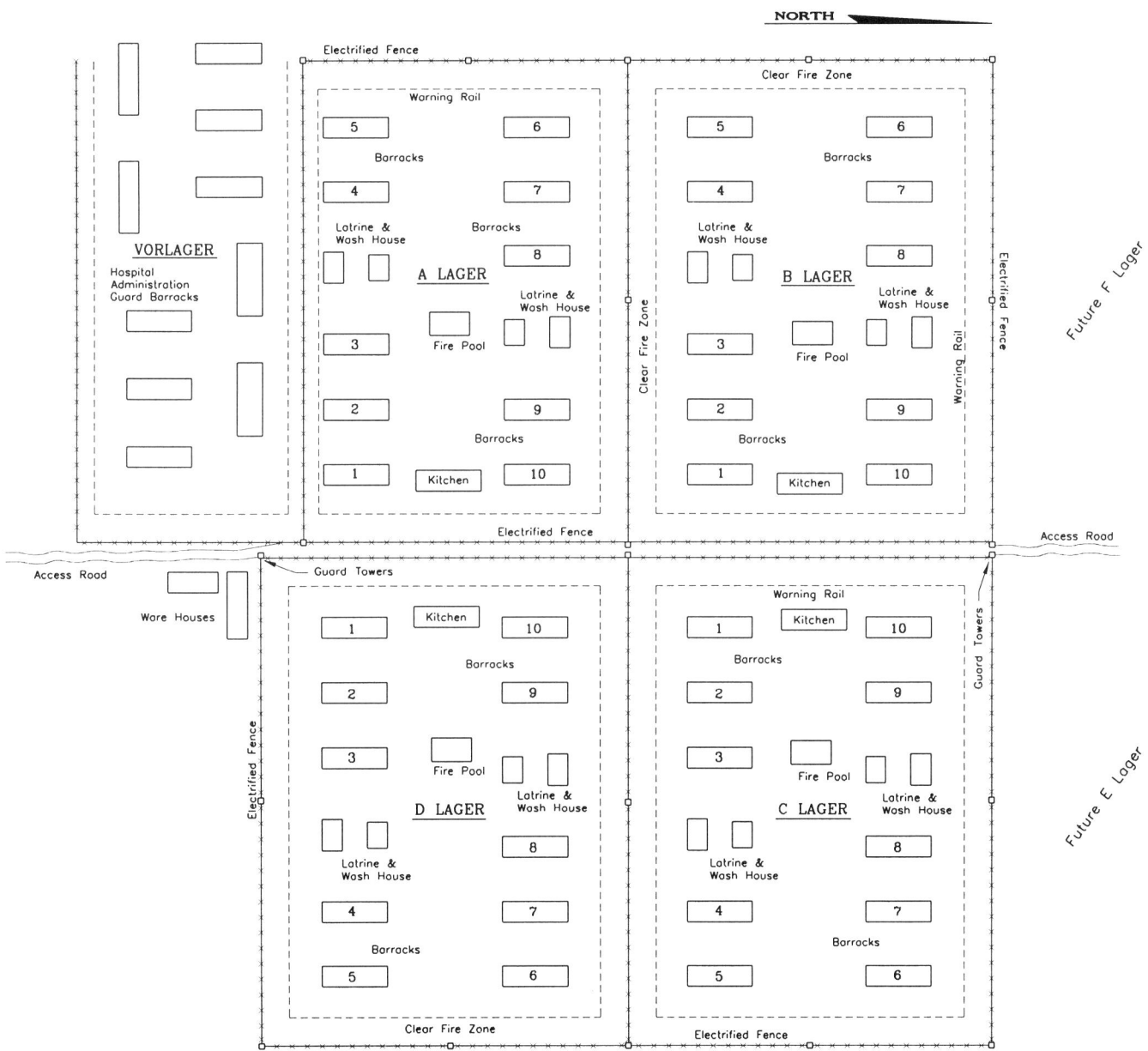

Stalag Luft IV was located at Grosstychow, Germany, and was used to hold Allied enlisted airmen. The radioman of the *Sunrise Serenade*, Andrew Senetsky, was among its first inhabitants on May 12, 1944. Later four other enlisted men of his crew would also arrive for a temporary stay. Due to the advancing Russian army, the camp was abandoned on February 6, 1945. The site of the former camp is now near Tychowo, Poland, due to changed country boundaries after the War. The above map was drawn from the best available resources including the memories of several former POW's held there, and may not be completely accurate.

central hallway running the entire length of the building. At the end of the hall was a small washroom without running water and also a pit latrine that was to be used only at night after lockdown. The rooms were approximately 15 x 25 feet and contained three tiers of bunks to accommodate 12 men along each wall. Each room had a small stove, which was fired with small coal brickettes made from coal dust. The POW's were issued only 6 to 8 of these small brickettes per day, which generated only a small amount of warmth.

Food and clothing were scarce, and men learned to ration whatever food could be obtained. If food arrived in cans, the guards would puncture each can so that it would quickly spoil if not soon eaten. The Germans feared that the prisoners would stockpile canned food for an attempted escape.

Efforts to escape through means of tunnels were attempted, but unlike some of those attempted at Stalag Luft III by the British, most of those at Stalag Luft IV were not highly organized. Though POW's did dig tunnels, the locations of such tunnels were not widely known among the other POW's in the Camp. After one particular tunnel was discovered, three German guards were said to have crawled inside to inspect it, when it suddenly collapsed at both ends, burying them alive. This tunnel was thought to have been ingeniously designed to collapse if the Germans entered it.

The barracks were generally all built on supports above the ground so that tunneling could easily be detected. Often times the guards would crawl under these barracks at night to listen to the conversations of the POW's. The prisoners in at least one barrack had saved all of their used razor blades that they were issued once every three weeks. These blades would be broken in half, and when the opportunity presented itself, a man would quickly dive under the barracks and place a blade into the wooden poles that supported the floors. This continued for some time, until one night the POW's made all kinds of noise, which caused the guards to release their dogs thinking there was a possible escape in progress. The frenzied dogs came in contact with the razor blades, and then the guards also went under the barracks to see why the dogs were yelping. The next morning blood and fur could be seen around and under the barracks, and several guards had their hands in bandages.

Although mail was a real morale booster to the POW's, it rarely came. If a package from home contained food, especially candy or cookies, it often disappeared before it left the guards' hands. Raymond Dean received his first letter from home while in Luft IV on October 10, 1944. It was his birthday that day, and it meant a great deal to receive a letter from home. Jim Gallagher had received a letter from Francis Smedley's mother while at this camp. Raymond Dean learned of Smedley's death from Jim's letter, and then sat down to write Mrs. Smedley a letter on November 17, 1944.

"Dear Mrs. Smedley, Read a letter that you wrote to Gallagher, and got your address. I am very sorry about Pappy, I don't know for sure what happened. The rest of the boys here are going to write you. We will all try and get together when we get back and talk things over. Bye, Raymond (Deenie)".

The Camp grew larger and larger as the War progressed. In July of 1944, two months after the Camp opened, the population was nearly 1,500 American airmen. By September it had grown to over 5,600 prisoners, and by December that number swelled to almost 8,300. The last official count taken in January 1945 just before the camp was evacuated was 8,708 American prisoners, 902 British prisoners, and 132 Russian prisoners. The American POW's alone would be enough airmen to fully load almost 871 Flying Fortresses with a full ten-member crew.

Andy Senetsky remembered quickly becoming an "old-timer" as he saw every new group of POW's arrive at the Camp. He and some of the other original POW's at Stalag Luft IV were part of the welcoming committee that showed the new arrivals where everything was located, and told of past policies and the tendencies of the guards. Some rules had at first been relaxed while the population was still low and manageable. One camp rule stated that the windows of the barracks were not to be used for exits. Since the doors were located at the end of the long hallways, the men would jump out the windows that were only about 4 feet off the ground. The guards had issued a few warnings, but they were evidently not taken seriously. On about June 19, 1944, a POW named Ralph Teague jumped out a window and then stood by the barracks. A guard had witnessed him go out the window and watched him for at least 5 minutes. Without warning the guard fired at Teague and killed him. After the War an investigation was conducted pertaining to his death.

Radioman Andy Senetsky was given a crude identification dog tag by the Germans upon his arrival at Stalag Luft IV. "Kgf. Lgr. 4d. Lw." translates into "POW Air Camp 4-Area D".
- *Collection of Andrew Senetsky.*

Though life at the Camp was an arduous experience, the prisoners managed to occupy their time throughout the seasons with a number of activities. During the summer and fall, the men played sports such as football or baseball outside, while a few ping-pong tables were set up indoors. Nearly every POW learned how to play cards or cribbage, which helped to pass the time. At Christmas, some decorations arrived from the YMCA. There were only enough decorations to decorate one barrack, and Raymond Dean's barrack was lucky enough to get them. Other POW's from around the camp came over to observe and enjoy the decorations.

It was about this time that many of the prisoners first became aware of a guard they had named "Big Stoop". He was like a giant, over 7 feet tall with hands twice the size of a normal man's hands. He was one of the cruelest guards the men would ever have to face. Prisoners were routinely called in for questioning and "Big Stoop" would backhand them across the face, which sent them sailing across the room. Some even claimed that he carried a stick with nails protruding from it, often striking prisoners. After the War was over, several rumors about this guard circulated. Some said he had been found in a barn with a pick in his head; others said he had been found beheaded near the railroad tracks; and one even reported seeing some ex-POW's pushing a wheelborrow down a road with his head inside it.

Tail gunner Raymond E. Dean was first processed into Stalag Luft VI where an official card was made about him. This card would travel in the German files through four different POW camps. Upon liberation he was able to find his card while searching through German records at the camp. - *Collection of Gwendolyn Dean.*

As January of 1945 arrived, the Russian Army was still advancing deeper into Germany. After much debate and hesitation, the Germans finally decided to evacuate Stalag Luft IV on February 6, 1945. Most of the men from the *Sunrise Serenade* had evidently never been aware of each other's presence at Stalag Luft IV, since they made little reference to seeing each other.

Through sharing the letter from Mrs. Smedley, Dean and Gallagher obviously knew that the other was there. Each prisoner blended in with the entire group, and as the numbers grew larger, it was not uncommon to have a once familiar face no longer be easily recognized. A prisoner's physical body also changed drastically so that a once recognizable man from the side or back was no longer recognizable. John Brown had gone into the POW camps weighing 155 pounds, and left weighing only 90 pounds.

Prison camps in the central part of Germany were being filled beyond capacity as those camps on the eastern and western fronts were being evacuated. The biggest problem facing the German command was where to take the POW's next. The prisoners from Stalag Luft IV were divided into several different groups. Raymond Dean and Andrew Senetsky, with about 3,000 of the estimated 10,000 POW's from Stalag Luft IV, were again put aboard railroad boxcars. These prisoners were evacuated shortly before the others were to begin marching west or south out of the Camp. John Brown was among the thousands to march west out of the Camp. Although the destinations of Brown, Dean and Senetsky after leaving Stalag Luft IV are known, the circumstances pertaining to Dusty Rhodes and Jim Gallagher are not as clear. It is believed they were also put aboard the railroad boxcars.

The Red Cross had the best intelligence as to the locations of the POW's on the march. Around the first part of March 1945, the American POW's were reported to be in three different regions of Germany. A group of 25,000 Americans with a total number of 80,000 POW's were scattered across a long line in southern Germany. A central line, consisting of men who were probably mostly from Stalag Luft III, numbered about 60,000. Columns of POWs moving across the northern part of Germany, including those from Stalag Luft IV, numbered in the range of 100,000 men. Sometimes these numbers were exaggerated since it was hard to distinguish marching POW's from German refugees heading in the same directions.

The railroad cars which Raymond Dean and Andrew Senetsky were aboard were packed with as many men as possible and then locked. This time there was an absence of a guard in the cars to watch the POW's. The prisoner numbers had grown so large that the Germans simply did not have enough guards to be with the men. Toilet facilities inside the cars were horrible. Usually a designated corner of the car was made for such uses, which only made conditions worse. Some men were fortunate enough to have a hole in the floor of their car to use for waste disposal purposes. The only light inside the car was from the daylight coming through the small holes in the roof. During the entire trip, the men inside the railroad cars were only allowed to have a total of two drinks of water.

THE ENLISTED MEN'S POW CAMPS
Brown, Dean, Gallagher, Rhodes, Senetsky

After being interrogated at the temporary holding site of Dulag Luft in southwest Germany, Andrew Senetsky was sent directly to Stalag Luft IV while John Brown, Raymond Dean, Jim Gallagher, and Dusty Rhodes were sent to Stalag Luft VI. After Stalag Luft VI was abandoned, all of the men were briefly together at Stalag Luft IV, but soon separated again when that camp was abandoned. Dean, Gallagher, Rhodes and Senetsky eventually ended up with the two officers of their plane, Griffin and McGrath, at Moosburg, while Brown went to a camp at Altengrabow and eventually was liberated at Bitterfeld.

The train began its slow departure from Stalag Luft IV and headed south in the direction of Berlin. The train made frequent stops because of damaged tracks due to Allied bombs and German movement of troops and equipment to the battle fronts. As the train pulled into Berlin, a bombing raid on the city had just started. The guards and railroad personnel left the train sitting in the yard with the POW's still aboard as they headed for the bomb shelters. The noise from the heavy bombs pounding the German capital city was deafening, and the POW's inside the dark cars could only wait helplessly until it was over. Fortunately, the bombing targets at this particular date were in another area of the city. During the transporting of prisoners in railroad cars, the Germans never marked the top of the cars to alert Allied bomber and fighter planes of their contents. The Germans reasoned that if the Allies would kill their own comrades by mistake, it would be less burdensome for the Germans to keep guarding them. Also, there would be no repercussions for the Germans if the Allies mistakenly did the killing.

Seven days after leaving Stalag Luft IV, Raymond Dean and Andy Senetsky with other fellow POW's arrived in southern Germany at Stalag XIIID, near Nuremberg. The conditions at Nuremberg weren't any better. The camp was filthy, not fit to inhabit. Ironically, Dean & Senetsky were now at the same camp where their fellow crewmen, George Griffin and John McGrath, were located. Around the same time, Jim Gallagher and Dusty Rhodes may have also arrived at this camp.

As the American Army closed in on Stalag XIIID, the Germans began to abandon yet another camp. By this time the War was decidedly already over for the Germans, but they continued the shuffling of POW's nonetheless. The Germans evacuated Nuremberg in early April 1945, with thousands of POW's once again finding themselves traveling down the back roads of Germany. The roads were littered with abandoned equipment and food parcels. German refugees were traveling in every direction not knowing which way to escape the approaching Russian and American armies. German troops were likewise in a state of confusion, either retreating or hurrying to the front lines, whichever their commanders dictated. The destination for the POW's, who now numbered well over 10,000, was Stalag VIIA at Moosburg. This camp was in extreme southeast Germany and was one of the last places the Allies had not overtaken. During this march, the German guards lost control of the columns and many POW's simply walked away. For many others, the relative safety of staying together was preferred since the end of the War was eminent. The German gestapo was no longer stopping and interrogating escaped POW's, but rather shooting them on sight.

The distance to Moosburg was about 90 miles. Over 30 miles was traveled the first day. Raymond Dean was so sure that they were about to be liberated that he traded his shoes for a pair of sheepskin lined English flying boots. This trade proved to be a mistake, since he blistered his feet so severely that the entire bottom of each foot was one large blister. Only by keeping in motion was he able to withstand the pain.

Communication with the Allied fighting forces was not yet synchronized, so a few American fighter planes strafed the POW columns, thinking that they were German soldier movements. Fortunately the many trees along the roads offered places to dive into as the planes dove down on the columns. Soon, reports of the positions of these POW columns were reported back to headquarters on a daily basis, and they were no longer mistaken for Germans.

Food was obtained in any manner possible. Farmhouses were regular stops to scavenge for whatever was available. Raymond Dean remembered coming upon one farmhouse.

> "We then found wheat in a barn and took a can full. We found four eggs and by pushing the pigs away from the trough, we retrieved some boiled potatoes. A German guard came around the corner, but turned the other way and acted as if he didn't see us. We returned to our group and I was always ashamed of the way I had acted. One friend said 'Deany, may I have some?' And I growled at him. I gave him some later, but not willingly. We were on the move so I discovered I could eat eggs raw. I downed two of them."

As the POW's approached Moosburg, the men had to cross the Danube River. The bridge, although still standing, was scattered with American bombs, apparently duds when they were dropped. Raymond Dean remembered having to step over them as they crossed the bridge. After all of the POW's had crossed, the bridge was exploded by the German army who was busy setting up artillery in a last ditch effort to stop the American advance.

Stalag VIIA at Moosburg, Germany, would be the final POW camp for six members of the *Sunrise Serenade* crew.
- Collection of Andrew Senetsky.

As the POW's arrived, the atmosphere around Stalag VIIA was full of the sounds of bombs being dropped and heavy artillery being fired from both sides. The air was full of American fighter planes that continually flew over the Camp while looking for targets. Any presence of German fighter planes had long been removed by the superior American forces who now ruled the skies. Every day the sounds of battle drew closer and closer until April 29, 1944, when a plane flew in low and the pilot wiggled its wings at the gazing POW's. Soon more and more planes flew in low, and then in the distance American tanks could be seen advancing. The German guards threw down their rifles to the POW's and now the roles were suddenly reversed. A brief exchange of gunfire between the American forces and the retreating Germans sent the POW's scrambling for cover on the ground. Raymond Dean remembered the final stages just before the camp was liberated:

> "One of the American tanks rumbled up to the fence and knocking it down, drove into the camp. They threw open the hatch and one of the occupants yells, 'Are any of you S.O.B.'s hungry?' Somebody yelled back, 'Why you dog-faced bastard, what do you think? What in the hell took you so long?' They started throwing out K-Rations and as the other tanks came up, we commenced to have a feast. I don't believe a person can express the feelings of a group of liberated prisoners with mere words. They commenced rounding up the Germans and asked if any of them had given us a bad time. There were a few of them who were just plain mean and ornery; these they roughed up a bit and then took them away to some place to hold as prisoners".

Long lines of American C-47 transport planes waited to evacuate thousands of the now ex-POW's from Stalag VIIA. The next stop would be Camp Lucky Strike for the men to rehabilitate before coming home. - *Collection of Andrew Senetsky.*

During the same time that Dean, Gallagher, Rhodes, and Senetsky were traveling through the various POW camps, John Brown had been separated into a different group of POW's who had begun a forced march across Germany.

Upon leaving Stalag Luft IV, Brown and thousands of other POW's had been forced to take a different route than those who had been loaded into railroad boxcars. The first day outside of the camp felt rather refreshing to most of the Kriegies, - the German name for a POW. They were glad to be away from the enclosures of barbed wire and were thankful for a change of scenery. As night-time came, the men were herded into a barn so tightly that there was not enough room for anyone to lie down. After a few days, almost all of the men had blistered and frostbitten feet. With the absence of sharp instruments to break the blisters, the men broke them with their fingernails and then tried their best to keep them clean. Some frostbite turned to gangrene which resulted in having to have feet amputated some even resulted in death. The German guards were equally weakened and sore with not much more provisions than their prisoners had. Soon the accumulated Red Cross parcels ran out. Water also became scarce. Every time the POW's marched through a town, they had to endure looking at the town well, while the guards threatened to shoot them if they tried to take any water. Often the men resorted to eating snow, or possibly getting water from a pond or lake. Under better circumstances, water obtained from a lake could be boiled first to remove any harmful bacteria in it.

At first the men thought that the marching would be only for a few days, but as each day came and went, it became obvious that they would be on the road for a long time. During the day, the men watched the thousands of American bombers with their trailing vapor trails heading for various targets. At night the British bombers could be heard as they likewise sought out prime German targets. The accommodations at night were usually in barns that hadn't been cleaned out in several years. The floors were usually just piles of manure that the POW's had to sleep on. The barns did, however, provide an occasional meal such as some wheat, livestock feed, or even stored vegetables. Usually the guards threatened to shoot any POW that took anything resembling food from the barns, so it was done rather quickly when the guards were not looking. The grain was usually full of rat and mice droppings and many POW's who were not accustomed to conditions outside of city life were said to have eaten quite a few of the droppings, thinking they were some type of grain. Others resorted to eating mice and rats, which often had to be eaten raw since a fire could not be made to cook them. Others enjoyed a meal of dog or cat meat while many others chose to eat grass. Many German farmers probably wondered what had happened to their dogs and cats as the Kriegies moved through the area. John Brown summed up his hunger for food in the following statement:

> "I never thought I would ever dig in a manure pile for something to eat, but if you get hungry enough, you will, and I did".

Many times the Germans refused to let anyone stop marching, not even to relieve themselves. A few men decided that they just had to stop and relieve themselves and were shot in the back of the head. From then on, the POW's had no choice but to go in their trousers. Dysentery was so widespread, they couldn't help themselves. Most POW's did not have a chance to bathe themselves of their filth for several months, until they were liberated. Many prisoners just simply couldn't continue the journey due to starvation and exhaustion. It is widely believed that most of these stragglers were killed, since very few were ever accounted for after the War. At day's end, the guards would divide the groups up into 150 or 200 men and place them inside barns that were generally all located in the vicinity of each other. The men were only allowed to sleep on the floor even though there were usually lofts full of hay or straw that would have made for better accommodations for sleeping. The Germans did not want the "filthy POW's" to contaminate the hay. Some men had tried to hide in the hay if the opportunity presented itself, but the Germans would affix their bayonets to their rifles and begin stabbing into the hay if they suspected someone was in there. Men usually huddled together and slept in pairs to help preserve body heat. The large group of marching men that John Brown was among had zig-zagged and wandered their way all across northern Germany, finally ending up south of Hamburg in the town of Uelzen on March 28, 1945. The distance traveled by foot since leaving Stalag Luft IV had been well over 350 miles. The men who were originally told before leaving Stalag Luft IV to prepare for only a 3-day march, had endured a march of 50 days.

The POW's, including John Brown, were then loaded onto boxcars at the town of Uelzen, where they were crammed together as much as 80 men per car. These old cars were designed to carry up to 40 men or 8 horses and were commonly referred to as "Forty & Eight" cars. They were much smaller than the present-day normal American boxcar. The Kriegies were once again handcuffed in pairs as they were put into the boxcars. As was done earlier on the trip by train from Swinemunde to Kiefheide, the prisoners removed the handcuffs. The instrument used to unlock the shackles was a key that was used to open powdered milk cans. John Brown described this useful little tool in this way:

> "Every Kriege worth his salt had at least one Klim can key. The Red Cross included a tin of powdered milk called 'Klim' which was milk spelled backwards. The Klim can key was attached to the tin for use in opening the tin. These little keys came in handy for lots of things. After we left Stalag IV, we were at one point loaded onto 'Forty and Eight' box cars (World War I type), only with us it was all they could cram into one car. Each two men were handcuffed together, but as soon as the doors were closed, out came those handy little Klim can keys and off came the handcuffs. They made excellent lock picks. I'm not sure if the Germans ever figured out how it happened."

The powdered milk came in 1 pound tins and was mixed with water. One POW described the mixture made from the powdered milk as tasting like rancid chalk. The prisoners eventually became accustomed to it and enjoyed it. The same could be said for the sour bread.

The right waist gunner, John G. Brown, endured over 350 miles of marching as well as over 250 miles of travel inside filthy railroad cars after leaving Stalag Luft IV. Upon liberation he weighed only 90 lbs. - *Collection of the author.*

Not all of the POW's were put aboard boxcars at Uelzen. Many continued to march north and east from Uelzen to the vicinity of Hamburg for another month until they were finally liberated. After a three-day and 140-mile journey by rail, John Brown and thousands of other POW's arrived at Stalag XIA at Altengrabow, Germany, on March 30, 1945. This small town was southwest of Berlin where the last stronghold of the German army was taking place to protect their capital.

At Stalag XIA there were prisoners originating from many different countries. Just about every nationality fighting in the War was represented there with a mixture of Russians, Indians, Hindus, Ghurkas, Poles, along with the familiar American, Canadians, and British. The latrines at Altengrabow consisted of crude slit trenches in the open. Many of the housing facilities were simply tents erected to house the many POW's now crammed into the camp. The only reason for stopping was because the Germans did not know what to do next. This gave the prisoners a much-needed time to rest The stay at Stalag XIA, however, was short lived, as the Germans once again decided to evacuate yet another POW camp. At this time the Russian forces were already attempting to take control of Berlin and the American forces were likewise closing in on the area. The Germans refused to give up, and on April 12th, the marching resumed in a southerly direction. By this time, most of the blisters on their feet had turned to calluses, and the weather was becoming more tolerable with spring arriving. The southward march continued for 14 more days and about 110 miles amidst retreating German forces going north toward Berlin.

The POW's crossed the Elbe River on April 26, 1945, at about 3:00 p.m. and walked into the hands of the 104th Timberwolve Tank Division of the United States 6th Army. The town was Bitterfeld, Germany, and ended 600 miles of traveling which had started three months earlier. At Bitterfeld, John Brown and his fellow liberated soldiers were taken to a school building to obtain food and rest. Most had endured those 600 miles of marching and travel by train while continuously on the move. The next day they were taken by truck to Halle, Germany, where they were deloused and then given new clothes for a plane ride to Reims, France. At Reims, every ex-POW was given the opportunity to send a free telegram home to their loved ones in the States.

Most of the other Americans who had been taken prisoner by the Germans were taken to Camp Lucky Strike at LeHavre, France. This camp was a huge tent city of ex-POW's arriving from the newly liberated camps all across Germany. Some men spent up to a month or more while their bodies were reconditioned to food, and they received medical treatment. The food given to the men was limited portions of eggnog, chicken, lean beef, milk, and hard candy. Many men had to be restrained from stuffing themselves with food since their bodies were not yet conditioned to receive a normal-sized meal. At least 20% of the ex-POW's were given injections of thiamin and niacin and also transfusions of blood and plasma. Some men had lost over 100 pounds since becoming a prisoner. If these young men had not been in the prime of their life, and in top physical shape before they became POW's, they would never have survived.

From LeHavre they were eventually put aboard ships for the journey back home to the United States. The estimated number of American POW's held by the Germans was around 85,000 men. This number combined with well over 100,000 British soldiers, countless Russian soldiers and many other nationalities made Germany one big prison camp. One of Hitler's last orders was to have all POW's murdered before they could be liberated. Fortunately many of the guards knew very well that their own countrymen were being well taken care of by the Western Allies, so they never followed through on this order.

While the majority of the American and British POW's were captured on the Western Front, many Germans were captured by the Russian Army on the Eastern Front. Thousands of these German POW's have never been accounted for to this day. The Germans and Russians were extremely brutal in their treatment of each other, especially in terms of soldiers taken prisoner. Some accounts state that up to 80% of all Germans taken prisoner by the Russians died in captivity; likewise 60% of the Russians taken prisoner by the Germans died in captivity. These numbers are hard to validate since the people of Germany did not have their own government until many years after the War, and were in no position to protest. Russia did nothing in terms of resolving the matter. In the years after the War, the United States compiled numbers on the Germans who were taken prisoner by the Russians. This number exceeded what the Russians would admit by nearly 1.7 million. As late as 1956, some Germans taken prisoner during World War II were still being released from Russia.

A group of unidentified Allied soldiers proudly display just one of the many souvenirs they would bring home from their ordeal in Europe. The reign of terror inflicted by the mighty German army had come to an end. - *Collection of Andrew Senetsky.*

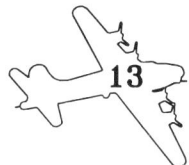

The Tiger's Tale

While many of his former crew of the *Sunrise Serenade* had been taken prisoner by the Germans, Robert "Tiger Bob" Lalumiere had been patiently waiting to recover from the April 11, 1944, incident in which he had been wounded in the ball turret. The May 1, 1944, crash of the *Sunrise Serenade* abruptly put an end to Lalumiere's hopes of someday returning to his crew.

The emotional pain of not being able to join his crew as they left without him for each new bombing mission was much worse than the physical pain from the wound to his right leg. Lalumiere also wondered if his replacement aboard the plane, Jim Gallagher, might possibly become his permanent replacement, requiring him to eventually finish his tour with another crew. One thing was certain, Lalumiere would not finish his tour of duty with the men with whom he had trained and flew combat missions. After the crew left for every new mission, Lalumiere remained at Deopham Green and prayed that his friends would return safely. Seven times the *Sunrise Serenade* and its crew left and then returned to inform Lalumiere of all that they had encountered. The missions seemed to be getting easier, since fewer planes were getting shot down. In the eleven bombing missions flown by the 452nd Bomb Group after Lalumiere had received his wound, only four planes from his Group had failed to return.

The May 1, 1944, mission to Brussels that brought down the *Sunrise Serenade* started out for Lalumiere like the previous ones in which he had not been a member of the crew. He would chat with the crew to find out where their target destination was, help get their flight gear together, and then wave to them as they boarded the plane and took off down the runway. Lalumiere was now able to walk around, so it would be very soon when he could again join the crew, possibly even the next mission.

As the planes began to return on the evening of May 1st around 8:30 p.m., Tiger Bob was anxiously waiting to catch a glimpse of the *Sunrise Serenade*. One by one the planes came in, but after failing to see the *Sunrise Serenade* as one of the first planes to land, he began to worry. He soon learned details from airmen aboard other planes about what had happened. Lalumiere stood on the tarmac in disbelief and wept as he now knew he might possibly never see his former crew again. He eventually headed back to his nissen hut while trying to obtain as much information as possible from various sources. The conflicting reports regarding the fate of his pilot, Francis Smedley, were not comforting. Airmen were trying to substantiate what they had seen, while also trying to hold out some glimmer of hope that he may have survived the crash.

While sorting through the personal items of his missing crew members, Lalumiere came across Harry Shoffner's diary which had been kept since February 6, 1944. Items belonging to missing airmen were supposed to be later shipped to their parents back in the United States, but often items seemed insignificant and were never returned. Lalumiere realized the importance of the diary and held it tightly, hoping that it would not be taken by another airman or thrown out.

Bob Lalumiere resumed his role in the ball turret aboard the *Silver Shed House* with a different crew after the *Sunrise Serenade* and his original crew had been shot down.
- *Collection of Sylvester Petri.*

Bob Lalumiere was soon assigned to the ball turret position on a plane known as the *Silver Shed House*. This plane was a newer plane which had come from the production plant in its natural metal color so the name was fitting. It had replaced the plane known as the *Shed House Mouse*, which was involved in a disabling incident on March 20, 1944. The pilot of the *Silver Shed House*, Jim Reynolds, was a well-respected and proven pilot within the 452nd Bomb Group. His crew often referred to their leader as "Big Jim". The *Silver Shed House* was in fact the plane on which Lalumiere had received his wound while substituting on the mission to Rostock, Germany, on April 11, 1944. Coincidentally, Jim Gallagher, who had taken over the duties in the ball turret position for Lalumiere on the *Sunrise Serenade*, had been originally assigned to Reynold's crew who were organized on April 1, 1944.

As the bombing missions continued, the plane known as the *Kickapoo Joy Juice* became the next victim of the Germans on May 8th. This plane had been flying off the right wing of the *Sunrise Serenade* when it was shot down. This was another loss for Lalumiere since the crew of this plane had shared the same hut as the crew of the *Sunrise Serenade*. In one week Tiger Bob had lost eleven friends with whom he had once spent a lot of time at their base. All airmen aboard the *Kickapoo Joy Juice* were lucky enough to escape the burning wreckage before it crashed into a street near Runingen, Germany, almost precisely where a B-24 Liberator had crashed the same day. The B-17 formation had been attacked by seventeen FW-190 enemy fighters coming from the one-o'clock position. The entire crew was taken prisoner and then their German guards stopped their transport vehicles by the wreckage of the plane for the crew to see. Soon the airmen met up with their fellow friends at the various POW camps, including those of the *Sunrise Serenade*, who were surprised to see them so soon.

The *Kickapoo Joy Juice* became the next plane from the 452nd Bomb Group to be shot down after the *Sunrise Serenade* had gone down. Ironically the enlisted men from both planes shared the same barracks. - *Collection of Dan Wilkerson.*

Later in the day on March 8th a second mission was flown; a plane, known as *My Achin' Back*, flown by Lt. Eugene A. Lohman took a direct hit of flak in the nose, and instantly killed the bombardier, 1st Lt. Robert L. Barrett. The impact pitched Barrett forward onto the bombsight and the bombs were subsequently salvoed. Fortunately the crew was over Cherbourg along the French coast, so they were able to limp back to England and land away from the enemy.

On the evening of May 10, 1944, Bob Lalumiere's new crew was alerted that they would fly the next morning. During the night, Tiger Bob wondered if he would still be skillful at managing his guns in the ball turret after being on the ground for an entire month. The next morning the crew was briefed on the target for that day, and to Lalumiere's amazement the target was Brussels, the site where the *Sunrise Serenade* had been lost. Following a successful mission, the crew returned safely to Deopham Green. They went to the "Hot News" briefing room, and then settled down in their huts for the evening. Lalumiere opened Shoffner's diary and began to write the events of that day:

> *"May 11, 1944 - Mission to Brussels was just what the doctor ordered for revenge. The flak was not bad, and we did a masterful job on the target. This was my first mission after the hospital. It was practically a Milk Run."*

This mission was memorable for the entire 452nd Bomb Group because fellow airman John S. "Herb" Steiner became the first man from that Group to complete his required 30 missions. Herb was flying aboard the plane known as *Inside Curve,* whose radioman, John Collier, had once been part of the *Sunrise Serenade's* crew during training.

The next day's mission was much different because the 452nd Bomb Group received their greatest loss of planes and crew members since becoming operational. The target for the May 12, 1944, mission was the synthetic oil factories at Brux, Czechoslovakia. The German *Luftwaffe* was waiting to attack the large formations of Flying Fortresses, which were comprised of many different Bomb Groups but particularly hit those of the 452nd the hardest. A group of about thirty-five Me-109 German fighters approached the formations to within 1,000 yards and then suddenly turned around and flew in the opposite direction. The P-51 Mustangs that were providing fighter support for the B-17's went after the German fighters, who later proved to be only decoys. The *Luftwaffe*, with many other fighters, then attacked the entire 45th Combat Wing, mainly from a head-on position and with other new flying tactics. Some estimates tallied the total number of fighters to be around three hundred FW-190's and Me-109's that came so close that the enemy pilots could be clearly seen in their cockpits. Many of the fighters were also shooting the feared 20mm shells, which burst all around and into the planes. The sky was filled with wreckage from planes along with many parachutes from both American airmen and also those of the German fighter pilots. The German parachutes had a yellow tint to them, so they were easily distinguished from the white ones of the Americans. Bob Lalumiere later wrote about this mission.

> *"May 12, 1944 - Mission to Brux, which was practically on the Russian border. We really caught hell and lost 16 ships. Lt. William Denham came back on one engine and got 9 fighters at least. Good crew. We were hit by 250 enemy fighters and it was rough. I don't mean maybe. Big Jim is really a calm and cool man like Smed was. Denham's crew shot down 16 fighters in two days - no "maybe's" in there. Leaves us with*

approximately 10 original crews left. Let's give them a real battle men. I thank God and Virgin Mary for protecting us again, as the escorts were snafued. P.S. - I must try to write some thoughts about my crew going down soon. I break down every time I think of it. Hurry back soon boys. I pray for you every night and I know the Lord is helping you boys. I'd give a million dollars for every flak gunner's hide in Brussels. How I miss my honey tonight."

Even though Lalumiere had just made it through a very tough battle with a new crew, his mind was still clearly on his missing friends from the *Sunrise Serenade*. It would take a little more time before he would feel the same comfort with his new crew that he had experienced with his former crew.

The mission to Brux had been well over 10 hours in duration, which at that time was the longest raid the 8th Air Force had ever attempted. As Lalumiere mentioned in his diary, only ten of the original crews to arrive with the 452nd Bomb Group in January were still flying. Among the planes of the 452nd Bomb Group to be shot down that day were *You've Had It, Princess Pat, Lucky Lady, My Achin' Back, The Punched Fowl, The Hard Way, Lady Stardust II, Duchess, Why Worry, Why Worry II*, and at least four other planes. Most of the losses were direct results of being hit by the guns from the German fighters; however, *You've Had It*, piloted by 2nd Lt. Otis Stogsdill, was struck by the falling wing of 2nd Walter V. Naylor's plane. The plane flown that day by 1st Lt. William E. Denham, named *The Big Noise*, sustained heavy damage. (Denham and the other three officers of his plane had once shared the nissen hut with the officers of the *Sunrise Serenade*.) As they were making their way back to England, Denham ordered the crew to throw everything out of the plane to lighten its load. The right waist gunner misunderstood the command and bailed out over enemy territory and was taken prisoner. The rest of the crew of *The Big Noise* made it safely back to England. The 96th Bomb Group, also flying in the 45th Combat Wing with the 452nd, also had a very rough day, losing 12 of their Flying Fortresses. The 8th Air Force lost a total of 46 heavy bombers that day, and had 412 others damaged during bombing missions to various targets. The loss of life for the 452nd Bomb Group on May 12th was 30 airmen who were confirmed killed. Nearly 90 other airmen were taken prisoner, and many others were badly wounded. The total number of airmen listed as "Missing In Action" for the entire 8th Air Force that single day was 430.

On May 16, 1944, four days after the terrible mission to Brux, Tiger Bob found time to record another entry into his diary.

"May 16, 1944 - No mission today. I'm just getting my full mind back from the bad luck of May 1st, Harry "Old Boy", so I'll try to carry on as Smed would want me to. I have flown two missions with old Jim Reynolds since my mishap. He's a good boy Smed, although you're still my pilot and I must carry on for the Serenaders."

The reference to Harry was in regard to carrying on the work that his former crew member of the *Sunrise Serenade*, Harry Shoffner, had started with the diary. Lalumiere also wrote about Francis Smedley, his former pilot, even though he didn't realize he had died in the crash.

During a mission to Berlin on May 19, 1944, the plane known as *Junior* from the 452nd Bomb Group was hit by flak and crashed near Althuttendorf, Germany. The entire crew, under the direction of 2nd Lt. Stephen A. Gaal, was taken prisoner. The same day another 452nd plane named *Rosalie Ann* was struck by another plane flying in a different formation. The impact cut the tail section off of the *Rosalie Ann* and forced the crew to bail out. Unfortunately two crew members could not escape the centrifugal force of the spiraling plane and were killed. Both of these crews were from the same Squadron as Lalumiere, the 730th, so more familiar faces were now gone.

The original crew aboard *Woolf Pack* were lucky and finished their required 30 missions in May of 1944. The plane would later be shot down with a different crew. The tail of *Smokey Liz II* is at the left of the photo. - *Collection of Irwin Math.*

The next mission credited to Bob Lalumiere occurred on May 23, 1944, and was to the Bretigny-Troye area located east of Paris, where the airfields and railroad installations were bombed. Lalumiere and the rest of his experienced crew were now flying as the lead plane in the formations. With only a few weeks until the secret D-Day assault upon the shores of France, almost every bombing campaign was now being aimed at crippling the Germans' ability to move men and equipment once the ground attack would begin. Only two planes from the 452nd Bomb Group had been lost due to enemy attacks, since the terrible losses at Brux eleven days earlier. The skies over much of Europe were beginning to reveal fewer enemy aircraft, so there was some relief for the bomber crews. The following account is from Lalumiere's diary:

> "May 23, 1944 - Mission to Troy, which is south of Paris, France. We hit the target of last resort which had already been bombed. We finished off the last two hangars. We led the entire 8th Air Force in and out with Jim Reynolds. This was a Milk Run, although it was fairly long. No one was hurt. Last target, the one we bombed, was an airfield in France. It no longer exists as of this date."

During the next two missions for the 452nd Bomb Group, Lalumiere and the crew of the *Silver Shed House* remained at the base. However, other crews from the Group returned to Berlin on May 24th to let the German high command know that they were not letting up on the pressure at any location. Even the once highly feared and fortified capital city of Berlin was now becoming routine for many of the crews. The 452nd Bomb Group did not lose any planes over Berlin, but the 8th Air Force lost 33 planes from various other Groups. The mission to Strasbourg, Germany, on May 27, 1944, resulted in a plane piloted by 2nd Lt. Milton M. Mard having to crash-land in France due to mechanical problems. Most of Mard's crew were also aboard one of the planes to go down on the fateful mission to Brux, in which they ditched their plane in the English Channel and returned to duty. This time, however, six of the crew were taken prisoner, but four managed to escape to Switzerland and evade capture.

The 452nd Bomb Group continued to pound the enemy on a daily basis at targets primarily in France, with fewer losses of planes and crew. On May 26th, John Collier aboard *Inside Curve* finished his missions and prepared to leave. His departure was another loss for Lalumiere, since he and Collier had been friends during their training days in the States.

Even Sunday was not reserved as a day of rest, so the enemy could not have any chance to regroup. The Sunday mission of May 28th had the crew of the *Silver Shed House* traveling to Magdeburg, Germany. The long and tiresome flight saw very meager flak, but those manning the guns on the ground were very accurate. One piece of flak barely missed Tiger Bob in the ball turret and came up through the right window of the plane, also just missing Sylvester Petri who was the right waist gunner. Petri had earlier been a waist gunner on *Invictus* and had switched to Jim Reynolds' crew just four days before his former crew were shot down. The mission to Magdeburg was Lalumiere's 19th mission, so he was just about caught up with others on this crew who had completed 20 missions.

During the flight his thoughts again turned to his former crew as the formation flew over Brussels, which had been the site of the *Sunrise Serenade's* crash. The Group hit a Ju-88 supply depot and destroyed it so well that they were given high praises from their commanding officers for their accomplishment.

The following day brought rest for Lalumiere and the rest of his crew. As Lalumiere was resting and still thinking about his close call with flak the previous day, other crews from their Group flew a mission to Leipzig, Germany. The flak during this mission had more devastating results than the previous day causing three of the Group's planes to go down. The crew of *The Round Tripper* bailed out after their plane struck another B-17 while under heavy enemy fighter attacks and was later hit by flak. Six members of this crew escaped while the other four were taken prisoner. The crew of *Princess Pat II* likewise bailed out after their plane was disabled by flak. One crew member whose parachute failed to open was killed. Another member of this crew was struck by flak and died while descending in his parachute. 2nd Lt. Stanley Lowell was piloting a veteran B-17 plane from the Group which his crew had inherited from another crew who had finished their tour. This unnamed plane was hit by friendly fire, which eventually caused three engines to shut down. Lowell and his crew crash-landed in a Belgian meadow near Grand Leez as two young Belgian boys on their bicycles stopped to witness the event. Lowell quickly obtained all the important documents inside the plane and burned them. The Germans soon arrived and took the entire crew prisoner before any members of the Belgian Underground could hide the crew.

One of Bob Lalumiere's closest friends after the loss of his former crew became Sylvester "Pete" Petri, who was a waist gunner on the *Silver Shed House*. Petri is shown posing on his bunk at their base. - *Collection of Sylvester Petri.*

On May 30, 1944, Lalumiere and his crew participated in the 452nd Bomb Group's mission to Reims, France. The main targets for the entire 8th Air Force that day were the industrial targets in Germany and railroad marshalling yards in Belgium and France. The *Silver Shed House* led the Group to their target at Reims where they encountered a large barrage of flak but were able to turn to the side of it and eventually bomb the railroad yards.

Three days later, Lalumiere again flew over the skies of Europe. With the planned D-Day invasion now only a few days away, both aircrews and ground crews of the Air Force were working around the clock. The Allied leaders were hoping that every important enemy airfield or marshalling yard would be struck before the invasion began. The following account is from Lalumiere's diary and would be the last time he took time to write down his thoughts.

> "Friday - June 2, 1944 - Mission to Bologne, France. 'Milk Run Deluxe'. Two ground rockets and 11 puffs of flak. Hit the heavy coastal guns I hope. Very chunky. Used P.F.F. ship. My 21st mission. Sure wish the boys were here for this last one. I'm pretty well confused on what to do after I complete this tour, if the Almighty permits. We're really getting a dirty rotten deal. Guess a gunner isn't appreciated no matter what. Hope I'm wrong. Miss everyone tonight."

The operation's officer at the base apparently had told some of the B-17 gunners in the Group that they would have to continue to fly until the War was over. At this point Petri had completed 25 of his required 30 missions, and Lalumiere was at 24. The reference to the gunners not being appreciated in Lalumiere's diary entry of June 2nd may have been from a forewarning of this order, and was probably the reason that he had quit writing entries into his own diary. All of the gunners had a "I don't give a damn" attitude according to Petri after that announcement was made. Thankfully the order turned out to be false, and may have started as a rumor that had been retold so many times that its true meaning had been lost.

On June 2, 1944, Bob Lalumiere and his crew flew a B-17 equipped with a PFF (Pathfinder Force) device that allowed them to bomb targets by using radar. The radar device is fitted where the ball turret would normally be located. The plane in this photo is *Johnny Reb*. - Collection of Irwin Math.

The 452nd Bomb Group, as well as the other Groups stationed in England, were now flying multiple missions every day to different targets. Part of the Group would be assigned to one target, while the other part would be flying to another one. The fortified coasts of France were heavily bombed with the hope that the soldiers crossing the English Channel on ships would face less resistance from the Germans.

On June 5th, Lalumiere and his crew returned to Bologne, France, to bomb more railroad yards and airfields. These missions were usually just over 2 hours in duration, and the crews loved them. The short bombing missions to nearby targets on the French coast were leading up to something big, and everyone was speculating on what it could be.

On D-Day, June 6, 1944, the 452nd Bomb Group flew three different missions. One was to Caen, France, and the other two were to Argentan, France. One of those missions that day is recalled in a diary kept by a fellow crew member of Lalumiere aboard the *Silver Shed House* named Sylvester Petri.

> "Invasion Mission To Coast. Briefed at 10:30 p.m. We suspected something, but were sure after we were briefed. "D-Day". We took off at 2:00 a.m. and assembled into formation. While assembling in the dark we could see flashes to the southwest - battle ships firing on shore batteries - everyone a bundle of excitement, but no one was talking. Bombs Away at 6:59 a.m. - about 20 minutes before the troops landed on the shore. We saw rockets while flying over the target coast. I'm sure glad we had a hand in this invasion. We had only 3 hours sleep, but were still waiting to go out again. The radio has been going all day - bombers are leaving here every 6 or 8 hours. May the "Good Lord" have mercy on our "Souls". This is a day for prayer alright. I'm glad we're 17,000 feet above all that "Hell". The weather is getting bad for flying, so I'll try to get some sleep."

On June 8th, the Group bombed the railroad bridges at Tours, France, hopefully to slow down the German reinforcements trying to reach Normandy. The weather that day was absolutely terrible with a cloud ceiling estimated to be at only 150 feet. The Bomb Group also flew missions on June 10th, 11th, and 12th, but Lalumiere and the crew of the *Silver Shed House* did not take part in these.

On June 14th, the *Silver Shed House* crew was again airborne and flew to Brussels where they bombed an important airfield with fragmentation bombs. After the bombs had been released, it was noticed that one had become hung up on the catwalk in the bomb bay. After some struggle from the crew's radio operator, Bob Hearn, it was finally freed and tossed out. The mission was considered an easy one, but some accurate flak was encountered along the way. The plane's navigator,

1st Lt. Joe Olson, completed his 30th mission on that day and began his preparations to leave the War and return to the States.

The next day the crew flew to Hanover, Germany, which was their longest mission since the end of May. The nearly eight hour mission encountered very heavy flak, but heavy cloud cover also kept the German fighters down. The German radar-controlled flak guns, however, could still seek and find their targets through the cloud cover. The B-17 formations were now flying with larger escorts of P-38's and P-51's to assist in the event of German fighter attacks. This was Mission No. 79 for the entire 452nd Bomb Group and much had happened since the *Sunrise Serenade* had gone down a month and a half earlier on Mission No. 42. Bomber crews were becoming more and more confident that they would complete their quota of 30 missions. Every day a few men, mostly those who had been with the Group from the very beginning, were trading their flying apparel for neatly pressed uniforms for their trip back to the States. The last loss of aircraft or crewmen from the 452nd Bomb Group had happened on May 29, 1944, which had been twenty missions earlier. Even though this was only 17 days by the calendar, it was an eternity for the men whose lives were held in the balance on every mission.

Another long trip to Bremen, Germany, on June 18th encountered plenty of heavy flak for the B-17's near the target, but none were fatally hit. Again the American fighter escorts of P-51's, P-47's, and P-38's were excellent in keeping any German fighters away from the formations. During take-off on this mission, the tail wheel of the *Silver Shed House* blew out, but Jim Reynolds was still able to become airborne. This caused some concern among the crew members later before landing, but Reynold's skill in the pilot's seat brought the plane to a landing without incident.

The next day, June 19th, Lalumiere and the rest of the *Silver Shed House* crew took the day off; however, other planes from the Group flew to Corme-Ecluse, France, which was north of the city of Bordeaux. The area over the target was partly obscured due to clouds and also the many lingering contrails left by previous planes. The long stretch of time during which no planes from the 452nd Bomb Group were shot down by the Germans was seemingly at its end when a direct hit of heavy flak struck the plane known as *Ain't Miss Behavin' II* over the target. The impact caused major damage, and also prevented the bomb bay doors from being opened. The crew was barely able to make it back to the English coast where they crash-landed about one half mile short of the runway at Wattisham, England. Upon impact the plane broke into pieces; however, the crew was able to get out and run to safety before the bombs aboard exploded. Another plane that day named *Dog Breath* had its No. 2 engine knocked out as the Group was attempting their third pass over the target since the first two passes were obscured. Again, flak hit *Dog Breath*, which this time took out the No. 1 engine. The plane and crew struggled as they made it to Spain where they were interred as part of the international agreement with neutral countries.

While Bob Lalumiere was continuing to participate in bombing missions against the Germans in late June of 1944, the surviving members of his former crew of the *Sunrise Serenade* were also having to deal with the War. At this time his copilot, Bill Hewett, was trying to formulate ways to escape the St. Gilles prison hospital. George Griffin and John McGrath were now nearing the end of their second month at Stalag Luft III. John Brown, Ray Dean, Jim Gallagher, Dusty Rhodes and Andy Senetsky were likewise getting accustomed to prison life at Stalag Luft IV and Stalag Luft VI. Harry Shoffner was secretly hiding in the Belgian Underground and trying to make contact with his ill wife back in the States or figure out how he could get back to his base at Deopham Green. Bob Lalumiere was continuing the work that all of his original crew had set out to accomplish together.

On June 20th, Bob Lalumiere and his crew remained at the base while other crews participated in a bombing mission to Magdeburg, Germany, which was accomplished without incident. The crew was still waiting for another chance to bomb more targets or possibly bring down more enemy fighters. Since becoming a member of the *Silver Shed House*, Lalumiere had brought down three enemy fighters. His total was now at five confirmed enemy planes shot down which would have made Tiger Bob an "Ace" had he been a fighter pilot. Fighter pilots had cameras in their planes which proved that they had indeed shot down an enemy plane. The gunners aboard the bombers, however, were usually not given proper credit for their accomplishments, since many different gunners were often firing at the same plane.

The continuous presence of enemy fighters was often due to the Flying Fortresses having to travel long distances to their targets, which gave multiple German fighter groups the opportunity to attack the planes along the route. It had been a goal of the United States 8th Air Force leaders to have bases located inside Russia from which to bomb targets in Germany as early as the fall of 1943. The Russian government responded only with a statement of "agreeing in principle" to this arrangement each time it was proposed, but they would never commit to arranging the final details. Bases located within the Russian border would drastically cut down on the amount of time needed to hit targets inside Germany, and could also be used to reload and strike Germany again on the way back to England. American leaders realized bases inside the eastern borders of

Russia could also be used to attack the industrial cities of Japan once an alliance with the Russians was established. In February of 1944, the logistics of such an operation were laid out in front of the Russian government at the Kremlin. The American leaders requested six bases, but were only given three bases located at Poltava, Mirgorod, and Piryatin. The Russians also greatly scaled back the amount of American personnel that they would allow to occupy these bases.

With the second World War less than one year from being over in Europe, the framework for the Cold War with Russia and the United States had seemingly just begun. Russia had earlier criticized the Americans and British for not starting a second battle front to relieve their armies on the Eastern Front. The Western Front against the Germans was finally started with the June 6, 1944, D-Day invasion at Normandy, France. Russia may have been thinking that their so-called Allies fighting against the Germans were in fact waiting for the Germans to do further damage to Russia. Josef Stalin had a great mistrust for the western Allies, and did not want them occupying any part of Russia; however, he did see opportunities to obtain Western technology by letting them use his bases. The guards that would be guarding the American B-17's at the Russian bases were ordered to document as much information about the planes as they could, or risk being sent to the dreaded Russian Front against the Germans. Stalin was also successful in obtaining a Norden bombsight from the Americans (something that even the British had not been able to do) before he finally authorized the use of the bases. Stalin also insisted that the Russian armies would protect the airbases, rejecting the efforts by the Americans to provide their own protection. The American leaders gave in to the Russians on that point fearing that they would anger the Russians and lose the use of the bases by persisting to use their own anti-aircraft defenses.

The first shuttle mission to Russia dubbed "Operation Frantic" occurred on June 2, 1944, when planes from the 15th Air Force stationed in Italy successfully used the air bases in Russia. On June 21, 1944, six Bomb Groups from the 13th and 45th Combat Wings stationed in England left for a 1,440 mile trip to bomb Germany and then land in Russia on a mission called "Frantic II". Among the formations flying in the 45th Combat Wing that day were the planes from the 452nd Bomb Group, including the plane with Bob Lalumiere and his crew. After a successful bombing of the Brabag Industrial Complex near Berlin, the 95th, 100th, and 390th bomb groups of the 13th Combat Wing landed at Mirgorod. The 96th, 388th and 452nd Bomb Groups of the 45th Combat Wing landed at Poltava, and the American escort fighters from the 4th and 352nd Fighter Groups landed at the Piryatin base.

During the trip to the Russian bases, a German plane had followed the American bombers to see where they would land. A German He-177 also flew over Poltava and Mirgorod just before sunset and photographed the neatly parked rows of American bombers at the two bases. The Germans quickly mobilized from their base located at Minsk, Russia, which had not yet been taken back by the Russian army. At 11:35 p.m. a warning was announced at Poltava indicating that German bombers were approaching, so the American airmen left their tents and headed for nearby trenches. To the dismay of the Americans, no Russian fighters had taken off yet to intercept the bombers, which started to raise suspicions. At 12:30 a.m. on June 22nd, German marker planes dropped high-intensity flares that lit up the entire base so the ensuing bombers could accurately hit their targets. The marker planes were followed by an estimated 80 German Ju-88 and He-111 bombers, which dropped their bombs with precision on the 73 parked Flying Fortresses. The Russian fighter planes at Poltava still did not take off to ward off the attack. The Russian leaders at Piryatin still refused to allow the American fighter planes to take off from that base. The Russian defenses located around Poltava turned out to be nothing more than some .50 caliber machine guns mounted on the backs of jeeps scattered around the base. The bombing continued until 1:45 a.m. as the airmen in the trenches helplessly watched their beloved planes being destroyed in front of them. After the German bombers left, another wave of planes soon came and began dropping anti-personnel bombs around the base, which lasted for another 20 minutes. At the end of the second attack, a magnesium flash bomb was dropped as a finale to illuminate the area again so the Germans could photograph the damage they had done.

When the bombing had stopped at Poltava, nearly every plane from the 452nd Bomb Group had been either destroyed or severely damaged. Planes from the 96th and 388th Bomb Group had also been hit as evidenced by this photo taken of a 96th Bomb Group plane. - *Collection of Chris Brassfield.*

Men began to crawl out of their trenches as fires continued to rage and ensuing explosions occurred everywhere around them. The Germans completely destroyed 43 of the B-17's, and the remaining planes all had heavy damage with only a few left in flyable condition. Also destroyed on the ground was 200,000 gallons of high-octane aviation fuel, which was equally devastating since it was in short supply. Of the planes damaged or destroyed, 24 of them belonged to the 452nd Bomb Group, including the one Jim Reynolds flew which was not the *Silver Shed House*. When Bob Lalumiere finally determined which plane had been theirs, it had been reduced to a melted pile of aluminum and wiring. Surprisingly only two Americans were killed and another 14 wounded during the attack. The Russians, however, faced heavier casualties with 25 people killed; mostly civilians working around the base. Lalumiere remembered seeing dogs running around the base carrying human body parts before those who were killed could be properly buried. The sight of the planes was equally devastating for the bomber crews who could only watch their planes continue to burn and explode. Most of the men had also lost their personal belongings that were aboard their planes.

Bob Lalumiere and other members of his crew had time to photograph sites around the Russian airfield. The plane shown is a Russian Ilyushin Il-2 "Shturmovik" anti-tank plane. Left to Right: Hubert Desaulniers, Bob Lalumiere, Sylvester Petri, Robert Hearns, and John Moody. - *Collection of Robert A. Lalumiere.*

The other American base in Russia, which contained the other B-17's, Mirgorod, was saved from the similar fate of those at Poltava. A navigational error by the German bombers sent to bomb Mirgorod resulted in them failing to find the base in the darkness. However, the flashes being made in the night from the bombs being dropped at Poltava gave the German bombers who were supposed to attack the Mirgorod base the necessary navigational direction to also bomb the base at Poltava.

Suspicion immediately began to surface that the Russians might have known about the impending attack upon the American bomber bases in Russia. Historical evidence produced after the fall of the Russian government 45 years later, supported the idea that Russia may have originally intended to let Germany and the American/British armies destroy each other before being drawn into the War themselves. Russia could then come with a massive force against all of them once they were weakened. The invasion of Russia by the Germans on June 21, 1941, had put an end to this plan. However, Stalin was still thinking of post-War settlements, and which country might be left with the strongest army after Germany was defeated. The prospect of having many American bombers easily destroyed on the ground by the Germans may have been just what Stalin had secretly wanted, so he did nothing to prevent it from happening.

It was rare for American airmen to have the opportunity to be so close to Russian aircraft, which were usually closely guarded. The plane is a Petlyakov Pe-2 attack bomber.
- *Collection of Robert A. Lalumiere.*

Russia had no intentions of giving up any German land that they had overrun, so any hint that the Americans had helped them acquire such territory would have to be dealt with after the War. The combined losses of the June 21, 1944, mission to Russia totaled 92 B-17's and B-24's, either shot down during the bombing mission or later destroyed on the ground at the bases. American leaders continued to use the bases on a periodic basis, but the relationship only worsened with the Russians. American B-17's were often fired upon by Russian anti-aircraft guns and even attacked by Russian fighter pilots. The Russians always had ludicrous excuses, such as saying that they could not determine if these large formations of B-17's might have possibly been captured by the Germans and were being used to attack their homeland. Excuses such as these held absolutely no validity, since the Americans always briefed the Russians when and where their formations would be flying.

Bob Lalumiere (left) and Sylvester Petri (right) pose with a Russian soldier in front of a British Hawker "Hurricane" fighter plane which was being used by the Russians through a lend-lease program. - *Collection of Robert A. Lalumiere.*

For the next eight days the airmen who were stranded in Russia without their planes patiently waited while arrangements were made to bring them back to England. Bob Lalumiere and Sylvester Petri took advantage of this waiting period and spent some time taking photographs of the area. Among some of the photos taken were the two men in front of a British Hawker Hurricane fighter plane, and other photos with some of the rest of their crew, and a Russian soldier. The Hurricane was being used by the Russians as part as a lend/lease program in which the British and the Americans were supplying Russia with military equipment to help fight the Germans. The stranded airmen were also allowed to visit an open market in Poltava to pass the time. Generally, the average Russian citizen was very friendly toward the Americans, but they had no control over the actions of their own government.

The route taken back to England after their planes were destroyed at Poltava involved almost five days of shuttling from airbase to airbase. Somehow the officers had been evacuated from Poltava before the enlisted men. This gave the enlisted men the feeling that the officers had been given preferential treatment in returning back to England. Bob Lalumiere remembered being with Sylvester Petri during this time and the details of the trip were recorded in Petri's diary. They took-off at 5:00 p.m. on June 29th in a C-87 plane and landed at Rostov, Russia, at 7:30 p.m. The next day they left Rostov at 7:00 a.m. in a C-87 and landed at Tehran, Iran, around 2:00 p.m. for fueling. An hour later they left Tehran and landed in Cairo, Egypt, at 10:00 p.m. On July 1st, they left Cairo in a C-47 cargo plane at 3:00 a.m., made a refueling stop at an unknown location, and arrived at Algiers, Algeria, about 2:00 p.m. After staying in Algiers for two hours, they took off and flew to Casablanca, Morocco, arriving there at 9:30 p.m. The next day the men toured the city while arrangements were made to fly on toward England. Later that day, their plane, a C-54, left Casablanca at 8:00 p.m. and arrived in Prestwick, Scotland, the following morning at 9:00 a.m. One hour later, the men left Prestwick and arrived at Hunnington, England, around 2:00 p.m. during a heavy rain. The men were then sent on to their base at Deopham Green by truck. Sylvester Petri, Bob Lalumiere, and other airmen from Poltava were some of the first men from their Group to arrive back at their base because they had been separated in Casablanca. The remaining men from their crew and others of the 452nd Bomb Group arrived the next day on July 4, 1944. Upon arrival at their base, all of the men were placed under high security until their identities could be proven. Bob Lalumiere was repeatedly interrogated by American officials in an attempt to determine if he was possibly a spy posing as Bob Lalumiere. He was asked questions referring to events in the United States such as how many feet were from home plate to first base on a baseball field, or how many players on a football team. Lalumiere, not being a sports enthusiast, could only guess at some of the questions being asked, but eventually was cleared.

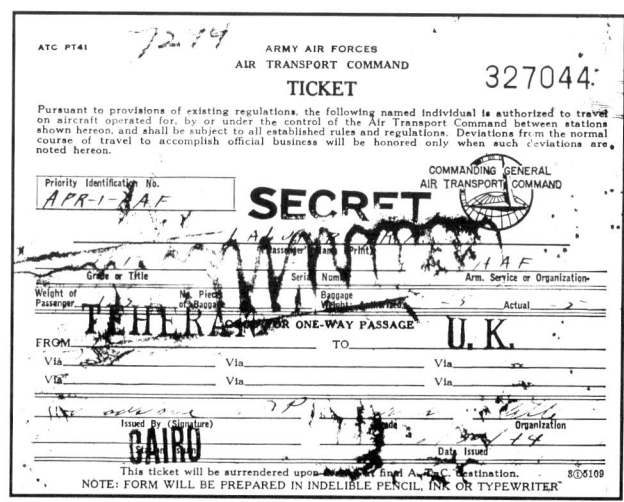

This ticket was issued to Bob Lalumiere by the Air Transport Command to travel between Teheran, Cairo, and the United Kingdom. - *Collection of Robert A. Lalumiere.*

In the time that Lalumiere and other fellow airmen had been absent from their base, the 452nd Bomb Group had flown nine more missions. If the Poltava incident had not occurred, Lalumiere and the rest of his crew would have all completed their required 30 missions. These last nine missions flown by the Group had all been relatively easy with no loss of planes.

On July 8, 1944, the crew boarded the *Silver Shed House* and took off for Rouen, France. This mission was to be the final one for waist gunner Sylvester Petri, pilot Jim Reynolds, and copilot Mark Liddell. Assembly that morning was in the early morning darkness and fears that the planes would collide were shared by the various crews. Due to some mechanical trouble with the plane, Bob Lalumiere and his crew could not fly in their No. 2 position in the formation as briefed. They eventually took up another location in the formation as they headed for the target. The flak encountered near the target was very heavy and accurate. The plane that had taken up the No. 2 position, *Marjorie Ann*, took a direct hit of flak in the No. 2 engine. The entire crew managed to bail out of the plane, with five escaping and the other five taken as prisoners. The plane flying off the right wing of Lalumiere's plane took a direct hit of flak and went straight down. The entire tail assembly of the plane had been completely shot off. Although three parachutes were apparently seen to open, only the left waist gunner survived. The danger encountered served as a reminder for several of the crew who were on their last mission to be thankful that their required bombing missions were now complete.

Bob Lalumiere finished his tour of duty with the 8th Air Force on July 11, 1944, with a mission to Munich, Germany. He and a few other members of his crew were flying with a new pilot that day since "Big Jim" Reynolds had finished his tour three days earlier. The mission to Munich was accomplished without any loss of planes for the 452nd Bomb Group. It had been 72 days since his original crew of the *Sunrise Serenade* had gone down on May 1, 1944. Since that date, 52 more missions had been flown by the 452nd Bomb Group, and during those, Lalumiere had logged his last 15. Robert "Tiger Bob" Lalumiere became the only crew member who had once flown combat missions on the *Sunrise Serenade* to complete his 30 bombing missions. After his quota of missions was complete, Lalumiere became an instructor to train new gunners how to operate the turret effectively to bring down German fighters.

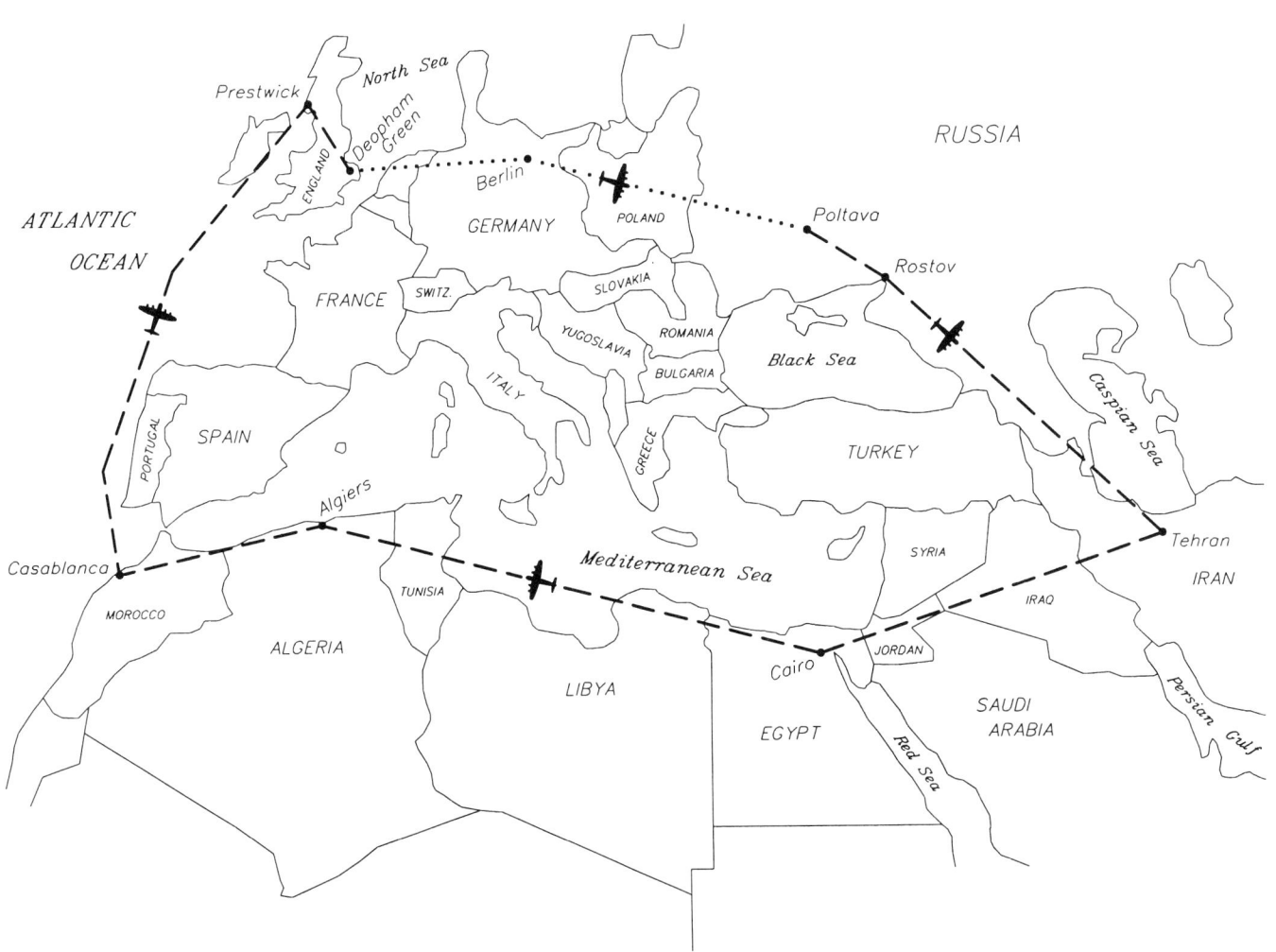

The shuttle mission to Poltava, Russia, on June 21, 1944, was supposed to be a routine flight where the crews would bomb Berlin on the way over and then reload in Russia and bomb a target on the way back to England the next day. The surprise German bombing attack by the *Luftwaffe* left nearly every 452nd Bomb Group plane destroyed on the ground, and the crews had to take the long way back to their base over safe air space. The crews arrived back at Deopham Green eleven days later.

The War Comes to an End

Many battles were still being won and lost by the 452nd Bomb Group, as well as the 8th Air Force as a whole, after the crew of the *Sunrise Serenade* was no longer playing an active role in winning the War. Isolation inside the prison camps meant that the men from the *Sunrise Serenade* could only hope that the strong leadership and desire to win that they had help started within their Group was now continuing without them. The skies over Europe were largely controlled by the American and British forces at the time Bob Lalumiere had finished his 30 missions on July 11, 1944. Less German fighter opposition was being encountered during the bombing missions by the entire mighty 8th Air Force. A once formidable German army was now rapidly retreating as more and more of their conquered land was being retaken. The Germans were, however, still making a concerted effort to produce more planes and artillery to defend their homeland. The 8th Air Force was attempting at this time to strike targets which would help the Allied forces on the ground and also strike targets to keep the German industry from rebuilding.

Six B-17's in the low formation fly toward Germany to increase the pressure being applied to the German industry that was struggling to rebuild from previous bombings.
- Collection of Sylvester Petri.

From July 11 to July 27, 1944, the 452nd Bomb Group had flown twelve missions without a single loss of planes. This included the July 18, 1944, mission to Kiel, Germany, which marked their 100th combat bombing mission. General James H. "Jimmie" Doolittle arrived for the celebration of the 100th mission in a B-26 Marauder, much to the excitement of the men at the base. The evening was one to remember for the combat weary airmen, with two USO shows featuring beautiful women performing on stage. Over 2,000 men were rewarded with a ham dinner as young women from the nearby towns and countryside arrived for a dance later in the evening. Any worries or stress from the bombing mission carried out earlier in the day were now gone. With their lives being held in the balance with each new day, the men wanted to enjoy themselves as much as they could before the War intruded in their lives again.

That intrusion came with a mission to Merseberg, Germany, on July 28th. All was going well until another combat wing mistakenly flew in front of the 452nd Bomb Group's formation which was already a few minutes into their bomb run over the target. The displaced air from the other planes caused the lead plane and also the deputy lead plane of the 452nd Bomb Group to collide with each other and explode. The Group's newest commanding officer, Col. Archibald Y. Smith, was flying in the lead plane as an eleventh crew member. The navigator and a waist gunner along with Smith were all blown clear of the plane, and parachuted to the ground. They were later taken prisoner. The remaining eight crew members were killed. The deputy lead plane faired only slightly better, with half of its ten-man crew surviving the crash.

As the month of August arrived, Col. William D. Eckert became the 452nd Bomb Group's new commanding officer. He was already the sixth different commanding officer since the Group began flying in combat. Two important changes took place during his command when the military leaders decided to reduce the bomber crews from ten airmen to nine. The reduction took place in the elimination of one waist gunner. A combination of factors including less German fighter opposition, fewer airmen available, and the idea that one waist gunner could handle both sides of the plane necessitated the change. The other major change was extending the quota of bombing missions from a required 30 to 35. This did little to boost the morale of the airmen who were experiencing heavy concentrations of flak near the targets on nearly every mission. Since the start of their participation in combat missions in February of 1944, the 452nd Bomb Group had seen the mission quota first raised from 25 to 30, then to a total of 35. After reaching the 25th mission many men had wished they could have begun earlier.

Also during the month of August 1944, the 8th Air Force lost 144 B-17 bombers, five being from the 452nd Bomb Group. Each one of these five planes was lost as a direct result of flak. During the month of September, four more planes from the Group were lost

113

as a direct result of flak. Many of the bombers now being hit by flak were able to continue flying, whereas in previous months the German *Luftwaffe* fighters would have quickly brought them down. Pilots who were flying planes that were badly damaged by flak were now able to stay in the air long enough to land in places like Belgium, Luxembourg, and France, which had previously been held by the enemy.

An event of historical importance occurred on September 11th, when the 452nd Bomb Group participated in the last shuttle mission to Russian bases, known as "Frantic VI". The 452nd Bomb Group had earlier visited the Russian bases on June 21, 1944, when the Germans had attacked their planes on the ground during "Frantic II". This would be the last time the American bombers would ever occupy Russian soil, and the 452nd Bomb Group had been selected as one of the groups to participate in the mission. The Russian bases were of little value now, and it was evident that the United States would not be getting access to bases inside Russia from which to bomb Japan. For most American leaders the attempts made to strengthen relations with the Russian government was considered a failure, and a one-sided affair. It was becoming more evident that post-War problems with Russia would likely exist since the Kremlin had shown a consistent pattern of non-cooperation and distrust with their so-called Western allies. Being the first to reach the German capital city of Berlin became the goal both for the Russian army and for the American and British armies. Some American leaders, however, would later be willing to let the Russian army take the brunt of the attack in this last German stronghold before moving in themselves. Both sides, never-the-less, saw Berlin as the prize by which history might later validate who had the better army.

The month of September also brought liberation to much of Belgium due to the efforts of the Allied ground forces and the air support from the bombers. For Bill Hewett and Harry Shoffner of the *Sunrise Serenade* the liberation of this country brought their first taste of freedom since being shot down four months earlier. The Allies were making advances, but the German army's resistance grew stronger as they pushed closer to the German homeland.

The month of October began with two bombers going down from the 452nd Bomb Group during the first week. On October 12, 1944, a veteran Flying Fortress that had begun with the Group eight months earlier finally met its end. During a mission to Bremen, Germany, the plane known as *Inside Curve* suddenly went out of control during assembly into formation over England. *Inside Curve* had been named by John Collier who had been the original radio operator of the *Sunrise Serenade*. The war-battled plane had faithfully flown 112 of the 147 combat missions flown by the Group. For its 113th mission, *Inside Curve* had been fitted with four new engines to add to its prominence. The unlucky crew was on their eighth mission, but their regular plane, *Little Miss America,* had been given to another crew that day. Prop wash, the invisible disturbance of air caused by a preceding plane, may have caused *Inside Curve* to go out of control and crash. Every crew member except the waist gunner, Paschal H. "Pat" Powell and the navigator, 2nd Lt. Sidney Solomon were killed. The ball turret gunner fell to his death trapped inside the ball turret. The pilot's hands were gripped to the controls so tightly that a crowbar had to be used to release them from the wreckage. Powell did not initially have his parachute attached until he saw it sliding by him while he was inside the middle section of the plane which had had both ends broken off. He quickly attached the parachute to his harness as he went out the jagged opening of the plane. As he was floating down, he vowed to God that he would serve Him for the rest of his life.

After that event, Powell was transferred to the 15th Air Force in Italy because his commanders thought that he might be a morale problem for his own Group. Often airmen who had traumatic experiences were a constant reminder to others in their Group of the reality of death, so they were often moved elsewhere. While in the 15th Air Force, Powell was later shot down and became a prisoner of War. The airman kept his promise to God, which he had made during his escape from *Inside Curve*, and became Reverend Powell upon his return to the States after the War.

The remainder of October was quiet until two planes collided during formation just a few miles west of Deopham Green on October 26th. The mishap claimed the lives of 16 airmen, but miraculously the tail gunners from each plane managed to bail out and survive.

The month of November started with the plane known as *Windy Lou* from the 452nd Bomb Group being hit by flak and going down on a mission to Ludwigshafen, Germany, on the 5th of November. Four days later the Group had a crew flying *The Lady Jeannette* involved in one of the most dramatic and decorated events in the history of the entire 8th Air Force during the War. During the November 9, 1944, mission to Saarbrucken, Germany, *The Lady Jeannette* was hit by flak just before going over the target, so it left formation. The pilot, 1st Lt. Donald J. Gott and his co-pilot, 2nd Lt. William E. Metzger, struggled to keep the plane aloft while three engines were either shut down or on fire. The communication system was down and hydraulic fluid fed the flames which ignited flares on the flight deck. The engineer was wounded in the leg and the radioman's arm had been severed. Metzger tried his best to apply first-aid to the stricken men while Gott jettisoned the bombs to lighten their load. Metzger ordered the remaining crew members who had not already bailed out to do so. One gunner's parachute was damaged beyond use, so Metzger gave him his to use. The radioman was now unconscious, so Gott and Metzger decided to attempt a crash landing in an attempt to save his life. As the plane, now completely engulfed in fire, was within a hundred feet of the ground, the fire reached the fuel tanks and the entire plane exploded. Upon impact the plane exploded again killing all remaining occupants aboard. Gott and Metzger were posthumously awarded the Medal of Honor for their courage and bravery in saving most of their crew and attempting to save the life of their radioman. *The Lady Jeannette* became the only B-17 Flying Fortress during World War II to have two Medal of Honor recipients aboard.

Both planes from the 452nd Bomb Group shown in this photo, the *Lady Jeannette* (left), and *The Uninvited*, were shot down on November 9, 1944. The *Lady Jeannette* became the only B-17 from the 8th Air Force to have two Medal of Honor recipients on the same plane. - *Collection of Irwin Math.*

Also on November 9th, two other planes, *Fiklebitch* and *The Uninvited*, had their bombing careers brought to an abrupt end. All crew members aboard *Fiklebitch* were killed while on their second mission when the plane crashed at sea. Those aboard *The Uninvited* survived after bailing out of their disabled plane while traveling for 30 minutes in a snowstorm with almost zero visibility. The entire crew was subsequently taken prisoner. A direct hit of flak had blown a 2-foot diameter hole in the wing just behind the No. 3 engine which also knocked out the No. 4 engine and the electrical system. Without a crew aboard, *The Uninvited* circled for a short time before finally crashing along the bank of a river near Minheim, Germany. Near the end of the month a return mission to Merseburg on November 25th had disastrous results for one plane from the Group while bombing the target through solid cloud cover at only 12,000 feet. The radar-controlled flak guns found their target when *Patches* took a direct hit and exploded. The crew, comprised of mostly new airmen who were flying on their first combat mission, were all killed. The co-pilot and bombardier were among the seven members of the crew who were veteran fliers with 26 and 34 completed missions respectively. For the bombardier, 1st Lt. James E. Hartmann, it would have been his final mission had he survived.

At this time, three members of the crew of the *Sunrise Serenade,* Bill Hewett, Harry Shoffner and Bob Lalumiere, were safely back in the States, while the rest of the crew were battling the extreme cold and otherwise miserable conditions of the POW camps in eastern Germany. The crash of their plane seven months earlier seemed like a long time ago, since a whole new way of life had descended upon the men coping inside the camps. They had now spent more time inside German prison camps than the entire time they had spent together in training and flying combat missions. Little did they know that their trials were more than half over. Every new day was a struggle just to survive; the future seemed so uncertain.

As the men of the *Sunrise Serenade* and hundreds of other bomber crews were enduring the effects of winter on the ground, thousands of airmen were also having to endure the extreme cold while flying bombing missions. The winter weather was keeping the majority of the Allied aircraft on the ground during much of the beginning of December. The first casualty for the month came on December 4th when intense barrages of flak encountered over the German cities of Weisbaden, Frankfurt and Koblenz brought down *Mon Tete Rouge II* and damaged 28 of the 452nd Bomb Group's other planes. A visit to the German capital city the next day to bomb a tank factory resulted in missing the planned target by seven miles and also claiming the lives of eight crew members when their plane crashed due to mechanical problems. On December 16, 1944, the German army took advantage of the poor weather situation and launched a major counteroffensive through the wooded country of the Ardennes and advanced 30 miles into Belgium and Luxembourg. The move completely surprised the Allied forces who believed that the German army would only further retreat as the War progressed. The German high command devised a plan to divide the American and British forces and retake the vital port city of Antwerp. The German advancement through the Allied lines created a bow in the line of defense and the ensuing battle became known as "The Battle of the Bulge". The German advance was finally halted at the Meuse River in late December, but not before inflicting heavy casualties on both sides.

On Christmas Eve of 1944, the 452nd Bomb Group put up a total of 64 aircraft, which was believed to be a record number of aircraft for a single mission from the Group. The formation bombed the airfield at Darmstadt, Germany, with only fair results. For one plane from the Group the day was tragic since a direct hit of flak brought down the plane and killed five of its crew. The next day no planes left the Deopham Green airfield in observance of Christmas; however, the 8th Air Force did dispatch over 400 heavy bombers from various other Groups.

On the final day of 1944, the 452nd Bomb Group suffered through a very rough day during a mission to attack an oil refinery at Hamburg, Germany. The German *Luftwaffe* had regrouped and decided to make one final effort of the year against the Flying Fortresses. Attacks upon the planes were made by an estimated 15 to 20 FW-190's coming in high and low on the tail. With their 20mm and 30mm guns blazing away at the heavy bombers, the German fighters performed roller coaster and swooper attacks as they came in pairs. After the battle subsided, the Germans had succeeded in knocking down five B-17's from the Group's 728th Squadron. Twenty-five other aircraft had received damage, but were able to stay in the air. The loss in experienced airmen totaled 13 dead and 32 taken prisoner. The American gunners retaliated with a confirmed four enemy aircraft shot down, seven possibly shot down and four others damaged. For most of the gunners aboard the bombers, this was their first major air battle. The mostly inexperienced German pilots scored a major victory since this was the heaviest loss of planes for the 452nd Bomb Group since the Poltava disaster on June 21, 1944, and the heaviest loss of planes due to German fighters since the Brux mission on May 12, 1944.

The costliest year for the American 8th Air Force had been 1944 in which approximately 2,750 heavy bombers had been lost. The losses for just the B-17 planes during this year amounted to approximately 1,930 planes, which equated to over 19,000 experienced airmen no longer available to help win the War.

The first mission of the new year for the 452nd Bomb Group was to an isolated railroad junction point in Germany, named Ehrang, on January 2, 1945. The location was just east of the Luxembourg border and was not supposed to have any flak batteries in the area. A force of 34 aircraft approached the target and was immediately met by a barrage of flak originating from four 88mm flak guns mounted on railroad cars parked on the tracks. The second burst brought down the deputy lead plane, *Rosalie Ann II*, flown by 1st Lt. William R. MacDougall. All members of the crew safely exited the plane, except the engineer who was killed. The next burst from the guns made a direct hit on the wing of the lead plane being flown by 1st Lt. Ralph R. Jones, sending it into a flat spin. The centrifugal force pinned the entire crew inside the plane, which then broke apart. In the tail gunner's position was 2nd Lt. John E. Everhart, who was in that position as the command observer radioing information to the pilot. Everhart managed to escape the plane after it broke apart and was the only survivor. Thirteen other aircraft received damage from the extremely accurate flak gunners. It was later learned that this was a flak battalion made up entirely of German women.

As the War dragged on it seemed to the airmen that every available German citizen must have been operating a flak gun on the ground. On January 10th, a plane from the Group was hit by flak over Cologne, Germany, and left formation. The temperature at the prescribed altitude of 27,000 feet was a bone-chilling 68 degrees below zero. Everyone had assumed that the plane had reached friendly territory and landed, but no trace of the plane or the crew were ever found. It was therefore presumed that the plane must have crashed into the North Sea or English Channel.

Mechanical problems also played a role in the loss of aircraft to the Group. Engine trouble for the *Panting Stork II* on January 5th forced it to land near Dieppe, France. The crew were advised by American personnel arriving in a jeep to guard the plane until it could be determined how to remove it from the area. For the next seven days multitudes of curious French citizens virtually turned their aircraft into a museum.

Near mid-January flak continued to be bothersome and severely damaged *Forbidden Fruit II*, killing the tail gunner. The mission to the U-boat ship yards at Hamburg on January 17th, and to the Rheine marshalling yards on January 20th resulted in five more planes from the Group being lost to flak, although two were able to land in Sweden. January of 1945 had produced very poor flying weather and only twelve missions were flown by the Group during the entire month, which was their lowest monthly total during the War.

During this time the crew members of the *Sunrise Serenade* who had been taken prisoner were now being marched along the frozen roads of Germany. The advancing Russian Army forced the Germans to abandon many eastern POW camps to avoid liberating Allied prisoners. As they marched, the POW's could see hundreds of American bombers' contrails every day as they flew toward their targets. Many weakened airmen directed their attention to the shiny specks at the end of the trails wondering if these planes might have originated from their own bases. Although they could not see the American faces inside those planes, there was comfort knowing that the planes carried their own comrades.

During the first week of February, the 452nd Bomb Group planes known as *Lady Satan, Slightly Dangerous, Lucky Lady II, Deuces Wild* and at least two other planes fell victim to the German flak guns.

Lady Satan ended her illustrious career having completed 85 bombing missions for the Group. On February 15, 1945, the 452nd Bomb Group celebrated its 200th combat mission after successfully bombing the secondary target, the marshalling yards at Cottbus, Germany. During the remainder of February, *Forbidden Fruit II* exploded after experiencing prop wash, and *Johnny Reb*, *Flatbush Floogie*, and one other plane were all shot down as a result of flak.

Forbidden Fruit II (center) flies among planes of the 388th Bomb Group, which was one of the three groups comprising the 45th Bomb Wing. The plane would be lost on February 17, 1945. - *Collection of the 452nd Bomb Group Association.*

The first twelve missions flown during the month of March 1945 were carried out with an occasional German fighter appearing and the usual flak, but no planes were brought down. On March 18th two planes collided over the English Channel as the 452nd Bomb Group was heading toward a routine mission to Berlin. The resulting crash left one entire crew dead, and two dead from the other crew. The following day produced a mission to Zwickau, Germany, where enemy fighters tried to regain at least part of the sky over Europe. Since hundreds of American bombers were leaving contrails behind them, this produced a cloud cover during an otherwise clear day. German Me-262 jet fighters used these contrails to cover their initial attack upon the bomber formations. For many B-17 airmen the mission to Zwickau was their first experience with the feared jet fighters who were upon them and gone before they could even return fire with their own guns. The attack by the jet planes occurred just before the bombs were dropped over the target and resulted in knocking down four of the 452nd Bomb Group's planes. The first casualty of the 452nd Bomb Group by a German jet-powered plane was believed to have been *Try'n Getit,* which crash-landed near Posen, Poland, which was now under Russian control. The same fate was true for another crew who landed near Radomsko, Poland, however, two planes known as *Smokey Liz II* and *Daisy Mae* were brought down by the jet fighters over German-occupied soil. The war with Germany was scarcely more than a month from being over, but the *Luftwaffe* had still been able to unleash its secret weapon, the jet fighter plane, against the Allied bombers. During the remainder of March, flak brought down *Rose-Etta* and *Hairless Joe*, and the weather and prop wash were blamed for bringing down two more planes from the Group.

One of the German cities to get bombed during the first week of April by the Group was Nuremberg, which had once been Hitler's pride, where he held mass rallies to gain strength for the Nazi Party. The city had long been the target of Allied bombers, but on April 5, 1945, the nearby Stalag XIIID was now empty for the first time. Many former crew members of the *Sunrise Serenade* had just evacuated the camp the previous day and had marched 17 miles to the town of Neumarkt on their way to Stalag VIIA at Moosburg. Unbeknownst to them, the planes responsible for the rumble of the exploding bombs in the distant city of Nuremberg were from their own Group.

Two days later on April 7th, the 452nd Bomb Group's mission was to the airfield at Kaltekirchen, Germany. The mission turned out to be reminiscent of the December 31, 1944, mission when the *Luftwaffe* had regrouped to attack the bombers. Somehow the German air force had managed to find and assemble forty to fifty Me-109's and FW-190's to attack the formation of 34 bombers. In addition to the typical German fighter planes, at least four Me-262 jet fighters also joined in the attack. The result was the loss of four planes from the Group, including at least two that had collided with the enemy fighters. From the four planes that were lost, 26 men had given their lives. It was later learned that the German plan that day was to ram the B-17's at the expense of the German pilot's life if necessary. It was a form of "patriotic suicide" not yet seen from the now desperate *Luftwaffe* pilots. The 452nd Bomb Group was issued the Distinguished Unit Citation for the mission. The gunners aboard the Flying Fortresses scored 14 enemy aircraft shot down, 10 possibly shot down and 10 others damaged that day.

Two other significant events for the Group also occurred during April of 1945. The first happened on April 9th when the last plane from the 452nd Bomb Group went down as a direct result of flak. The crew safely landed their damaged plane on a dirt road near Darmstadt, Germany, which had just been taken by the Allied ground forces the previous day. The second event happened on April 15th. A veteran bomber from the 452nd Bomb Group, named *E-Rat-Icator,* was one of 38 aircraft to be loaded with a new type of napalm fire bomb for a raid on the port city of Royan, France. *E-Rat-Icator* returned from the mission just like it had been doing for the past 14 months during its compilation of 125 missions. This plane was one of the only original B-17's from the 452nd Group to survive the War. The *Sunrise Serenade* had once sat only two planes away from *E-Rat-Icator* at the Deopham Green airfield when both planes were still flying. Near the end of the War, the Germans still held several port cities in France, even though the rest of France had been liberated for some time. Besides Royan, the Germans also held St. Nazaire, La Rochelle, Lorient, Dunkerque and a few other cities. Dunkerque remained held by German troops until two days after the War with Germany was over.

The Reincarnation survived the War, however, not unscathed. A mishap on March 20, 1944, severed the nose of the plane, which at that time had been named the *Shed House Mouse*. The 466th Sub-Depot rebuilt this plane from other damaged aircraft, hence the name. - *Collection of the 452nd Bomb Group Association.*

"Bombs Away" was a scene that was repeated thousands of times before the Germans were finally subdued. The plane in the foreground was lost on March 21, 1945. - *Collection of the 452nd Bomb Group Association.*

The final mission for the 452nd Bomb Group occurred on April 21, 1945, with a mission to the marshalling yards at Ingolstadt, Germany. No fighters were encountered and only a few meager puffs of flak were occasionally seen as just a token reminder that some Germans on the ground had still not given up the fight. The historic and final combat mission was the 250th for the Group. For many of the airmen the day was marred by the absence of one plane returning from the target. Except for the co-pilot, 2nd Lt. George V. Pringle who had completed 29 previous missions, this had been the first mission for the rest of the crew including the pilot, 2nd Lt. Frank B. Bell. Pringle was flying with the crew only as an experienced pilot to give Bell any assistance if needed during his first mission. After entering a cloud bank, *Slienthe Je Vahr* (Gaelic for *"To a Long & Healthy Life"*) stalled and fell to the left and then went into a fatal spin. The plane temporarily leveled off just enough for the navigator, 2nd Lt. James W. Boehling, to bail out of the nose of the plane. Again the plane went into a steep dive and exploded in mid-air, killing all those aboard. Witnesses on the ground thought that lightning had initially struck the plane, which caused it to go out of control. Boehling landed safely on the ground near Landau, Germany, and returned to headquarters two days later.

The following week the majority of the German POW camps were liberated, including great masses of Allied POW's who gathered around Stalag VIIA at Moosburg. For the most part, the American bombing campaign that had started three years earlier was nearly finished. Small pockets of German resistance continued until the end of the first week in May, especially around the capital city of Berlin, which kept the Allied ground troops busy. On May 7, 1945, Germany accepted the unconditional terms of surrender at Reims, France, by General Alfred Jodl on behalf of the German government.

During the 5-year period of World War II, the American factories produced nearly 98,000 aircraft of various designs which were used to help win the War. The 452nd Bomb Group's participation in the War, resulted in a loss of over 200 Flying Fortresses due to either enemy action or operational accidents. Credit was given to the Group's gunners for shooting down 96½ German aircraft, possibly destroying 45, and damaging 58 others. The Group had gone through nine commanding officers during combat, which was more than any other Bomb Group during the War. The number of aircraft dispatched to bomb German targets from the 452nd Bomb Group during their nearly 15 months of operation totaled 7,279. The total tonnage of bombs dropped by the Group amounted to 16,466 tons.

It is estimated that the entire 8th Air Force lost nearly 3,200 B-17's in combat, with another 2,500 so badly damaged that they were not operational. In addition to these numbers, thousands of B-24's, B-25's, B-26's, and an array of fighter planes were also lost. The losses of personnel for all branches of the 8th and 15th Air Forces during the War is estimated at 24,288 killed in action, second only to the infantry, and 18,699 missing in action. Another 18,804 were wounded and over 31,000 were taken prisoner by the Germans.

The thousands of liberated POW's, including the remaining crew of the *Sunrise Serenade*, were loaded into many different ships at La Havre, France, for the ride back home to the States near the end of May 1945. During the trip back to the United States, some ships struck icebergs in dense fog. This created a mixed sound of scraping and also an array of horn blasts from nearby ships in an attempt to stay away from each other. Several ships did collide while trying to maneuver around the icebergs, but fortunately none sank. A few men began to panic during the commotion, as they now feared that their lives would be lost at sea at the end of the War. As the ships began to arrive in the United States the first week of June, many passed by the Statue of Liberty. The sight made even the most hardened men break down and weep, for they knew that they were finally home.

John Brown, Jim Gallagher, Ray Dean, Dusty Rhodes, and Andy Senetsky had all become separated from each other during the past year and so they came home on separate ships. George Griffin and John McGrath were the only members of the *Sunrise Serenade* who had remained together during their entire time in prison and also during their voyage home. McGrath and Griffin were placed aboard an Italian ship, which was far removed from the luxurious *Queen Elizabeth* they had traveled to England in 18 months previously. McGrath had developed an abscessed tooth during the first day of the voyage home. He finally had to have the ship's dentist pull the tooth so he could eat. Since the tooth was not decayed, the problem was blamed on the continuous poor diet while being a POW. The trip across the Atlantic seemed like an eternity for the men who were trying to visualize what their girlfriends and wives had once looked like. Pictures or other items of remembrance had long been lost or confiscated by the Germans. For most men the pleasant memories of home had been completely blurred by the atrocities that the War had revealed.

As ships brought home the American servicemen from the War, many openly wept as the Statue of Liberty came into view, for they now knew that they were finally home.
- *Collection of the author.*

Estimated World War II Deaths Per Country:

Country	Military Deaths	Civilian Deaths	Total Deaths
Russia	9,000,000	17,000,000	26,000,000
China	1,300,000	10,000,000	11,300,000
Germany	3,250,000	3,600,000	6,850,000
Poland	850,000	6,000,000	6,850,000
Japan	1,500,000	300,000	1,800,000
Yugoslavia	300,000	1,400,000	1,700,000
Romania	520,000	465,000	985,000
France	340,000	470,000	810,000
Hungary	200,000	600,000	800,000
Austria	380,000	145,000	525,000
United States	450,000	-	450,000
Italy	330,000	80,000	410,000
Great Britain	326,000	62,000	388,000
Czechoslovakia	7,000	315,000	322,000
Holland	14,000	236,000	250,000
Greece	19,000	140,000	159,000
Belgium	10,000	75,000	85,000
Finland	79,000	-	79,000
Canada	42,000	-	42,000
India	36,000	-	36,000
Australia	29,000	-	29,000
Albania	28,000	-	28,000
Bulgaria	19,000	2,000	21,000
Spain	12,000	-	12,000
New Zealand	12,000	-	12,000
South Africa	9,000	-	9,000
Norway	5,000	-	5,000
Luxembourg	5,000	-	5,000
Denmark	4,000	-	4,000

The above numbers are an approximation only, and errors probably exist for each individual country. The total deaths that occurred during World War II, both military and civilian, will never be fully known. Even the total number of deaths from the United States has never been fully and accurately documented. It is estimated that Russia alone may have had up to 30 million total casualties. The civilian deaths for each country is also hard to determine since the effects of the War had a lasting impact on each nation, and many died due to disease and starvation after the War. In 1943 it is estimated that 3,000,000 civilians from India died due to famine. The civilian deaths for the United States may be as high as 6,000. Poland lost nearly 17% of its entire prewar population largely due to the deaths of those killed in the concentration camps. Russia and Germany each lost nearly 10% of their prewar population, while it is estimated that the United States lost less than 0.5% of its prewar population.

After the War

In the years following World War II, many American men returned to the United States only to find themselves in a strange environment. Young immature boys who had left home for the War, had now returned completely changed and grown up in just a couple of years. During those years they had made countless new friends, many of whom were killed beside them. The horrible images they witnessed would be imprinted in their minds for the rest of their lives, no matter how hard they tried to forget. Many, who were just barely twenty years old, had seen the worst that life could offer, and getting back into a routine, civilian life was not easy.

The Armed Services tried to make the transition easier. Most of the servicemen, including those of the *Sunrise Serenade*, were given a sixty-day furlough to go home upon arrival back in the States. For most servicemen it was just a quiet walk up to the front door of their youth and a tearful hug for their parents. The big parades and celebrations held immediately after the War had quieted down long before the majority of the men had returned home. Pictures adorning the walls showing brothers or other relatives who had not returned were a constant reminder of the sacrifices that were made for victory. After the furlough was over, the men were shuffled around to various locations for a couple of months, but were usually given their choice of camps until they received their official discharge papers.

Once they were discharged, many servicemen found themselves unemployed. For many, their only specialized training included how to drive a tank, fire artillery, or operate a gun on a bomber. These skills were no longer needed, so a new line of work needed to be learned. The Servicemen's Readjustment Act of 1944, popularly referred to as the GI Bill of Rights, provided unemployment and education allowances and home, farm, and business loans for millions of World War II veterans. This was the much-needed boost to get the returning War heroes back into the mainstream of the American workplace.

The surviving crew members of the *Sunrise Serenade* were like many of the other men who returned from the War. Some made it back to living a relatively normal life while others struggled daily with the shadows of War. Some were able to slide back into their old lives; others searched for years before finding a way of coping; and still others never quite got past their experiences during the War.

William J. Hewett, the co-pilot, was one of those who searched for years before finding what he wanted to do after the War. Upon returning to the States in late 1944, Bill Hewett spent lengthy hospitalizations and had several operations on his hand at Wakeman General Hospital in Indianapolis, Indiana. His badly burned hand was a constant reminder of May 1, 1944, when the *Sunrise Serenade* caught fire and crashed. It was two years later in November 1946, before Bill was relieved from active duty. Returning to his boyhood home in Cleveland, he was filled with expectations regarding his future. However, it did not take him long to realize the War had changed him, and he felt a need to broaden his horizons. Bill felt something was missing and was sure that he could find it outside of Cleveland, Ohio. He enrolled in and eventually graduated from the American Institute of Foreign Trade (Thunderbird) in Phoenix, Arizona. He traveled the world constantly looking for ways to fill a void within him and finally settled for five years in the Canary Islands. During this time, Bill also filled the void in his life with alcohol, which seemingly helped him to get by day by day. In 1963, once again back in Cleveland, Bill admitted and accepted that he was powerless over alcohol and with the help of a twelve-step program began a new and sober life of recovery and work with alcoholics. While attending the Rutgers School of Studies in Alcoholism in 1966, he joined the staff of the Hazelden Foundation in Center City, Minnesota.

Nearly fifty years after the War was over, the copilot, Bill Hewett, was awarded the Prisoner of War Medal on February 7, 1993. The presentation was made by Major General John Roth, commander of the 81st Army Reserve Command.
- *Collection of William J. Hewett.*

Those many years of winters in northern Minnesota then became memories when Bill moved to Tequesta, Florida, located in northern Palm Beach County. During his residence in Florida, Bill tried to fill up his time with work indoors, volunteering, and hobbies such as golf, backgammon and gliding. Bill's emptiness continued until he invited God to become his personal savior and manage his life. Bill credits his spiritual awakening to his twelve-step alcoholism program. At his church, Bill eventually became elected as a deacon. In 1984 while attending his church, Bill married Jennie and became a new husband and step-father to two daughters.

Though Bill eventually got his life turned around after the War, he still carries memories of those years. In fact, Bill and his wife Jennie have kept in contact with the Belgian couple who saved him after he escaped from the Germans during the liberation of Belgium. They also made an emotional visit back to the former 452nd Bomb Group's airfield at Deopham Green, England. Still other memories were stirred when Bill was recently presented with a copy of Tom Brokaw's book, "The Greatest Generation" on his 82nd birthday. He accepted the book with pride and gratitude knowing that he had the opportunity to serve with such men as those mentioned in the book. Bill, now at age 83, and his wife, Jennie, continue to live in Florida.

One of those men Bill Hewett served with was the original ball turret gunner, Robert "Tiger Bob" Lalumiere, who also searched for a way to cope with the memories of war. He returned to the United States in November of 1944, and after one week of being home, married his high school sweetheart, Rita. He was then sent to Atlantic City for debriefing, so Bob and his new wife decided to honeymoon at the Ambassador Hotel where rooms had been arranged by the military for fatigued serviceman and their wives. While traveling to Atlantic City by bus, Bob was apprehended by two policeman and told to go with them. Rita was told to go on ahead and check into the hotel without him. Because Bob was among the airmen to fly a mission to the Russian base at Poltava on June 21, 1944, he was interrogated by the military for 48 hours. This was the second time he had been interrogated about the Poltava mission -- the first being at Deopham Green, England, upon returning to base from that mission. The police had somehow been previously made aware of Bob's time spent in Russia and either wanted to find out more about the Russians or make sure he was not a Russian spy. After the interrogation he finally arrived at the hotel to find that the single beds in the rooms had been wired together to force the fatigued servicemen to sleep with their wives in an effort to calm them down. The War was always on Bob's mind, and even troubled him when he slept. He constantly kept thrashing in bed during the night so much that Rita finally separated the beds, which upset those in charge of the hotel. Bob eventually transferred to Lake Lure, North Carolina, to another rest and relaxation facility for fatigued and wounded airmen. As time progressed, and Bob distanced himself from the fighting overseas, he finally began to sleep better and leave the War behind him. He finally recovered enough to be assigned to Columbia Airbase, Columbia, South Carolina, as a gunnery instructor where he remained until his discharge on September 27, 1945.

Bob Lalumiere was the first combat veteran from his hometown of Haverhill, Massachusetts, to be separated from the military since he had the most points gained toward discharge. He proudly wore his Purple Heart, Distinguished Flying Cross, and Air Medal with five oak leaf clusters, among other citations. After returning home, Bob was a foreman for a shoe tape factory and also owned a laundromat and dry cleaning store. He spent ten years as a Haverhill firefighter before going to work as a sales engineer for a shoe machinery company. As the company grew, Bob opened an office in Carlisle, Pennsylvania, where he stayed until his retirement in 1984. He and Rita raised eight children - four boys, and four girls. From these children they were blessed with sixteen grandchildren, and two great-grandchildren. After retiring, Bob and Rita spent six months in Florida, four months in Maine, and the rest of each year visiting family. Bob fought a courageous battle with cancer for several years before having his voice box removed in 1999. He used an electro-larynx to speak and was on his way to his old self again - still the "Tiger". Cancer finally overtook Bob and he died on February 19, 2000, at the age of 77. He is buried in the Elmwood Cemetery at Haverhill, Massachusetts.

Sometimes these wartime experiences provided men with career options that they might not have had otherwise. That was the case for James E. Gallagher, the substitute ball turret gunner, when he returned to the United States after being liberated from the German POW camps. Since he had joined the Armed Forces immediately out of high school, he was only 19 years old when the War ended. Jim decided that the military life would be well suited for him as a career and became the only member of the *Sunrise Serenade* to stay in the Armed Forces after the War. Post-war assignments took Jim back to the countries where he had once bombed targets, such as France and Germany. Working as a mechanic, Jim helped to keep the United States Armed Forces strong during the Cold War with Russia. While stationed in Paris, France, he met his future wife, Denise, at a military PX store in July of 1957. Six years later they were married, and Jim retired from the Air Force. Jim and his wife moved to Malega, Spain, where he operated a tavern. Two sons were born while in Spain, but the marriage was short-lived, and he and his wife separated in 1965. Jim returned to the United States while his wife returned to France with his two young sons. Even though Jim had retired from the Air Force, he could never leave the military way of life behind him. The constant moving around in the military combined with the atrocities of the War seen at such a young age made it difficult ever to adjust fully to civilian life. Jim spent the rest of his life living in the Vancouver, Washington, area and rarely, if ever, had contact with his family in France. Jim died on October 28, 1995, at the age of 71. He is buried in the National Military Cemetery in Portland, Oregon. Jim's former wife and two sons continue to live in Paris, France.

Jim Gallagher, the replacement ball turret gunner, became the only crew member of the *Sunrise Serenade* to continue a career with the military after the War had ended. - *Collection of Sean Gallagher.*

Many relationships suffered because of the War. Young men often came home to find that their sweethearts had changed because of the long separations. Many didn't find that out until after a quick marriage upon arrival back in the States. That was the case for Andrew Senetsky, Jr., the radioman, who married his high school sweetheart during his 60-day furlough in Dickson City, Pennsylvania. After the furlough, he chose to be transferred to Fort Dix, New Jersey, to await being processed out of the military. It was during their first year of marriage that both realized that the wedding had been a mistake. During the nearly three and half years he had been away from home, both he and his girlfriend had changed. Neither were the same person that they had remembered. The sudden joy of seeing each other again after the end of the War prompted their marriage, but that ended after just one year. They remained friends, however, until her death in 1997. Andy obtained a job as an inspector at Chaberlain Corporation in Scranton, Pennsylvania, where shell casings were made for the Korean and Viet Nam Wars. He remained at this job until his retirement. Andy, now at age 79, still resides in Pennsylvania close to the area he has always called home.

Some relationships did work out though. The engineer and upper turret gunner, Norbert E. "Dusty" Rhodes, returned to the rural life just outside of Williamsburg, Pennsylvania, after spending a short time in Miami and in St. Petersburg, Florida, where he was formally discharged from the Armed Forces. Upon his arrival home, he married his high school sweetheart, Esther, who had anxiously waited for his return from overseas. Dusty was employed at Beasly Rebuilders where he built engines until his retirement 35 years later. The couple had one son, Randall, who died in 1989 at the age of 40 as a result of a brain tumor. Dusty loved to build radio-controlled airplanes and boats, and also enjoyed traveling around the country to see new places. Dusty died on June 16, 1991, at the age of 69 and is buried in the Royer Cemetery at Williamsburg, Pennsylvania. His wife, Esther, continues to live in the Williamsburg area.

John J. McGrath, the navigator, also married his pre-War sweetheart, Alice, within a year after returning to his hometown of Langhorne, Pennsylvania. He even returned to work at his pre-War employer, Rohm & Haas in October 1945, three months before he officially separated from the military. John became an industrial engineer at Rohm & Haas and worked at this company for 37 years until his early retirement. While working, John received his Industrial Management degree from Temple University in 1962 through night classes. After retirement, John obtained a real estate license and sold real estate, and also worked part-time for Rohm & Haas for four more years. Retirement enabled John to devote more time to playing tennis, which he loved since early childhood. From the 1980's to the present, John has been ranked as one of the top 5 tennis players in the world in his age division, and has also been ranked number one on two occasions. The national tennis rankings have allowed him to travel to Europe, where he has visited some of the places where he was stationed during the War. John continues to make the headlines in the tennis world and is currently ranked No. 1 in the United States, and his team is ranked No. 1 in the world. He and Alice have four children; two girls and two boys, eight grandchildren, and one great-grandchild. John, now at age 81, and his wife Alice, live in Langhorne, Pennsylvania, and spend their winters in Florida.

Sports played a major role in another of the crew member's acclimation into civilian life. George D. Griffin, the bombardier, resumed playing baseball upon his arrival back in the United States at the position of catcher. He first played professional baseball at Oneonta, New York, in a Class C league. Later he played AAA baseball for the Tigers in Toledo, Ohio; the White Sox at Charleston, West Virginia; the Red Sox at Scranton, Pennsylvania; and on an independent team in Toronto, Canada. During this time George was married in 1948, and a son was born in 1953. His professional baseball career spanned 14 years before he retired from the sport. After baseball, George became self-employed selling retail office machinery and insurance, and he also worked in the trucking industry. George remarried after the death of his first wife. George, now at age 78, and his wife Phyllis, presently live in Florida and spend their summers in North Carolina.

George Griffin, the bombardier, resumed his professional baseball career after returning home from the War. In this photo George is playing catcher for the Oneonta, New York, Red Sox. - *Collection of George D. Griffin.*

A few of the crew from the *Sunrise Serenade* returned to the United States and started careers working with airplanes. If Francis C. Smedley, the pilot of the *Sunrise Serenade*, had not been killed, he would have probably continued to fly airplanes. He had once written to his mother that as soon as he came home from the War he would become a commercial airline pilot in order to take care of her better financially. Sadly, Francis only became a statistic of the War to most of the world, but his friends and crew would forever hold the memory of him as a great leader and caring individual.

Left waist gunner Harry C. Shoffner was one crew member who did start a career working with airplanes. Harry was one of the first crew members to return home from the War in mid-October of 1944, after Belgium was liberated. In 1946 he returned to Kansas University to earn an Aeronautical Engineering degree. Harry graduated in 1949 and soon after accepted a position with Convair in San Diego, California, as an aeronautical engineer. Due to lay-offs at Convair, Harry worked for a short time in Burbank, California, before being called back to Convair in 1952. Another lay-off forced him to relocate to St. Louis a few years later to work for the McDonald Douglas Corporation. Harry C. Shoffner died of a sudden heart attack at the age of 52 on May 15, 1972. At the time of his death, Harry was working for McDonald Douglas and he and his family lived in Bridgerton, Missouri. Harry is buried at Glen Abbey Memorial Park in Bonita, California. His wife, Mary Lou, moved back to San Diego after Harry's death where she presently lives.

One of the happiest days of Harry Shoffner's life was when he reunited with his wife, Mary Lou, and young son, Larry, in October of 1944. The prolonged effects of the War would cause that happiness to be greatly diminished as the years went by for the former waist gunner. - *Collection of the author.*

When right waist gunner, John G. Brown, returned to the United States he began working on a survey crew with the Virginia Department of Highways until a lifelong friend suggested he apply for a job with Capital Airlines in Washington D.C. where he worked. John obtained a position as an aircraft mechanic at Capital Airlines and stayed there for 20 years. While working for Capital Airlines, John met his sweetheart, Donna, whom he later married. When Capital Airlines was taken over by United Airlines, John and many others were transferred to San Francisco, California. He continued to work for United Airlines and retired with a total of 37 years in the airline business. John, now at age 77, and his wife Donna, currently reside in Oregon. The couple have a son and a daughter, four grandchildren, and two great-grandchildren.

It took Raymond E. Dean a few years before he got back into the business of flying. The former tail gunner returned to Montana upon arrival back to the United States where he purchased 160 acres of farmland and leased an additional 250 acres. He purchased a tractor and plow with the back wages he had accumulated while being a POW of the Germans. He also borrowed some other equipment from his father as payment for helping on the home place. He then began to farm. During the next year, he married his younger brother's school teacher, Gwendolyn. Raymond and she raised four children - two boys and two girls. In 1949 Raymond realized his childhood dream of flying and, utilizing the G. I. Bill, learned to become an aerial spray pilot. In 1958 they moved to Star Valley, Wyoming, where he became the test pilot and manager of quality control for CALL-AIR, a manufacturer of agricultural airplanes. He traveled to various parts of the continental United States as well as New Zealand

and South America demonstrating these planes. In 1967 they moved to Albany, Georgia, where he became the test pilot for Aero-Commander and later Maul Aircraft in Moltrie, Georgia. Later he returned west and after a season in Hawaii dusting sugar cane, he began his own business, Desert Air Ag, in the alfalfa and potato country of Terreton, Idaho. After retiring in 1987, he created in his back yard a log house from a pile of bug-killed Lodge Pole pine. He numbered each log, dismantled it and trucked it up to Bigfork, Montana, where he rebuilt it, added the finishing touches, and called it home until 1996 when they sold it. They moved to Farmington, New Mexico, to escape the severe Montana winters, since Raymond had developed Post Traumatic Stress Disorder and diabetes resulting in a severe heart condition. Raymond passed away on June 26, 1998, at the age of 74 and is buried in the National Cemetery in Santa Fe, New Mexico. His family described him as a devoutly religious man who was deeply loyal to his family. He was also loyal to his former pilot and friend.

Raymond Dean, the tailgunner, fulfilled his lifelong dream of becoming a pilot after the War. Raymond (right) and son, Alan, stand in front of one of their planes used for aerial crop spraying in the mid 1980's. - *Collection of Gwendolyn Dean.*

Raymond and his wife traveled to Europe in 1990 and 1991 to many of the sites associated with the War. They toured Germany as well as Brussels, Belgium, where they learned that Smedley's body had been moved to a military cemetery near Liege, Belgium. They also visited with an eye witness of the *Sunrise Serenade's* demise, and visited the site of the crash. He brought home a few souvenirs of the plane; one of which was a piece of the bullet-proof glass.

The crew of the *Sunrise Serenade* had returned home one by one, usually among unfamiliar faces of other weary soldiers aboard transport ships. Some came home much earlier than others, such as Harry Shoffner who was liberated from the Belgian Underground, Bill Hewett who escaped from the Germans, and Bob Lalumiere who finished his 30 combat missions. John Brown, Raymond Dean, Jim Gallagher, Dusty Rhodes and Andy Senetsky, all who had been separated during their time in the German prison camps, would remain separated even after the War ended. Only John McGrath and George Griffin stayed together during their entire time overseas and came back to the United States together. The bond they built between them in the POW camps would continue over the years; they would occasionally see each other or contact each other through letters or telephone calls. They shared a common experience beyond being just crew members on the same plane. It was easier for them to talk about it openly with each other than with someone who had not shared their same experiences.

For the rest of the crew, the day they were shot down, May 1, 1944, was the last time many of them would ever see each other again. An occasional Christmas card was exchanged between a few of the men, but most did not keep track of each other's addresses, and some moved to different locations. Harry Shoffner had a tough time dealing with the effects of the War after he returned home. He never discussed what had happened during the War even with his own family, so he made no attempt to contact former crew members to relive the past. His crew never fully knew the details about his experiences in the Belgian Underground. The same was true for Bob Lalumiere and Bill Hewett who survived their own harrowing experiences without most of their former crew ever knowing what had happened to them. One of Bob's only meetings with a former crew member occurred in 1946 when he and Andy Senetsky briefly met.

One year after the War, Andy Senetsky (left) and Bob Lalumiere met to discuss what each other had been through. This meeting would be the last time the former radioman and ball turret gunner would ever see each other again.
- *Collection of Robert A. Lalumiere.*

Two members who did share their experiences were John Brown and Dusty Rhodes who met briefly once after the War. John related this story many years later:

> "The last time I saw any of the crew was May 1, 1944. I think some of the guys and I may have been in the same camp, but I didn't know it. Dusty Rhodes and his wife came to see us in Virginia about five years after the War. I was repairing a tire in the garage with the big door open. I noticed a car stop out front, and a man got out and walked up to the garage. He stood there looking at me without saying a word. I thought to myself that he would say something sooner or later. Finally it hit me like a ton of bricks. It was Dusty. He and his wife had driven down from Pennsylvania. We had a really great visit, but it turned out to be the last time we would ever see each other again. Ray Dean dropped by once but we were not at home, so I missed seeing him. I really find it hard to believe that both of these guys are both gone. There was a time when we all felt we were invincible."

Dusty Rhodes also met with Ray Dean a few years after the War and talked about their war-time experiences. It lasted all night. It was a conversation shared only by Dusty and Ray, as their wives found it difficult to relate. They both felt it was good for them to reflect and discuss what had happened during the War since few others around them could truly understand. It was the first and last time that those two would see each other after the War.

The brother of Francis Smedley, Vincent, did contact John McGrath to learn more details about his brother's death and the crash of the *Sunrise Serenade*. Vincent had lost his only brother and was seeking closure to the many questions he still had about his death. Bob Lalumiere and John McGrath did meet for the first time 55 years later in an emotional meeting. Neither had known what each other had experienced after the *Sunrise Serenade* failed to return to its base.

The navigator, John McGrath (left), and the ball turret gunner, Bob Lalumiere, reunited for the first time in 55 years in January of 1999. The very emotional meeting proved that the bonds formed among men who fought together during the War are not easily broken. - *Collection of John J. McGrath.*

As the years passed by, time put distance between the former crew members of the *Sunrise Serenade*. Some would die without the other members of the crew ever knowing. Most inwardly relished the thought of having a former crew member of the *Sunrise Serenade* contact them, but each would wonder if the others wanted just to forget about the past, so contact was rarely initiated. For most of the young men serving their country during the War, it wasn't just about one country fighting against the other, but rather the War involved their own personal fight to somehow stay alive just long enough to return home. This collective idea of personal survival helped to create stable and well-trained bomber crews who in turn depended upon each other, such as those who flew aboard the *Sunrise Serenade*.

The pilot, Francis C. Smedley, never had the chance to marry or raise children. The last two years of his life were, in a sense, spent preparing to die for his country so that others might have that chance he never had. - *Collection of the author.*

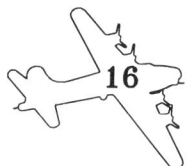

Fighters, Flak and Fear

Bomber crews were constantly faced with the fear and reality of dying during every mission. Each time a bomber took off, its crew faced many factors that could lead to their demise. Of these factors, some were a minimal threat - weather, mechanical problems or pilot error. However, the major factors that brought down the majority of the American heavy bombers were the German fighter planes and the ground based anti-aircraft guns that produced flak. Rarely was there a mission when at least one or both of these were not encountered, usually in heavy concentrations. The tactics used by bomber crews to evade the fighters and the flak were very different since each had its own unique characteristics. The menacing flak fired from the anti-aircraft guns was generally aimed at entire formations, while the German fighters were usually more discriminating, picking out individual planes for their targets.

Fighters

The German *Luftwaffe* was very impressive and had a wide range of aircraft at their disposal. Among these were nearly 25 different styles of bombers, 28 different styles of fighters, and at least 15 different styles of planes used for transport, reconnaissance, sea-landing, and anti-tank operations. In addition to these planes, the *Luftwaffe* utilized many planes from their Italian ally, and also those which were taken from Czechoslovakia, Poland, The Netherlands, and other countries they overran.

The Messerschmitt Me-109 German fighter was widely known to Allied bomber crews. The Focke-Wulf FW-190 was the other fighter primarily used by the *Luftwaffe* against the Allied bombers - *Collection of the author.*

The primary fighter planes that the German *Luftwaffe* used against the B-17 Flying Fortresses were the Focke-Wulf FW-190 and the Messerschmitt Me-109 (also known as the Bf-109). Certain models of the FW-190 could attain a maximum speed of 408 mph while the somewhat slower Me-109's speed was a maximum of 386 mph. These speeds were certainly faster than the Flying Fortress's normal cruising speed of 150 mph when loaded with bombs, or its maximum unloaded speed of 287 mph. The Me-109 was the most extensively produced fighter plane in history - 35,000 built between 1935 and 1945.

Though the B-17's were slower than the fighter planes, they still had numerous ways to counter attack the fighters. The Boeing B-17 Flying Fortresses were designed to be able to defend themselves against the German fighters with their armament, sometimes with up to thirteen .50 caliber guns. The German fighters respected these guns, not only because of their size, but because the bombers flew in formations which could have many of these guns from different planes firing in unison at any particular fighter. Formation flying was one way the American bombers counter-attacked the German fighters. It was crucial that a bomber stay in formation because if a bomber became separated from the main formation, the German fighters could focus on that single plane. Once a particular bomber became separated from the rest of the formation it was almost always doomed if the formations happened to be where the German fighters were attacking. Every gunner on a crippled B-17 tried his best to fight off the enemy attackers, but the overwhelming number of fighters often prevailed.

The most heavily armored version of the FW-190 fighter, the FW-190A-8, carried two 20mm fixed forward-firing cannons in the root of the wings, two 20mm fixed forward-firing cannons in the leading edges of the wing, and two 13mm fixed forward-firing machine guns in the upper part of the forward fuselage. This particular model also had a nitrous oxide power boost system for faster acceleration and additional fuel capacity in the rear-fuselage tank.

Most Me-109 fighters contained two 20mm fixed forward-firing cannons in the leading edges of the wings and two 7.92mm forward-firing machine guns in the upper part of the forward fuselage. The Me-109G model, still in production at the end of the War, was heavily armed with a 30mm cannon and two 13mm machine guns.

The German 13mm machine guns were comparable in size to the American .50 caliber machine guns; however, the much larger 20mm and 30mm cannons were greatly feared. The German 7.92mm machine guns were the only disadvantage over the Flying Fortress in terms of fire-power since they were of a slightly smaller caliber.

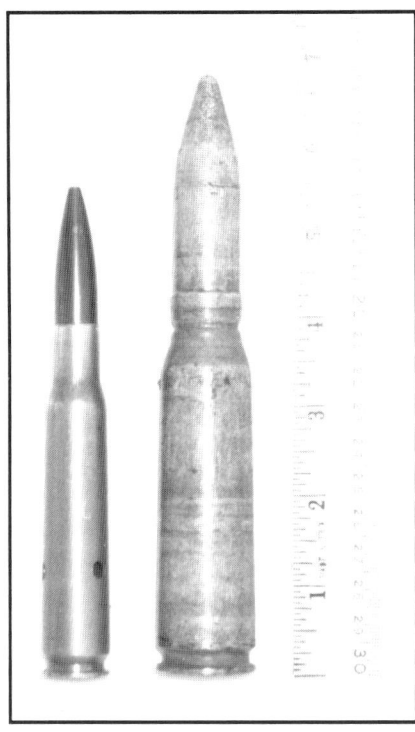

The .50 caliber shell, (left) was used by the gunners aboard the B-17's, and was noticeably smaller than the 20mm shell used by the German fighters. An even larger 30mm shell was also used by the German fighters. - *Photo by the author.*

Another counter attack used by the Americans against the German fighter planes was the use of escort fighters for the bombers. These fighters were mainly three different planes; the Lockheed P-38 Lightning, the Republic P-47 Thunderbolt, and the North American P-51 Mustang.

The P-38 was the first American fighter to escort the heavy bombers. The fastest version obtained a maximum speed of 414 mph which immediately gave itself a slight advantage over the best German fighter, however many models could only attain a speed of 390 mph which compared closely to the German Me-109. The P-38's armament consisted of one fixed forward-firing 20mm cannon in the nose and four 0.50 caliber fixed forward-firing machine guns in the nose. It could also carry an external bomb and rocket load weighing up to 4,000 lbs. The range of a P-38 was usually only 400 miles; however, a later model of the P-38 was developed with extra fuel tanks that could attain a range up to 2,600 miles.

The P-47 could travel even faster than the P-38. It had a maximum speed of 435 mph, with a specially designed model that could travel up to 470 mph. The P-47 contained eight .50 caliber fixed forward-firing machine guns in the leading edges of the wings, plus an external bomb and rocket load up to 2,500 lbs. This plane was the largest and heaviest (19,426 pounds) fighter plane used during the War. The appearance of this large fighter somewhat resembled a milk bottle, so it was often referred to as a "seven-ton milkbottle" or a "jug". The United States built 15,683 of these massive fighter planes between 1942 and 1945 - more than any other U.S. fighter escort planes.

The most famous of the three American fighter escorts, however, was the P-51, which could achieve a maximum speed of 440 mph, which was nearly 50 mph faster than most of the German fighters in active service. The armament on the P-51 consisted of six 0.50 caliber fixed forward-firing machine guns in the leading edges of the wings, plus an external bomb and rocket load up to 2,000 lbs. The P-51 was best known for its ability to escort the bomber formations the entire mission, since it had a basic range up to 950 miles and an extended range of over 2,000 miles with additional drop fuel tanks. Prior to the arrival of the P-51, the fighter escorts generally had to leave the bomber formations and turn back due to low fuel levels if the mission was an extended distance. When the fighter escorts left, the bombers then became vulnerable to the German fighters who had often patiently waited until the escorts had left. Many deem the P-51D Mustang the best fighter plane used during the War. It was aerodynamically built and powered by a British Rolls-Royce engine. The pilots who flew the P-51's logged 213,873 missions in Europe alone, while destroying 4,950 enemy planes. Bomber crews were always relieved to see the fighter escorts and affectionately called them their "Little Friends".

The North American P-51 Mustang became the workhorse of the escort fighters. It was 50 mph faster than the conventional German fighters and had a range of over 2,000 miles. - *Collection of Merle Olmsted.*

Upon the arrival of the Flying Fortresses to the War in 1942, the German fighters were initially hesitant to engage the bombers due to the intimidation of the many guns aboard the plane. As the War progressed more and more tactics were developed by the Germans to find the vulnerable areas on the B-17's. They soon learned that an attack from the head-on position was the most successful tactic that a German fighter could use against the B-17F model. This continued until bomber crews repeatedly spoke out about the lack of protection from the front end. In late 1943 the B-17F was redesigned to carry two extra forward facing 0.50 caliber machine guns in a chin turret that was operated by the bombardier. The *Sunrise Serenade* was one of these newer models of the Flying Fortress, which was designated as the B-17G.

Protection against bullets coming from German fighters was minimal inside a B-17. The thin aluminum covering of the plane was easily penetrated by almost any caliber of gun used by the German fighters. Usually the fighters would try to disable the entire plane by either shooting at the engines or aiming for the pilots. Armor plating inside a Flying Fortress was placed at the back of the two pilots' seats, the front and rear of the top turret position, the rear of the radio operator's seat, the backside of the ball turret position, the forward side of the two waist gun positions and the front side of the tail gunner's position as he was looking back. The specifications for the thickness of the armor plating was designed to only stop a .30 caliber bullet or German equivalent. This design thickness was not even sufficient to stop stray .50 caliber bullets being fired from other Flying Fortresses, let alone a 20mm or larger shell being fired from a German fighter.

Despite the months of intense training that a B-17 gunner received, shooting down a German fighter was not an easy task. Firing at a moving target going one way while your plane was going at a different speed in another direction required much skill and intuition to correctly place the shots. As soon as a little black speck resembling a fighter had been sighted, it took only seconds for it to pass by the bomber. The gunners had to have a keen eye and react without hesitation once a German fighter was first sighted. The crew of the *Sunrise Serenade* was officially credited with shooting down six German aircraft during their 20 missions. Some bomber crews were credited with shooting down more than six fighters; however, this number was probably considered high since most crews only lasted an average of ten missions. The first of these six planes claimed by the *Sunrise Serenade* occurred on their second mission, which was to Posen, Poland, on February 20, 1944. The tail gunner aboard the *Sunrise Serenade*, Ray Dean, described the eventful occurrence in his writings after the War:

> "*On this mission I received credit for shooting down a German fighter, a Ju-88. This plane came in on the tail and when I finally stopped him, he was less than fifty yards away. His left engine caught fire and he went into a spin; I never saw the pilot bail out. The ball turret gunner, Bob Lalumiere, also got credit for a German fighter this day. I was very afraid, but also proud that I had been able to function well under fire. On this day I fired nearly 3,000 rounds of ammo through those two .50 caliber machine guns.*"

The Ju-88 was a twin-engined German fighter/bomber, more correctly described as a Junkers Ju-88. Typically this plane was used by the Germans as a level bomber or night fighter and was not commonly seen by B-17 crews. Due to the increased need to stop the American bombers, the Ju-88 was occasionally used against the bombers. This four-passenger German plane was much slower than the FW-190 or the Me-109 fighters, but shooting down one of these impressive planes was still considered an honor. The Ju-88 was the first plane to bomb a British city during the Battle of Britain and by the end of the War over 15,000 had been built. Bob Lalumiere, in the ball turret position of the *Sunrise Serenade,* was also credited with shooting down a Ju-88 during one of their later missions.

During an intense battle between the B-17's and the German fighters, the intercom inside the bombers was alive with the gunners calling out the various fighter positions, such as at the three o'clock position, to ensure that every gunner knew the direction from which their plane was being attacked. The engineer and upper turret gunner of the *Sunrise Serenade*, Dusty Rhodes, was credited with shooting down at least one FW-190 during one of their missions and gave this account of the German *Luftwaffe* during the crew's first trip to Berlin on March 6, 1944:

> "*The fighters came at us. To my right I could see small black dots in the distance. I watched them as they circled around and then I recognized them. They were Focke Wulfs and Messerschmitts and they were getting set for an opening. They came in at us head on, guns blazing away and cannons lobbing 20mm shells at us. The 20mm shells burst with little white puffs of smoke. Those planes flew into a hail of lead from every turret and gun in the formation, the likes of which I have never seen. Our fighter escort was after them, and a furious air battle started. A group of Messerschmitts started to fire red bursting rockets at us. They all missed due to perfect evasive action on our part. One of the Messerschmitts crashed right square into one of the Fortresses in another formation. Both ships burst into flame and pieces of metal started to fly in all directions.*"

Among the more advanced planes used by the Germans were the turbojet fighters, which entered the War in late 1944. One of the more widely known

German turbojet planes was the Me-262, which first flew in testing stages as early as March 1942 and had been in the planning stages since 1938. This plane had a maximum speed of 540 mph, making it over 100 mph faster than the American P-51 Mustang. Constant meddling in the German aircraft industry by Adolph Hitler hindered the production of this advanced plane until he finally authorized it in November 1943, but only as a high-speed bomber. Hitler was still preoccupied with inflicting revenge upon England, and a jet-powered bomber was to be his answer. The *Luftwaffe* was in dire need of having the Me-262 as a fighter to intercept bomber formations, but Hitler was incensed at the idea of producing planes that were primarily for defensive purposes only. By late 1944, a redesigned model of the Me-262 was eventually utilized to intercept bomber formations, and carried four 30mm fixed forward-firing cannons. This plane became the world's first jet to see aircraft-to-aircraft combat in October of 1944 even though both the Americans and the British were desperately working on their own version of a jet aircraft. Slightly over 1,000 of the Me-262's were produced, however less than 100 actually saw combat and most were destroyed on the ground. This technically superior weapon had been rendered useless because it had entered the War at such a late stage. The German high command had estimated that only 200 to 250 of these aircraft would have been needed to stop the daily Allied bomber raids, and possibly turn the direction of the War around in favor of the Germans.

Another German-produced plane of World War II was the remarkable Me-163 Komet. The Komet used a liquid-propellant rocket motor to propel it to speeds nearing 600 mph. The armament consisted of two 20mm or 30mm fixed forward-firing cannons in the root of the wings. The major drawback of this plane was its limited range of just 22 miles. The airbases for these planes had to be positioned along known bomber routes to have any hope of bringing down one of the Flying Fortresses. Certain models of the Me-163 were fitted with upward firing guns that fired when the shadow of a bomber activated a photocell connected to the guns of the Me-163 passing underneath.

Despite the heavy losses inflicted upon the German fighter planes by the Allied planes and from the meddling of the German hierarchy, approximately 105 German fighter pilots each had over 100 planes shot down to their credit. Erich Hartmann was the top German ace with 352 kills to his credit, however only seven of these were American planes. Francis "Gabby" Gabreski was the top American ace in the European Theater with 28 kills to his credit, with Robert S. Johnson following closely with 27 kills. Hartmann chose to fly an Me-109 while Gabreski and Johnson both flew P-47's with the 56th Fighter Group. This Group led all 8th Air Force fighter groups with the most enemy aircraft destroyed.

The German *Luftwaffe* had over 100 fighter pilots with over 100 kills each. Field Marshall Erhard Milch (center) leads Egon Mayer (left), Walter Oesau (back), and Adolph Galland (right) on an inspection tour of JG26. Josef Wurmheller stands at far left. Career kills for these men are Oesau-117; Galland-103; Mayer-102; and Wurmheller-102.
- *Collection of the author.*

German Fighter Aces
With over 100 Kills against all Countries

Name	Kills	Name	Kills	Name	Kills
Erich Hartmann	352	Fritz Tegtmeier	146	Friedrich Obleser	120
Gerhard Barkhorn	301	Albin Wolf	144	Franz-Josef Beerenbrock	117
Gunther Rall	275	Kurt Tanzer	143	Hans-Joachim Birkner	117
Otto Kittel	267	Friedrich-Karl Muller	140	Jakob Norz	117
Walter Nowotny	258	Karl Gratz	138	Walter Oesau	117
Wilhelm Batz	237	Heinrich Setz	138	Heinz Wernicke	117
Erich Rudorffer	224	Rudolf Trenkel	138	August Lambert	116
Heinz Bar	221	Walter Wolfrum	137	Wilhelm Crinius	114
Hermann Graf	212	Horst-Gunther von Fassong	136	Werner Schoer	114
Heinrich Ehrler	208	Otto Fonnekold	136	Hans Dammers	113
Theodor Weissenberger	208	Karl-Heinz Weber	136	Berthold Korts	113
Hans Philipp	206	Joachim Muencheberg	135	Helmut Lent	113
Walter Schuck	206	Hans Waldmann	134	Kurt Buhligen	112
Anton Hafner	204	Alfred Grislawski	133	Kurt Ubben	110
Helmut Lipfert	203	Franz Schall	133	Franz Woidich	110
Walter Krupinski	197	Johannes Wiese	133	Reinhard Seiler	109
Anton Hackl	192	Adolf Borchers	132	Emil Bitsch	108
Joachim Brendel	189	Adolf Dickfeld	132	Hans Hahn	108
Max Stotz	189	Erwin Clausen	132	Bernhard Vechtel	108
Joachim Kirschner	188	Wilhelm Lemke	131	Victor Bauer	106
Kurt Brandle	180	Gerhard Hoffman	130	Werner Lucas	106
Gunther Josten	178	Franz Eisenach	129	Gunther Lutzow	105
Johannes Steinhoff	178	Walther Dahl	129	Eberhard von Boremski	104
Ernst-Wilhelm Reinert	174	Heinrich Sterr	129	Heinz Sachsenberg	104
Gunther Schack	174	Franz Dorr	128	Adolf Galland	103
Emil Lang	173	Rudolf Rademacher	126	Hartmann Grasser	103
Heinz Schmidt	173	Josef Zwernemann	126	Siegfried Freytag	102
Horst Ademeit	166	Dietrich Hrabak	125	Friedrich Geisshardt	102
Wolf-Dietrich Wilcke	162	Wolf Ettel	124	Egon Mayer	102
Hans-Joachim Marseille	158	Herbert Ihlefeld	123	Max-Hellmuth Ostermann	102
Heinrich Sturm	158	Wolfgang Tonne	122	Josef Wurmheller	102
Gerhard Thyben	157	Heinz Marquardt	121	Rudolf Miethig	101
Hans Beisswenger	152	Heinz-Wolfgang Schnaufer	121	Werner Molders	101
Peter Duttman	152	Robert Weiss	121	Josef Priller	101
Gordon Gollob	150	Erich Leie	121	Ulrich Wernitz	101

American Fighter Aces
With 12 or more Kills fighting against the Germans

Name	Kills	Name	Kills	Name	Kills
Francis "Gabby" Gabreski	28.00	Gerald W. Johnson	16.50	Donald S. Bryan	13.33
Robert S. Johnson	27.00	John T. Godfrey	16.33	George Carpenter	13.33
George E. Preddy	26.83	Charles E. "Bud" Anderson	16.25	James L. Brooks	13.00
John C. Meyer	24.00	Donald M. Beerbower	15.50	Willard Millikan	13.00
David Schilling	22.50	Samuel J. Brown	15.50	Glennon Moran	13.00
Fred J. Christiansen	21.50	Richard A. Peterson	15.50	Harry A. Parker	13.00
Ray S. Wetmore	21.25	William Whisner	15.50	Robert W. Stephens	13.00
John J. Voll	21.00	Jack T. Bradley	15.00	Felix Williamson	13.00
Walker Mahurin	20.75	Robert W. Foy	15.00	Lowell K. Brueland	12.50
Donald Gentile	19.83	Ralph K. Hofer	15.00	Quince L. Brown	12.33
Glenn E. Duncan	19.50	John D. Landers	14.50	Michael Brezas	12.00
Leonard K. Carson	18.50	Joe H. Powers, Jr.	14.50	Clyde B. East	12.00
Glenn T. Eagleston	18.50	Henry W. Brown	14.20	George W. Gleason	12.00
Walter C. Beckam	18.00	Bruce W. Carr	14.00	Howard D. Hively	12.00
Herschell H. Green	18.00	Robert C. Curtis	14.00	Kenneth G. Ladd	12.00
Hubert Zemke	17.75	Kenneth Dahlberg	14.00	Robin Olds	12.00
John B. England	17.50	Wallace N. Emmer	14.00	Leroy Schreiber	12.00
Duane W. Beeson	17.33	James A. Goodson	14.00	Norman Skogstad	12.00
John F. Thornell	17.25	Arthur F. Jeffrey	14.00	William Sloan	12.00
James S. Varnell	17.00	Donald H. Bochkay	13.83		

Notes: Several factors can be attributed to the higher number of kills made by the German fighter pilots. The German fighter pilots were generally engaged in active service during the entire six years of the War, whereas the American pilots were on a rotation basis during only the last three years. The Germans also scored many kills against inferior aircraft being flown by the countries they overran at the beginning of the War. The German totals shown are from every country they fought against during the War; however, the American totals shown represent only those pilots fighting in Europe against the Germans. Walker Mahurin, George Preddy and John Landers also had at least one kill each fighting against the Japanese. Richard I. Bong was the top American ace of the entire War with 40 kills fighting against the Japanese.

Flak

The Germans produced massive numbers of Fliegerabwehrkanone or "Flak" guns to protect their ground troops and also to shoot down heavy allied bombers. The main purpose of flak was to cause the bombers to divert or abort from dropping their payload accurately on the target. Light Flak guns referred to those guns which generally utilized the rapid firing 20mm shells. These guns were highly effective at shooting down low-flying aircraft, but were useless against the high-flying bomber formations. Light Flak was considered to be all shells up to 36mm in diameter. Medium Flak guns had a longer range than the Light Flak guns. This longer range allowed the Medium Flak guns to be used to defend the German cities, but used contact-bursting shells only, which meant that they had to actually hit their target. The Medium Flak was all shells measuring from 37mm to 59mm in diameter. The most effective flak used by the Germans against the bombers was the Heavy Flak, which included all shell sizes from 60mm to 159mm in diameter. The most famous gun in the Heavy Flak category was the 88mm version.

The Heavy Flak used a shell that exploded at a predetermined height to match the altitude of the bomber formations. The 88mm gun had been in production since 1928 and was first tested by the Germans in battle during Spain's civil war between 1936 and 1939. Many airmen referred to this gun or its exploding shells as "ack-ack" which was taken from the German word "Achtacht" (eight-eight). Four models of the 88mm guns existed (18, 36, 37, and 41). By the end of the War in 1945 more than 25,000 of these guns had been produced by the Germans. The guns fired shells up to an altitude of 49,000 feet and at a rate of three shells per minute. This altitude was more than sufficient to penetrate the altitude of the bomber formations. Most anti-aircraft batteries were equipped with four guns, although heavier batteries with six guns were also used. The batteries were positioned around almost every German occupied city that had any type of military significance such as an airfield, factory, or railroad yard. The batteries were also positioned along the French and Belgium coasts and along known bomber flight paths. The first flak encountered was usually as the bombers passed over the English Channel or North Sea to the enemy coast. This was generally the tell-tale sign for the bomber crews that they had reached the coast, which also proved to be true as they were leaving the coast on the return trip.

As the bombers were approaching their target, the loader of the 88mm gun was handed a shell which he placed nose-down into a tube under and next to the open breech. The cartridge revolved slowly as the device on the nose of the shell was being pre-set by electro-mechanical means to explode at the proper altitude, depending on the proper flight path of the bombers. At the beginning of the ring of an alarm bell, attached to the supports of one of the hydraulic recoil tubes, the loader lifted the cartridge out of the tube and shoved it into the breech; he had only seconds to perform this task. At the precise moment that the bell stopped ringing, he pulled the lanyard that was attached to the firing mechanism. Other members of the crew were busy bringing new shells from the stockpile nearby. A typical 88mm gun crew consisted of a leader and eight men. Most of the larger flak guns all operated in a similar fashion. The smaller guns such as the 20mm and 37mm flak were loaded with shells held in magazines. These were rapid-firing guns and required a constant reloading as the shells were quickly fired at lower flying aircraft.

The most famous anti-aircraft gun used against the Allied bombers was the 88mm. The *Sunrise Serenade* was brought down by flak units using both the 88mm and 105mm flak guns.
- *Collection of the author.*

The Germans generally always knew that the bomber formations were headed their direction. Radar detection units known as Wuerzburg detected the bombers and relayed the direction and altitude to waiting flak batteries. Once the route was determined, those flak batteries along that path would determine the time-delay needed on the shells to explode at the proper altitude to match the bombers. As soon as the German fighter planes quit attacking the bomber formations, the bomber crews knew that the flak would soon begin. The German fighters knew the extreme danger of the exploding flak and did not pursue the bombers into the area which it was being fired. Large black puffs of seemingly harmless flak began to appear ahead of the bombers. Soon the planes were completely surrounded by the flak that produced large explosions and violently shook the planes. The flak shells were machined so that upon explosion the shells would break apart into many pieces which had a lethal radius of over 50 meters. These pieces of flak often ripped through the thin covering of the bombers with deadlier force than the shells being fired from German fighters. Inside the planes the crew all put on flak jackets and helmets to protect their bodies from the flying pieces of the shells. The most intense flak usually happened when the bombers were on their final bomb runs and could not deviate from their course to fly away from the concentrations. A direct hit of flak into a bomber was usually fatal. A near miss was likewise usually fatal since the exploding shell sent pieces flying into the cockpit or gas tanks, causing them to catch fire.

One of the awards that a German flak gunner could receive was the Army Flak Badge. This badge was bestowed with 16 points being the requisite, or could be awarded without reference to the number of points for any act of bravery or merit in the conduct of performing the anti-aircraft mission. Any anti-aircraft battery credited with downing an enemy aircraft without the support of other batteries was awarded 4 points, but if other batteries assisted in downing the aircraft, only 2 points were awarded. Each member of the four batteries that shot down the *Sunrise Serenade* would have probably been awarded 2 points each. Searchlight crews in support of the batteries who were credited with a first detection were awarded 1 point. When a flak battery commander had half of his company awarded the badge, he then became eligible himself for the award. The crews operating the 88mm and larger flak guns would paint a ring around the barrel of their gun with every new plane that they had helped to bring down.

The German Army Flak Badge was awarded to flak gunners on a point system involving the shooting down of Allied planes. The anti-aircraft batteries that were involved in shooting down the *Sunrise Serenade* each received 2 points. A total of 16 points was needed to be awarded the medal.
- *Collection of the author.*

The prestigious Knights Cross Medal was awarded to only 195 Germans who operated the anti-aircraft guns. Of this number 165 were members of the Luftwaffenflak, 13 from the Heeresflakeinheiten, 8 from the Waffen-SS-Flak, and 6 from the Marine-Flak. Six German officers also earned the Oak Leaves for their leadership of the flak battalions.

It is estimated that it took 16,000 rounds of 88mm Flak 36 or 8,000 rounds of the improved AA shell to shoot down a single enemy plane. Since the main purpose of the flak was to primarily cause the bombers to divert or abort from dropping their payload accurately on the intended target, it was not intended to aim for individual planes. Timing, however, for the flak gunners was very critical since an 18-lb. 88mm shell fired at maximum range would take nearly 25 seconds to reach the altitude. In that amount of time the bombers would have flown an additional 2 miles.

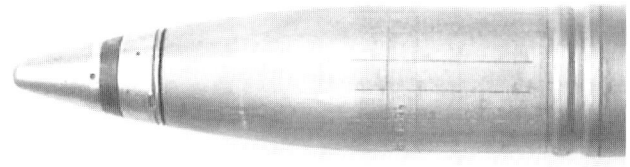

The nose of the 88mm anti-aircraft shell held the timer that caused it to explode at the predetermined altitude of the bombers. Upon detonation the scored bullet burst into many fragments producing "flak". The entire shell including the casing was over 42" long. - *Collection of the author.*

It was rare that any bomber while flying through a barrage of flak did not receive some damage. The pilot of the *Sunrise Serenade*, Francis C. Smedley, gave this account of flak during their first mission to Berlin on March 6, 1944:

> "Hours passed, and then we approached the plum, Berlin. There she stretched before us, for miles and miles. She looked immense and peaceful. Then the flak came up at us. Never in my life had I seen such a barrage of hot, bursting metal. It held me spellbound for it appeared like hell. Pieces of ragged metal peppered our ship so that it sounded like large balls of hail hitting a metal roof. Our engineer called over the intercom that over 20 holes had been ripped in the fuselage, but there was no serious damage. Honestly, we were scared stiff. Through all of this we still maintained a steady course, straight for our target. Nothing, absolutely nothing was to keep us from that."

The flak that brought down the *Sunrise Serenade* on its fateful mission of May 1, 1944, was a combination of 88mm flak and 105mm flak. A total of 260 shells were fired at their bomber formation from four different flak battery positions. The German units inflicting the damage to the *Sunrise Serenade* were from the schw. Flakabteilung 553 (o) RAD and the gem. Flakabteilung 402 (v) RAD. The "schw." designated the 553rd unit as being a heavy unit, and they probably operated 88mm guns, which were in a flak battery somewhere in the Brussels vicinity. The (o) designated this unit as being a stationary or permanent battery. The "gem." designated the 402nd unit as being a mixed unit that utilized both 88mm and 105mm guns. The (v) designated this unit as being a mobile battery which was probably mounted on railroad cars in the Schaerbeek marshalling yard that was bombed. Such flak originating from railroad cars was known as "Eisenbahn flak". Both units were part of the Reichsarbeitdienst (RAD), which was the official German Labor Party.

The RAD was formed in July of 1934 and was similar to the American Civilian Conservation Corps (CCC). Before the War, the German RAD took part in drainage improvement work, tree removal operations, road construction and similar projects. As the War developed, the RAD units became directly involved with War operations. The RAD units served on all fronts during the War with many of them directly involved as anti-aircraft units under the control of the *Luftwaffe*. Along the Western Front, such as at Brussels, Belgium, the RAD saw service as RAD Flak Batteries. By late 1944 there were at least 60,000 RAD troops known to have served in the RAD Flak Batteries. The Reichsarbeitdienst was dissolved with the collapse of the Third Reich on May 8, 1945.

The crew of the *Sunrise Serenade* had entered the War at a particularly bad time when the anti-aircraft guns and the German fighters were at their peak. Thirty-percent of the entire German arsenal produced during 1944 consisted of flak guns. During 1944 the German industry produced nearly 66,000 flak guns to be used against the Allied bombers. The total number of flak guns produced by the German army from 1939 to 1945 totaled over 182,000.

Fear

Many airmen mentally broke down under the intense stress and fear that was created by the flak. The constant explosions and the sounds of metal pieces ripping through their planes caused many to lose control of their emotions and subsequently refuse to fly again. The term "flak happy" was used to describe such an airman who had become overly terrified of the flak. Every airman had fear, but most were able to deal with it in such a manner as not outwardly to show it to the other crew members. Although the presence of German fighters also created fear, the majority of the crew members aboard a Flying Fortress could fire back at the oncoming planes, which gave them a better sense of being in control.

After the War had ended, the American Psychological Association interviewed nearly 4,500 airmen to determine the extent of fear in well-trained and combat-experienced soldiers. The results of the survey, which interviewed men from every position on the plane, concluded that 99% of all airmen had experienced fear to some degree. The survey also showed that as the missions increased the fear of dying also increased.

Symptoms of fear while flying inside a bomber included a rapid-beating heart, dry mouth, sweating, sensations in the stomach, trembling, and sometimes losing control of bodily functions. After the mission was complete, the airmen were often fatigued, depressed, restless, had obsessive thoughts or bad dreams, and over-reacted to loud sounds. Many airmen could not sleep after a particularly tough mission and climbed back into their planes the next day after a long and hard battle through the night only to repeat the process again.

Every Flying Fortress crew member experienced having to fly through flak, and nearly every crew member experienced the threat of a German fighter attack. These two threats were on the minds of the airmen immediately after take-off for every new mission since the Germans were always prepared to meet them. The airmen generally never worried about mechanical problems since they had tremendous faith in the ground crews who prepared their planes before every new mission. Likewise, most airmen had faith in their pilot's ability to fly their plane through bad weather. It was the presence of the German fighters and flak that produced the fear of dying during every new mission.

Anti-aircraft flak was encountered on nearly every mission by the bomber crews. Every black puff of smoke was in fact an exploding 88mm or larger shell producing hundreds of smaller fragments that ripped through the thin covering of the planes. For most airmen the fear of being killed by flak was greater than being shot by a German fighter plane. The bomber crews could do little to combat the flak as they steadily flew right through it having committed to the final bombing run. - *Collection of the 452nd Bomb Group Association.*

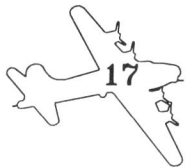

A Tale of Two Smedleys

During the research of the *Sunrise Serenade*, an interesting discovery was made that links together two airmen with the same last name. The official government documents pertaining to the crash of the *Sunrise Serenade* and its pilot, Francis C. Smedley, are contained in the Missing Air Crew Report #4492. Mixed in with this report are pages that pertain to another B-17 Flying Fortress that was also hit by flak over Belgium on May 1, 1944. Aboard this second plane was an airman named S/Sgt. Emile E. Smedley. The Air Force personnel apparently mixed up the two planes when processing the paperwork and possibly thought that the two different Smedleys were the same man since both planes were both shot down on the same day over Belgium.

Emile E. Smedley bailed out of a B-17 over Belgium the same day that the *Sunrise Serenade* crashed and killed Francis C. Smedley. The Air Force would later mix up the two men while processing the Missing Air Crew Reports. - *Collection of Sharon Schaming.*

Emile E. Smedley's flight that day began on the morning of May 1, 1944, at approximately 9:30 a.m., when his B-17 Flying Fortress took off from its airfield at Great Ashfield, England. This plane was part of a formation of bombers from the 550th Squadron of the 385th Bomb Group made up from the 934th Combat Wing of the 3rd Air Division. Their intended target that morning was Legrosseiller, France, although their flight path would also take them over western Belgium. The pilot of this plane, 2nd Lt. Russell Novotny, was flying a plane nicknamed the *Stork*, aptly named because his wife was pregnant. As their plane was flying toward the target, the crew noticed another B-17 ahead of them that appeared to be damaged and on auto-pilot without a crew aboard. Closer examination of this plane revealed that one of the airmen of this plane had his parachute tangled on the rear horizontal stabilizer bar of the plane. The crew of the *Stork* attempted to catch up with this plane and try a mid-air rescue of the airman. However, as they approached the plane, their own plane took a direct hit of flak near Lichtervelde, Belgium, which caused them to abort this planned rescue.

All members of the *Stork* bailed out over German occupied Belgium except the pilot and co-pilot, who stayed with the plane and miraculously managed to fly it back to England. S/Sgt. Emile E. Smedley successfully parachuted to the ground and was captured near Gistel, Belgium. He was later taken to Stalag Luft IV in Germany for the remainder of the War. That same evening the *Sunrise Serenade* was also flying over Belgium with 1st Lt. Francis C. Smedley at the controls. The direct hit by flak into the *Sunrise Serenade* caused it to subsequently crash, killing Francis C. Smedley whose parachute had apparently become tangled on the rear horizontal stabilizer bar of his plane.

Remarkably the circumstances of Francis C. Smedley's death were similar to the airman caught on the plane that the crew of the *Stork* had been trying to catch that morning.

The following story, which further details the May 1, 1944, mission by Emile E. Smedley's crew, was provided by the co-pilot Fred M. "Fritz" Hageter. This story was published in the *Stars & Stripes* magazine immediately after the pilot and co-pilot had successfully returned to their base. (The reference to being over France when the incident occurred is incorrect. It was often difficult for the airmen to determine when they were over France or Belgium, since German flak erupted from both coasts as the planes flew over them.)

An Eighth AAF Bomber Station, England - A pilot and co-pilot had to make a difficult decision recently on an Eighth AAF Flying Fortress bombing attack on the Nazi rocket gun installations on the French coast, and happily they were right. 2nd Lieutenant Russell A. Novotny, 27-year-old first pilot of a Fortress, from Cedar Rapids, Iowa, and the co-pilot, 2nd Lieutenant Fred M. Hageter, 23 years of age, of 1408 N. Center St., Bethlehem, Pennsylvania, had their ship hit by flak just before the IP (Initial Point), and with better than two engines out, they made it from enemy territory back to England.

In the words of Lt. Novotny, "It was a terrific experience, and I thank God we are alive to tell it. Just before turning on the IP a heavy concentration of Flak hit us in the #2 and #4 engines and left wing. The #2 engine we had to feather immediately, but the #4 was completely out of control, and the prop just windmilled. A burst of flak tore a hole in the left wing, and made flying level even more difficult. We were about ten miles from the coast, still in enemy territory, and we decided to turn back, hoping to make it to England before anything more happened."

"Rather than risk the lives of the crew through a ditching experience or crash landing, we offered them the choice of staying with us, or bailing out, and the other eight men chose to "hit the silk". Before leaving the ship the bombardier salvoed the bombs in an empty field, hoping not to hit any friendly French inhabitants. The engineer was the last to leave, and I am certain all the chutes opened, and the eight boys are safe. About this time we crossed over another group of flak guns and we suffered another two or three hits, one puncturing the #3 engine, and it started to smoke. All together now we had about 200 holes in the Fortress "STORK" and we felt like a flying sieve. The #1 engine was our only good one, and we got some power from the #3. Our altitude was the thing that saved us from ditching, and we were able to make the English coast."

"I had to fly most of the way back alone, for Lt. Hageter was busy throughout the ship, making ready for a possible ditching. The bomb bay doors would not close mechanically, and he had to crank them shut by hand, using the only available tool, a screwdriver. He threw overboard all loose and extra equipment, and made the ship as light as possible. In the meantime I tried to get the most out of the remaining engines, and soon spotted the shoreline. The flames in the #3 engine by this time were growing worse and were licking back towards the gas tank in the wing. I knew we couldn't make it back to our own field, and decided to set the "Stork" down at the first field we could get in to. The radio was out, and along with the instrument panel board, was burning slightly. We had no means of contacting the field, just had to come in for a landing."

Lt. Hageter by this time had made his way back into the cockpit and was helping Lt. Novotny to bring the ship into the final approach of the runway. As the left tire had been hit by flak, and had burned to a crisp, they didn't put their wheels down, but came in for a belly crash landing, and a pretty one it was too. As soon as the ship came to a stop, the two fliers jumped out and took off from the vicinity of the plane, for she had broken out into flames throughout the wing structures and with the gas still left in the tanks, the danger of explosion was eminent.

Said Lt. Hageter, *"It was a damn good landing too, even if I do say it myself. Lt. Novotny did a beautiful job and sure deserves a lot of credit. If only the whole crew could have made it back. I am sorry about that. Some day I wish to hell we could all get together again and go back and pound the devil out of those bastards in Germany."* Lt. Novotny and Lt. Hageter added a personal touch to the story when they related how they shook hands a half dozen times during the course of the flight, once when they succeeded in feathering the #2 prop, again when all the boys bailed out safely, and again when they sighted the English coast, and finally when the plane came to a stop on the runway. Two brave men had completed a dangerous but heroic task, and were happy.

Wilbur R. Dennis
1st Lieut., PRO
385th Bomb Group
1 May, 1944

In May of 1999, Emile E. Smedley, was contacted at his current residence in Pennsylvania. Emile confirmed that he was indeed a waist gunner who had bailed out from a B-17 on May 1, 1944, over Belgium. Additional contacts were made with other members of his crew including his co-pilot Fred M. Hageter; ball turret gunner Lloyd A. Winegarner; bombardier Earnest O. Lundgren; navigator Franklin P. Murdock; and waist gunner Raymond E. Smith. Many of these former crew members then contacted each other for the first time in 55 years.

Besides the Missing Air Crew Report being incorrect, another error was detected at an American airmen memorial wall, at the Imperial War Museum at Duxford, England. This memorial lists all American airmen from the 8th and 9th Air Force who were killed while flying from bases in England during World War II. Listed among the names on this wall is Emile E. Smedley, though the wall should have contained the name of Francis C. Smedley instead. Personnel at this museum have been subsequently notified, and plans have been made to correct the name on the memorial.

Francis C. Smedley and Emile E. Smedley were not closely related to each other, even though they each had the same last name. The name is not a very common American last name, so two different Smedley's both bailing out of B-17 Flying Fortresses after both being hit by flak on the same day over the same country is a remarkable coincidence.

Raymond J.	Small
Win R.	Smalley
Irving	Smarinsky
Robert B.	Smart
Robert C.	Smart
Harold E.	Smathers
Thomas A.	Smecik
Emile E.	Smedley
Harold C.	Smelser
Eldon L.	Smeltzer
Emil	Smetana
Orville P.	Smets
Harvey C.	Smetzer
Frederick W.	Smickitter
James S.	Smidy

The memorial wall at the Imperial War Museum at Duxford, England, had mistakenly listed Emile E. Smedley as among those who died instead of Francis C. Smedley. - *Imperial War Museum photo.*

Behind the Plane's Name

It was rather fitting that the B-17 bomber named the *Sunrise Serenade* had succumbed to the affects of war in the same year that Glenn Miller who recorded the song, "Sunrise Serenade", also became a victim of the War. Francis Smedley's plane was named after that song because it reminded him of his mother. The song evoked memories of his mother enjoying her favorite song at their Wisconsin home.

In 1938 the music "Sunrise Serenade" was written by popular songwriter Frankie Carle, with the lyrics by Jack Lawrence. Initially the song was performed and recorded by Carle as a theme song for his own band. Glen Gray and his Casa Loma Orchestra next recorded the tune on February 17, 1939, for Decca Records. However, the song did not become a hit until it was recorded by Glenn Miller on April 10, 1939, at Victor Studios in New York City. The song was on the front side of a record that included Glenn Miller's theme song, "Moonlight Serenade". Sunrise Serenade was a Bluebird recording designated as B 10214-A. The backside, B 10214-B, was recorded a few days earlier on April 4, 1939, with these musicians:

   Trombones: Glenn Miller, Al Mastren, Paul Tanner
   Trumpets: Bob Price, Leigh Knowles, Dale McMickle
   Reeds: Hal McIntyre, Stanley Aronson, Wilbur Schwartz, Tex
       Beneke, Al Klink
   Rhythm: Chummy MacGregor, Allan Ruess, Rolly Bundock,
       Frank Carlson
   Vocalists: Marion Hutton, Ray Eberle, Tex Beneke

Although Glenn Miller's instrumental version of "Sunrise Serenade" did not contain any vocals, the song was already known for its early morning feeling of freshness, newness and challenge, which had been portrayed through Jack Lawrence's lyrics for the song.

Miller was born in 1904 as Alton Glenn Miller at Clarinda, Iowa. At a young age, Miller and his family moved to North Platte, Nebraska, and it was here that he first got his musical start when his father brought home a mandolin for him to play. Miller later moved to Colorado where he attended high school at Fort Morgan, and where he later attended college at the University of Colorado at Boulder. Before starting his own band, Miller led a busy career as a dance band and studio trombonist. He worked in the bands of the American bandleaders Ben Pollack in 1927, and with Red Nichols from 1929-1930. In 1934 he worked with the Dorsey Brothers Band, and later joined the English bandleader Ray Noble in 1935 as a trombonist and arranger. Finally in 1937, Miller formed his own swing orchestra, though the band struggled for the first couple of years. In 1939 the band began to receive extensive radio airplay during their engagements at the Meadowbrook Ballroom in New Jersey and also at the Glen Island Casino in New York. That year several of Miller's songs became instant hits, including "Sunrise Serenade". Other hits included "Little Brown Jug", their theme song "Moonlight Serenade", and their biggest hit "In the Mood". In 1941 Miller recorded "Chattanooga Choo Choo" which was the first record in almost 20 years to sell over a million copies. Miller also enjoyed fame with the hit songs "Pennsylvania 6-5000" and "(I've Got a Gal In) Kalamazoo".

The *Sunrise Serenade* was named after a popular Glenn Miller song. Both the plane and Glenn Miller were victims of the War during the same year. - *Collection of the author.*

The Glenn Miller Orchestra continued to perform through the summer of 1942 when Miller stunned the music world and disbanded his orchestra to enlist in the United States Army on October 7, 1942. Miller was assigned to the Army Specialist Corps where he began to work with a new band. His appointment to the rank of Captain came after many months of convincing his superior officers that he could modernize the existing army band and ultimately improve the morale of the fighting men. Miller was transferred to the Army Air Corps where he formed the 42-piece all-star Army Air

Force Band. During the remainder of 1942 and most of 1943, the band entertained World War II service personnel with regular radio broadcasts in the United States. Finally in late 1943 Miller and his new band were shipped out to England to entertain the troops.

In less than one year, the Glenn Miller Army Air Force Band engaged in over 800 performances with the broadcasts being heard by millions. Miller personally made over 300 appearances in concerts and dances to entertain the troops in England.

On the evening of December 14, 1944, the night was unusually quiet around London, England. The normal crowds of British and American servicemen at the popular nightclub, Piccadilly Circus, were uncharacteristically absent for a Friday night. Even the Germans, for no apparent reason, had decided not to send their usual nightly bombardment of V-1 Rockets into the city. Glenn Miller finished his performance and went to attend a late night party given by a former bandleader Jack Hylton. Miller was the last to leave the party as he and Hylton walked outside together. As Miller looked up into the cold night sky, he remarked to Hylton "Well Jack, it'll soon be over now", referring to the War in general. After a shake of hands and an exchange of goodbyes, Miller left his friend just after 1:30 a.m. and headed for a waiting airplane.

Glenn Miller, then 33, and another passenger, Lt. Col. Norman Baessell, boarded a single-engine plane piloted by John Morgan. The plane, a Noorduyn C-64A Norseman owned by the United States Air Force, took off from a Royal Air Force base near Bedford, England, at 1:55 a.m. Miller's plane headed across the English Channel for Paris, France, to set up concerts for Allied troops. The plane disappeared over the English Channel in a slight fog, and no trace of the crew was ever located. After an intense 12-day search, which produced no clues to the lost aircraft, Miller's disappearance was finally officially reported to the news media. Miller, who will always be remembered for his quote, "*It don't mean a thing if it ain't got that swing!*", had often wished that he could get closer to the fighting with the rest of the men overseas.

Bad weather or contact with a German fighter plane were originally thought to have been the most plausible reasons for Miller's disappearance. However, in the mid 1980's a Royal Air Force navigator named Fred Shaw, a veteran of World War II, dug out his old logbook after seeing the film "*The Glenn Miller Story*" which chronicled Miller's life. Shaw's bomber crew, which was part of a larger squadron, had aborted a mission to Siegen, Germany, on December 15, 1944. On their return to England, the squadron let loose their 4,000-pound bombs over the English Channel rather than land at their airfield with them aboard. The bombs, which were time-delayed, exploded just above the surface of the water. Shaw remembers at this instant seeing a small plane spiraling out of control toward the water. In his own words Shaw recalls: "*Around it I could see the sea bubbling and blistering with the exploding bombs. As each bomb burst, I could see the blast wave from it radiating outwards…It was obvious to me that airplane below was in trouble. Eventually, I saw it disappear into the English Channel.*"

The downed plane was not reported, but Shaw's story was corroborated by other squadron members. In 1985, Britain's Ministry of Defense wrote a letter to Shaw conceding his theory as certainly possible. The Ministry of Defense also said that they now leaned toward this theory as being the most likely solution to the mystery of Glenn Miller's plane.

After Shaw's death, his logbook containing the incident, which possibly involved Glenn Miller, was put up for sale by Sotheby's auction house. In April of 1999, a 76-year-old businessman from Boulder, Colorado, paid $35,000 to own the logbook. Its buyer had a long-time interest in the disappearance of Glenn Miller, and had served in the Army Air Corps during World War II.

SUNRISE SERENADE
Good mornin', good mornin' you sleepy head.
It's dawnin', Stop yawnin', Get out of that bed.
Say the air is soft as silk. It's time to get the mornin' milk.
Come on. Wake up! Get up!
Look at the grass, silver in the sun, heavy with the dew.
Look at the buds you can almost see how they're breakin' thru.
Look at the birds feedin' their young in the sycamores.
But you better get on with your mornin' chores.
Just take a breath of that new mown hay and the sugar cane.
Looks like tonight there should be a moon down in lover's lane.
There you go, day dreaming when it's time that you obeyed that SUNRISE SERENADE.

Official Documents

Immediately after an American bomber or fighter plane was reported missing, a Missing Air Crew Report (MACR) was initiated for that aircraft at the reporting airfield. The purpose of the MACR was to compile as many facts pertaining to the missing plane as possible into one file while the recollections of eye-witnesses were still fresh. The compilation of this data proved to be invaluable for Air Force personnel in aiding them to inform the parents or wives of the missing airmen.

After the *Sunrise Serenade* had become officially missing, a file pertaining to the plane and its crew was assigned as MACR #4492. A complete list of the individual crew members' names, ranks and serial numbers, as well as their next of kin's addresses was some of the first information to be entered into the report. Other information included data pertaining to their mission such as their intended target, weather conditions, and crash location.

One of the most important items in the report were statements made by those persons who were believed to have last knowledge of the aircraft. Two pilots who gave statements, and were also flying in the same formation when the *Sunrise Serenade* was shot down, were 2nd Lt. Howard K. Morehouse and Lt. Chester W. Austin. (Morehouse was flying off the right wing of the *Sunrise Serenade* in a plane named *Kickapoo Joy Juice*, and Austin was flying a plane known as *Frivolous Sal*. The *Kickapoo Joy Juice* was shot down one week after the *Sunrise Serenade* went down, and the crew of *Frivolous Sal* was one of the few original 452nd Bomb Group crews to complete their 30 missions).

Other pages in the MACR were known as "Casualty Questionnaires" which were included if any members of the crew had been killed. These questionnaires were filled out by individual crew members after the War was over to further substantiate the facts that were gathered immediately after the crash. (Due to limited space, these pages are not shown among the other pages of MACR #4492 that follow). Crew members from the *Sunrise Serenade* who filled out the questionnaire were Harry Shoffner, John Brown, Norbert Rhodes, Raymond Dean, and George Griffin.

The Germans also compiled documents pertaining to the crash of the *Sunrise Serenade* in order to properly award those anti-aircraft gunners involved in its demise.

Noted on the first page of the German document is a statement stating that Battle Groups 3 and 4 Fighter Division had not claimed the downing of this plane. This was important to note since many bombers that were initially disabled by anti-aircraft flak were then subsequently shot down by German fighters. The ground flak gunners often never got credit for making the initial hits on many bombers because the fighter planes eventually brought down those crippled bombers and, therefore, received the awards. The four small open circles on the German map shown on page 149 represent the locations of the four flak batteries involved in the downing of the *Sunrise Serenade*. The arcs coming from these circles indicate the range and action of the flak guns.

The reference in the German document to the *Sunrise Serenade* being called a "Fortress II" instead of a "B-17G Flying Fortress" was a term associated with the British bombers. In addition to their own Halifax and Lancaster bombers, the British did fly some B-17G versions of the Flying Fortress, which they and the Germans both referred to as being a "Fortress II".

In the 1980's the majority of the Missing Air Crew Reports became declassified and available to the public. The MACR pertaining to the *Sunrise Serenade* officially became declassified by authority of Declassification Project 785072 on September 10, 1982. Thousands of these reports were photographed and placed on 4"x6" microfiche cards for permanent records at the National Archives at College Park, Maryland. Unfortunately many of the records had deteriorated over the years, and those sheets that were carbon papers of the originals did not photograph well. Some pages were completely illegible, but through extensive research and also with assistance from National Archive personnel, who viewed the originals, the pages have been completely retyped as they appeared in the file. Some of the pages in the report pertaining to another aircraft were inadvertently mixed in with those of the *Sunrise Serenade*. These pages were not retyped, nor do they appear among those in the following pages. A further explanation as to why these pages were mixed in the wrong report is more fully explained in Chapter 17. The retyped pages from MACR #4492 that follow do contain some obvious errors such as the omission of individual names and contradictory data.

1, May, 1944 1900	13, May	KU 1732
Brussel		
Type: Fortress 949		
730 HB Squadr	1st. Lt. SMEDLEY	Francis C. 0-747347 dead
452 Group		
Airfield	2nd. Lt. HEWETT	William John 0-754005 o
Deopham Green 142		
	2nd. Lt. GRIFFIN	George Donald 0-673797 capt
	2nd. Lt. Mc.GRATH	John Joseph 0-692327 capt
	T/Sgt. SENETSKY	Andrew Jr. 13100429 capt
	T/Sgt. RHODES	Norbert Elroy 33257190 capt
	S/Sgt. DEAN	Raymond Eugene 19124173 capt
	S/Sgt. BROWN	John Gibbon 13121490 capt
	S/Sgt. GALLAGHER	James Edward 13041523 capt
	S/Sgt. SHOFFNER	H.

. . . .

Report of downing and capture
Air District Command Belgium - Northern France of 1 May 1944 (finished at 2400)

Case No.	Downing by:	Time	place of crash	type of plane	cap'd	fate of the crew dead	fugitive	remarks
6)	Anti-Aircraft	1900	Capelle St. Ulric 12 km west-north-west Brussels KU 1733	Fortress II	8 8 men captured 1) Second Lieutenant 2) Second Lieutenant 3) Second Lieutenant 4) Staff- Sergeant 5) Tech- Sergeant 6) Tech- Sergeant 7) Staff- Sergeant	1 1 dead 1) First- Lieutenant	1 1 man fugitive 1) Staff- Sergeant	Hewett, W.J. 0-754005 Griffin, G. 0-673797 McGrath, J. 0-692327 Dean, R.E. 19124173 Senetsky, A. 13100429 Rhodes, N.E. 33257190 Brown, J. 13121490 Smedley, F. 0-747347 Shoffner

Airbase Command E (v) 220/XI
Place: Brussel - Evers

Date of Crash:	1, May 44, at 1900 hours
Place of Crash:	Capelle - St. Ulric, approx. 12 km northwest of Brussels
Aircraft type:	Fortress II
Identification:	Star black on gray background
Kind of landing:	Crashed on fire
Kind of Capture:	Flak

Disposition of the Crew

1 man DEAD

1. 2nd Lt. Smedley, Francis, 0 747347

Place of Burial: Will follow

8 men captured	Place of Capture
1. 2nd Lt Hewett, Will. J., 0 754005	Near Zellik
2. S Sgt Dean, Raymond E., 19124173	Near aircraft
3. S Sgt Senetsky, Andrew, 13100429	Brussel Bv. Lambermont
4. S Sgt Gallagher, Jam. E., 13041523	Near Kas
5. S Sgt Brown, John, 13121490	Near Kas
6. T Sgt Brodes, Norb. E., 33257190	Near Kas
7. 2nd Lt Grath, Mc. John, 0 692327	Near Kas
8. 2nd Lt Griffin, George, 0 673797	Kfs. Best camp

KU 1731

Identification Tags

John J. McGrath	O 692327
Brown, John G.	13121490
Raymond E. Dean	19124173
Norbert E. Rhodes,	33257190
Francis C. Smedley,	O 747347
James E. Gallagher,	13041523
Andrew Senetsky,	13100429
Rhodes, Norbert E.,	33257190 identification card
William John Hewett,	O 754005 identification card and miscellaneous

---

DATE AND TIME AIRCRAFT
WAS LAST SEEN _1 May 1944 - Time 19.00_   CASUALTY NO. _KU 1731_

PLACE OF CRASH _Brussel_

TYPE OF AIRCRAFT _Fortress_

REPORTING OFFICE _Transport Brussel_

NAME	RANK	SERIAL NUMBER	CAPT'D WOUNDED DEAD	PLACE OF INTERNMENT
Mc GRATH, John Joseph - . - Penna.	2nd/Ltn.	0-692327	Captured	Stalag Luft
GRIFFIN, George Donald 7 January 1922 - N.Y.	2nd/Ltn.	0-673797	Captured	Stalag Luft
SENETSKY, Andrew Jr.	T/Sgt.	13100429	Captured	Stalag Luft
RHODES, Norbert Elroy	T/Sgt.	33257190	Captured	Stalag Luft
DEAN, Raymond Eugene	S/Sgt.	19124173	Captured	Stalag Luft
BROWN, John Gibbon 1 December 1922	S/Sgt.	13121490	Captured	Stalag Luft
HEWETT, . . .	2nd/Ltn.	- . -	Wounded	- . -

Downing Number KU 1731   1st. Follow up Report from 6 June 1944

NAME	RANK	SERIAL NUMBER	CAPT'D WOUNDED DEAD	PLACE OF INTERNMENT
GALLAGHER, James Edward	S/Sgt.	13041523	Captured	Stalag Luft
SMEDLEY, Francis C.	1st/Ltn.	0-747347	Dead	??

REMARKS:
    Stalag Luft; 23 May 1944 / We.

First Lieutenant Francis C. Smedley	Mrs. Clara W. Smedley (Mother) Route Number One, Box 32, Oconto Falls, Wisconsin.
Second Lieutenant William J. Hewett	Mr. George Hewett, (Father) 3312 Aberdeen Road, Shaker Heights, Cleveland, Ohio.
Second Lieutenant George D. Griffin	Mr. O. J. Griffin (Father) Roxbury, New York.
Second Lieutenant John J. McGrath	Mrs. Frances M. McGrath (Mother) Station Avenue, Langhorne, Pennsylvania.
Technical Sergeant Norbert E. Rhodes	Mrs. Lola Rhodes, (Mother) Rural Free Delivery Number Two, Williamsburg, Pennsylvania.
Technical Sergeant Andrew Senetsky, Jr.	Mrs. Anna Senetsky 404 Main Street, Dickson City, Pennsylvania.
Staff Sergeant John G. Brown	Mrs. Mary S. Brown (Mother) 415 Bradley Street, Abingdon, Virginia.
Staff Sergeant Raymond E. Dean	Mr. Dorwell D. Dean, (Father) Valier, Montana.
Staff Sergeant Harry C. Shoffner	Mrs. Mary Lou Shoffner, (Wife) Route Number Three, Lawrence, Kansas.
Staff Sergeant James E. Gallagher	Mrs. Beatrice Gallagher, (Mother) 934 Western Avenue, Pittsburgh, Pennsylvania.

MISSING AIR CREW REPORT

1. ORGANIZATION: Location   *Station 142*   : Command or Air Force   *8 AF*
   Group *452nd Bomb Gp (H)* : Squadron *730th Bomb (H)*   Detachment
2. Specify: Point of Departure: *Station 142*   : Course
   Intended Destination   *Metz*   : Type of Mission   *Bombing*
3. Weather conditions and visibility at time of crash or when last reported:
   Scattered Clouds - Visibility Good 5056 N - 0416 E
4. GIVE: (a)Date *1 May 44* Time *Approx 1900* and Location *5 Miles west of Brussels*
   of last known whereabouts of missing aircraft.
   specify whether (X) Last sighted   ( ) Last contacted by radio.
                   ( ) Forced down   ( ) Seen to crash or ( )information not available.
5. AIRCRAFT WAS LOST OR IS BELIEVED LOST AS A RESULT OF: Check only one.
       ( ) Enemy Aircraft   (X) Enemy Anti-Aircraft   ( ) Other
   circumstances as follows
6. AIRCRAFT: Type, model and series   *B-17G*   AAF Serial No.   *42-37949*
7. ENGINES: Type, model and series   *R-1820-97*   AAF Serial No.
           (a) *SW 114*   (b) *SW 1011*   (c) *SW 1049*   (d) *SW 1052*
8. INSTALLED WEAPONS   (Furnish below Make, Type and Serial number)
           (a) *991543*   (b) *684162*   (c) *650722*   (d) *649685*
           (e) *398005*   (f) *630834*   (g) *398004*   (h) *676698*
           (i) *684349*   (j) *215060*   (k) *866176*   (l) *927590   684670*
9. THE PERSONS LISTED BELOW WERE REPORTED AS: (a) Battle Casualty   *X*
                                        or (b) Non-battle Casualty
   NUMBER OF PERSONS ABOARD AIRCRAFT: Crew   *10*   : Passengers   *None*
                                                      Total   *10*
10. (Starting with pilot, furnish the following particulars: If more than
    10 persons were aboard aircraft, list similar particulars on separate
    sheet and attach original to this form).
                              NAME IN FULL

Crew Position	Last Name First	Rank	Serial No.
1. P	Smedley, Francis C.	1st Lt.	O-747347
2. CP	Hewett, William J.	2nd Lt.	O-754005
3. N	McGrath, John J.	2nd Lt.	O-692327
4. B	Griffin, George D.	2nd Lt.	O-673797
5. TT	Rhodes, Norbert E.	T/Sgt.	33257190
6. R	Senetsky, Andrew(NMI)Jr.	T/Sgt.	13100429
7. BT	Gallagher, James E. Jr.	S/Sgt.	13041523
8. RW	Brown, John G.	S/Sgt.	13121490
9. LW	Shoffner, Harry C.	S/Sgt.	
10. TG	Dean, Raymond . E.	S/Sgt.	19124173

11. IDENTIFY BELOW THOSE PERSONS WHO ARE BELIEVED TO HAVE LAST KNOWLEDGE
    OF AIRCRAFT, AND CHECK APPROPRIATE COLUMN TO INDICATE BASIS FOR SAME:
                          (Check one column only)

Name in full (Last name first)	Rank	Serial Number	Contacted by Radio	Last Sighted	Saw Crash	Forced Land
1. Morehouse, Howard K.	2nd Lt.			X		
2. Austin, Chester W.	1st Lt.			X		
3.						

(over)

12. IF PERSONNEL ARE BELIEVED TO HAVE SURVIVED, ANSWER YES TO ANY OF THE FOLLOWING STATEMENTS: (A) Parachutes were used __X__, (b) Persons were seen walking away from seen of crash _____, (c) any other reason SPECIFY
_____

13. ATTACH AERIAL PHOTOGRAPH, MAP, CHART, OR SKETCH, SHOWING APPROXIMATE LOCATION WHERE AIRCRAFT WAS LAST SEEN, *Approx. 5 miles west of Brussels.*

14. ATTACH EYEWITNESS, DESCRIPTION OF CRASH, FORCED LANDING, OR OTHER CIRCUMSTANCES PERTAINING TO MISSING AIRCRAFT., See Statement Below.

15. ATTACH A DESCRIPTION OF THE EXTENT OF SEARCH, IF ANY, AND GIVE NAME, RANK AND SERIAL NUMBER OF OFFICER IN CHARGE WERE *No search by this Group*.

Date of Report _____ *6 May 1944* _____

Signature of preparing officer
C. M. CRONIN
1st Lt. AC
Gp Stat O

Following information obtained by S-2, 452nd Bomb Gp. at interrogation after mission:

Aircraft B-17G 42-37949 was hit by flak over the target area, and about three minutes after bombing, at approximately 5 miles west of Brussels the #2 engine, the cockpit and the bomb bay were seen on fire. Nine chutes were observed to blossom from the plane - tenth man seen escaping from the nose of the ship snagged his parachute on the aircraft and it was ripped from him. The aircraft was seen to hit the ground and explode.

German Documents

Flakgruppe Brüssel
-Ord.Offz.- (Ic)
Br.B.Nr. 277/44 geh.

Gefechtsstand, 14.5.44. 13

Betr.: Abschuss einer Firtress II am 1. 5. 44, 19.00 Uhr bei Capelle St. Ulric bei Ternath ca. 12 km WNW Brüssel. Jägergradnetz N J 5 4.

Stellungnahme
zum
Antrag auf Anerkennung eines Abschusses.

Beim Angriff mehrerer viermot. Feindverbände am 1. 5. 44 von 18,46 bis 18,56 Uhr auf die Industrieanlagen Brüssel-Schaerbeek bekämpften die am Flugplatz Melsbroek eingesetzten 1./schw. Flakabteilung 553 (o) RAD, 2./schw. Flakabt. 553 (o) RAD, 3./gem. Flakabteilung 402 (v) RAD und 4./gem. Flakabteilung 402 (v) RAD, einen aus Richtung 7 anfliegenden Verband.

Die Schüsse lagen gut am Feind. Bei 2 Maschinen brannte der rechte, äussere Motor mit starker Rauchfahne. Eine Maschine wurde von der Besatzung verlassen. Die Maschine scheerte daraufhin aus dem Verband aus und ist um 19.00 Uhr bei Capelle St. Ulric bei Ternath 12 km WNW Brüssel, Jägergradnetz N J 5 4 abgestürzt.

Diese Tatsachen werden bewiesen durch die Zeugenaussagen und die Gefechtsberichte.

Jafu 4 und 3. Jad-div. haben auf vorstehenden Abschuss keinen Anspruch erhoben.

Ich bitte daher um Anerkennung des Abschusses
für die oben angeführten Batterien.

---

ergruppe Brüssel
Flakabteilung 691(v)   Fp.N   L 51520   Lgpa.Brüssel
Gefechtsstand, den 11.5.1944

Abschußmeldung.

1.) Abschußzeit: 1.5.1944 um 19,00 Uhr.
2.) Abschußhöhe: 5400 m.
3.) Typ: Fortress II.
4.) Aufschlagort: Capelle-St.Ulric bei Ternath, ca. 12 km WNW Brüssel.
    Jägergradnetz: N J 5 4.
5.) beteiligte Einheiten:
    1./schw.Flakabt. 553 (o) RAD
    2./schw.Flakabt. 553 (o) RAD
    3./gem. Flakabt. 402 (v) RAD
    4./gem. Flakabt. 402 (v) RAD
    beteiligte fremde Einheiten (auch Jäger): keine.
6.) Schicksal der Besatzung: 1 Toter, 8 Gefangene
7.) Staffelkenner: Nicht feststellbar, 100% Bruch.
8.) Angabe ob einzeln fliegende Maschine oder Abschuß aus Verband:
    Abschuß aus Verband.
9.) Vernichtungsart: helle Rauchfahne, senkrechter Absturz, Fallschirmabsprung, brennender Absturz.

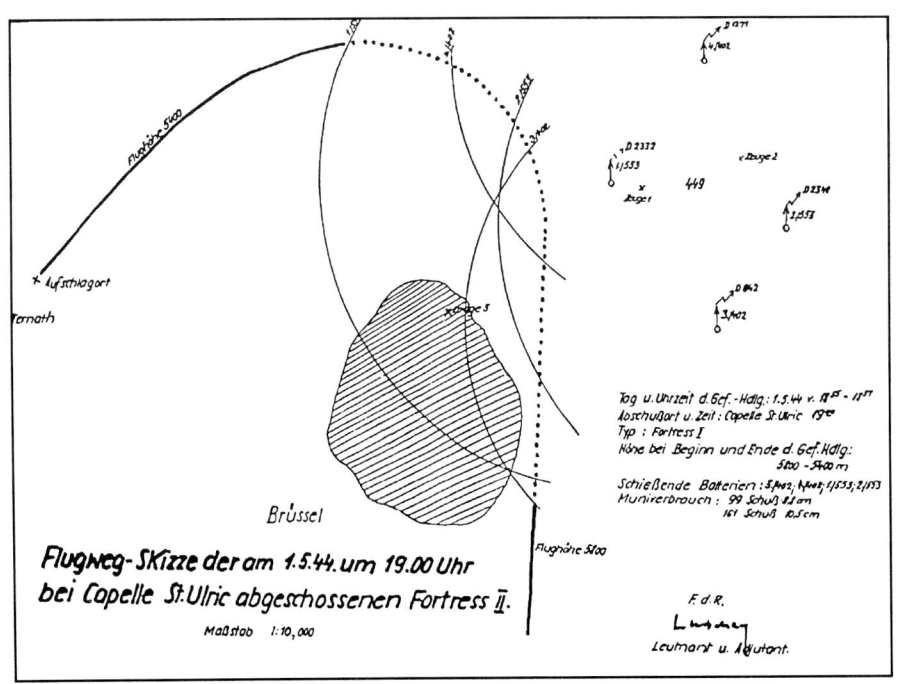

Flugweg-Skizze der am 1.5.44. um 19.00 Uhr bei Capelle St.Ulric abgeschossenen Fortress II.
Maßstab 1:10,000

Translation of the German Documents

Air Defense Group - Brussels
- Ordinance Officer - (Intelligence/Security)
Letter File No. 277/44 Secret

Command Post, May 14, 1944

Concerning: Shooting down of a Fortress II on May 1, 1944, 19:00 Hours at Sint-Ulriks-Kapelle near Ternat, approx. 12 km WNW of Brussels. Grid location N J 5 4.

Statement
for
Application for acknowledgement of a shooting down.

During the attack, by several four-engine enemy formations on May 1, 1944, from 18:46 until 18:56 on the industrial building near Brussel-Schaerbeek, the airfield of Melsbroek stationed units attacked 1./ 553rd Stationary Heavy Air Defense Unit - German Labor Service; 2./ 553rd Stationary Heavy Air Defense Unit - German Labor Service; 3./402nd Mobile Mixed Air Defense Unit - German Labor Service; and 4./ 402nd Mobile Mixed Air Defense Unit - German Labor Service, were fighting a formation coming from direction 7.

The shots hurt the enemy considerably on two planes the right engine was burning with strong smoke development. On one plane the crew abandoned. The plane left the formation and came down at 19:00 Hours at Sint-Ulriks-Kapelle near Ternat, 12 km WNW of Brussels, Grid location N J 5 4.

This fact is proved by several witnesses and the battle bulletins.

Battlegroups 4 and 3, Fighter Division have not claimed the shooting down of this plane.

I therefore request the acknowledgment of the downing.

    for the above mentioned Batteries.

(Signature)

Air Defense Group - Brussels Command Post,   May 11, 1944
691st Mobile Air Defense Unit Field Post No. L 51320,   Post Office Box Brussels

Shooting Down Report

1.) Date and time: May 1, 1944 at 19:00 Hours.
2.) Height of downing: 5400 meters
3.) Type: Fortress II
4.) Location of Crash: Sint-Ulriks-Kapelle near Ternat,
   12 km WNW of Brussels.
   Grid location: N J 5 4.
5.) Participating Units:
   1./ 553rd Stationary Heavy Air Defense Unit - German Labor Service
   2./ 553rd Stationary Heavy Air Defense Unit - German Labor Service
   3./ 402nd Mobile Mixed Air Defense Unit - German Labor Service
   4./ 402nd Mobile Mixed Air Defense Unit - German Labor Service
   Other outside units involved (such as Fighters): None.
6.) Fate of Crew: 1 killed, 8 captured.
7.) Squadron markings: Not determined, 100% destroyed.
8.) Specify whether a lone plane or shot down from a formation:
   Shot down from a formation.
9.) Way of destruction: Bright smoke trail, perpendicular fall,
   parachutes jumping out, on fire as it crashed.

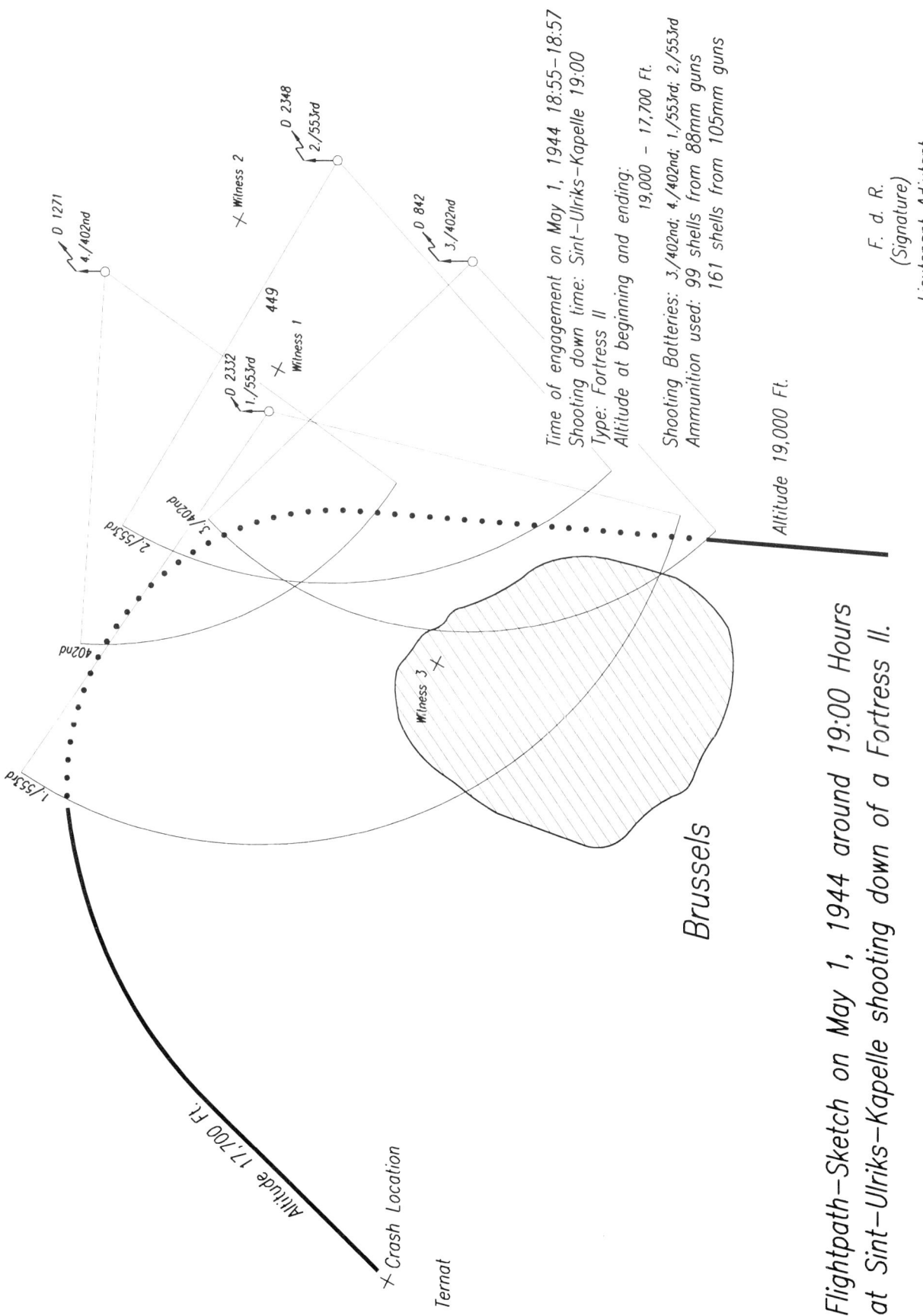

Flightpath-Sketch on May 1, 1944 around 19:00 Hours at Sint-Ulriks-Kapelle shooting down of a Fortress II.

Scale 1:10000

PLANES THAT SERVED WITH THE 452nd BOMB GROUP

© 2000 Jerry Penny

Serial #	Name	Pilot	Date	Final Fate
41-9019			July 10, '44	Crashed into by plane #43-37631 on the runway. (Damaged on runway again on 9-05-44).
42-6153	Good Pickin'	Jarrett	Aug. 08, '43	Assigned to training at Pyote, Texas. Later assigned to training at Dalhart, TX, on 8-26-44.
42-30123	Big Dick		Febr. 25, '44	Crashed near Regensburg, Germany. (388th BG Plane w/ 452nd BG crew)
42-30572			July 25, '43	Assigned to training at Pendleton Field, Oregon, then to various other bomb groups.
42-30575			July 31, '43	Assigned to training at Geiger Field, Washington, then to various other bomb groups.
42-30600			Febr. 11, '43	Assigned to training at Pendleton Field, Oregon. (Written-off on 12-18-43).
42-30755			Oct. 23, '43	Assigned to training at Pendleton Field, Oregon.
42-30756			Oct. 19, '43	Assigned to training at Geiger Field, Washington.
42-30800	Cock O' the Walk	Colvin	Febr. 29, '44	Crashed near Bienrode, Germany, due to flak. (388th BG plane w/ 452nd BG crew).
42-31242	Patty Jo	Salles	May 19, '44	Mid-air collision w/ #42-38145 over England. (388th BG plane w/ 452nd BG crew)
42-31318	Belle of Broadway	Turner	Febr. 10, '44	Crashed near Diepholz, Germany, due to mid-air collision w/ #42-39961.
42-31319	Tangerine	Wilson	Apr. 26, '44	Crashed on take-off from base due to mechanical problems.
42-31322	Mi Amigo	Kreighauser	Jan. 30, '44	Trans. to the 305th BG. (Later crashed near Sheffield, England, on 2-22-44). "My Friend"
42-31325	(None)	Lorenzi	Febr. 08, '44	Crashed near Le Cardonnois, France, due to enemy fighters.
42-31330	Dog Breath	Graham	June 19, '44	Crash landed in Spain due to flak and interned.
42-31331	Mon Tete Rouge	Butterworth	Mar. 04, '44	Crashed near Nienburg, Germany, due to enemy fighters. "My Red Head"
42-31332	Frivolous Sal	Austin	July 04, '45	Returned to the United States after the War.
42-31334	Three Cads and a Lad	Evers	Apr. 12, '44	Crashed in the North Sea near Clacton, England, due to mechanical problems.
42-31337	Hell's Cargo	Sweeney	Mar. 06, '44	Crashed near Fassburg, Germany, due to flak and enemy fighters.
42-31338	Hard To Get	Smith	Febr. 10, '44	Crashed near Kemmel, Belgium, due to enemy fighters.
42-31341	Breaks of the Game	Mittman	Mar. 04, '44	Crashed near Staaken, Germany, due to enemy fighters.
42-31345	Lady Stardust II	Marecek	May 12, '44	Ditched in the English Channel due to enemy fighters.
42-31348	Swing Shift Baby II	Ferguson	Dec. 31, '44	Crashed near Rhade, Germany, due to enemy fighters. (a.k.a. "Terry-A-Long").
42-31350		Kuhlmeier	Apr. 08, '44	Caught fire upon landing due to battle damage.
42-31352	Iron Bird	Mayek	Apr. 09, '44	Crashed in the Baltic Sea near Laaland, Denmark, due to enemy fighters.
42-31354	Dixie Jane	Sorensen	Aug. 04, '44	Crashed in the North Sea near Helgoland, Germany, due to flak.
42-31358	Princess Pat II	Parvin	May 29, '44	Crashed near Goddula, Germany, due to flak.
42-31359		Lerum	June 21, '44	Crashed near Rheinberg, Germany, after mid-air collision w/ #42-102662.
42-31360	Smokey Liz	Downey	Sept. 28, '44	Forced landing near Brussels, Belgium, due to flak. (Salvaged on 11-14-44)
42-31361	The Punched Fowl	Arey	Aug. 04, '44	Crashed in the North Sea near Helgoland, Germany, due to flak.
42-31366	Old Outhouse	Owens	Apr. 07, '45	Crashed near Stadthagen, due to a mid-air coll. with an Me-109. (a.k.a. "Snake Eyes").
42-31368		MacSporan	Dec. 24, '44	Crashed near Higham, England, due to battle damage.
42-31371	Lucky 13	Stephens	Mar. 23, '44	Crashed near Vaassen, Holland, due to a mid-air collision w/ an FW-190.
42-31373	Flakstop	Wagner	Mar. 06, '44	Crashed near Staphorst, Holland, due to enemy fighters.
42-31382	Angel II		July 18, '44	Caught fire due to an electrical short after being loaded with bombs. - Scrapped.
42-31525	Shed House Mouse	Reynolds	Mar. 20, '44	Had entire nose taken off by bomb dropped from another B-17. (See below)
42-31525	The Reincarnation			Rebuilt and renamed. (See above). Returned to the USA after the War on 6-28-45.
42-31780	Windy Lou	Leith	Nov. 05, '44	Crashed near Kessenich, Germany, due to flak.
42-31784	Section Eight	Suckow	Apr. 29, '44	Ditched in the North Sea due to flak. Crew returned to base.
42-31810		Anderson	June 21, '44	Crash landed near Skovde, Sweden. Interned until Oct. 1944.
42-31919	Evanton Babe	Schimmel	Mar. 06, '44	Damaged by fighters near Emmen, Germany. Crew bailed out. Pilot returned alone.
42-31934	Marie Helena	Smith	Aug. 08, '44	Crash landed in France due to flak. (Returned to the USA after the War 7-05-45)

Serial	Name	Pilot	Date	Fate
42-32070	(None)	Patterson	Apr. 09, '44	Crashed near Nakskov, Denmark, due to flak and enemy fighters.
42-32082	Passionate Witch II	Cook	Mar. 28, '44	Crashed near Chateaudun, France, due to flak.
42-32083	Flatbush Floogie	Marksian	Febr. 26, '45	Crashed near Liszki, Poland, due to flak.
42-32087	Old Glory	Graber	Aug. 06, '44	Landed near Resmo, Sweden, and interned due to mechanical problems.
42-32116	Heigh Ho Silver		Mar. 11, '44	Transferred to the 457th BG. (Returned to the United States on 5-27-45).
42-37853	Leading Lady		Apr. 18, '44	Salvaged due to unknown circumstances.
42-37941	Lucky Lady II	Bodet	Apr. 09, '44	Crashed near Lingerau, Germany, due to enemy fighters.
42-37946	The Worry Bird	Truex	Febr. 08, '44	Crash landed near Goderville, France, due to enemy fighters.
42-37947	Princess Pat	Davis	May 12, '44	Crashed near Daxberg, Germany, due to enemy fighters.
42-37949	**Sunrise Serenade**	**Smedley**	**May 01, '44**	**Crashed near St. Ulriks-Kapelle, Belgium, due to flak.**
42-37950	Dinah Might	Sharpless	Febr. 10, '44	Ditched in the Zuider Zee area of Holland due to enemy fighters.
42-37951	Mavoureen	Huffman	Febr. 20, '44	Crashed near Haldagerlille, Denmark, due to enemy fighters.
42-37954	Hank from Dixie	Wilson	Mar. 08, '44	Crashed near Toppel, Germany, due to enemy fighters.
42-37956	The Hard Way	Thomas	Apr. 20, '44	Crashed in the English Channel near Calais, France, due to flak.
42-37960	Delta Girl	Noell	Febr. 10, '44	Crashed near Dankern, Germany, due to enemy fighters.
42-38124			Mar. 27, '44	Salvaged due to unknown circumstances.
42-38145	Rosalie Ann	Gaither	May 19, '44	Crashed near Buckenham, England, due to mid-air coll. w/ #42-31242 from 388th BG.
42-38157	Four Freedoms	Olson	June 21, '44	Destroyed on the ground at Poltava, Russia, by enemy bombers.
42-38202	BTO in the ETO	Hernandez	June 21, '44	Crashed near Biala Podlaska, Poland, due to enemy fighters.
42-38211	Sleepy Time Gal	MacDonald	Mar. 08, '44	Crashed near Nienburg, Germany, due to enemy fighters.
42-39841	Wacky Woody	Lupole	Jan. 26, '44	Crashed near Saarbrucken, Germany, due to fighters. (96th BG plane w/ 452nd BG crew).
42-39858			Mar. 25, '44	Salvaged due to unknown circumstances.
42-39902	The Big Noise	Denham	May 12, '44	Crash landed at base due to heavy battle damage. (Returned to the USA on 7-05-45).
42-39903	Marjorie Ann	Hale	July 08, '44	Crashed near Ymare, France, due to flak.
42-39909	Annony Miss		Sept. 09, '44	Crashed during practice take-off and landings at base. (Returned to USA on 6-28-45).
42-39916	Eastward Hup	Callow	Mar. 16, '44	Crashed near St. Quentin, France, due to enemy fighters. (a.k.a. "Westward Ho").
42-39917	Pretty Baby	Holland	Febr. 24, '44	Crashed near Jornstorf, Germany, due to flak and enemy fighters.
42-39920	Karen B	Nelson	Apr. 29, '44	Crashed near Rurrlo, Holland, due to flak.
42-39933	Star Eyes	Young	Mar. 23, '44	Crashed near Rodenbeck, Germany, due to enemy fighters.
42-39934	My Achin' Back	DeVore	Nov. 02, '43	Transferred to 100th BG. (Later crashed near Watenbuel, Ger., on 3-15-44 due to flak).
42-39936	Bar Fly	Boyd	Apr. 09, '44	Crashed near Nakskov, Denmark, due to fighters.
42-39937	Duchess	Hemer	May 12, '44	Crashed near Rudersdorf, Germany, due to enemy fighters.
42-39939			May 12, '44	Apparently crashed on mission to Brux, Czechoslovakia. Exact fate and crew unknown.
42-39940	Dixie Jane	Jameson	Febr. 08, '44	Crashed near St. Pierremont, France, due to being out of fuel.
42-39941	Lucky Lady II	Noble	May 12, '44	Crashed near Sougne-Remouchamps, Belgium, due to flak.
42-39954	Paper Doll	Yates	Mar. 23, '44	Crashed near Oppenwehe, Germany, due to flak.
42-39955			Febr. 06, '44	Crashed on runway due to blown out tire and collapsed landing gear.
42-39961	Bad Check	Tiska	Febr. 10, '44	Crashed near Hemsloh, Germany, due to mid-air collision w/ #42-31318.
42-39970	E-Rat-Icator		June 28, '45	Returned to the USA after the War. Battle damaged many times.
42-39971	Little Chum	Wands	Apr. 21, '44	Crashed near the 95th BG airfield at Horham, England. Exact cause of crash unknown.
42-39972	Our Buddy	Money	Dec. 31, '44	Crashed near Rotenburg, Germany, due to enemy fighters.
42-39973	Inside Curve	Miller	Oct. 12, '44	Crashed near Ingham, England, due to a mechanical problems or prop-wash.
42-39974	Punchboard	Racener	Apr. 09, '44	Forced landing near Vaerlose, Denmark, due to enemy fighters. (Captured by Germans).
42-39976	My Achin' Back	Martin	May 12, '44	Crash landed near Kongen, Germany, due to enemy fighters.
42-39977	Hard To Get	Compton	Febr. 09, '44	Crashed after take-off near Wymondham, England, due to mechanical problems.
42-39978			Mar. 07, '44	Salvaged due to unknown circumstances.

Serial	Name	Pilot	Date	Notes
42-39981	Rugged But Right	Haakenson	Apr. 29, '44	Crashed near Burg, Germany, due to enemy fighters.
42-39985	Duchess of Fubar	Brennan	Mar. 23, '44	Crashed near Rengershausen, Germany, due to enemy fighters.
42-39990	Junior	Gaal	May 19, '44	Crashed near Althuttendorf, Germany, due to flak.
42-39995	Cow Town Boogie	Schimmel	Apr. 11, '44	Forced landed and interned near Angelhome, Sweden, due to mechanical problems.
42-40003	Ol' Gappy		June 28, '45	Returned to USA after War. Trans. from the 379th BG. (157 missions flown - 8AF record).
42-97069	Mon Tete Rouge II	Downey	Dec. 04, '44	Crashed near Messerich, Germany, due to flak. "My Red Head"
42-97083	Flatbush Floogie	Gardner	Apr. 11, '44	Crashed near Minsen, Germany, due to flak.
42-97094	Why Worry II	Mard	May 12, '44	Ditched in the English Channel due to enemy fighters.
42-97130	The Avenger III	Lacti	Mar. 07, '44	Transferred to the 390th BG. (Later crashed near Ludenscheid, Ger., on 9-09-44, flak).
42-97143	You've Had It	Stogsdill	May 12, '44	Crashed near Wicker, Germany, due to falling wing of plane #42-92735.
42-97175	Lady Satan	Bayless	Febr. 06, '45	Crashed near Kirn, Germany, due to flak.
42-97195	Miss Minneapolis	Wynne	Mar. 13, '44	Transferred to the 96th BG. (Later crashed near Wittstedt, Germany, on 8-04-44).
42-97200	(None)	Robinson	Mar. 28, '44	Crash landed near Chateaudun, France, due to flak.
42-97206	Woolf Pack	Friddle	Sept. 25, '44	Crash landed near Houthulst, Belgium due to battle damage.
42-97209	(None)	Hochstetter	May 12, '44	Crashed near Bodenrod, Germany, due to enemy fighters.
42-97220	Kickapoo Joy Juice	Morehouse	May 08, '44	Crashed near Runingen, Germany, due to enemy fighters.
42-97222	Deuces Wild	Tyner	Febr. 06, '45	Forced landing near Charleville, France, due to flak.
42-97235	(None)	Naylor	May 12, '44	Crashed near Merzhausen, Germany, due to enemy fighters.
42-97236			Apr. 23, '45	Crashed upon landing at base. Co-pilot error while taking instructions.
42-97247		Reilly	June 21, '44	Destroyed on the ground at Poltava, Russia, by enemy bombers.
42-97256	Big Time Operator	Zimmerman	June 21, '44	Destroyed on the ground at Poltava, Russia, by enemy bombers.
42-97283		Jackson	June 21, '44	Destroyed on the ground at Poltava, Russia, by enemy bombers.
42-97306	Lady Janet	Sorenson	June 21, '44	Damaged at Poltava, Russia, by enemy bombers. (Salvaged on 8-17-45).
42-97308	Hairless Joe	Moore	Mar. 31, '45	Crashed near Ochsenhausen, Germany, due to enemy fighters.
42-97345	Ramblin' Wreck	Duckworth	July 03, '45	Returned to the United States after the War.
42-97349	Silver Dollar		May 31, '45	Returned to the United States after the War.
42-97361	The Punched Fowl	Halbleib	May 12, '44	Crashed near Ohren, Germany, due to enemy fighters.
42-97371	(None)	Atkinson	May 12, '44	Crashed near Echzell, Germany, due to enemy fighters. (a.k.a."Hairless Joe")
42-97375			Mar. 01, '45	Slated for the 452nd, but apparently never left the United States.
42-97390		Thomas	June 21, '44	Destroyed on the ground at Poltava, Russia, by enemy bombers.
42-97525	Invictus	Stephens	Mar. 08, '44	Crashed near Rothensee, Germany, due to enemy fighters.
42-97529	Dinah Might II	Boy	Apr. 09, '44	Crashed near Puttgarden, Fehmarn Island, Germany, due to enemy fighters.
42-97534	Patches	Cohen	Nov. 25, '44	Crashed near Schweinfurt, Germany, due to flak.
42-97549	Round Tripper	Brogan	May 29, '44	Crashed near Rocquigny, France, due to flak. (Also possible slight mid-air collision w/ #?)
42-97616	Hi Blower	Smith	July 28, '44	Crashed Merseburg, Germany, due to mid-air coll. w/ #42-97764. (96th BG plane w/ 452nd BG crew)
42-97628		Pesch	Jun. 21, '44	Destroyed on the ground at Poltava, Russia, by enemy bombers.
42-97663		Price	Mar. 04, '44	Transferred to the 457th BG. (Later crashed near Godincihum, France, on 3-26-44).
42-97666	Lucky Lady	Kostuch	Dec. 31, '44	Crashed near Hellwege, Germany, due to enemy fighters.
42-97697		Hankins	Oct. 02, '44	Crashed near Brackelhoxter, Germany, due to flak.
42-97700			June 29, '44	Transferred to the 96th BG. (Returned to the United States on 6-28-45).
42-97764	Now Go!	Franklin	July 28, '44	Crashed near Merseburg, Ger. (96th BG plane w/ 452nd crew). Mid-air coll. w/ #42-97616
42-97780			April 28, '44	Transferred to the 401st BG. (Returned to the USA after the War on 6-06-45).
42-97786	The Hard Way II	Thomas	May 12, '44	Crashed near Koblenz, Germany, due to enemy fighters.
42-97808	(None)	Lowell	May 29, '44	Crash landed near Grand-Leez, Belgium, due to flak.
42-97852		Stiles	Aug. 14, '44	Crashed near Strasbourg, France, due to flak.
42-97864	Why Worry	Patrick	May 12, '44	Crashed near Mershausen, Germany, due to enemy fighters.

Serial	Name	Crew	Date	Notes
42-97901		Koprowicz	Mar. 19, '45	Crash landed near Radomsko, Poland, due to enemy jet fighters.
42-97904	The Lady Jeanette	Gott	Nov. 09, '44	Crashed near Saarbrucken, Germany, due to flak.
42-97935	Rose-Etta	Lane	June 21, '44	Destroyed on the ground at Poltava, Russia, by enemy bombers.
42-97977		Rosholt	Mar. 21, '45	Crashed near Ahaus, Germany, due to flak.
42-97987			Oct. 01, '44	Crashed on runway due to landing gear failure. (Returned to the USA on 6-28-45).
42-102397	C'est La Guerre	Skoglund	Jan. 17, '45	Crashed near Guderott, Germany, due to flak. "That's the War".
42-102499		Harris	June 21, '44	Destroyed on the ground at Poltava, Russia, by enemy bombers.
42-102513	Swing Shift Baby	Davis	Sept. 25, '44	Crashed over Luxembourg after crew bailed out due to flak.
42-102514		Nelson	June 21, '44	Destroyed on the ground at Poltava, Russia, by enemy bombers.
42-102535	Lovely Lady	Williams	July 31, '44	Crashed near Munich, Germany, due to flak.
42-102541	Ain't Miss Behavin' II	Wright	June 19, '44	Crash landed near Wattisham, England, and destroyed by fire.
42-102572	Why Worry III	Mard	May 27, '44	Crashed near Avoudrey, France, due to enemy fighters.
42-102575			Aug. 25, '44	Crash landed into ditch near runway after battle damage and brake failure.
42-102587		Oswalt	June 21, '44	Destroyed on the ground at Poltava, Russia, by enemy bombers.
42-102615	Forbidden Fruit II	Knoll	Febr. 17, '44	Crashed near Tiberham, England, while forming due to prop-wash.
42-102622		Gaither	June 21, '44	Destroyed on ground at Poltava, Russia, due to enemy bombers.
42-102631			Aug. 08, '44	Overran and crashed at the end of runway due to pilot error.
42-102649	Lady Geraldine	Hattrem	Apr. 04, '44	Transferred to the 100th BG. (Returned to the United States on 6-01-45).
42-102650		Hayes	June 21, '44	Destroyed on the ground at Poltava, Russia, by enemy bombers.
42-102660	Lovely Lady	Armm	Dec. 28, '44	Ran into plane #43-38822 after skidding off the runway. (a.k.a. "Sack Time Sioux").
42-102662		Kirk	June 21, '44	Crashed near East Preignitz, Germany, due to mid-air collision w/ #42-31359.
42-102665		Antol	June 21, '44	Destroyed on the ground at Poltava, Russia, by enemy bombers.
42-102691		Meyers	June 21, '44	Destroyed on the ground at Poltava, Russia, by enemy bombers.
42-102931	Fiklebitch	Mowery	Nov. 09, '44	Crashed in the North Sea near Lowestoft, England.
42-102963		Sorenson	June 21, '44	Destroyed on the ground at Poltava, Russia, by enemy bombers.
42-107036	The Big Noise II	McKenzie	Apr. 11, '44	Force landed and interned at Rinkaby, Sweden.
42-107037		Eisele	Mar. 23, '44	Crash landed near Caister-on-Sea, England.
42-107048	Tangerine	Mills	June 21, '44	Transferred to the 303rd BG. (Later crashed near Cambrai, France, on 6-12-44).
42-107049		Reynolds	July 06, '45	Destroyed on the ground at Poltava, Russia, by enemy bombers.
42-107073	Silver Shed House	Gilbert	Aug. 09, '44	Returned to the USA after the War.
42-107087	Big Barn Smell	Slanin	May 12, '44	Ditched in the North Sea near Great Yarmouth, England, due to flak.
42-107089		Skurka	May 08, '44	Crashed near Buedesheim, Germany, due to enemy fighters.
42-107091	Forbidden Fruit	Reynolds	June 21, '44	Crashed into a truck while landing on runway after battle damage.
42-107093	Panting Stork II	Schaller	Jan. 05, '45	Destroyed on the ground at Poltava, Russia, by enemy bombers.
42-107174		Bradshaw	Aug. 09, '44	Crash landed near Buchy, France, due to flak. (a.k.a. Nippon'Ese)
42-107225	Smokey Liz II	Caldwell	Mar. 19, '45	Crashed near Eindhoven, Holland, due to flak.
43-37542	Liberty Belle		May 28, 45	Returned to the United States after the War.
43-37543		Skinner	June 07, '44	Transferred to the 306th BG. (Later crashed near Cambrai, France, on 6-12-44).
43-37545			June 21, '44	Destroyed on the ground at Poltava, Russia, by enemy bombers.
43-37558	Lady Be Good	Gay	Jan. 05, '45	Crash landed near Sarralbe, France, due to flak after crew had bailed out.
43-37563			July 10, '44	Collided with plane #41-9019 on runway due to brake failure.
43-37631			July 05, '45	Returned to the United States after the War.
43-37634	Feather Merchant	Seger	Dec. 31, '44	Crashed near Ritterhude, Germany, due to enemy fighters.
43-37644		Birch	June 11, '44	Transferred to 96th Bomb Group. (Later crashed near Steenwjik, Holland, on 3-24-45).
43-37645	That's All Jack	Traynelis	Dec. 31, '44	Crashed near Tauenbrueck, Germany, due to enemy fighters and flak.
43-37673	Lucky Lady III	Marksian	Febr. 06, '45	Crash landed near Assigny, France, due to battle damage.

Serial	Name	Pilot	Date	Fate
43-37726		Caswell	Dec. 24, '44	Crash landed near near Melsbroek, Belgium, due to battle damage.
43-37744	Final Approach	Green	Oct. 05, '44	Crashed near Venlo, Holland, due to flak.
43-37745	Mug Wump	Betts	Jan. 17, '45	Forced landing near Kalmar, Sweden, due to flak and interned.
43-37747		Hanson	July 08, '44	Crashed near Boubiers, France, due to flak.
43-37753			June 29, '45	Returned to the United States after the War.
43-37802	My-Assis-Dragon		July 05, '45	Returned to the United States after the War.
43-37807			July 06, '45	Returned to the United States after the War.
43-37814	Richter's Wreckers		Apr. 05, '45	Crashed while landing at base.
43-37817	Mollita		July 12, '44	Crash landed near base due to being out of fuel.
43-37824			July 03, '45	Returned to the United States after the War.
43-37829	(None)	Bickford	Sept. 28, '44	Crashed in northern Luxembourg due to flak after crew had bailed out.
43-37833	The Uninvited	Bickford	Nov. 09, '44	Crashed near Minheim, Germany, due to flak.
43-37834		Lockwald	June 29, '44	Transferred to 457th Bomb Group. (Later crashed near Wetzleben, Germany, on 9-28-44).
43-37841			Apr. 05, '45	Skidded off wet runway and crashed. (Returned to the USA on 7-06-45).
43-37853			July 03, '45	Returned to the United States after the War.
43-37878			Oct. 04, '44	Crashed somewhere on mission to Munster, Germany.
43-37905			July 08, '44	Transferred to the 379th BG. (Returned to the United States on 7-3-45).
43-37906		Specht	Oct. 26, '44	Crashed near Caston, England, after mid-air collision with #43-38696.
43-37915			Aug. 12, '44	Trans. to 100th BG. Later force landed in Russia during Warsaw supply drop on 9-18-44.
43-38093			July 11, '45	Returned to the United States after the War.
43-38119		Parmely	Sept. 03, '44	Ditched or crashed in the English Channel near Guernsey Island due to flak.
43-38179	Chastain's Kindergarten	Chastain	Mar. 21, '45	Crash landed at base and destroyed by fire due to battle damage.
43-38185	Lacka Sacky	Betts	Dec. 04, '44?	Battle damaged and made crash landing in Belgium.
43-38193			June 28, '45	Returned to the United States after the War.
43-38201		Eccles	Sept. 30, '44	Crashed at base due to landing gear not being down. Battle damaged.
43-38205		Daniel	Mar. 19, '45	Battle damaged and forced landed at Maastricht Airfield, Holland.
43-38231	Try'n Getit	Knox	Mar. 19, '45	Crash landed near Posnan, Poland, due to enemy jet fighters.
43-38318	Da Poiple Boid	Moynihan	Apr. 25, '45	Ran off runway struck a mobile lighting unit. (Returned to the USA on 7-06-45).
43-38356	Slienthe Je Vahr	Bell	Apr. 21, '45	Crashed near Landau, Germany. - Explosion due to lightning? "To a Long & Healthy Life"
43-38358	Slightly Dangerous	Fry	Febr. 03, '45	Battle damaged and forced landed near Rinkaby, Sweden. (Returned to USA on 8-13-45).
43-38368	Daisy Mae	Ettredge	Mar. 19, '45	Crashed near Zwickau, Germany, due to enemy jet fighters.
43-38421	Flak Magic	Schewel	July 11, '45	Returned to the United States after the War. (a.k.a. "N for Nan").
43-38513	Never Had It So Good		Sept. 17, '44	Transferred to the 96th BG. (Returned to United States on 6-01-45).
43-38533		Halik	Jan. 17, '45	Crashed near Sittensen, Germany, due to flak.
43-38614	Utah Gal		June 28, '45	Returned to the United States after the War.
43-38696		Bragg	Oct. 26, '44	Crashed near Caston, England, after mid-air collision with #43-37906.
43-38698		Payne	Febr. 16, '45	Crashed near Sundern, Germany, due to flak.
43-38702			July 03, '45	Returned to the United States after the War.
43-38822			Dec. 28, '44	Skidded off runway then struck by plane #42-102660 which had skidded off runway.
43-38868		Richardson	Apr. 07, '45	Crashed near Schwarmstedt, Germany, after being rammed by an enemy Me-109.
43-38876		Porter	Mar. 26, '45	Crashed near Crettingham, England, after mid-air collision w/ #43-38402 from 34th BG.
43-38879		Bishop	Mar. 18, '45	Crashed in the English Channel after mid-air collision w/ #43-38982.
43-38917	Not Today Cleo	Kerber	July 03, '45	Returned to the United States after the War.
43-38921		Jones	Jan. 02, '45	Crashed near Ehrang, Germany, due to flak.
43-38943		Larson	Jan. 10, '45	Presumed crashed in North Sea or English Channel. No trace of plane.
43-38982		Booth	Mar. 18, '45	Crash landed near Woodbridge, England, after mid-air collision w/ #43-38879.
43-38989			July 03, '45	Returned to the United States after the War.

Serial	Name	Pilot	Date	Fate
43-39007			Dec. 25, '44	Returned to the United States after the War.
43-39089			June 29, '45	Returned to the United States after the War.
43-39143	You've Had It	Robinson	July 06, '45	Returned to the United States after the War. (Involved in runway accident May 1945)
43-39326	Flak Shy Lady		June 29, '45	Returned to the United States after the War.
43-39355			May 30, '45	Returned to the United States after the War.
43-39358			June 20, '45	Returned to the United States after the War.
43-39439	Jeannie w/ the Light Brown Hair	Remmenga	June 28, '45	Returned to the United States after the War. (a.k.a. "Cyanide for Hitler").
44-6001		Skinner	June 21, '44	Destroyed on the ground at Poltava, Russia, by enemy bombers.
44-6011		Forman	June 21, '44	Destroyed on the ground at Poltava, Russia, by enemy bombers.
44-6137			June 03, '44	Transferred to the 96th BG. (Later mid-air coll. w/ #43-38746 on 1-29-45).
44-6152			Mar. 05, '45	Crash landed at base due to landing gear collapse.
44-6153			June 11, '44	Transferred to the 96th BG. (Returned to the United States on 6-02-45).
44-6165	Lady Gay		Febr. 20, '45	Crash landed at base due to landing gear collapse.
44-6560	Puddin's Pride	Knox	July 03, '45	Returned to the United States after the War.
44-6578	Rusty Dusty		Dec. 07, '44	Transferred to the 91st BG. (Later taxi-collision w/ #43-38306 on 4-04-45).
44-6601	Lucky Lady	Belton	Jan. 20, '45	Crashed near Midwound, Holland, due to flak.
44-6816		DuMond	Mar. 30, '45	Crashed near Littleport, England. Cause thought to be prop-wash.
44-6827	Hi Blower		June 28, '45	Returned to the United States after the War.
44-6905	Virginia		June 29, '45	Returned to the United States after the War.
44-6909	Annony Miss		Febr. 04, '45	Transferred to the 384th BG. (a.k.a. "Achtung Adolph"). Salvaged by the 9th AF.
44-6940			May 27, '45	Salvaged due to unknown circumstances.
44-8015	Johnny Reb	Emmett	Febr. 22, '45	Broke apart and crashed near Pfaffenhoffen, Germany, due to prop-wash.
44-8081			June 28, '45	Returned to the United States after the War.
44-8181		Arnt	Jan. 10, '45	Crashed into the bomb dump at 100th BG base due to icing on wings.
44-8201	Rosalie Ann II	McDougall	Jan. 02, '45	Crashed near Trier, Germany, due to flak.
44-8249	(None)	Kenworthy	Dec. 24, '44	Crashed near Prum, Germany, due to flak.
44-8308			Aug. 26, '45	Returned to the United States after the War.
44-8365	Virginia		Oct. 08, '45	Transferred to the 94th BG. (Returned to the United States 6-07-45).
44-8491		Meneley	Dec. 27, '45	Landed at Menvielle, France, due to being low on fuel.
44-8514	Lassie Come Home		Oct. 23, '44	Transferred to the 100th BG. (Later crash landed in Europe 12-29-44).
44-8518		Wagoner	Dec. 05, '44	Crashed near Lingen, Germany, due to mechanical problems.
44-8519			June 07, '45	Returned to the United States after the War.
44-8522			Oct. 24, '44	Transferred to the 94th BG. (Returned to the United States 6-07-45).
44-8527			Febr. 06, '45	Landed at Menvielle, France, due to being low on fuel.
44-8531	Miassis Dragon	Gill	Apr. 07, '45	Crashed near Schwarmstedt, Germany, due to enemy fighters.
44-8575			Sept. 01, '46	Salvaged by the 9th Air Force.
44-8602		Smith	Jan. 17, '45	Force landing at Bulltofta, Sweden, due to flak.
44-8609			June 06, '45	Returned to the United States after the War.
44-8634	Ida Wanna	Sharp	Apr. 07, '45	Crashed near Heide, Germany, due to fighters.
44-8703			June 28, '45	Crash landed on German airfield due to flak. (Returned to the USA after the War).
44-8706			Febr. 14, '45	Transferred to the 457th BG. Salvaged by 9th Air Force on 10-30-45.
44-8799	Manchester Misses	Schaller	Dec. 29, '45	Returned to the United States after the War.
44-8841			Apr. 28, '44	Struck a power shovel parked near the taxiway. (Returned to the USA 12-13-45).
44-8875			Jan. 04, '46	Returned to the United States after the War.
44-8908			Oct. 29, '45	Returned to the United States after the War.
44-83264	Scrappy Jr.		June 28, '45	Returned to the United States after the War.
44-83473			July 03, '45	Returned to the United States after the War.

Plane Names of the 452nd Bombardment Group

- Achtung Adolph
- Ain't Miss Behavin'
- Ain't Miss Behavin' II
- Ain't Miss Behavin' III
- Angel
- Angel II
- Angel Mine
- Anony Miss
- Avenger
- Bachelor's Den
- Bad Check
- Balcony Seat
- Bar Fly
- Bar Fly's Revenge
- Batson's Bastards
- Belle of Broadway
- Berlin Rooster
- Big Barn Smell
- Big Noise (The)
- Big Noise II (The)
- Big Time Operator
- BIOYA
- Borrowed Time
- Breaks of the Game
- BTO in the ETO
- Buffagator
- Can Do It
- Cap'n Crow
- Case Ace (Cat Ass)
- C'est La Guerre
- Chastain's Kindergarten
- Cock O' the Walk
- Cocktail Siren
- Contrail Chaser
- Cow Topsy Boogie
- Cow Town Boogie
- Cyanide For Hitler
- Da Poiple Boid
- Daisy Mae
- Daisy June
- Delta Girl
- De R.I.
- Deuces Wild
- Dinah Might
- Dinah Might II
- Dixie Jane
- Dog Breath
- Dol
- Down For Double
- Dragon Lady
- Dream Gal
- Duchess of Fubar
- Dynamite
- ETO - Balcony Seat
- E-Rat-Icator
- Eastwood Hup
- Easy Does It
- Edna Sheila
- Eight Ball
- Evanton Babe
- Feather Merchant
- Feudin' Wagon
- Fiklebitch
- Final Approach
- Flak Magic
- Flak Shy
- Flak Shy Lady
- Flakstop
- Flatbush Floogie
- Forbidden Fruit
- Forbidden Fruit II
- Four Freedoms
- Four Winds
- Four-Fan Ann
- Frivolous Sal
- Ghost Bomber
- Gin Rickey
- Good Pickin'
- Grade "A"
- Gruesome Crewsome
- Gunners Paradise
- Gypsy
- Hairless Joe
- Hank From Dixie
- Happy Valley
- Hard Way (The)
- Hard Way II (The)
- Hard To Get
- Hel'en Berlin
- Hell's Angels
- Hell's Cargo
- Hi Blower
- Hog
- Home Sweet Home
- Home Sweet Sue
- Hot Rock (The)
- Ida Wanna
- Impatient Virgin
- Inside Curve
- Invictus
- Iron Bird
- Jeanne D'Arc
- Jeannie
- Jeannie with the Light Brown Hair
- Johnny Reb
- Junnie "K"
- Junior
- Karen B
- Karen B II
- Karen B III
- Karen B IV
- Karen B V
- Kickapoo Joy Juice
- Lacka Sacky
- Lacka Shacky
- Lady Be Gay
- Lady Be Good
- Lady Dog Breath
- Lady Gay
- Lady Janet
- Lady Jeanette
- Lady Moe
- Lady Satan
- Lady Stardust
- Lady Stardust II
- Lassie Come Home
- Leading Lady
- Liberty Belle
- Little Chum
- Little Colonel
- Little Dudette
- Little Miss America
- Lovely Lady
- Lucky 13
- Lucky Lady
- Lucky Lady II
- Lucky Lady III
- Manchester Misses
- Many Happy Returns
- Marie Helena
- Mary Jane
- Mary Jane II
- Marjorie Ann
- Mavoureen
- Miassis Dragon
- Miss America
- Miss Anonymous
- Miss Behave
- Miss It
- Miss Tena
- Mo-Feudin'
- Mollita
- Mon Petit Rouge
- Mon Tete Rouge
- Mon Tete Rouge II
- Mug-Wump
- My Achin' Back
- My-Assis-Dragon
- My Darling Lee
- "N" for Nan
- Never Had It So Good
- Nippon'Ese
- Now Go!
- Not Today Cleo
- Our Buddy
- Old Outhouse - Never a Dry Run
- Pandamonium
- Panting Stork
- Panting Stork II
- Paper Doll
- Pappy's Pride
- Passionate Witch
- Passionate Witch II
- Patches
- Patty
- Peg Of My Heart
- Perils of Pauline
- Pistol Packin' Mama
- Pretty Baby
- Pretty Baby II
- Princess Pat
- Princess Pat II
- Princess Pat Ches
- Puddin's Pride
- Punchboard
- Puppy Breath
- Purple Shaft
- Quivering Queenie
- Ragged But Right
- Ramblin' Wreck
- Raunch
- Reddy Teddy
- Reincarnation (The)
- Richter's Wreckers
- Rinkaby
- Rosalie Ann
- Rosalie Ann II
- Rose
- Rose-Etta
- Round Tripper
- Rusty Dusty
- Sack Time Sioux
- Satan's Sister
- Scrappy
- Scrappy Jr.
- Sea Biscuit
- Section Eight
- Section Eight II
- Section Eight III
- Sentimental Journey
- Shed House Mouse
- Short Snoozer
- Short Snorter
- Silver Shed House
- Six Bounders
- Sky Hawg
- Sky Hog
- Sky Queen
- Sleepy Time Gal
- Slienthe Je Vahr
- Slightly Dangerous
- Smokey Liz
- Smokey Liz II
- Snake Eyes
- Solid Comfort
- Star Eyes
- Stars and Stripes
- Sunrise Serenade
- Sweet Adeline
- Sweet Eloise
- Sweet & Low
- Sweet Stuff
- Sweet and Slow
- Swing Shift Baby
- Swing Shift Baby II
- Tangerine
- Tennessee Cavalier
- Terry-a-Long
- Tina
- Tina Tangerine
- That's All Jack
- Three Cads and a Lad
- Thunderbird
- Tim Tyler's Luck
- Top Hat
- Try'n Getit
- Twice?
- Umbriago
- Uninvited (The)
- Up N Front
- Up'N Atm
- Utah Gal
- Virgin on the Verge
- Virgin Wolf
- Virginia
- Virginia Wolf
- Wacky Woody
- War Weary
- Wars End
- Westward Ho
- Wham Bam Thank You Ma'm
- Whatsup Doc
- Why Worry
- Why Worry II
- Wild Hare (The)
- Windy Lou
- Woolf Pack
- Worry Bird (The)
- You've Had It

Target Locations of the 452nd Bombardment Group
Febr. 5, 1944 – April 21, 1945
Missions 1 - 250

#	Date	Target
1.	2-05-44	Romilly
2.	2-06-44	Romilly
3.	2-08-44	Frankfurt
4.	2-10-44	Brunswick
5.	2-13-44	No. France
6.	2-20-44	Posen - Tutow
7.	2-21-44	Brunswick
8.	2-24-44	Posen
9.	2-25-44	Regensburg
10.	2-29-44	Brunswick
11.	3-03-44	Berlin
12.	3-04-44	Berlin
13.	3-06-44	Berlin
14.	3-08-44	Berlin
15.	3-09-44	Berlin
16.	3-15-44	Brunswick
17.	3-16-44	Ausgburg
18.	3-18-44	Augsburg
19.	3-20-44	Frankfurt
20.	3-22-44	Berlin
21.	3-23-44	Brunswick
22.	3-26-44	No. France
23.	3-27-44	Bordeaux
24.	3-28-44	Chateaudun
25.	4-01-44	Ludwigshaven
26.	4-08-44	Achmer-Rheine
27.	4-09-44	Posen - Warnemunde
28.	4-10-44	Courcelles
29.	4-11-44	Rostock
30.	4-13-44	Augsburg
31.	4-18-44	Luneburg
32.	4-19-44	Lippstadt
33.	4-20-44	Northern France
34.	4-22-44	Hamm
35.	4-24-44	Friedrichshaven
36.	4-25-44	Dijon
37.	4-26-44	Hildesheim
38.	4-27-44	Northern France
39.	4-29-44	Berlin
40.	4-30-44	Clermont
41.	5-01-44	Northern France
42.	5-01-44	Metz - Brussels
43.	5-07-44	Berlin
44.	5-08-44	Berlin-Brunswick
45.	5-08-44	Northern France
46.	5-09-44	Juvincourt
47.	5-11-44	Brussels
48.	5-12-44	Brux
49.	5-13-44	Osnabruck
50.	5-19-44	Berlin
51.	5-20-44	Belgium
52.	5-22-44	Kiel
53.	5-23-44	Bretigny - Troye
54.	5-24-44	Berlin
55.	5-25-44	Liege
56.	5-27-44	Strasbourg
57.	5-27-44	St. Valery
58.	5-28-44	Konigsburg
59.	5-29-44	Leipzig
60.	5-30-44	Reims
61.	5-31-44	Schwerte
62.	6-02-44	Wimereaux
63.	6-02-44	Achers
64.	6-03-44	Wimereaux - Boulogne
65.	6-04-44	Le Chatelet
66.	6-04-44	Villeneuve - St. Georges
67.	6-05-44	Cap Grisnez
68.	6-06-44	Caen
69.	6-06-44	Argentan
70.	6-06-44	Argentan
71.	6-07-44	Nantes
72.	6-08-44	Tours
73.	6-10-44	Merlimon Plage
74.	6-11-44	Pontabault
75.	6-12-44	Bernay - St. Marrin
76.	6-14-44	Brussels
77.	6-15-44	Misburg
78.	6-15-44	No. France
79.	6-18-44	Bremen - Hanover
80.	6-19-44	Corme Ecluse
81.	6-20-44	Magdeburg
82.	6-21-44	Berlin
83.	6-21-44	Ruhland - Elsterwerda
84.	6-22-44	Melun
85.	6-23-44	No. Paris
86.	6-24-44	Bremen
87.	6-25-44	So. France
88.	6-29-44	Wittenburg
89.	7-04-44	So. Paris
90.	7-06-44	No. France
91.	7-06-44	No. France
92.	7-07-44	Leipzig
93.	7-08-44	Rouen
94.	7-11-44	Munich
95.	7-12-44	Munich
96.	7-13-44	Munich
97.	7-14-44	So. France
98.	7-16-44	Stuttgart
99.	7-17-44	No. France
100.	7-18-44	Kiel
101.	7-19-44	Schweinfurt
102.	7-20-44	Wetzlar
103.	7-21-44	Regensburg
104.	7-24-44	St. Lo
105.	7-25-44	St. Lo
106.	7-28-44	Merseburg
107.	7-29-44	Merseburg
108.	7-31-44	Munich
109.	8-01-44	So. France
110.	8-02-44	No. Paris
111.	8-04-44	Bremen
112.	8-05-44	Magdeburg
113.	8-06-44	Berlin
114.	8-07-44	No. France
115.	8-08-44	No. France
116.	8-09-44	Eindhoven
117.	8-11-44	Mulhouse
118.	8-13-44	No. France
119.	8-14-44	Ludwigshaven
120.	8-18-44	Burron - Marlotte
121.	8-24-44	Ruhland
122.	8-25-44	Politz
123.	8-26-44	Brest
124.	8-27-44	No. Germany
125.	8-30-44	Bremen
126.	9-01-44	No. France
127.	9-03-44	Brest
128.	9-05-44	Stuttgart
129.	9-08-44	Mainz
130.	9-09-44	Dusseldorf
131.	9-10-44	Nuremberg
132.	9-11-44	Chemnitz
133.	9-13-44	Bischofsheim
134.	9-13-44	Diosgyor
135.	9-17-44	Deelen
136.	9-19-44	Weisbaden
137.	9-21-44	Ludwigshaven
138.	9-25-44	Ludwigshaven
139.	9-27-44	Mainz
140.	9-28-44	Merseburg
141.	9-30-44	Bielefeld
142.	10-02-44	Kassel
143.	10-03-44	Nuremberg
144.	10-05-44	Munster
145.	10-06-44	Berlin
146.	10-07-44	Lutzkendorf
147.	10-09-44	Mainz
148.	10-12-44	Bremen
149.	10-14-44	Cologne
150.	10-15-44	Cologne
151.	10-15-44	Helgoland
152.	10-17-44	Cologne
153.	10-18-44	Kassel
154.	10-19-44	Mannheim
155.	10-25-44	Hamburg
156.	10-26-44	Hanover
157.	10-30-44	W. Germany
158.	11-02-44	Merseburg
159.	11-04-44	Neunkirchen
160.	11-05-44	Ludwigshaven
161.	11-06-44	Rheydt
162.	11-09-44	Saarbrucken
163.	11-10-44	Wiesbaden
164.	11-11-44	Oberlahnstein
165.	11-16-44	Duren area
166.	11-21-44	No. Germany
167.	11-25-44	Merseburg
168.	11-26-44	Hamm
169.	11-27-44	Bingen
170.	11-29-44	Hamm
171.	11-30-44	Lutzkendorf
172.	12-04-44	Giessen
173.	12-05-44	Berlin
174.	12-10-44	Koblenz
175.	12-11-44	Giessen
176.	12-12-44	Darmstadt
177.	12-18-44	Mainz
178.	12-24-44	Darmstadt
179.	12-26-44	Andernach
180.	12-28-44	Koblenz
181.	12-29-44	Lunebach
182.	12-30-44	Kassel
183.	12-31-44	Hamburg
184.	1-02-45	Ehrang
185.	1-03-45	Fulda
186.	1-05-45	Hanau
187.	1-07-45	Cologne
188.	1-08-45	Lunebach - Waxweiler
189.	1-10-45	Cologne
190.	1-15-45	Augsburg
191.	1-17-45	Hamburg
192.	1-20-45	Rheime
193.	1-21-45	Mannheim
194.	1-28-45	Hohenbudburg
195.	1-29-45	Bielefeld
196.	2-03-45	Berlin
197.	2-06-45	Chemnitz
198.	2-09-45	Fulda
199.	2-14-45	Tachau - Sonneberg
200.	2-15-45	Cottbus
201.	2-16-45	Hamm
202.	2-17-45	Farnkfurt
203.	2-19-45	Osnabruck
204.	2-20-45	Nuremberg
205.	2-21-45	Nuremberg
206.	2-22-45	Freiburg - Ulm
207.	2-23-45	Ansbach
208.	2-25-45	Munich
209.	2-26-45	Berlin
210.	2-27-45	Leipzig
211.	2-28-45	Kassel
212.	3-01-45	Ulm
213.	3-03-45	Dedenhausen
214.	3-04-45	So. Germany
215.	3-05-45	Chemnitz
216.	3-08-45	Langendreer
217.	3-09-45	Frankfurt
218.	3-10-45	Dortmund
219.	3-11-45	Hamburg
220.	3-12-45	Swinemunde
221.	3-14-45	Hanover
222.	3-15-45	Oranienburg
223.	3-17-45	Ruhland - Plauen
224.	3-18-45	Berlin
225.	3-19-45	Zwickau
226.	3-20-45	Hamburg
227.	3-21-45	Handorf
228.	3-22-45	Frankfurt
229.	3-23-45	Hengstey
230.	3-24-45	Plantlunne
231.	3-26-45	Plauen
232.	3-28-45	Hanover
233.	3-30-45	Hamburg
234.	3-31-45	Zeitz - Erfurt
235.	4-03-45	Kiel
236.	4-04-45	Kiel
237.	4-05-45	Nuremberg
238.	4-06-45	Gera
239.	4-07-45	Kaltenkirchen
240.	4-08-45	Grafenwohr
241.	4-09-45	Munich - Reim
242.	4-10-45	Zerbst
243.	4-11-45	Donauworth
244.	4-14-45	Royan - St. Georges
245.	4-15-45	Royan
246.	4-16-45	Pas de Lillan
247.	4-17-45	Dresden
248.	4-18-45	Straubing
249.	4-19-45	Karlsbad
250.	4-21-45	Ingolstadt

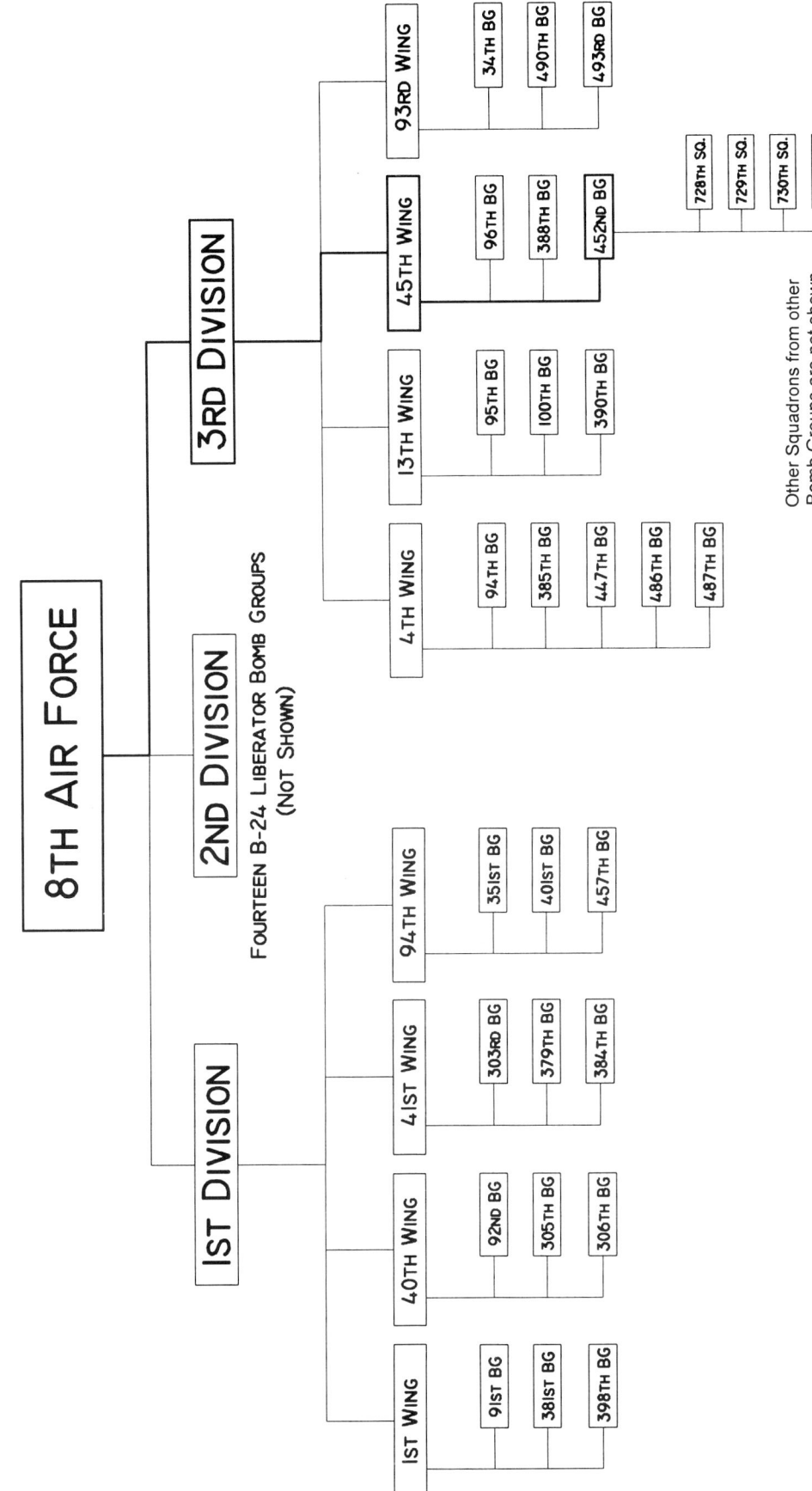

Acknowledgements

During the research and writing of this book, I was very fortunate to interview many men of outstanding bravery, courage, and valor. Each one is truly an American hero, although most would personally shun this title. One reoccurring praise that I kept hearing from these men was one of thankfulness to God for bringing them back home to their parents or their own young families. Some miraculously were the only survivors while the rest of their crew was killed. I must also give my foremost thanks to God for allowing me the opportunity to meet such men of integrity and for continually directing me the past few years while writing this book. By knowing these men I have been able to see an entirely different generation through their eyes.

My late friend Vincent A. Smedley's love for his brother, Francis, inspired me to write this book about his brother's plane and crew. Sadly, before Vince died in March of 1997, he never learned much about the other men that flew with Francis or the many details that I have uncovered during the past few years. Vince's wife, Marie Smedley, had also been an inspiration to me as we learned together of the many details pertaining to Francis Smedley's plane and crew before her death in September of 1999. Many times we thought of how Vince would have loved to have known about every new detail that presented itself.

I am also greatly indebted to the surviving wives and crew members of the *Sunrise Serenade* who supplied me with invaluable information regarding their World War II experiences. John & Donna Brown; Gwen Dean (wife of Raymond); Denise Bonfiglio (former wife of James E. Gallagher); George & Phyllis Griffin; Bill & Jennie Hewett; Bob & Rita Lalumiere; John & Alice McGrath; Esther Rhodes (wife of Norbert); Andy Senetsky; and Mary Lou Shoffner (wife of Harry). Other family members of the crew who also helped are Wyatt Parsons (grandson of Raymond Dean); Sean Gallagher (son of James Gallagher); Larry and Nancy Shoffner (children of Harry Shoffner); Kim Berringer (granddaughter of John McGrath), and Daniel Lalumiere (son of Bob Lalumiere).

My sincerest appreciation is extended to my friend Sally Olson and also to my wife, Sharon Penry, who both provided me with many hours of proofreading, encouragement, and ideas during the process of writing. They were able to transition many areas of the book into a sequential story.

Special recognition must be given to the secretary of the 452nd Bomb Group Association and combat veteran, Henry J. "Hank" North, who has answered literally hundreds of my inquiries pertaining to facts, planes, and airmen of the 452nd Bomb Group. Hank had always made himself available to quickly research new details that I needed. Without his assistance this book would only be a fraction of what it has become.

I also want to express my appreciation to 452nd Bomb Group combat veteran, Ed Hinrichs, whose book "*Missing Planes of the 452nd Bomb Group*" provided me with many details and quick references to crew lists as I researched the other planes and crews that went down during the Group's operation. Ed's passion and love for the history of the 452nd Bomb Group is unsurpassed. He, too, has made himself available to me an innumerable amount of times, often at short notice. Ed also provided the framework for the information regarding the many planes that served with the Group that are listed on pages 150 to 155. He painstakingly searched and identified the serial numbers of every B-17 that served with the 452nd Bomb Group. With this list of planes we were then able to add the details pertaining to each plane.

Many combat veterans of the 452nd Bomb Group provided me with the names of their planes and often very detailed accounts of their planes and crews. Some have written lengthy letters or recalled events during long telephone conversations while others could offer only simple facts to verify or disprove certain events or plane names. Many of these men deserve much more praise from me than just individually listing their names, but to sort through them would be very difficult based upon the information they were able to provide. With that said, the following men provided the framework for many details portrayed in the chapters pertaining to the combat missions of the 452nd Bomb Group.

William H. Abbott, Ernie Alban, Charles E. Anderson, Marvin L. Armstrong, Hugh T. Atkinson, Michael A. Barbara, Edward R. Betts, Kenneth F. Bickford, James W. Boehling, James F. Bottenfield, Clyde T. Boy Jr., Robert J. Brennan, Henry Buchanan, Harry F. Burgess, Harold E. Burrell, William C. Caldwell, Winecke F. Carpenter, Clyde V. Cassill, John P. Chopelas, John Collier, Frank M. Console, Robert M. Cook, Arthur E. Crowe, Conrad N. Desmarais, Joseph Di Marco, Francis E. Dugo, Frank S. Ebey, Gerald E. Elliot, John E. Everhart, Harold G. Fulmer, Stephen A. Gaal, Thomas G. Garten, Hubert Gay, Tony P. Gill, Ralph P. Goldsticker, Warren R. Good, Vencel V. Gordon, Louis W. Graber, Clark G. Graham, Earl F. Green, Russell W. Gustafson, George A. Haakenson, Lewis T. Haas, Russell D. Haas, Verne D. Hale, Gerald J. Hanus, Fred B. Heckman Jr., Buell E. Hoagland, Stan Hodsdon, Hal D. Holland, Floyd E. Holman, Frank "Sam" Houston, William J. Howe, Nelson L. Jack, Lake H. Jameson,

Paul F. Jenkel, Grady B. Jolly, Edward M. Kaminski, Ralph L. Karkow, Robert F. Kerr, Luther B. King, Patrick J. King, Ray E. King, Samuel K. Kniffen, Howard W. Kordatzky, Frank Kottlowski, Robert T. Krout, Joseph F. LaFrance, Douglas E. Leinweber, Raymond W. Lentz, Eugene A. Lohmann, Stanley Lorek, Robert O. Lorenzi, Stanley Lowell, Truman L. Manning, Milton M. Mard, Milan Marecek, Claude C. Martin, Clyde J. Martin, Daniel Mason, Irwin Math, Thomas E. McDannold, Merland E. McDowell, Charles M. McKeag, James M. McLelland, Gene Meese, Gilbert J. Meneley, Nickolas Menza, Lowell "Mike" Millisor, Arthur H. Mills, Virgil G. Mims, Arthur Mittman, Nick Moramarco, James A. Morris, Lawrence S. Moses, Charles J. Mueller, Thomas E. Murray, Hugh E. Noell, Norman E. Parnell, Shirley A. Parvin, Arnold O. Pederson, John J. Pesch, Rev. Paschel H. "Pat" Powell, Ernest Racener, Kenneth R. Raske, George P. Remmenga, William L. Roche, Merle E. Rohlfs, Wilburn C. Rowden, John A. Safarik, Duncan Sanderson, Clem A. Schaller, Warren R. Schewel, C. Herbert Shulman, George A. Silva, Paul E. Simerly, Robert H. Smith, Durwald L. Sorenson, John B. Stellitano, Richard L. Thayer, Edwin W. Thomson, Carl E. Tyner, Daniel G. Viafore, Claude Waite, Teddy F. Weatherford, Fred K. Whitlinger, Daniel D. Wilkerson, and Edward S. Wodicka.

It has been brought to my attention that several of the men I have listed above have now passed away, and it would be difficult for me to try to list who they are. Hundreds of other men who served with the 452nd Bomb Group were not contacted, but I'm sure they would have been just as helpful as the ones with whom I corresponded.

The following wives, children, or relatives of 452nd Bomb Group veterans also contributed information about their husband's, father's, or uncle's crew and planes: Susan Birbeck (daughter of Lucius C. Birbeck), Douglas Boren (son of James R. Boren), Randy Jolly (son of Grady B. Jolly), Mrs. Grady C. Justice (wife of Grady C. Justice), Elizabeth Lanigan (wife of Vincent C. Lanigan), Betty Mason (wife of Daniel Mason), George Paulk (son of George P. Paulk), Joseph L. Petri (nephew of Sylvester Petri), Jo Petri-Terry (daughter of Sylvester Petri), Kate Reynolds (wife of James Reynolds), and Claire Saucedo (wife of James M. Saucedo).

Combat veterans of the 8th Air Force who supplied information, but who were not part of the 452nd Bomb Group, are Richard Crippen, Fritz M. Hageter, Robert K. Morgan, Merle Olmsted, Emile E. Smedley, Claude Watkins, Bob Wills, Lloyd Winegarner, Robert F. Yeager.

Yvonne Daly-Brusselmans helped provide details pertaining to the events of Harry Shoffner in the Belgian Underground. Her book "*Anne Brusselmans, Mission Accomplished - My Mother*" was invaluable in helping to understand how her mother and other brave Belgian citizens saved many allied airmen from the Germans.

Doris P. Jackson at the National Archives in College Park, Maryland, provided assistance in obtaining Missing Air Crew Reports and help in deciphering many unreadable pages.

Arlene Leonard and Ed Polic of the Glenn Miller Historical Society provided much of the information about Glenn Miller and his orchestra.

Special thanks to the staff at Service Press who expertly worked to print this book and answered many of my questions throughout the process.

My contacts in Europe who have greatly helped search for details and provided much-needed information include Christoph Awender, Oisten Berge, Alison Birley, Andreas Brekken, Cynrik De Decker, Ivo De Jong, Geert De Vos, Jean-Marc Fort, Wolf Hess, Martin J. Jeffery, Monsieur Jungbloed, Ross McNeil, Holger Mueller, Simon Orchard, Lars-Uwe Rudek, Andreas Thaler, and Gunther Vogel.

Additional information and assistance was provided by Ben Bolling, Gareth Collins, Ted Darcy, Cheryl Davis, Fred Dijkstra, Gina Earle, Roland Geiger, John Kahl, Jay Karamales, George D. Kasparian, Teresa Krysl, Darrell McCoy, Mike Miller, Sandy Mutchler, George F. Nafziger, Andrew Petro, Jason Pipes, Dick Pumphrey, Bob and Sharon Schaming, and Gene Thomsen.

My sincerest apologies are offered to anyone who has assisted in the writing of this book that I have failed to personally mention.

Bibliography

Barnes, Marvin E. *452nd Bombardment Group, 3rd Edition.* Charlotte, North Carolina: Delmar Printing Company, 1980.

Bauer, Lt. Col. Eddy. *Illustrated World War II Encyclopedia, Volume I.* Westport, Connecticut: H. S. Stuttman, Inc., 1978.

Bradley, Clyde W. *A Wartime Log.* Unpublished, date unknown.

Chant, Chris. *Aircraft of World War II.* New York, New York: Barnes & Noble, Inc., 1999.

Daley-Brusselmans, Yvonne. *Anne Brusselmans - Mission Accomplished: "My Mother".* Yvonne Daley-Brusselmans, 1993.

Davis, Larry. *B-17 in Action.* Carrollton, Texas: Squadron/Signal Publications, Inc., 1984.

Forman, Wallace R. *B-17 Nose Art Name Directory.* North Branch, Minnesota: Phalanx Publishing, 1996.

Freeman, Roger A. *The Mighty Eighth: A History of the US Eighth Air Force.* Garden City, New York: Doubleday & Company, Inc., 1970.

Freeman, Roger A. *Mighty Eighth War Diary.* London: Jane's Publishing Company Limited, 1981.

Freeman, Roger A. *Mighty Eighth War Manual.* London: Jane's Publishing Company Limited, 1984.

Freeman, Roger A. *The B-17 Flying Fortress Story: Design - Production - History.* London: Arms & Armour Press, 1998.

Hinrichs, Edward T. *Missing Planes of the 452nd Bomb Group, 2nd Edition.* Forest Lake, Minnesota: Edward T. Hinrichs, 1995.

Infield, Glenn B. *The Poltava Affair.* New York, New York: MacMillian Publishing Co., Inc., 1973.

Jablonski, Edward. *Flying Fortress: The Illustrated Biography of the B-17's and the Men Who Flew Them.* Garden City: Doubleday & Company, Inc., 1965.

Kaplan, Philip and Smith, Rex Alan. *One Last Look.* Abbeville Press, 1983.

Ludden, Robert W. *Barbed Wire Interlude.* Alexandria, Virginia: Robert W. Ludden, 1945.

Mackersey, Ian. *Into The Silk.* New York, New York: W. W. Norton & Company, 1958.

McDowell, Earnest R. *Flying Fortress: The Boeing B-17.* Carrollton, Texas: Squadron/Signal Publications, Inc., 1987.

Mueller, Werner. *German Flak In World War II.* Atglen, Pennsylvania: Schiffer Publishing Ltd., 1998.

Mueller, Werner. *The 88mm Flak.* West Chester, Pennsylvania: Schiffer Publishing Ltd., 1991.

Neary, Bob. *Stalag Luft III: A Collection of German Prison Camp Sketches.* North Wales, Pennsylvania: Bob Neary, 1946.

O'Donnell, Joseph P. *The Shoe Leather Express - Book II: Luftgangsters Marching Across Germany.* Joseph P. O'Donnell, 1986.

O'Donnell, Joseph P. *The Shoe Leather Express, Third Edition.* Joseph P. O'Donnell, 1982.

Powell, Dr. P. H. "Pat". *Inside Curve and Beyond.* Columbus, Georgia: Brentwood Christian Press, 1995.

Whelan, James R. *Fighter Aces of WW II*. Washington, D.C.: Regnery Gateway, 1991.

Various issues of the 452nd Bomb Group Association's *Poop From The Group* newsletters and past and present membership directories from the 452nd Bomb Group Association.

The unpublished diaries of Harry C. Shoffner, Robert A. Lalumiere, and Sylvester Petri.

The unpublished memoirs of Raymond E. Dean.

The many personal letters from the various mothers, and from the crew members of the *Sunrise Serenade*.

The Missing Air Crew Reports from the National Archives pertaining to 452nd Bomb Group crews.

About the Author

Jerry Penry, a 34-year-old registered land surveyor in the state of Nebraska, has authored *The Atkinson & Northern Railroad* in 1991 and co-authored *The Cowboy Line* in 1998. Both books deal with railroad-related topics concerning the area near his hometown, Atkinson, Nebraska. He has also written numerous historical articles for the *Nebraska Surveyor* newsletter as well as several unpublished manuscripts on railroad, surveying, and World War II related subjects. The *Sunrise Serenade* is his most complete work to date, giving one final tribute to the many veterans of World War II he has come to know over the years, many who have already passed from this life. He now resides in Milford, Nebraska, with his wife and two children, Sarah and Andrew.